Montréal: A History

MONTRÉAL
A History

Robert Prévost

Translated by Elizabeth Mueller
and Robert Chodos

Canadian Cataloguing in Publication Data
Prévost, Robert, 1918–
Montréal: a history
Translation of: Montréal: la folle entreprise.
Includes index.
ISBN 0-7710-7034-9
1. Montréal (Québec) – history.   I. Title.

FC2947.4.P7313 1992   971.4'28   C92-094379-9
F1054.5.M857P7313 1992

Typeset at McClelland & Stewart
Printed and bound in Canada

Originally published in 1991
under the title *Montréal ... la folle entreprise* by
Les éditions internationales Alain Stanké Ltée.
1212 rue St-Mathieu
Montréal, Québec
H3H 2H7

Published in English in 1993 by
McClelland & Stewart Inc.
The Canadian Publishers
481 University Avenue
Toronto, Ontario
M5G 2E9

Contents

Foreword

In 1939, Montréal was getting ready for a sumptuous celebration of its three hundredth anniversary. The city appointed a commission to plan and carry out a program of festivities and named the dean of city council, Léon Trépanier, as its director general. Trépanier, who had represented Lafontaine ward since 1921, resigned from council to devote his full attention to his new responsibilities.

A former journalist who had worked first at *La Presse*, then as news editor of *Le Devoir* under its founder, Henri Bourassa, and finally at *La Patrie*, Trépanier was interested in history. When some people had been willing to tear down the Château de Ramezay so that Gosford Street could be extended towards the harbour, it was through Trépanier's vigorous efforts that the historic building had been saved and an overpass built instead. To help him with his duties as director general, Trépanier surrounded himself with historians, including the president of the Société Historique de Montréal, Ægidius Fauteux.

One of the members of this learned group was a young journalist with a passion for history, Robert Prévost. His first article had been published in *L'Illustration Nouvelle* under the editorship of Louis Francoeur in 1934, and for five years he had been working on popularizing Canadian history. Prévost quickly came up with the idea of publishing a magazine, *Canadiana, Revue du IIIe Centenaire* (Canadiana: magazine of the three hundredth anniversary). Trépanier enthusiastically endorsed the idea, and in the inaugural issue he announced that the commission he headed would be sponsoring a competition leading to the publication of a popular history of Montréal.

Unfortunately, all the fine ideas that were announced would never be carried out on the scale that had been anticipated. Because of the war,

Montréal's celebration of its three hundredth anniversary was a modest one. Léon Trépanier got involved in the successful Victory Bond campaign of 1941. Early that same year, *Canadiana* ceased publication and the idea of publishing a popular history of Montréal was abandoned.

Half a century passed. In 1988, when the Corporation Montréal 1992 was established to oversee the celebration of Montréal's 350th anniversary, it occurred to us at Stanké that we should publish the popular history of Montréal that had been planned for the tricentenary. The obvious person to write this history was Robert Prévost. He had never stopped writing, he had built up a splendid collection of files over the years, and Stanké had already published three of his books.

If we are not mistaken, the last popular history of Montréal appeared more than a century ago. *L'histoire populaire de Montréal* by A. Leblond de Brumath, an eminent teacher who would later become principal of the Académie Commerciale de Montréal, was published by Granger Frères, booksellers, in 1890, and was offered as a prize to night-school students by the Banque Ville-Marie that same year.

It is certainly not too soon to offer Canadians an account that brings the history of Québec's largest city up to date. And it is never too late to do something worthwhile.

Les Éditions Internationales Alain Stanké
Montréal

Preface

In this last decade of the twentieth century, skepticism is a widespread phenomenon. Doubting the authenticity of sincere altruism, the reality of the miraculous and the existence of a genuine spirit of sacrifice, people are skeptical about the motives of many figures in history.

How can we believe that Isaac Jogues, having suffered the most appalling agony at the hands of the Iroquois, his wounds eaten away by gangrene, would agree to return to his tormentors as an emissary of the governor of New France, this time to be burned to death? Without suspecting them of seeking personal gain, how can we acknowledge that seventeen young men from Ville-Marie would sign their wills and go out to face hundreds of natives who had sworn to drive the French from Montréal Island – all of them losing their lives in the confrontation? How can we understand what would lead people whose birth destined them for lives of great honour in France – such as the Sulpician François de Salignac de Lamothe-Fénelon, half-brother of the famous writer and archbishop of Cambrai of the same name – to choose to devote themselves instead to evangelization in the forests of the New World?

There are any number of examples. How can we explain the fortuitous encounter of Jérôme Le Royer de La Dauversière and Jean-Jacques Olier, who – never having met before – both went at the same time to seek support from Pierre Séguier, chancellor to the king and guardian of the seal of France, and fell into each other's arms as they entered the chancellor's house? The friendship that grew out of this encounter would be a key element in the founding of Ville-Marie.

And why did the priests and laypeople who founded the Société de Notre-Dame de Montréal to encourage the evangelization of native people decide to establish their settlement near the Ottawa River rather than near the existing settlement of Québec, when the rational thing to do would have been to consolidate the colony's forces at a time when it was reeling under the impact of repeated Iroquois incursions?

The small ships that appeared in front of Québec in the fall of 1641, bearing Sieur de Maisonneuve and his handful of pioneers, were greeted with joy by the French settlers living at the foot of Cap aux Diamants. But their joy lasted only until they learned that this new contingent had come not to provide reinforcements for them but rather to found a new settlement near the Lachine Rapids. "May God will," wrote the Jesuit superior, Father Barthélemy Vimont, after they landed in Québec, "that the Hiroquois will not block the way when we try to go farther."

Governor de Montmagny of New France was persuaded to oppose the plan on grounds of the Iroquois threat. He believed, as the historian Dollier de Casson wrote, that "this project would never be able to withstand their incursions," adding that the new company's scheme was so absurd that the best name that could be given to it was *"la folle entreprise"* – the foolish venture.

Let us see what would happen to this "foolish venture" over the next three hundred and fifty years.

Robert Prévost

Adam's Will

———— >< ————

When Christopher Columbus returned from his voyage across the Sea of Darkness in 1492, did he know that he had not reached Grand Cathay or Cipangu? Some historians maintain that he did: he was aware that he had reached a new continent that blocked the way to the spices and other riches of the Orient.

In any case, Spain and Portugal claimed ownership of all the lands and islands that had been discovered and would be discovered towards the west – sovereigns did not pay much attention to freedom of the seas in those days. Pope Alexander VI – Rodrigo Borgia – gave sanction to these claims in a bull that demarcated the two countries' zones of influence, dividing them along a meridian running through the Cape Verde Islands.

France was still oriented towards the Mediterranean and the east, and its Valois rulers were not greatly upset at the papal decision. Nevertheless, King François I did express some resentment at it; according to a famous remark attributed to him, he said he would like to see the will in which our father Adam bequeathed lands that no one had yet taken possession of to the kings of Spain and Portugal alone.

In 1523, Giulio de' Medici became pope under the name of Clement VII. He allied himself with François I, forming the League of Cognac against Charles V in 1526. The same year, King François appointed the bishop of Lisieux, Jean Le Veneur, *grand aumônier* of France. Bishop Le Veneur was a good friend of Cardinal Ippolito de' Medici, the pope's nephew. When François stopped at Mont-Saint-Michel in 1532, on his way to bring Brittany under the French crown, he was greeted by the temporary temporal officer – Jean Le Veneur.

Over the years, a succession of daring captains set sail for the Americas.

Jean Parmentier, backed by the powerful shipowner Ango, sailed to New-foundland (whose rich fishing grounds had been a destination for Breton fishing boats since the beginning of the sixteenth century) and to Brazil. In 1524 the Florentine navigator Giovanni da Verrazano, sailing for France and supported by Rouen bankers, reached Cape Breton. And in 1509 Captain de Ruffose, of Honfleur, returned from the "new lands" with seven armed "savages" in traditional clothing, along with their canoes, on board his ship *La Bonne Aventure*.

Meanwhile, Jean Le Veneur's skilful manoeuvring brought about a change in Alexander VI's bull. Le Veneur persuaded his friend Ippolito de' Medici to take up the matter with his uncle, and as a result Clement VII modified the initial decree so that it applied only to known lands and not to lands that other kingdoms might claim.

Among the mariners who had become familiar with western shores was one Jacques Cartier, who knew the waters of Newfoundland and had sailed the coast of Brazil. It is said that Cartier was related to the treasurer of the abbey at Mont-Saint-Michel, and that may be how Jean Le Veneur became interested in the new world. Le Veneur presented Cartier to the king as a captain who was experienced enough to lead an expedition to America, and he may even have offered to invest part of his personal reserve in the voyage.

And so, on April 20, 1534, Cartier left Saint-Malo with sixty-one sailors on two ships. He made an exceptionally rapid crossing and reached the Baie des Châteaux – what we know as the Strait of Belle Isle – twenty days later. The object of the voyage was clear: "To discover certain islands and coun-tries where it is said that great quantities of gold and other riches are to be found."

He was disappointed that the lands along whose coasts he sailed were so infertile. It should not be referred to as *Terre Neuffue* (Newfoundland), he wrote, because he had not found a single *charetée de terre* (cartload of earth); it was, rather, "the land that God gave to Cain." He made his first contact with natives, who had come to hunt seals.

Cartier then sailed south along the coast of Newfoundland and reached the Magdalen Islands. He named the first island he reached Brion, after Phi-lippe de Chabot, seigneur de Brion, grand admiral of France. Here nature was more generous: "One arpent of this land is worth more than all of Newfoundland."

Then Cartier entered the Baie des Chaleurs, retraced his steps, anchored in a large inlet at whose head Port-Daniel now stands, explored the coast in detail in small boats, and made contact with natives again. "Their land is more temperate than Spain, and the most beautiful that could ever be seen," Cartier concluded.

On July 23, at the head of the Baie de Gaspé, Cartier formally took possession of the territory in the name of François I. The natives here, like the others Cartier had met, were hospitable – so much so that their chief agreed to let two of his sons go with the captain, who promised to bring them back. Dressed in shirts, livery and red caps, the natives left the land of their ancestors for new horizons.

Cartier sailed for Anticosti Island, rounded its east end and sailed upstream along its north coast as far as the west end. At this point a strong west wind developed and the captain brought together his pilots, officers and sailors to help him decide what to do. In the situation that faced them, knowing nothing about the conditions of navigation farther upstream and fearing the storms that were common in Newfoundland waters at that time of year, they decided it would be best to return home. They reached Saint-Malo on September 5.

Mount Royal Enters History

On his first voyage, Cartier had explored the Gulf of St. Lawrence but he had not reached the mouth of the river. Less than two months after his return, on the "second to last day of October" 1534, Grand Admiral Chabot granted him a new commission to "complete the navigation of the lands you have already begun to discover." The king supplied 3,000 livres to furnish three ships – the *Grande Hermine*, the *Petite Hermine* and the *Émerillon* – with equipment and provisions for fifteen months.

Domagaya and Taignoagny, the two natives Cartier had brought with him to France, had no doubt learned enough French to carry on a conversation, and they told Cartier about the great river, about Canada, about Stadacona and Hochelaga. Perhaps, in their metaphorical way of speaking, they had allowed the possibility of the existence of gems and precious metals to shimmer in front of the Europeans' eyes. And perhaps François I wanted a loyal servant of the king on board. In any case, when the expedition left Saint-Malo on May 19, 1535, an important figure was part of it: "Claude de

Pontbryand, son of the seigneur of Montréal and cupbearer of *monseigneur le Daulphin*." He will play a significant part in our story.

Bad weather separated the ships, and they were not reunited until July 26, in the Baie des Châteaux. Domagaya and Taignoagny indicated the "route and the beginning of the great Hochelaga River and the route towards Canada, which became ever narrower." The two guides added that the river was "so long that no one has ever been to its end," undoubtedly leading Cartier to believe that this was the much-sought-after great passage to Japan and China. Such a misapprehension is hardly surprising: a century later the explorer Jean Nicolet landed on the shores of Lake Superior in mandarin dress to meet Blackfeet whom the French had taken for Chinese.

The flotilla sailed up the St. Lawrence, entered the Saguenay and then continued up the St. Lawrence and anchored near an island where hazel bushes grew in profusion: "Therefore we named it *l'isle es Couldres* [Hazel island, today Île aux Coudres]." Seven or eight leagues upstream they came upon thirteen islands close together, "which is the beginning of the land and province of Canada." With the help of their two interpreters, Cartier and his sailors had little difficulty making contact with the natives, and Donnacona, "the lord of Canada," appeared in front of them with ten boats. Domagaya and Taignoagny told Donnacona about their stay in France. Cartier drew up alongside him and had bread and wine brought to the chief.

The flotilla had reached the Île d'Orleans, which Cartier named Bacchus because of the vines he found there. Deciding that it might be risky to venture farther upstream with his three ships, he anchored the two larger ones in the St. Charles River and carried on in the *Émérillon*. Appearing before Cartier with more than 500 men, women and children, Donnacona tried to dissuade him from continuing the voyage.

Cartier explained "that he was under the command of his master the King to go as far forward as he possibly could." Taignoagny had promised to go with Cartier, but now he changed his mind. The next day Donnacona approached Cartier again, this time with presents, offering him two young boys and a young girl. The girl, between ten and twelve years old, was the daughter of his own sister. Then a day later, three "devils" dressed in dogskin, with blackened faces and wearing horns as long as their arms, gesticulated in front of the ships. Cudouagny, their god had contacted Hochelaga: there would be so much ice and snow upstream that Cartier and his sailors would die.

On September 19 the *Émérillon* left Stadacona with two boats, taking advantage of the rising tide. In the account of this voyage, the banks of the

Natives greet Jacques Cartier at Hochelaga in 1535. (Drawing by Andrew Morris, lithographed by Napoléon Sorony, New York, 1850.)

great river are described as a virtual paradise, with the best lands that could ever be seen, covered with beautiful trees and vines laden with grapes. Everywhere there were hospitable natives who worked diligently at fishing and "came to our ships in as friendly and familiar a manner as if we had been from their country."

Cartier had left Canada behind him. On September 28, the *Émérillon* reached a large lake, Lac Saint-Pierre, from which there appeared to be no navigable outlet upstream. Since it was "the time of year when the water is lowest," Cartier decided to use the boats to continue the voyage. Claude de Pontbriant was among the gentlemen who came with him. On October 2, more than a thousand people greeted them with as fine a welcome "as any father ever gave to his child." Children were brought to Cartier so that he could touch them. Cartier had presents distributed, and then the French withdrew to their boats for the night, while the natives danced and lit fires on the beach.

The next day Cartier visited Hochelaga. The village was surrounded by tilled fields, full of "the wheat of their land, which is like the millet of Brazil." It was a large town, with "about fifty houses, each about fifty paces long or more, and twelve to fifteen broad, built all of wood, with roofs and sides made of strips of bark or of wood." Each house had individual rooms for families and a communal room with a fire, as well as a garner for storing food.

The town was built in a circle and surrounded by a wooden palisade in three tiers lashed together, with horizontal pieces running between them. As the account of the expedition describes it, "At several points along the wall are galleries of a kind, with ladders ascending to them, provided with rocks and stones for its guard and defence."

Cartier climbed the slopes of the mountain and looked out on the panorama that was visible from the summit. "This mountain we called Mount Royal," the account notes. The view stretched more than thirty leagues and included the Laurentians, the Adirondacks and the Green Mountains, as well as "three fine conical mountains" closer to where he stood. These were no doubt the mountains of the Montréal region: Saint-Bruno, Beloeil and Rougemont.

This is the oldest description we have of the original settlement on Montréal Island. According to historians, the natives belonged to the Iroquois Confederacy of Five Nations. They were sedentary, not "nomadic like the natives of Canada and Saguenay, although the Canadians are subject to them, along with eight or nine other peoples along the river."

The natives clearly thought that Cartier had supernatural power of some kind, for their chief, the *agouhanna*, completely crippled on his deerskin, asked Cartier to touch his legs and arms, and then gave him the band of cloth studded with hedgehog quills that served as his crown. "And at once many sick persons were brought to the captain [Cartier], some blind, others with but one eye, others lame or impotent and others again so extremely old that their eyelids hung down to their cheeks."

No doubt moved to have such trust placed in him, Cartier devoted "a pair of hours" to making the sign of the cross over the sick natives and then reading the Passion of Jesus Christ in the Gospel. After that gifts were distributed and trumpets were sounded.

On October 4, the explorers returned to the *Émérillon*. They left the next day and after six days' sail reached the St. Charles River, where the other crew members had built a fort for the winter.

Did Cartier Land at Gros Saut?

———————— ✄ ————————

Montréal Island is flanked by two natural barriers that made all upstream navigation impossible until canals were built: the Lachine Rapids in the St. Lawrence, which were finally circumvented by the Lachine Canal, and the Sault au Récollet or Gros Saut in the Rivière des Prairies, between the parish of Sault-au-Récollet and the point where the Cartierville Bridge now stands.

More than sixty years ago, an architect with a passion for history, Aristide Beaugrand-Champagne, advanced the hypothesis that Jacques Cartier reached Montréal Island not through the St. Lawrence, as everything written about the expedition had maintained up to that time, but rather through the Rivière des Prairies. To a navigator sailing upstream towards Montréal along the north shore of the St. Lawrence, he explained, the Rivière des Prairies would appear to be the natural continuation of the river. And this, he argued, is precisely the route that Cartier took.

Beaugrand-Champagne came to this conclusion by analysing a number of maps. He pointed out that Cartier himself drew a map on the basis of the rough charts that he made as the ship progressed up the river; this map is mentioned in two letters, one of them written by Cartier's nephew, Jacques Noël. Cartier's map has never been found, but according to Beaugrand-Champagne it undoubtedly served as the model for all subsequent maps of the St. Lawrence.

All but one of the place names identified on the earliest map drawn after Cartier's first voyages are on the north shore of the St. Lawrence. Moreover, native villages were located primarily on the north shore: Huron villages as far as the St. Maurice River, and then Iroquois villages from there to Lake St. Francis.

Beaugrand-Champagne, who wrote extensively on the Iroquois, endeavoured to reconstruct the network of Iroquois paths crisscrossing Montréal Island. The Iroquois village of Hochelaga, it appears, had a population of about 3,500; built as it was with the capacity to beat back aggressors, its site must have been considered a strategic one. Considering the region Iroquois land, the inhabitants oversaw canoe traffic on both sides of the island and levied tribute on non-Iroquois who wished to use any of the rivers of the archipelago: the St. Lawrence, the Rivière des Prairies or the

This statue of Jacques Cartier in Montréal's Saint-Henri district, the work of the sculptor Arthur Vincent, was unveiled in 1893. It was the first monument to the mariner of Saint-Malo.

Rivière des Mille-Îles. They even maintained outposts, notably one at the mouth of the L'Assomption River some sixty kilometres downstream from Montréal and another one sixty kilometres farther on at the present site of Lanoraie. The view from this second outpost encompassed the whole width of the river and no canoe coming out of the maze of islands off Sorel could escape the Iroquois sentinels' vigilance.

  The Iroquois also needed paths leading out of Hochelaga that gave them safe and quick access to the rapids that broke the steady flow of the St. Lawrence and the Rivière des Prairies and to the two ends of the island (the upstream end opens out onto Lac des Deux-Montagnes and the Ottawa River).

On October 3, 1535, along with twenty well-armed sailors and gentlemen including Claude de Pontbriant, Cartier walked from the shore where they had landed to the Iroquois village along "as beaten a path as can possibly be seen." After about "a league and a half," they met "one of the leading lords of the village." They still had not reached their destination. The account adds that the group walked through "the most beautiful land, the best that could be seen, full of oak trees, as beautiful as any in the forests of France, under which the ground was completely covered with acorns." After they met the "lord," they continued "on, and about half a league from there, we began to see tilled fields." It was in the midst of these fields that "the town of Hochelaga is situated."

These passages are perplexing. If – as was long thought – Hochelaga was at the foot of the mountain, about where McGill University is now, why did Cartier have to walk two leagues from the St. Lawrence to reach it, unless he anchored his boats farther downstream? On the other hand, two leagues would be a reasonable distance from the foot of Gros Saut in the Rivière des Prairies.

Beaugrand-Champagne also advanced another argument for his thesis. There was at one time an oak forest between the bank of the Rivière des Prairies at the Gros Saut rapids and the north slope of Mount Royal. However, he maintained, in all the digging of the subsoil of the island between the mountain and the St. Lawrence, no trace was found of the trunks of old oak trees. As an architect, Beaugrand-Champagne presumably had the opportunity to visit a number of construction sites personally.

Is this why no one has ever conclusively determined the site of the old Iroquois village, even though a settlement of 3,500 people would have to leave fairly substantial traces in the subsoil? Were people looking in the right place? The question has attracted the attention of many scholars and been the subject of much ink, but it remains a mystery.

Why "Montréal"?

————————— >< —————————

Embedded in the railing of the lookout on Mount Royal, overlooking the panorama of the city, is an elegant bronze plaque. The inscription on the plaque purports to explain the origin of the city's name: "On October 2nd, 1535, Jacques Cartier, discoverer of Canada, climbed this mountain under the guidance of the Indians of the village of Hochelaga and, impressed with the beauty of the landscape displayed before his eyes, gave it the name of Mount Royal, 'from which the city of Montréal took its name.'"

This explanation, although endorsed by the Jacques Cartier quatercentenary committee in 1934, is only a hypothesis. True, Cartier did write in the account of his voyage that his view from the mountain was a panoramic one and he "had a view of the land for more than thirty leagues round about," but he made no connection between the beauty of the panorama and the name he chose for the mountain. The account says simply, "We named this mountain Mount Royal," and elsewhere refers to "the mountain mentioned earlier, which we named Mount Royal." Nothing more.

In 1642 the Jesuit superior, Father Barthélemy Vimont, said that the island "took its name of *Montréal* or *Mont royal* from the sight of a beautiful mountain that is found there." But that was a century later. Was Father Vimont's remark based on an oral tradition?

The explanation that Mount Royal's name came from the beautiful landscape before Cartier's eyes seems a natural one. It brings to mind another apparently natural explanation: that the Rivière des Prairies was so named because it flows through beautiful prairies. However, the Jesuit *Relations* give a different explanation. The name came from the circumstance that "a certain man named des Prairies" sailed into the river by mistake instead of continuing up the St. Lawrence where his boat was expected. Father Paul Le Jeune no doubt got this story from Samuel de Champlain, who had used the name Rivière des Prairies for the river twenty years earlier.

We might ask ourselves, If it seemed to this "man named des Prairies" that the Rivière des Prairies was the continuation of the St. Lawrence, why would Cartier not have been subject to the same misapprehension? But let us get back to *Montréal*.

There is no shortage of hypotheses. A French historian, Eugène Guernier, even wrote that when Cartier set out on his second voyage he received an order from François I to give "the first city that is founded" the name of Montréal in honour of Cardinal Ippolito de' Medici, then archbishop of Monreale in Sicily. It will be recalled that Cardinal de' Medici, the nephew of Pope Clement VII, had persuaded his uncle to modify his predecessor Alexander VI's bull that gave Spain and Portugal exclusive possession of all lands to be discovered to the west. "The Norman city of Monreale," Guernier concluded, "thus became the godmother of the city of Montréal." Pressing his point, he added that the king may have secretly wanted to honour the memory of William II of Sicily, who had founded Monreale in the twelfth century.

There is also another hypothesis, at least as good as these; in fact, I believe it is more plausible.

At the time Cartier climbed the slopes of Mount Royal, there had for five hundred years been at least twenty places called *Montréal* in France. Each was a citadel or blockhouse built on a height of land in a strategic location. We know that the name undoubtedly came from "mont royal" (*mons regalis*). One of these Montréals, in the old county of Périgord, was the castle of the great Pontbriant family.

Pierre de Pontbriant, born in the castle of Amboise, where his father was deputy governor to the young Count of Angoulême, the future François I, was lord of this Montréal. He had two sons, François and Claude. François was governor of Limoges and high seneschal of Limousin, while Claude, as noted earlier, was "cupbearer of *monseigneur le Daulphin*," that is, of the eldest son of King François I. We know that Claude de Pontbriant – by this time *dit Montréal* – was at Cartier's side on Mount Royal. Can we not imagine that the captain might have wanted to please this special shipmate by giving the place a name that evoked both his family's castle and his own name?

A description of the rest of Cartier's voyage is beyond the scope of this book. Let us just say briefly that the crews wintered at Stadacona, where they became ill with scurvy, which killed twenty-five of them. In the spring of 1536, Cartier decided to abandon the *Petite Hermine* because he didn't have enough hands to sail it.

Only four or five men escaped the illness, and it is unlikely that Claude de Pontbriant *dit Montréal* was among them. He was clearly ill when he returned to France, for he died the same year, on November 3, 1536. We know the precise date because François I paid a certain sum of money to François de Boucart, who had become cupbearer to both the dauphin and his brother, the Duc d'Orléans, to cover arrears relating to the wages for this office from that date, "the day on which Pontbriant died." And perhaps on that day not only did the dauphin lose his cupbearer but Montréal lost its godfather as well.

Champlain at the Lachine Rapids

It was not until the early seventeenth century that Europeans were again seen in the waters around Montréal Island. Fishermen regularly visited the banks of Newfoundland, and Basques hunted whales in the St. Lawrence estuary, especially opposite the mouth of the Saguenay. In 1542-43 Jean-François de La Rocque, Sieur de Roberval, tried in vain to establish a settlement at the foot of Cap Rouge, upstream from Stadacona, under the name of *France-Roy*. After that, however, there does not appear to have been any serious attempt to set up a colony on the banks of the St. Lawrence.

Their Most Christian Majesties, as they liked to call themselves, did want to look for the mysterious passage leading to the Orient, discover sources of gems and precious metals and, at the same time, encourage the evangelization of the natives. However, they hesitated to use the royal coffers for these purposes. Instead, they used a system of privileges: in exchange for the exclusive right to engage in the fur trade, companies made a commitment to bring missionaries and settlers to New France. Shrewd as this policy appeared, it led only to disillusionment. It would be 1663 before Louis XIV, at the instigation of his minister Jean-Baptiste Colbert, decided to end the rule of the companies and take the colony under his wing.

In 1600 Pierre de Chauvin, Sieur de Tonnetuit, who had turned to commercial interests after a military career and owned four ships, sailed up the St. Lawrence to engage in the fur trade and built a house at Tadoussac. This was four years before the founding of Acadia, and historians believe that Tadoussac is the oldest site of continuous European settlement in Canada. On one of his maps, Samuel de Champlain drew this house and identified it as the "dwelling place of Captain Chauvin from the year 1600." A replica of this house was built in 1942, in exactly the same place where the remains of the original stockade, which had burnt to the ground, were found. And in Honfleur, at 52-54 rue Haute, you can see the extensively remodelled home of the Sieur de Tonnetuit.

Pierre de Chauvin died early in 1603, and his commission passed to Aymar de Chaste, governor of Dieppe. De Chaste also had a military career behind him, having commanded an expedition to the Portuguese Azores and fought the Calvinists, capturing the Île d'Oléron and bringing Dieppe under Henri IV's control. For these acts of service he deserved a reward and was given the commission of Pierre de Chauvin, who had served under his command. He put François Gravé, Sieur du Pont, who had accompanied Chauvin to Tadoussac, in charge of continuing his companion's mission.

François Gravé had brought two natives back to France. To go with him as recorder on a new expedition, Gravé chose Samuel de Champlain, who had undertaken a voyage to the West Indies in 1598-99. To the best of our knowledge, Gravé and Champlain would become the first Europeans to see Montréal Island since Jacques Cartier.

Gravé and Champlain sailed from Honfleur on the *Bonne-Renommée* on March 15, 1603. The ship was delayed by ice floes, one of them more than eight leagues long, and did not arrive at the Grand Banks until May 2. Eighteen days later it reached Anticosti Island, "which is the entrance to the river of Canadas."

Many places already bore names that have stuck. The sailors identified *Gachepé, Mantanne, le Pic* (Bic), *Tadousac* and, at the mouth of the Saguenay, *la poincte de Sainct Matthieu ou autrement aux Alouettes*.

Champlain met a large aboriginal population, led by the great *sagamo* Anadabijou, at the mouth of the Saguenay, and took advantage of the opportunity to record extensive observations about the natives: beliefs, feasts, clothes, food and other customs and traditions. His account would appear under the title *Des Savvages, ov Voyage de Samvel de Champlain de Brovage fait en la France Novvelle* (Savages, or the Voyage of Samuel de Champlain of Brouage to New France).

The explorers sailed a fair distance up the Saguenay, then continued up the St. Lawrence towards their ultimate destination of "the saut": Saut Saint-Louis, which we know today as the Lachine Rapids. They anchored at "a narrowing of the river of Canadas" that Champlain referred to as Québec – the first time this term was used to designate Cartier's Stadacona. Champlain must have noticed that the narrowing of the river made this a suitable location for a settlement, and he would found Québec there five years later. Sparkling quartz crystals attracted his attention: "Along the coast of Québec, there are diamonds in the slate rocks, and they are better than those of Alençon."

The explorers then proceeded to Trois-Rivières, already known as a trading post under that name; in 1599, Pontgravé told Pierre de Chauvin that he had gone there. "It would in my judgement be a place fit for habitation," Champlain noted, "and it could be fortified quickly." He added that "a settlement at Trois-Rivières would be beneficial to the freedom of several nations, who don't dare to come there, because of the Iroquois, who line both sides of the river of Canadas." The colonizer in Champlain comes through clearly here, although it would be thirty-one years before he would send Sieur Laviolette to establish a permanent settlement at Trois-Rivières.

On the last day of June, the explorers reached the mouth of the Rivière des Iroquois – what we know today as the Richelieu River – and then "the entrance to the *saut*, sailing before the wind." They skirted an island that Champlain would later name St. Helen. "I assure you that I have never seen a torrent of water flow so impetuously," Champlain observed. They walked a distance of a league beside the rapids, concluding that no craft could clear them.

The natives here gave Champlain a fairly exact description of the course of the St. Lawrence above Montréal, which included the Cascades, Cèdres and Coteau-du-Lac rapids, Lake St. Francis, Long Sault and five other rapids that mark the river before it reaches the Lac des Entouhouronons (Lake Ontario) and then the other Great Lakes. Champlain quickly asked if the waters of the last great lake flow towards Gaspé and was told that they didn't, "which makes me believe that it is the South Sea." In fact, however, they were far from the Gulf of Mexico, through which they hoped eventually to cross the continent and reach the fabled lands of the Orient.

The goal of the voyage had been accomplished, and there is no doubt that Champlain saw Montréal Island, at the head of navigation, as the ideal strategic location for a future settlement. He would spend some time there eight years later with a view towards implementing such a plan.

The year 1603 also saw the death of Aymar de Chaste, under whose protection Gravé and Champlain had sailed. His gravestone can be seen in a small chapel behind the choir in Saint-Rémi Church in Dieppe. A short distance farther back, a simple monument notes that here, "on August 19, 1942, two Canadian soldiers fell."

The First Clearing of Place Royale

—————————————— >‹ ——————————————

Samuel de Champlain's efforts over the next four years were concentrated primarily in Acadia. After de Chaste's death, the exclusive privilege to carry on the fur trade was given to Pierre Du Gua, Sieur de Monts, again undoubtedly as a reward for military service under Henri IV. Most of the people who appear in our history in these very early years of the seventeenth century were Huguenots or former Huguenots, faithful servants of a king who had only recently renounced his Calvinist faith. It is believed that Champlain also came from a Protestant family, and this may be why his birth record has never been found.

After playing a central role in the founding of Acadia and especially of Port-Royal, Champlain returned to France. In 1608 he set out again, and on July 3 of that year he founded Québec at the point where the St. Lawrence narrows – the strategic location he had noticed five years earlier.

In December 1610 he married Hélène Boullé, a girl from Saint-Germain-l'Auxerrois parish in central Paris who was about thirty years younger than he was and who would enter a convent after her husband's death. Then in 1611 Champlain again set sail for Québec. After he arrived at his destination he went to Saut Saint-Louis where he traded with the natives. But his expedition also had another purpose; he wrote that he had come "to meet the savages and to identify an appropriate place for a settlement." The idea of founding Montréal was already in his mind.

While he waited for the natives to arrive, Champlain examined the surrounding area "to find an appropriate place to locate a settlement and to prepare the land to build it there." He went through the woods as far as Lac des Deux-Montagnes, then retraced his steps until he chose "a small place, the farthest upstream that small boats and launches can reach easily." He called it Place Royale. Here along a small river (the Saint-Pierre, which has since disappeared as a result of drainage works and canalization), he found more than twenty hectares of land that he described as *"désertés"* – in other words, cleared. He noted that previously "savages worked the land there"; these would have been the Iroquois who greeted Cartier in 1535.

Champlain noted the presence of grasslands "which would feed as many cattle as one could wish," an abundance of vines and small fruits, and wildlife on the land and in the water in such quantity "that while we were at the *saut* we did not lack anything."

He quickly set about clearing Place Royale. Making use of a deposit of "earth thick with clay, very good for making bricks or for building," he built a twenty-metre-long wall on a nearby island, planning to return on another voyage and see whether it had been damaged by the water during the winter. Finally, he had two gardens laid out and planted them to check the fertility of the soil. The seeds "grew perfectly and quickly, which shows that the land is good." Champlain left nothing to chance.

Offshore, he recognized an island that he had noticed in 1603, "about three quarters of a league in circumference, where a good and strong town could be built." He named the island Île Sainte-Hélène, St. Helen's Island, probably in honour of his young wife, who after their wedding had gone back to her parents to wait until she was of marriageable age.

On the day that Expo opened in Montréal in 1967, a monument consisting of a slab of stone from St. Helen's Island was unveiled at the Pointe du Vert Galant in Paris. If you turn to the left after reading the inscription on the monument, you see the Rue de l'Amiral-de-Coligny, on which stands the Église Saint-Germain-l'Auxerrois, where Champlain and Hélène Boullé were married in 1610.

Champlain had brought back with him from France a native named Savignon, who now served him as an interpreter. Champlain sent Savignon to meet his compatriots, who had promised to come in large numbers to trade in furs. Savignon went as far as Lac des Deux-Montagnes; coming back, he saw an island where there were so many herons "that the air was completely covered with them." When a young man named Louis heard this, he wanted to go hunting, and he set out with Savignon and Outetoucos, a Montagnais captain. Unfortunately, on their way back their canoe capsized in the rapids and only Savignon survived the accident. The historian Laverdière believes that it was on account of this young Frenchman that the great rapids were named Saut Saint-Louis.

When the flotilla of canoes arrived, natives went to recover Outetoucos's body and buried it on St. Helen's Island. They said that their enemies, had they found the body, would have cut it in quarters and hung the pieces on trees "to displease them."

Back in La Rochelle, Champlain went to see Sieur de Monts to report on the voyage. Unfortunately, de Monts had lost his partners. The furs of Canada were a matter of dispute among merchants. The merchants of Saint-Malo claimed the right to the furs because Jacques Cartier had taken possession of the country – "as if the town had contributed to the cost of the discovery," Champlain noted. While Champlain had no commercial interest of his own, he was aware that pursuing his explorations and consolidating the infant colony depended on the fur trade. The merits of those who took the risks of the trade had to be recognized. "It is not reasonable," he quite rightly noted, "that if they took the sheep, the others should have the fleece."

The First Mass

There is no doubt that Champlain's virtue and lack of interest in personal gain were appreciated in high places; he returned to Canada endowed with a royal commission naming him lieutenant to Henri de Bourbon, prince of Condé, who became viceroy of the country in 1612.

The next year, Champlain undertook the burden of a futile expedition that almost cost him his life. In the past he had used the services of one Nicolas Vignau, who had wintered with the natives. In 1612, back in Paris, Vignau told Champlain that he had seen the much-sought-after north sea. He had seen the wreck of an English ship there, only seventeen days' journey from Saut Saint-Louis. Vignau repeated his story several times, and even signed a declaration affirming it before two notaries in La Rochelle.

On May 27, 1613, Champlain left St. Helen's Island with Vignau, three other Frenchmen and a native. After twelve days' journey up the Ottawa River, marked by rapids and portages, they reached the Île des Allumettes, where the sage Tessouat reigned. At one point, when Champlain had wrapped the rope of his canoe around his hand to haul it along the bank, an eddy violently swept the boat away. It was only because the boat fell between two rocks that Champlain was saved from being dragged into the current.

Other natives joined the little group. Vignau's answers became evasive, and Champlain increasingly began to doubt that he had been telling the truth. Vignau insisted that his story was true. Champlain reported to Tessouat what Vignau had said and asked the sage to supply him with canoes and men to go farther upriver, as far as the north sea. Tessouat unmasked the impostor: "You are surely a liar; you know well that every night you lay at my side with my children, and you got up there every morning; if you went to those peoples, it was in your sleep!"

The natives threw themselves at Vignau "as if they wanted to eat him or tear him apart." One of the captains said to Champlain: "Do you not see that he wanted to make you die? Give him to us, and we promise you that he will not lie any more!" Champlain threatened to have him hanged and strangled if he had made up the story. Vignau threw himself on his knees, admitted that he was a liar and begged for mercy. Champlain insisted that the natives should not molest him; he wanted to bring Vignau back to Saut Saint-Louis and present him to the French, who were there to trade in furs and "to whom he would have to carry salt water."

Champlain's voyage was not completely useless: he set out again for Saut Saint-Louis at the head of forty canoes laden with furs. Before the end of August he was back in France. Already, Montréal Island was a pivotal point for trade. It was also an important centre of evangelization, for Champlain never lost sight of this second objective.

Not knowing where to turn to find missionaries, he raised the subject with Louis Houel, controller-general of the salt mines of Brouage, who recommended the Récollets. The Estates-General were meeting in Paris at the time, and Champlain took advantage of the occasion to secure the agreement of the cardinals and bishops participating in the meeting. He also asked for financial support, which amounted to 1,500 livres: that was enough to pay the cost of the voyage and food as well as priestly ornaments for the first four Récollets who came to New France, under the leadership of Father Denis Jamet.

On April 24, 1615, the *Saint-Étienne* under Captain François Gravé set sail from Honfleur. The ship anchored at Tadoussac and the voyage continued by boat to Québec and then to Saut Saint-Louis. After meeting the natives there, Champlain crossed the island to the Rivière des Prairies. Here on June 24, Father Jamet and one of his companions, Father Joseph Le Caron, said the first mass in New France since the coming of Jacques Cartier. Three hundred years later, the St. Jean Baptiste Society erected a monument in a park in the north Montréal neighbourhood of Ahuntsic to recall this event.

Ahuntsic is named for a young convert from Huronia, a follower of Father Nicolas Viel, one of two Récollets who arrived at Québec in 1622. On June 25, 1625 – ten years virtually to the day after the mass of 1615 – Viel and Ahuntsic ventured by canoe into the rapids of the Rivière des Prairies. Their boat capsized and they drowned. From that time on the rapids were

In front of the Sault-au-Récollet parish church, two statues evoke the memory of
the Récollet missionary Nicolas Viel and his convert Ahuntsic, who died in the
rapids of the Rivière des Prairies in June 1625.

called the Sault au Récollet or the Gros Saut (in 1928, the construction of a
hydroelectric dam off Île de la Visitation made the river higher and sub-
merged the rapids). Two modest statues in front of Sault-au-Récollet
church evoke the memory of the missionary and his convert.

Until 1625, the Récollets were the only missionaries who devoted
themselves to the evangelization of the native peoples of New France. That
year, the first Jesuits arrived under Father Charles Lalemant, but they barely
had time to settle before Québec was occupied by the Kirke brothers in

1629. Three years later, King Charles I of England agreed to return New France to his brother-in-law, Louis XIII, who had finally agreed to pay the balance owing on his sister's dowry. The Jesuits returned to Québec under their new superior, Father Paul Le Jeune, who became the first editor of the Jesuit *Relations*. It was primarily through reading the *Relations* that the promoters and members of the Société de Notre-Dame de Montréal developed their ardour for founding Ville-Marie.

Three Enterprising Promoters

—————————— ➤❧ ——————————

The Jesuit *Relations* contributed greatly towards making the missions of New France known. But it may be going too far to maintain, as some have, that the *Relations* were responsible for the development of a plan to found a settlement on Montréal Island.

It was not until 1637 that the *Relations* mentioned Montréal for the first time. That year Governor de Montmagny, who had arrived in Québec after Champlain's death, undertook a voyage upstream. He wished to see the little settlement at Trois-Rivières, established three years earlier, as well as the Rivière des Iroquois; after Cartier's visit the Iroquois had left the banks of the St. Lawrence, and they now used this tributary to gain access to the great river to attack their enemies. Montmagny took Father Le Jeune with him and went as far as Saut Saint-Louis.

In his account of the voyage, Le Jeune included a description of the Hochelaga archipelago and especially Montréal Island (which "appears to be cut in the middle by a double mountain") and Île Jésus ("beautiful and large, it is named the *Isle de Montmagny*"). On the way back they pursued a moose. "If all voyages in New France pass as pleasantly as this one," the missionary remarked, "the attraction will be too great, and the body may benefit more than the spirit."

Around this time, the tax collector in the district of La Flèche on the Loir River in the French province of Maine was one Jérôme Le Royer de La Dauversière, whose worldly profession did not prevent him from having an interest in good works. He visited the poor in Maison-Dieu hospital in La Flèche, volunteered to be the guardian of orphans, and acted as procurator of the Confraternity of the Blessed Sacrament. In explaining how the idea of establishing a settlement on Montréal Island came to La Dauversière in 1634, we need to avoid being too dogmatic, for allowance should be made both for a rational hypothesis and for the miraculous.

One of La Dauversière's sons reported that starting in 1630, after the Le Royers were consecrated to the Holy Family, Jérôme had the impression that the Divine Master was commanding him to work towards founding a congregation of hospital nuns. He revealed his thoughts to Father François Chauveau, chaplain for day students at his alma mater, the Jesuit college in La Flèche. "A pious delusion," Father Chauveau answered him. The following year, La Dauversière again felt the intervention of the Divine Master, with an important detail added: the community-to-be would establish a house in Montréal!

Jérôme Le Royer de La Dauversière was a student at the Jesuit college from 1608 to 1617. The building now houses La Flèche's military school, the Prytanée Militaire, where an inscription in Saint-Louis chapel recalls La Dauversière's presence. There is no doubt that he remained in contact with his former teachers and fellow students. Among these fellow students were Father Charles Lalemant, who studied philosophy at La Flèche from 1609 to 1612 and later became the first Jesuit superior in Canada (1625-29), Father Paul Le Jeune, a philosophy student at the college starting in 1615 and Jesuit superior in Canada after 1632, and Father Barthélemy Vimont, who would celebrate mass to mark the founding of Ville-Marie in 1642, to name only a few. Montréal may not have been mentioned in the *Relations* until 1637, but it is very likely that the first Jesuits who worked in New France maintained contact with their colleagues in La Flèche.

Pierre Chevrier, Baron de Fancamp, a very rich gentleman who supported good works, was a close friend of La Dauversière's and stayed in La Dauversière's house from 1634 on. Baron de Fancamp, who later became a priest, wanted to become involved in the great plan that animated his host and suggested that he go to Paris to solicit the support of influential figures.

The next episode in the story involves an astonishing accident of timing. Pierre Séguier, chancellor to the king and guardian of the seal of France, was well known for his generosity. He and Claude de Bullion, the superintendent of finances, had helped the Récollets considerably in founding their community in Faubourg Saint-Laurent. La Dauversière decided to knock on the chancellor's door. The same day, so did a Parisian named Jean-Jacques Olier.

Ordained a priest in 1633, Abbé Olier had been a missionary under Vincent de Paul. He decided to devote himself to the training of young priests, a goal emphasized by the Council of Trent, and planned to start a seminary in Paris. This plan would be realized with the founding of the Vaugirard seminary in 1641, which marked the beginning of the Society of Saint-Sulpice, or Sulpician order.

La Dauversière entered Chancellor Séguier's house by one end of the corridor, Olier by the other. Never having seen each other before, they fell into each other's arms. La Dauversière told Olier about his plan to establish a settlement on Montréal Island to encourage the conversion of the natives. Olier, perhaps imagining it as a place to send missionaries who would graduate from his future seminary, immediately gave him a hundred gold pieces, "telling him that he wanted to be part of the plan."

Neither Jérôme Le Royer de La Dauversière nor Baron de Fancamp nor Jean-Jacques Olier would ever cross the Atlantic. But they formed the trio that would bring together enough influential personalities to eventually establish the Compagnie de Notre-Dame de Montréal. The plan would be implemented on the ground starting in 1642 by another trio, whose members all came from the province of Champagne in northeastern France.

The Plan Takes Shape

———————— >< ————————

The three promoters of the plan continued their efforts to recruit prestigious collaborators. In about 1639, Baron de Fancamp settled on Rue Cassette in Paris, where he was better able to lobby members of Parisian society to join the movement. It was probably through his efforts that another figure known for his generosity, Baron de Renty, became involved. The company was slowly taking shape, but before the project could be launched, the necessary land on far-off Montréal Island still had to be procured.

When Cardinal Richelieu founded the Company of One Hundred Associates in 1627, Jean de Lauzon, a *maître des requêtes* (solicitor), was one of the first members of the company and almost immediately became its intendant. The influential Lauzon took advantage of his involvement to have large expanses of land in New France granted to him and members of his family, notably the seigneury across the river from Québec that would bear his name. In 1636, Jacques de Girard, Seigneur de la Chaussée, received

Montréal Island – no less – as a gift. However, in an act of retrocession two years later, he acknowledged that he had "accepted the concession only to give pleasure and lend his name to the Sieur de Lauzon, in whose possession it had always remained."

In a conversation with La Dauversière, Father Lalemant, now procurator for the Canadian missions in Paris, offered to go meet Lauzon (who was living in the southeastern province of Dauphiné, where he had been appointed intendant) and find out how he felt about the island. An unverified report of the meeting suggests that Lauzon agreed to grant ownership of the island for the "modest" sum of 150,000 livres. In any case, it appears that the Company of One Hundred Associates took back the island, perhaps because Lauzon had obtained it through a figurehead. On December 17, 1640, the company granted La Dauversière and Baron de Fancamp "a large part of Montréal Island located on the St. Lawrence River and between Lac St. Pierre and Lac St. Louis, taking this part of the island to the point that looks to the northeast and taking in its entire width towards the southwest as far as the Mountain of Montréal, which has given this island its name."

The new owners also received another part of the island, on the other side of the mountain, as well as a huge tract of land on the north shore of the St. Lawrence, stretching two leagues from the Rivière des Prairies past the Rivière de l'Assomption and extending six leagues back from the riverfront.

There were a number of conditions attached to the grant. The new seigneurs could "build trenches or walls only insofar as is needed to protect against incursions by the savages," while the Company of One Hundred Associates reserved the right to build forts or a citadel wherever the company deemed it appropriate, "even on the Mountain of Montreal." This condition recalls the blockhouses with which the heights of land designated *Montréal* in France were generally equipped. Finally, La Dauversière and Baron de Fancamp could not grant lands to people who already lived in New France "but only to those who want to cross the ocean for this purpose so that the colony will grow further in this way."

The partners who had formed a group around the original promoters and supported them with their money and influence probably knew as early as the spring of 1640 that they had won the opportunity to build a settlement on Montréal Island. At that time, they shipped twenty cases of food, tools and supplies to Québec. They asked the Jesuit superior, Father Le Jeune, to take responsibility for the shipment and made arrangements for the construction of a warehouse in Québec's Lower Town.

The project was thus well underway, and the departure of an initial contingent of settlers was planned for 1641. But the expedition needed a leader who was suited to a responsibility of this sort. Once again, it was Father Lalemant who took the initiative. He knew a gentleman from Champagne who appeared to have all the qualities required for such a venture and told La Dauversière about him, indicating where this rare jewel could be found. La Dauversière went to dine there; during dinner, without revealing his purpose, he began to talk with each of the other diners in turn, making sure everyone heard the details of the venture.

One of La Dauversière's table companions was especially curious about the project. Paul de Chomedey, Sieur de Maisonneuve, said he wanted to talk about the plan and told La Dauversière that "to avoid debauchery" he wanted to distance himself from Paris and would devote himself to this work "wanting nothing but the honour of serving God and his master the king in the calling and profession of arms which he had always carried." This conversation was reported by Dollier de Casson, a Sulpician and Montréal's first historian, to whom we will return further on.

The indefatigable La Dauversière, the prime mover behind the Société de Notre-Dame de Montréal, got busy recruiting settlers. There are at least 200 contracts involving potential settlers in notaries' records in La Flèche and Nantes; every one bears La Dauversière's signature. It was also La Dauversière who proceeded with the necessary purchasing for the venture; all kinds of supplies were packed into the *"magasin de Montréal"* in La Flèche, between the Hôtel-Dieu and the Loir.

The partners who supported La Dauversière with their money worked anonymously for the most part, so that no complete list exists. However, the names of a number of them are cast in bronze on one of the plaques at the base of the Obelisk in Place Royale that honours Montréal's pioneers.

"If All the Trees on the Island...."

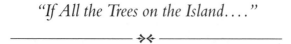

During a visit to the statue of the Virgin in Notre-Dame Cathedral in Paris, the partners chose the name Ville-Marie to designate the future settlement on Montréal Island, no doubt as a symbol of the mystical objective of their venture. The founding of the settlement was planned for 1641.

The first recruits crossed the Atlantic on board three small ships. The first ship weighed anchor in the spring of 1641 with ten men on board; they were probably of Norman origin since the ship left from Dieppe. The joy with which this little contingent was greeted in Québec was short-lived. Québec was threatened by Iroquois incursions; its small population, precariously settled at the foot of Cap aux Diamants, had hoped that the ship would bring precious reinforcements.

The remaining two ships left La Rochelle on May 9. One ship carried Sieur de Maisonneuve with twenty-five men and a priest who was being assigned as chaplain to the Ursulines, while the other ship's passengers were the Jesuit Jacques de La Place, who was going to help his colleagues in Québec, twelve men and a very determined woman whom we have not yet mentioned, Jeanne Mance. This last ship reached Québec after a three-month voyage. The new contingent of pioneers joined the ones from Dieppe, who had already arrived and had quickly begun to unpack the twenty cases shipped the previous year. Unfortunately, however, their haste proved futile, for the ship bearing the leader of the expedition had to return to France three times because of storms, and it probably did not reach New France until September. Three or four men were lost on the voyage, and the surgeon as well!

There could no longer be any question of "going any farther upriver than Kebec this year," wrote Father Barthélemy Vimont, the new Jesuit superior, "and may God will that the Hiroquois will not block the way when we do try to go farther." By now, the Iroquois threat had reached the point where the French were even considering the possibility of abandoning Québec. In this atmosphere, the disappointment that greeted the plan to establish a settlement on Montréal Island should not be surprising. "This venture," Father Vimont added, "would seem as rash as it is simple and bold, were it not based on the power of the one who is always present for those who never undertake anything except according to the divine will."

Dollier de Casson, the Sulpician historian quoted earlier, reported that Governor de Montmagny was persuaded to oppose the partners' plan on the grounds that the European population of the entire colony was not more than 200. It was an absurd plan, a *"folle entreprise"* – a foolish venture. There could have been no doubt in the governor's mind that this argument was well founded. He reminded Sieur de Maisonneuve that the Iroquois had recently broken off peace talks and had overrun the area around Lac Saint-Pierre. Still, Montmagny understood the mystical objective of the promoters of the Ville-Marie settlement. He offered to give Maisonneuve

Île d'Orléans, so that in a crisis the residents of the new settlement could join with the small population of Québec, forming a nucleus that would be better able to resist attack.

But the Paris partners owned most of Montréal Island, and Maisonneuve did not regard himself as being in a position to substitute his own authority for theirs. His response to Montmagny was a historic one: "Sir, what you say to me would be good if I had been sent to deliberate and choose a site. But since it has been determined by the Company that sent me that I would go to Montréal, it is a matter of honour for me, and you will approve, that I will go there to start a colony, even if all the trees on the island were to turn into as many Iroquois!"

This response was not reported by anyone who was there, and the Jesuit *Relations* did not record it word for word. We owe its preservation to Dollier de Casson, who wrote his *Histoire du Montréal* thirty years later, noting that all his sources were oral ones. However, since Dollier arrived in New France in 1666, it is reasonable to suppose that he would have known several people who were there at the time of Maisonneuve's conversation with Montmagny.

Good Knight of Malta that he was, the governor could not be insensitive to such determination and persuasive logic, especially with regard to a project whose fundamental purpose was evangelization. He decided to go to Montréal Island himself in the autumn to participate in choosing a site for the future settlement.

It has been suggested that Sieur de Maisonneuve did not go to Montréal Island on that expedition but was busy unloading the ships instead. This is unlikely, as two of the ships had arrived several weeks before his own. It is true that the *Relations* do not mention Maisonneuve specifically but say only that "the governor, Father Vimont and several other people well versed in knowledge of the country arrived at the place that was chosen for the first settlement." Given Maisonneuve's mandate, however, it would be surprising if he did not consider it essential to participate in choosing the site. According to Dollier de Casson, after his proud reply to Montmagny, Maisonneuve added, "As for the season, because it is too late, with your agreement I will be satisfied to go observe the place with the most nimble of my people before winter to see where I can encamp with my whole company next spring." And so possession was taken of the island "in the name of the Compagnie de Montréal."

The First Winter in New France

——————————— >< ———————————

Paul de Chomedey was born in Neuville-sur-Vanne, some thirty kilometres west of Troyes. The church where he was baptized on February 15, 1612, is still standing, and behind it is an elegant monument to his memory. One tower of the family manor is also still standing.

Paul's father, Louis, was seigneur of a number of domains. In 1614 he bought the fief of Maisonneuve from a man named Charles Palluau as an endowment for his young son. This area is still known today as the "*bois de Palluau.*" The name of the fief was added to Paul's family name.

Very little is known about Paul de Chomedey's childhood and youth. Our only information comes from Dollier de Casson, according to whom he chose the profession of arms when he was thirteen years old. He fought in Holland, and he was so virtuous that he learned to play the lute to fill his leisure time, which he did not want to spend in debauchery like his companions.

It appears that he may have been in Paris looking for a job just as he was turning thirty. Visiting a lawyer one day, he came across a copy of the Jesuit *Relations*, which spoke of Father Charles Lalemant, recently returned from Canada. He wanted to meet this missionary, hoping to find an occupation that could take him away from worldly affairs. And so Lalemant suggested to La Dauversière that he make contact with Maisonneuve.

As procurator in Paris for the Jesuits of New France, Father Lalemant rendered valuable services to the promoters of Ville-Marie. Apart from his role in recruiting Maisonneuve, it was also largely through Lalemant's efforts that Jeanne Mance — who, as noted earlier, arrived in Québec on board one of the ships that preceded Maisonneuve's — decided to devote herself to the project at its outset.

Like Maisonneuve, Mance was from Champagne. There is a solemn black marble statue to her memory under the trees in a small park in front of the cathedral in the town of Langres, where she was born in 1606. In her youth she oversaw the education of her young brothers and sisters. The hospitals of Langres were filled with soldiers wounded in the Thirty Years' War, and it was here that she probably began administering first aid. This helps us understand the services that she would provide in Ville-Marie during the skirmishes with the Iroquois.

In the spring of 1640, she learned that a cousin of hers, Nicolas Dole-beau, nephew of the Duchesse d'Aiguillon, was in Langres. Nicolas's brother Jean was a Jesuit missionary who had just set out for far-off New France. A year earlier, brave Ursuline nuns and sisters of the Hôtel-Dieu had also crossed the Atlantic to devote themselves to the care of the young and the sick in Québec.

Hearing of this work no doubt helped clarify Mance's vocation. The Duchesse d'Aiguillon – Cardinal Richelieu's niece – had been patroness of the nuns responsible for providing Québec with a hospital, a *Hôtel-Dieu*. In Paris visiting her cousin, Nicolas Dolebeau's only sister, Mance spoke of her hope of doing missionary work. Father Lalemant encouraged her enthusi-astically. Then a worthy Récollet, Father Rapin, introduced her to a very rich marquise, Angélique Faure, widow of Claude de Bullion, who, as already noted, had helped found a Récollet community in Faubourg Saint-Laurent.

Probably inspired by the Duchesse d'Aiguillon's generous patronage of Québec, the Marquise de Bullion wanted to do the same for the future set-tlement of Ville-Marie. After several visits, Mance agreed to take charge of the project. La Dauversière was very happy to have a nurse among his first recruits, and so Jeanne Mance set sail on the first of the two ships that left La Rochelle.

The fall of 1641 was well advanced by the time Maisonneuve found a suitable solution to the problem of where the almost sixty people who had accompanied him to New France should spend the winter. A rich man in his seventies living near Québec, Pierre de Puiseaux, Sieur de Montrénault, held two seigneuries, Sainte-Foy and Saint-Michel (Sillery), and he offered them as an outright gift to the Compagnie de Montréal. The manor at Sil-lery was one of the finest dwellings in the colony, and Madame de la Peltrie, lay foundress of the Ursulines, was already living there. Sieur de Maison-neuve, Jeanne Mance and some joiners could spend the winter there, along with Pierre de Puiseaux. Meanwhile, most of the settlers could stay in the house at Sainte-Foy and use the oak trees that surrounded it to build the boats they would eventually require to travel to Montréal Island and carry the tools and other things they would need to found their settlement.

January 25 was Paul de Chomedey's saint's day. To mark the occasion, and perhaps to inject a note of gaiety into the stifling silence of winter, Jeanne Mance gave some gunpowder to a man named Jean Gory. The ten-sion between the newcomers and the small population of Québec arising out of the decision to establish a settlement on Montréal Island does not appear to have faded. In any case, when Gory set off an old cannon, he found himself behind bars. At whose initiative were the salvos fired? The governor collected testimony from witnesses.

"A woman named Mademoiselle Manse who lives with the Sieur de Maisonneuve," said the mason Robelin, who signed with a flourish. The baker Jean Cailliot said that Sieur de Maisonneuve got angry with the workers "when they did not obey Mademoiselle Mance." Pierre Laimery added that "Mademoiselle Mance is in command of the workers in the service of the Compagnie de Montréal" with regard to "what is in the house as Sieur de Maisonneuve understands it." Gory himself said that his leader took advice "from the woman named Mance." This story shows that Jeanne Mance did not lack determination and that Sieur de Maisonneuve had full confidence in her. Her influence over the people around her was substantial enough that some writers have called her the co-founder of Ville-Marie.

When Gory was freed, Maisonneuve greeted him affectionately; this did not help the situation. Might this incident have been a preliminary indication of the tensions that in later years would so frequently arise between governments in Québec and those in Montréal?

Was Montréal Founded on May 17 or May 18?

———————————— ✢ ————————————

Much has been written about whether Montréal was founded on May 17 or May 18, 1642, but as we will see, it is a pointless question.

The coming of spring was the signal to leave for Montréal Island. It is clear that Governor de Montmagny did not hold a grudge against Maisonneuve, either for the defiant response Maisonneuve had given him when he had suggested establishing the settlement on Île d'Orléans or for the Gory incident. In fact, Montmagny wanted to accompany the expedition, even in the face of the Iroquois threat, so that he could authorize its leader to take possession of the island.

The expedition left Sillery on May 8 on board a pinnace and a barge that had been extensively refitted or perhaps even built from scratch during the winter. Apart from the governor, Maisonneuve and Mance, three other distinguished passengers accompanied the settlers: Madame de La Peltrie, who would spend the winter in Ville-Marie; the still energetic Pierre de Puiseaux; and the Jesuit superior, Father Barthélemy Vimont.

As noted earlier, the partners of the Compagnie de Montréal had chosen the name of Ville-Marie for the future settlement in honour of the Virgin Mary. For a long time, people made a distinction between the name of the settlement and the name of the island, which was always Montréal Island. The name Ville-Marie retained official status in documents and correspondence, and some people clearly wanted to give it a note of permanence. As late as 1818, when a biography of Marguerite Bourgeoys was printed in Montréal, the title page specified that the work was appearing à Ville-Marie, chez Wm. Gray, rue St. Paul.

Historians depend principally on two sources for information about the founding of Montréal: Father Vimont and the Sulpician Dollier de Casson. As noted earlier, Dollier de Casson wrote his Histoire du Montréal thirty years after the founding of the settlement. His account was not based on any documents; his only source was his memory of what people had told him. His manuscript is no doubt important on an anecdotal level and provides many details that give us an excellent idea of how the first Montréalistes lived. It has to be acknowledged, however, that his word cannot be taken as the equal of Vimont's when it comes to citing an exact date. Vimont was there when Montréal was founded and celebrated the first mass. Furthermore, in his capacity as Jesuit superior in the colony, he reported on the event within the year to the provincial of the Jesuits in France, Father Jean Filleau, in his Relation de ce qui s'est passé en la Novvelle France en l'année 1642.

According to Dollier, the boats arrived early in the morning of May 18, and after mass the holy sacrament was exposed. "The whole of this day," he wrote, "was passed in devotions, thankgivings and hymns of praise to the Creator." In his account, the founders resorted to using fireflies as sanctuary lamps, which was "altogether fitting ... considering the rudeness of this savage country." The account continues: "Next day, these ceremonies over, they began to make arrangements for the post they were in. At first everyone was under canvas, as in Europe in the army, later they worked hard by cutting stakes and in other ways to surround the place and to safeguard themselves against the surprises and affronts to be feared from the Iroquois." In sum, Dollier reports that Ville-Marie was founded on May 18 and that actual work did not begin until the next day.

Now let us look at Father Vimont's account: "On May 17 of the present

This bas-relief on the Maisonneuve monument in Montréal's Place d'Armes shows Father Barthélemy Vimont saying mass at the founding of Ville-Marie.

year 1642, the Governor placed Sieur de Maison-neufve in possession of the Island, in the name of the Gentlemen of Montréal, to begin the first buildings; Rev. Fr. Vimont sang the *Veni Creator*, said Holy Mass, exposed the Holy Sacrament, so that Heaven would grant an opportune beginning to this project; then the men immediately were set to work; they built a small fortress of large stakes to keep themselves protected against their enemies."

Not only is this an eyewitness account, but its description of how the day was spent also seems more realistic. The Iroquois could burst out of the forest at any moment. Whatever the religious fervour of this small group of people, it is hard to see them spending the whole first day in prayer and waiting until the next day to build an initial rudimentary fortress. On the contrary, Vimont tells us, the settlers were put to work building a small fortress of large stakes "immediately after" the mass. It would have required more time to build this shelter if it had been necessary to cut down trees; however, Samuel de Champlain had cleared Place Royale in 1611. The pioneers would have found right there all the wood they needed to build the palisade.

Fortunately, the Iroquois do not appear to have been aware of the establishment of the outpost and left the settlers in peace for many months. This was especially fortuitous since some of the men had stayed in Québec to finish building the warehouse, while others took care of shipping the equipment left in Sillery. As a result, Maisonneuve could count on only about twenty men to build the barricade and the small fort and make sure they were defended.

A Small Mustard Seed. . . .

During the mass he celebrated at the founding of Montréal, Father Vimont ventured a prediction: "What you see is but a grain of mustard seed but it is sown by hands so pious and so moved by the aspect of faith and piety that Heaven must doubtless have vast designs since it uses such workmen and I have no doubt that the seed will grow into a great tree, one day to achieve wonders." To anyone with a passion for history, seeing the aluminum and glass skyscrapers that bear witness to the extent to which the Ville-Marie of those first days has become a great international city, that statement is a haunting one.

Montréal's rise has been due largely to its geographical position. It stands at the foot of the turbulent rapids that prevented any navigation farther upstream until canals were built, and at the confluence of rivers that in the early days of the colony were the only means of communication. Fur traders had already taken advantage of this latter feature, making Saut Saint-Louis an important trading post. Dollier de Casson aptly noted, "If we take into account convenience for trade, since this place is the farthest to which pinnaces can ascend, there is no doubt that the spot is one of the best in the country for the inhabitants because of the trade they can do there with the savages who come down the river in canoes thereto, from all the nations living higher up the river."

There is no doubt that canalization work done on the Québec City-Montréal portion of the St. Lawrence River starting in the nineteenth century contributed greatly to Montréal's development. It allowed the city's harbour facilities to accommodate ever-larger ships and made it possible for Montréal to win a clear victory in its rivalry with Québec City. As a saying has it, *l'avenir est à l'ouest* – the future is in the west. The opening of the St.

Lawrence Seaway in 1959, allowing large freighters to penetrate the heart of the continent, provided Toronto with the opportunity to become Canada's greatest city at the expense of Montréal. Economists now see this steady westward movement as more than just coincidence. And with the phenomenal growth of air transportation, attention is now turning towards Calgary, Vancouver....

The rest of the year 1642 was quiet. One after another, the colonists left their makeshift dwellings and settled in houses built within the stockade. The colonists hoped that ships coming from France would bring encouraging news, and they did. There were now forty-five partners in the Compagnie de Montréal, and they had voted an additional 40,000 livres for the embryonic settlement. Twelve men came to augment the initial contingent, including Gilbert Barbier, known as le Minime, a skilled joiner to whom La Dauversière entrusted several artillery pieces to consolidate the defence system of the palisades. Eight years later, Sieur de Maisonneuve would grant Barbier the first parcel of land located outside Ville-Marie, in Point Saint-Charles; Barbier's daughter, born in 1663, would be the first Canadian to take the veil in the future Congrégation de Notre-Dame. She would also be the first person to undergo surgery for cancer caused by wearing too prickly a hair-shirt; this operation was performed in 1700 by the surgeon Michel Sarrazin, and she lived thirty-nine more years after it.

Also in 1642, at Governor de Montmagny's orders, construction was begun on a fort at the entrance to the Rivière des Iroquois (today's Richelieu River), the Iroquois' main route to the St. Lawrence. This undertaking protected both Ville-Marie and Trois-Rivières and may have struck fear into the hearts of the Iroquois, who were armed by the Dutch.

People needed a large dose of courage to settle in a place that was far away from everything and could be raided by cannibals, so that they ran the risk of ending up in a cooking pot! To realize what was involved, it is sufficient to read about the indescribable fate that awaited Algonquins who fell into Iroquois hands in the 1642 Relation. The Iroquois roasted three two-month-old babies slowly on a spit in the presence of their mother and then savoured their flesh. "These wolves devoured their prey," Father Vimont reported. "Some threw themselves on a leg, some on a chest. Some sucked the marrow from the bones, some opened a head to take out the brain. In a word, they ate people with as much appetite and more joy than hunters would eat a boar or a deer."

Soon after the middle of March 1643, the frame of Ville-Marie's main building was completed. A cannon was hoisted there to mark the feast of St. Joseph "with the noise of artillery." This was a rash gesture, perhaps, for people who did not want to attract attention. Was it this joyous blast that brought the existence of Ville-Marie to the attention of the Iroquois? Or did an Iroquois party notice the fort while giving chase to a group of Algonquins? In any case, the news spread. In early June, the *Montréalistes* would experience their first losses.

The First Cross on Mount Royal

In 1611, as we noted, Samuel de Champlain built a brick wall on an island across from Place Royale, to see how far the waters rose at their highest point. Did Sieur de Maisonneuve, thirty-one years later, choose a place for his settlement that was too low or too close to the river's edge?

In late December the waters swelled, invaded the grasslands around the enclosure, filled the ditches that protected the palisades and knocked on the door of the main settlement. Maisonneuve quickly had a cross erected near the Saint-Pierre River, in the hope that heaven would restrain the flood, and he promised that if his wish came true he would carry another cross up to the top of the mountain. "Just at midnight," wrote Father Vimont, "and just as we were celebrating the Birth of the Son of God on earth," the waters stabilized and then receded, "placing the inhabitants out of danger and the Captain in execution of his promise."

In the next few days Maisonneuve had a heavy cross made and a path cleared, and on January 6, Epiphany, he carried it on his shoulders to "the peak of the mountain," where Father François Du Peron, who would spend the winter in Ville-Marie, said mass. This first procession in Montréal is pictured in a stained-glass window in Notre-Dame Basilica on Place d'Armes.

Father Vimont wrote about the settlers who were spending their first winter on Canadian soil in very laudatory terms. He marvelled that "the French who are here, by and large, are very different from one another in age and character and almost all come from different parts of the country, but in will they are one, working towards the same goal: the glory of God and the salvation of these poor Savages."

This stained-glass window in Notre-Dame Basilica on Place d'Armes shows Sieur de Maisonneuve climbing the slopes of Mount Royal, carrying a heavy cross that he would plant on the mountaintop.

The first winter passed in perfect harmony, his account went on, and no one was ill, "something that has never been seen in any new settlement here." He took note of the location's beauty, its rich land and abundance of meadows. The natives would happily settle here if a way were found to protect them against their enemies.

It was a well-travelled area, for the St. Lawrence was a boulevard. Towards the end of February 1643, twenty-five warriors stopped there, with women and children, on their way to fight the Iroquois. Two or three days later, another group of natives arrived; they were on a hunting

I

Liber matrimoniorum In aedibus B. Mariæ Montis regalis factorum.

1643
1. Anno Domini 1643 die 7 Martij Ego Imbertus Duperon Societ. Jesu Sacerdos Josephum Oumasasikweie et Joannam Mitigoukoue rebus Baptizatos et iam dudum, more patrio matrimonio ~~iunctam~~ coniunctos In aedibus B. Mariæ Montis regalis interrogavi eorumque mutuo consensu habito, Sollemniter per verba de præsenti matrimonio ritu Christiano facto coniunxi, præsentibus testibus

2. Anno Dni 1643 die 9 Martij Ego Anto[nius] Societ. J. Sacerdos Carolum ... et Magdalenam Argabine rebus Baptizatos et iam dudum more patrio matrimonio coniunctos In aedibus B. Mariæ Montis regalis interrogavi eorumque mutuo consensu habito Sollemniter per verba de præsenti matrimonio ritu Christiano facto coniunxi, præsentibus testibus

In 1643, Father Joseph Antoine Poncet performed the first wedding in "Montis Regalis." He married two natives, Joseph Oumasasikweie and Joanne Mitigoukoue. The *Liber matrimonium* was written in Latin.

expedition. Their chief, whose name was Oumasasikweie, was baptized and benefited from his new status by taking a wife in a church ceremony. This was the first time that such an occasion had been celebrated in Ville-Marie, according to Vimont's account. On March 9 the uncle of this first convert, Tesswehas, "Captain of all these lands," whom the French called "le Borgne of the Isle," was baptized along with his wife.

Oumasasikweie's wedding may have been the first in Ville-Marie, but the chronicler could not say the same of his baptism, for on July 28, 1642, Father Joseph Antoine Poncet had baptized a little four-year-old Algonquin, "the first fruit that this Island has borne for Paradise."

But the *Montréalistes* would not live in peace and harmony for much longer. The first sacrifice of their blood, spilled to ensure the survival of their little settlement, was not long in coming.

Because the French had come to an agreement with the first natives they had met along the great "river of Canadas," the Hurons and the Algonquins, they had unwittingly become an object of hatred for the enemies of those natives. It has been written that if the route of French penetration of the continent had been the Hudson River rather than the St. Lawrence, exactly the opposite would have happened.

It didn't help matters that the Dutch in New Amsterdam – present-day New York – armed some Iroquois tribes, especially the Mohawks, against the French, with a view towards increasing their profits from the fur trade. The Mohawks lived in three villages near the Dutch. "They trade mostly for muskets," the *Relations* reported. "They now have three hundred, and they use them skilfully and boldly."

In early June 1643, Iroquois assembled in "a place popularly [called] *la Chine* [China]" decided to conduct an initial strike against the settlement. This was the location at the head of the rapids from where canoes left for the west – and from where, it was hoped, they would eventually reach Grand Cathay. It is still called Lachine, written now as one word.

Some forty Iroquois attacked six men, carpenters and woodcutters, surprising them in the midst of their work. Only ten of the Iroquois actually fell on the men while the others moved towards the palisades to give the impression of an attack on the settlement; they were past masters of deception. Three of the Frenchmen were immediately killed and scalped while the other three were taken prisoner. Only one of them escaped; he returned to Ville-Marie in a damaged canoe after filling the holes with grass. There is no doubt that the two others were cruelly tortured to death.

The survivor reported that the Iroquois had hidden a large quantity of furs that they had taken in a confrontation with a group of Hurons. Maison-neuve allowed the settlers to go take them, and he distributed them to his men "without keeping any for himself." The names of the three men whose bodies were found after the Iroquois left are preserved in the *Liber defunc-torum* in the Ville-Marie parish register: Guillaume Boissier, from Limousin; Bernard Berté, from Lyon; and Pierre Laforest *dit* Lauvergnat, who, as his name suggests, was from Auvergne. They head a long list of pio-neers whose names are written in blood in our history, and let us salute them.

A Rescuer from Champagne

In the early summer of 1643, Governor de Montmagny visited the *Montréal-istes* just as they were mourning the loss of five of their companions and brought them very encouraging news. Favourably impressed with the devotion of the Société de Notre-Dame de Montréal, the king had donated a 350-ton ship, the *Notre-Dame*, to the society. The partners had quickly sent the ship out with a varied cargo of relief supplies for the new settle-ment. The king's generosity should not be surprising: after all, this small group of men and women, with no thought of material gain for themselves, were bringing out more colonists to New France than had syndicates of wealthy merchants aiming to obtain the exclusive right to carry on the fur trade.

The governor also told Sieur de Maisonneuve that some forty new recruits were sailing to Ville-Marie to reinforce the settlement. In addition, the king had authorized Montmagny to build a fort supplied with cannons "and other things needed for war" so that Ville-Marie's small population would be in a better position to resist Iroquois incursions.

The reinforcements arrived in Ville-Marie in September. Their leader was a man who would render valuable services to the settlement. Like Maisonneuve, Louis d'Ailleboust was thirty-one years old, and he too was from Champagne, having been born in the village of Ancy-le-Franc. His father, Antoine, was a counsellor to the prince of Condé, and his grand-father, Jean d'Ailleboust, was one of the first physicians to King Henri IV, who had elevated him to the nobility.

Louis d'Ailleboust was known for his skill in the art of fortification. He had the initial palisade replaced with a solid wall flanked by four bastions. He recommended to the settlers that they plant good French wheat instead of the peas and corn they had planted before; the yield had not been enough to feed either their families or the natives, who were coming to Ville-Marie in increasing numbers as a result of the generous welcome they received from the French.

D'Ailleboust was also able to tell Jeanne Mance that an anonymous benefactor had decided to endow Ville-Marie with a hospital. Thanks to this woman's generosity, the new contingent included ten workers whose task was to build the hospital. The benefactor insisted that her anonymity be respected; we know that she was Angélique Faure, Marquise de Bullion, the rich widow of the superintendent of the royal finances.

Accompanying Louis d'Ailleboust to New France were his wife, Marie-Barbe de Boulogne, and her sister, Philippine Gertrude. They were from Ravières, another village in Champagne. As we have seen, Madame de La Peltrie had spent the winter in Ville-Marie, no doubt to make sure that Jeanne Mance was not the only woman there. Now, "seeing that Mademoiselle Mance had plenty of help from her own sex," she decided to return to Québec with her companion.

The generous Pierre de Puiseaux, who had donated his two seigneuries to the Société de Notre-Dame de Montréal, became ill with paralysis. "His brain having become enfeebled with age," he said that he would like to regain possession of his old properties so that he could go to France in search of a cure. Sieur de Maisonneuve provided for his return, and the members of the society "did not abandon him even to the grave; he had great need of this help, for he was then seventy-seven or seventy-eight years old, and he had spent his long life in incredible toil, both in New Spain where he had accumulated his wealth and in New France where he had spent it."

Once the dispatches to be placed on the last ships sailing for France before winter set in were completed, serious work was begun on repairing and strengthening the settlement's structures of defence under d'Ailleboust's leadership.

Iroquois prowled around the settlement regularly, looking for an opportunity to obtain more French scalps. The settlers and workers were unhappy with Maisonneuve's refusal to lead an attack on these native parties that stalked the forest close to Ville-Marie. None of them had developed the cunning needed for forest skirmishes, Maisonneuve explained. Furthermore, he argued, they would run the risk of being at a numerical disadvantage on expeditions of this sort, and losses in battle would threaten the implementation of the mandate that had been entrusted to him.

Gradually, people began to grumble that perhaps their commander was not so much cautious as afraid. These complaints were reported to Maisonneuve, who clearly did not want slander of this sort to spread. He decided to take advantage of the first opportunity to demonstrate that the allegation against him was not true; such an opportunity arose in late winter.

Dogs were used to stand guard around the fort. This was a very old practice: before piers were built linking Saint-Malo to the mainland, the town of Saint-Malo-en-l'Isle was saved by mastiffs on its fortifications at night. This episode from the distant past is recalled by the Venelle aux Chiens, an alley opposite the Saint-Vincent gate, at the entrance to Rue Jacques-Cartier. In Ville-Marie, according to Dollier de Casson, a dog named Pilote had been trained to lead the canine scouting parties sent into the woods. On the morning of March 30, 1644, the dogs' howling bore an important message: they had discovered Iroquois lurking behind the trees.

The Battle of Place d'Armes

————————— ✧✦ —————————

"Our enemies are in the woods. Are we never going to see them?"

"Yes, you will see them," Maisonneuve replied. "Get ready to march right away. But be as brave as you have promised to be: I will lead you!"

The expedition almost ended badly. However, the *Montréalistes* had an opportunity to realize that their commander's reservations had indeed been prompted more by caution than by cowardice.

It was the very end of March. Everywhere the snow was thick. Ville-Marie was linked to the outside by a single beaten path, along which wood cut in the neighbouring forest was hauled to the settlement for the construction of the hospital. The natives moved easily on their snowshoes. The French did not have enough snowshoes, nor were they as skilled in using them. No matter: Sieur de Maisonneuve did not want to be suspected of cowardice any more. Some thirty settlers went out to the woods to face the enemy. Once there, they found out that about 200 Iroquois were waiting for them, ready for an ambush. They were short of powder. They had to retreat quickly behind the protection of the wall, going back along the beaten path.

With his second pistol, Maisonneuve fells a feathered chief who has grabbed him by the throat. (Bas-relief, Maisonneuve monument, Place d'Armes.)

Maisonneuve was the last to withdraw, making sure that the wounded were already under cover.

Maisonneuve, whom the Iroquois recognized as the commander of the settlement, would be a highly valued prize if taken. It was left to one of their chiefs to capture him. All of his men having retreated to the safety of the fort, Maisonneuve faced the enemy alone, a pistol in each hand. The feathered warrior harried him from such close range "that he almost always had him on his shoulders." A first shot missed its target: the chief ducked when he saw Maisonneuve take aim. He got up and jumped at Maisonneuve's throat, but Maisonneuve felled him with the second pistol. While the Iroquois rushed forward towards their chief to take him away, Maisonneuve returned to the fort to everyone's great relief. Even then, he could have been killed by friendly fire: an inept settler lit a cannon pointed towards the road, but it did not go off.

It was a painful experience. The *Montréalistes* lost three more of their comrades: Guillaume Lebeau, from La Rochelle; Jean Mattemasse, from Bordeaux; and Pierre Bigot, from Saintonge. They realized that they had been foolhardy and they no longer thought that their leader lacked courage. They swore that they would not risk his life again.

Despite the constant Iroquois threat, the settlers went out to the fields, sickles in their hands and muskets slung across their backs. Two statues at

These statues at the base of the Maisonneuve monument in Place d'Armes show Charles Le Moyne, musket slung across his back, reaping wheat, while an Iroquois, hatchet in hand, lies in wait for settlers busy with the harvest.

the base of the Maisonneuve monument in Montréal's Place d'Armes are an apt representation of Ville-Marie's beginnings. One is of an Iroquois crouching in the underbrush, hatchet in hand, watching the settlers at work. The other is of the pioneer Charles Le Moyne, wary as he holds a handful of wheat and harvests the fruit of his labour.

Also in 1644, a company of soldiers sent to strengthen the colony's defence arrived in New France, along with another contingent of pioneers bound for Ville-Marie recruited by the Société de Notre-Dame de Montréal. They all set sail under the leadership of one Captain de La Barre, who in La Rochelle posed as a devout man. In his belt he wore "a large rosary with a large crucifix that he kept in front of his eyes almost all the time." There was no hesitation in giving responsibility for the voyage to such an "apostolic man."

Occasionally, there were periods of respite for the *Montréalistes*, as Iroquois pressure was not constant, and during these periods it was possible to stroll under the trees. It was during one of these periods that Sieur de Maisonneuve found out that Captain de La Barre was not quite as "apostolic" as he wanted people to believe.

This fake often went walking in the woods with a native maiden. He made her pregnant – the Sulpician Dollier de Casson uses the vulgar term *engrosser*. (Before becoming a priest, Dollier had served for three years under Marshal de Turenne as a cavalry captain, and he never completely gave up his rugged military manner. Thus, in describing the *Montréalistes'* pathetic return to the fort in the snow after their sortie against the Iroquois, pursued by natives "well mounted on snowshoes," he willingly acknowledges "that they were like cavalry, and we in comparison were barely infantry.") After a few months Maisonneuve, recognizing that La Barre had "nothing holy about him except his rosary and his false manner," made arrangements to have him sent back to France.

Early in 1645, the Iroquois set a variety of traps for the settlers, but they emerged unscathed. They were undoubtedly more careful and they had learned the art of the ambush. In any case, they always went out to the fields in groups, and at the sound of the bell at noon they returned to the fort together to eat.

One day the Iroquois posted a scout in a tree with luxuriant foliage; after the settlers returned to work, he was to indicate where to attack them. At the sound of the bell, the settlers all came out at the same time, and they stationed their sentries for the afternoon under that very tree. The unfortunate "crow" spent the rest of the day on his perch: "He was neither seen nor heard." The settlers heard the story after the event from some other natives.

Tribulations of the First Hospital

As already noted, ten workers arrived in Ville-Marie in September 1643 to build a hospital. The Marquise de Bullion had followed through in carrying out her generous plan.

Given the donor's wish to remain anonymous, few people knew her identity. Among those who did know the secret were Jeanne Mance, whom the marquise had received in her private mansion on Rue Plâtrière (now Rue Jean-Jacques Rousseau) in Paris; Father Rapin, who had introduced Mance to the marquise; Father Charles Lalemant, procurator in Paris for the New France missions; and Jérôme Le Royer de La Dauversière.

The Duchesse d'Aiguillon and her prestigious uncle, Cardinal Richelieu, had donated a little over 40,000 livres to found the Hôtel-Dieu in Québec. The marquise wanted to give at least as much, and she paid 42,000 livres in hard cash – "louis, double louis, gold crowns, quarter crowns and coins" – to La Dauversière and the secretary of the Société de Notre-Dame de Montréal, Bertrand Drouart. She no doubt appreciated the value of the gold louis all the more in that it was her late husband who had struck the first louis in his capacity as Louis XIII's treasurer.

On January 12, 1644, the act establishing the *Fondation pour les malades dans l'Isle de Montréal* (Foundation for the Ill on the Island of Montréal) was signed before the notary Chaussière in Paris. The signatures of Drouart and La Dauversière are on the contract, in their capacities as secretary and *procureur* of the *compagnie des Assocyez pour la conversion des Sauvages de la nouvelle France en l'Isle de Montréal* (Company of Partners for the Conversion of the Savages of New France on the Island of Montréal). The marquise's signature, however, is not. She is designated simply as a person "who does not want to be known in this world" and who wishes "to build and found a hospital on the Island of Montréal in the name and to the honour of St. Joseph to provide treatment, care, medicine and food for the poor sick people of the country and educate them in what they need for their health."

La Dauversière noted that 4,000 livres had already been spent to hire, feed and maintain the ten workers sent out to Montréal Island in June of the previous year (1643) to begin the construction work and 2,000 more would be set aside for their maintenance in the current year. The beneficiaries of the gift undertook to invest the remaining 36,000 livres to provide an annual income to go to the future hospital. The marquise stipulated that if "the Island of Montréal should become completely uninhabited and abandoned both by the French and by the Savages with no hope that they would ever return and the hospital should become useless," the foundation's capital should be paid as an irrevocable gift to the Hôtel-Dieu in Paris.

In the fall of 1643, Louis d'Ailleboust had brought Jeanne Mance the news that the Marquise de Bullion had decided to carry through her plan. Maisonneuve had had a small temporary hospital set up inside the fort. The marquise no doubt thought that construction work on the future Hôtel-Dieu had been progressing rapidly since the arrival of the ten workers: she

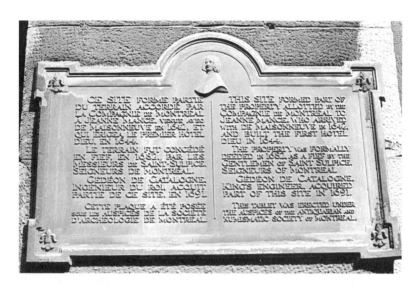

This plaque at the corner of Saint-Paul and Saint-Sulpice streets indicates the site of the first hospital.

had a variety of furnishings and an additional 2,000 livres sent to Mance. But the real situation was very different.

We find out what the workers were really working on from the *Journal des jésuites*. In October 1645, Father Jérôme Lalemant, superior of the New France missions, arrived in Ville-Marie and found that all the wood needed for the frame of a house intended for the Jesuit missionaries had been prepared. Just as they were getting ready to put up the walls, Maisonneuve received an order from France to use all the workers for something else, "that is to build a hospital, for which they had received a lot of money in the last few years, and yet no work had been begun."

This is an eyewitness account and there can be no serious doubt about its accuracy. Does this mean that, for Mance, housing the missionaries and evangelizing the natives was a greater priority than caring for the sick – especially the settlers who came back wounded after Iroquois incursions? In any case, Maisonneuve was wondering how to tell the Jesuits delicately about this order when Father Lalemant took responsibility for informing them. Some held him responsible; as he wrote, "they made trouble for me, as if it were I who had prevented it."

Maisonneuve put a parcel of land with four linear arpents (230 metres) of riverfront and stretching fifty arpents (2.9 kilometres) back from the river at the disposal of the future hospital. However, Mance quickly realized that

La maison de Mlle Mance, as Ville-Marie's first hospital was called, built in 1645 a short distance from the fort. (Drawing by the historian Aristide Beaugrand-Champagne based on old documents.)

The chapel of the old Hôtel-Dieu, at the corner of Saint-Paul and Saint-Sulpice streets, was used by the *Montréalistes* as a parish church.

because of the Iroquois she could not develop this holding for the benefit of the institution and she returned most of the land to Maisonneuve, retaining only seven square arpents (24,000 square metres).

There was not enough space for the hospital inside the fort and so it was built on a small height of land a little less than half a kilometre upstream, at the present corner of Saint-Paul and Saint-Sulpice streets, where a bronze plaque with a bust of Jeanne Mance marks the site for passersby. Its location sheltered it from spring floods, and it was surrounded by a solid palisade and a ditch.

This first hospital in Ville-Marie was referred to as *la maison de Mlle Mance*. The first hospital nuns who came from La Flèche to take responsibility for the Hôtel-Dieu stayed here, as did the first Sulpicians while their seminary was being built.

Two Voyages to France

——————— ⇥⇤ ———————

In 1645, ships from France brought Maisonneuve sad news: his father had died. He had to return to France to take care of family affairs arising out of his father's death. Mance entrusted him with a letter for the Marquise de Bullion, asking her to establish another income so that Mance and her servant could live without drawing on the income that had been set aside for the poor and sick in the hospital. She said she was embarrassed to appeal to the marquise's generosity once again, but she added that "I would fear eternal reproach if I failed to inform you of the need that I know is there."

Maisonneuve entrusted Louis d'Ailleboust with governing the settlement while he was away. On September 20, 1645, a peace treaty was agreed to at Trois-Rivières between the French, the Algonquins and the Hurons on one side and the Iroquois on the other. The negotiations, punctuated by exchanges of gifts featuring wampum necklaces and beaver skins, were conducted in four languages, and the event concluded with a feast offered to 400 natives. The natives acknowledged the peace in a symbolic way: "It is going well. We are all eating together and all have the same dish." Unfortunately, it would only be a temporary truce, but D'Ailleboust took advantage of the period of calm to complete the work on Ville-Marie's defences.

Little is known about Maisonneuve's stay in France. He probably divided his time between his native Champagne and Paris, as the partners in the Société de Notre-Dame de Montréal had not seen him for four years. Once he had completed his business, in 1646, he was in a hurry to return to the colony. It may have been he who brought back the Marquise de

Bullion's reply to Mance: she had turned 20,000 livres over to the partners, with which they were to establish an income for Mance "so that you can serve the poor without being an expense to them." She added, "My desire to give you the things you need is greater than your desire to ask me for them." Dollier de Casson commented that the marquise "well knew that in charity there are valuable letters of exchange for the next life."

Maisonneuve, however, could not give Mance the letter personally. He had hardly reached Québec when another ship brought him a letter from La Dauversière, asking him to come back quickly to France. According to Dollier de Casson, Maisonneuve's mother had "conceived a ruinous plan for a second marriage"; in addition, his brother-in-law had been murdered. Of the alleged whims of Louis de Chomedey's widow we know nothing more, but we do know that Dollier's memory was faulty regarding the second reason. François Bouvot, husband of Maisonneuve's half-sister Jacqueline de Chomedey, was indeed murdered by a cousin of Jacqueline's, Sieur de Médavie, but this did not happen until 1651. Four years after that, Jacqueline herself died at the murderous hand of the same cousin!

In reality, it was undoubtedly administrative matters that prompted Maisonneuve's return to France. The previous year (1645), the Company of One Hundred Associates had ceded its fur-trading privileges to the Compagnie des Habitants, formed by prominent residents of New France. Maisonneuve's intention to cross the Atlantic again in the fall was not the only reason he did not return immediately to Ville-Marie: he also had to attend a meeting of the new company in Québec.

The proceedings at this meeting appear to have been marked by dissension. "Members of the council," reported the *Journal des jésuites*, "tried mightily to have their wages increased and to be compensated for their services, which caused such confusion that people were ashamed. M. de Maisonneuve did not want to sign, so that nothing was signed for these bonuses." The chronicler does not specify the auspices under which Maisonneuve attended this lively meeting, but it was undoubtedly as a representative of the Société de Montréal.

To give an idea of the wealth that the fur trade could bring, in 1646 the Compagnie des Habitants harvested more than 160 poinçons of beaver pelts. The poinçon is an old unit of volume that represented 200 pounds of furs, and furs sold at ten francs a pound. And there were other skins as well, notably moose.

Maisonneuve reported the stance he had taken to La Dauversière, who supported it unreservedly. The founding of the Compagnie des Habitants was a blow to Governor de Montmagny's authority, resulting in irregularities that the Conseil du Roi (Louis XIV was still only eight years old) wanted to correct. Thus a triumvirate was established, made up of the governor of the colony, the Jesuit superior and the governor of Montréal.

There was talk of replacing Montmagny. He may have expressed some dissatisfaction, or the king's advisers may have anticipated that he would not be happy with the establishment of the new triumvirate. We are told that the governorship was offered to Maisonneuve, but he refused, suggesting that it be given to Louis d'Ailleboust instead. It is not surprising that Maisonneuve would have been approached. Not only did he have an impeccable reputation, but there was also another factor in his favour: three members of the Conseil du Roi belonged to the Société de Montréal. La Dauversière and his close collaborators had chosen their associates well!

In the summer of 1647, Maisonneuve finally saw his beloved Ville-Marie once again. Maisonneuve told d'Ailleboust that he was wanted in France as soon as possible. D'Ailleboust sailed on board the *Notre-Dame* on October 21, and on August 20, 1648, he returned to Québec as governor of New France. Montmagny received him courteously, in fact ceremoniously, and left for France a month later.

Pierre Gadois, Montréal's First Habitant

While he was in Paris, Maisonneuve took the opportunity to meet with the leaders of the Société de Notre-Dame de Montréal. The partners owned 85,000 hectares of land on Montréal Island, but they didn't want to keep any of this immense holding for themselves. They all held prestigious positions, and they had got together only to pursue a completely selfless goal: to encourage the evangelization of the native tribes.

So far, the *Montréalistes* had lived a communal life, working in the fields during the day and then spending each night in the fort. Now the partners decided that the time had come to allow settlers to occupy their own concessions. This was the only formula that would make it possible to put the colony on a permanent footing.

When Maisonneuve returned to Ville-Marie in 1647, he made arrangements to carry out the partners' wishes. The first beneficiary of the new

The signatures on this first deed of concession can easily be made out: Paul de Chomedey (Maisonneuve); Pierre Gadois, who accepts the forty arpents granted to him; Louis Goudreau, master surgeon of Villemarye; César Léger, master toolmaker, witness; and Jean de Saint-Père, notary. Léger had married Pierre Gadois's daughter Roberte, who in 1650 took Louis Prudhomme as her second husband.

settlement policy was Pierre Gadois, from the village of Igé in the county of Perche west of Paris (now in the department of Orne), where he is recalled by an inscription in the church.

On January 4, 1648, Gadois was granted forty arpents of land in front of the notary Jean de Saint-Père. The archivist É.-Z. Massicotte has determined that the boundaries of this piece of land would coincide with the present Saint-Pierre Street in the east, McGill Street in the west, Saint-Paul Street in the south and Ontario Street in the north, representing an area of about 300,000 square metres. If Gadois were alive today, he would be the owner of an empire: real-estate values in downtown Montréal were estimated at $3,000 a square metre in 1988!

In 1661, Gadois fought the Iroquois, although he was by then sixty-eight years old. "An old man named Pierre Gadois," Dollier de Casson reported, "the first *habitant* of this place, was greatly noticed and gave a good example to everyone: it is said that this man, decrepit though he was, fired on the Iroquois as vigorously and actively as a twenty-five-year-old, without anyone being able to stop him."

Let us also remember the other pioneers who were granted land in the first five years: Jean Desroches, Simon Richomme, Blaise Juillet *dit* Avignon, Louis Prudhomme, Gilbert Barbier, Jean Descaries *dit* Le Houx, Urbain Tessier *dit* Lavigne, Jacques Archambault and Nicolas Godé.

Jean Desroches married Françoise Godé in 1647, and they had thirteen children. Simon Richomme, from Samuel de Champlain's native town of Brouage, died in February 1655 after an accident involving a falling tree. Blaise Juillet, from Avignon, also came to a sad end: he drowned near Île Saint-Paul (the present Nuns' Island) in April 1660 as he was fleeing a party of Iroquois. He left four children, all of whom had children of their own.

Louis Prudhomme, from Pomponne near Meaux just east of Paris, saved the life of Major Lambert Closse in 1653. A brewer and later a captain of militia, he married Pierre Gadois's daughter Roberte and they had seven children, of whom at least six had children of their own. Gilbert Barbier, from the region of Nevers on the Loire south of Paris, was a master carpenter and became treasurer of Montréal. His daughter Marie founded the first community of the Congrégation de Notre-Dame in Québec and then succeeded Marguerite Bourgeoys as superior general of the order.

In 1654, while passing through Québec, Jean Descaries met Michelle Artus, a young woman from Bousse near La Flèche in Anjou who had recently arrived in the colony. They immediately fell in love, and the notary Guillaume Audouart, called to the warehouse of Montréal, drew up the marriage contract. Three sons and a daughter from this marriage would have children of their own.

Urbain Tessier *dit* Lavigne, born in Château-la-Vallière in the archdiocese of Tours, was a woodcutter. He married Jacques Archambault's daughter Marie, and ten of their children would themselves marry. The Iroquois burned their house in 1651. Some of their descendants carried on a long but futile struggle to have the courts recognize that they still had rights to Place d'Armes.

Jacques Archambault was born in the village of Dompierre-sur-Mer, right near Rochefort-sur-Mer on the Atlantic coast. In 1988, his descendants put up a plaque to his memory in the village church. He almost lost his life when the Iroquois burned the house of his son-in-law, Urbain Tessier. He and his wife Françoise Tourault, also from Dompierre-sur-Mer, had seven children.

Nicolas Godé came from Igé in Perche, the same village as Pierre Gadois, whose sister Françoise he married. He was killed by the Iroquois in October 1657, at the same time as the notary Jean de Saint-Père. Françoise survived him by many years, and was considered Montréal's first centenarian. When she died in 1689 the priest announced her age as 103, but this was probably somewhat exaggerated.

This list could be much longer, because during his term as governor Maisonneuve signed no fewer than 123 acts of concession. We are only going as far as 1653 because on March 30 of that year Louis Séguier, secretary to the Montréal partners, ratified the concessions made until then to confirm the land titles. This precious document is preserved in the archives of Saint-Sulpice seminary on Notre-Dame Street in Montréal. Louis Séguier – who that same year was named provost of the guilds of Paris – was a cousin of Chancellor Pierre Séguier, in whose house, as noted earlier, the initial chance meeting between Jérôme Le Royer de La Dauversière and Jean-Jacques Olier had taken place.

On the Brink of the Abyss

————————— ✦ —————————

Unfortunately, the peace concluded at Trois-Rivières in September 1645 did not last. This was only to be expected, as Iroquois treachery was legendary.

During the winter the Iroquois burned Fort Richelieu at the mouth of the Richelieu River, their route to the St. Lawrence. The fort was not garrisoned, and the French may have made the ill-fated decision that it was no longer useful. In the spring the Iroquois formed bands to harass the Hurons and the Algonquins, who were sufficiently unafraid that they were busy hunting and fishing. This was the beginning of the destruction of these tribes by the Iroquois, even though all three groups had at one time been part of the same nation.

Maisonneuve's return helped put minds at rest. "There was such a fright throughout Canada," reported Dollier de Casson, "that hearts were frozen by the excess of fear, especially in such a forward outpost as Montréal." Governor de Montmagny, Dollier wrote, dissuaded new arrivals from settling in Montréal, "saying it did not appear that the settlement could survive." Maintaining the settlement would not have been humanly possible, he acknowledged, "were it not that God was part of the effort."

It is time to note the presence in Ville-Marie of Charles Le Moyne. Born in Dieppe, he had arrived in New France in 1641 at the age of fifteen. He spent four years with the Hurons to learn native languages and then joined the garrison at Trois-Rivières in 1645. The next year he settled permanently in Ville-Marie, where he would spend the rest of his life. His sons would win such fame that they would earn the title of "Maccabees of New France."

Charles Le Moyne, whose statue stands at the base of the Maisonneuve monument, was one of Montréal's most admirable pioneers. In the spring of 1648 some Iroquois arrived outside the settlement, giving the impression that they wanted to engage in negotiations. Le Moyne and Thomas Godefroy, Sieur de Normanville, an interpreter who had spent several years with the Hurons, went out to meet them. Against his companion's advice, Godefroy went forward recklessly and was surrounded by the Iroquois. Le Moyne quickly pointed his gun at three Iroquois who were near him; one offered to go get Godefroy, but he did not come back. Le Moyne brought the two others back to the fort, and the next day Godefroy was freed. Unfortunately, he would be killed by the Iroquois four years later. After Le Moyne captured the two Iroquois, he and Nicolas Godé captured two more Iroquois who were spotted on a sandbar.

Even if "a poor man, ten paces from his door, was not safe," the Montréalistes held their own courageously. They had become experienced in the art of avoiding ambushes, and in 1648 they lost only one person, Mathurin Bonenfant, killed at the age of twenty-five. The thought of abandoning the settlement did not enter their minds. Not only did Maison-neuve begin granting concessions, as already noted, but work was begun on building a mill to grind wheat. In this way the Iroquois would understand that the French were not "inclined to abandon this glorious land to them."

People were glad to see Louis d'Ailleboust return in August, endowed with his commission as governor, but the ships also brought sad news: Montréal had to compete for the partners' devotion with missions in the Levant. One of them had left 80,000 livres in his will for the establishment of a diocese in New France, but the bequest had become invalid "because this matter had not been diligently attended to."

Cardinal Mazarin, Cardinal Richelieu's successor, had authorized the formation of a mobile detachment made up of forty soldiers that could be deployed wherever the Iroquois threat was most intense. As commander of this detachment, the new governor appointed his nephew, Charles-Joseph d'Ailleboust des Muceaux, who was a member of both the Société de Notre-Dame de Montréal and the Compagnie des Habitants. The presence of these soldiers on constant alert in Ville-Marie relieved some of the pres-sure of the settlers' daily grind.

But the *Montréalistes'* troubles were not over. In 1649 the ships again brought bad news: Father Rapin, who had introduced Jeanne Mance to the Marquise de Bullion, had died; the Société de Notre-Dame de Montréal was still in disarray; and La Dauversière was not only seriously ill but also near bankruptcy, having committed his own resources and guaranteed those of others to found and consolidate Ville-Marie. Mance, who had gone to Québec, heard all this news. She was not an indecisive woman. If she returned to Montréal she would miss the fall departure of the fleet for France, so she decided to leave for France immediately. She wrote to Maisonneuve, letting him know of her departure.

New France was in a critical situation. The Iroquois had decided to annihilate the Hurons. They destroyed Saint-Joseph mission, which housed 400 families, and killed the missionary Antoine Daniel, the first Jesuit mur-dered in Huronia. Then they destroyed Saint-Ignace mission, brutally tor-turing to death Father Jean de Brébeuf and Father Gabriel Lalemant. A cen-tury and a half later the description of this tragedy in the Jesuit *Relations* made such an impression on the painter Francisco Goya that he rendered it in two paintings, which are now in the museum at Besançon, France. Finally, the missionary Charles Garnier died in the destruction of Saint-Jean mission.

The Iroquois, wrote Dollier de Casson, "having no more cruelties to carry out farther up because there were no more Hurons to destroy, turned to Montréal Island." Not only Ville-Marie but the whole colony teetered on the brink of the abyss.

Sparing the Whole Country by Saving Montréal

———————— ✥ ————————

In France the energetic Jeanne Mance spoke to many people and revived their flagging altruism. The partnership was reorganized. The partners recognized their collective interest in Montréal Island through a mutual deed of gift *inter vivos* covering the fort, the *habitations* and the outbuildings; all their heirs were permanently excluded from this agreement. Mance may have foreseen the day when another company would have to take over from the partners and realized that at that point it would be essential to produce clear titles.

Abbé Jean-Jacques Olier, who had been curé of Saint-Sulpice in Faubourg de Vaurigard since 1642 and had founded a seminary for young clerics there, became one of the directors of the society. Louis Séguier was confirmed as secretary and La Dauversière, who had regained his health, was confirmed as *procureur*.

Mance found that the Marquise de Bullion's generosity had not diminished: the marquise gave her a large sum of money to recruit more settlers. She never left the private mansion on Rue Plâtrière without having received some purses full of money, so that one day her porters noticed that she was heavier on the journey out than on the journey in – leading her to take the precaution of using a different chair.

To increase the hospital's income, the Société de Notre-Dame de Montréal also granted it 200 arpents of land in the "place found most convenient." This turned out to be the Saint-Augustin fief on Lac aux Loutres, the future Point Saint-Charles.

When she returned to Ville-Marie in late September 1650, Mance found the settlement more threatened than ever. It was with horror that she learned of the martyrdom of the missionaries, whose devotion she had appreciated, and the annihilation of the Huron nation, whose survivors

Lurking in the midst of felled trees, two Iroquois watch a group of settlers working in the fields. (Painting by Charles Cockburn.)

could be seen opposite Montréal Island as they made their way to Québec, where they hoped to benefit from French protection. The number of Hurons exterminated by the Iroquois has been estimated at 30,000. The Iroquois were now in a position to attack Ville-Marie.

The year 1651 thus began on a very ominous note, as it did not take long for the Iroquois to make their presence felt. "Not a month of this summer passed," Dollier de Casson wrote, "without our roll of slain being marked in red at the hands of the Iroquois." He illustrated this statement with some anecdotes, "all others being beyond the memory of man, the sole authority I can use."

On May 6, Jean Chicot and the mason Jean Boudart were surprised by ten or so marauders. Chicot hid under a tree while Boudart went back towards his house to take refuge there with his wife, but she had carefully barred the door. It was too late: the couple fled. The Iroquois quickly caught up with Madame Boudart. Her husband came back to try to save her, but it was a futile effort, and he died under the Iroquois' blows. His wife was spared "to make a cruel meal of her" – the Iroquois tried to take as many prisoners as possible for the pleasure of slowly burning them to death.

Three settlers ran to the scene: Charles Le Moyne, Jacques Archambault and a third whose identity we don't know. Some forty Iroquois fell on them. They retreated to the hospital – it was open and Mance was there alone. Le Moyne (whose cap had been pierced by a bullet) and his companions endeavoured to bring her to the fort; then they went out looking for Chicot.

May 6, 1651 is recorded as the date of the burial of Jean Boudart, but not of Jean Chicot, who didn't enter the *Liber defunctorum* until June 8, 1667. After spotting his hiding place, the Iroquois tried to capture him, but he defended himself so vigorously that they scalped him right there, even taking a piece of his skull. The Iroquois left him for dead but he survived, living sixteen more years after this cruel experience.

On June 18, four *Montréalistes* took refuge in a small redoubt after being surprised by the Iroquois. A fifth, "one of our old *habitants* named Lavigne" (probably Urbain Tessier *dit* Lavigne), joined them, emerging unhurt after sustaining sixty to eighty gunshots while running through felled trees. Other settlers burst out of the fort. The Iroquois, crouched behind the felled trees, made the mistake of firing first; when they got up to flee, the French picked off some thirty of them.

The Iroquois sustained much higher losses in these skirmishes than the French, but they had plenty of reinforcements, while the ranks of the settlers were being thinned out. "In the daytime," wrote Dollier de Casson, "no one dared go four steps from one's house without a rifle, a sword and a pistol."

Maisonneuve decided to require everyone to take refuge in the fort. The hospital was closed temporarily, and Jeanne Mance came into the fort as well, bringing her sick and wounded to the temporary location she had used earlier. It had been hoped that the pioneers would settle on their own lands and develop them. Now, however, the colony was turning in on itself. What would become of it? To make sure the enemy didn't burn the hospital, Maisonneuve garrisoned it with a small party of soldiers, armed with cannons and guns for firing stones.

Once again, it was Jeanne Mance who intervened to save Ville-Marie. The Marquise de Bullion had given her 22,000 livres for the hospital. She offered the money to Maisonneuve to use to recruit more people. "I am confident that my conscience is clear," she told him. "Use this money to recruit people to make the whole country safe by saving Montréal!" In November Maisonneuve left for France.

Enter Lambert Closse

————————— ❧ —————————

When he left Ville-Marie, Maisonneuve put Charles Joseph d'Ailleboust des Muceaux, whose mobile detachment had just been increased in strength to seventy soldiers, in command of the settlement. Before sailing, he no doubt paid his respects to the new governor, Jean de Lauzon, who had succeeded Louis d'Ailleboust on October 13, 1651. Maisonneuve sailed on a Dutch ship on November 5.

Maisonneuve hoped to recruit 200 men during his stay in France. "If I do not get at least a hundred," he said, "I won't go back and we will have to abandon everything, for the settlement will really be untenable!" Three years earlier the Hundred Associates had increased Maisonneuve's compensation from 3,000 to 4,000 livres, but he was responsible for the soldiers' wages and maintenance. When Lauzon arrived, he cancelled the 1,000-livre increase and insisted that Maisonneuve pay in advance to equip ten soldiers whom he had promised to add to Ville-Marie's garrison. When these soldiers arrived on December 10, they were so poorly dressed that people thought they were seeing ghosts.

Dollier de Casson could not understand Governor Lauzon's spite. After all, Ville-Marie was a kind of dike, capable of at least partially holding back the Iroquois waves flooding towards Québec, where they "didn't even always respect his own family." This was an allusion to the governor's son, also named Jean, the high seneschal of New France, who was killed on Île

CLOSSE

With no more marauding Iroquois to watch out for, Lambert Closse and the faithful dog Pilote watch Montrealers pass by in Place d'Armes.

d'Orléans in June 1661 in an Iroquois raid. Was Lauzon still bitter because he had not been able to make the profit he had hoped for from the grant of Montréal Island, which the Hundred Associates had taken back because it had been obtained through a figurehead?

We have not yet introduced another person who has won the admiration of every historian, Raphaël Lambert Closse, and it is time to make his acquaintance. Very little is known about his ancestry, but it is probable that he had a record of military service to his credit when he arrived in

Ville-Marie. Maisonneuve had full confidence in him and gave him full authority over the garrison. In 1648 Maisonneuve gave him the title of sergeant-major, which he retained until his untimely death at the hands of the Iroquois in 1662. Closse used dogs to track down the Iroquois and trained them as sentries. The sculptor Philippe Hébert immortalized him in bronze, and at the base of the Maisonneuve monument he holds Pilote before sending her out on the trail of the enemy.

In 1651 the Iroquois tightened the vise on Ville-Marie. There were only about fifty French settlers left, the Jesuit *Relations* reported: "This place would be an earthly paradise were it not for the terror of the Iroquois, who make their presence felt almost all the time."

On Sunday, June 18, 1651, the *Montréalistes* engaged in combat with some fifty Iroquois, killing their captain and wounding several warriors. Four of the *Montréalistes* were wounded, and one of them, a native of Limousin named Léonard Lucos *dit* Barbot, died two days later, leaving his wife and a one-year-old daughter. The Iroquois were no more merciful towards women they captured than towards fighting men. In the Jesuit *Relations*, Father Paul Ragueneau reported the fate of a Frenchwoman taken captive: "She was cruelly burned by these barbarians after they tore off her breasts and cut off her nose and ears."

Martine Messier from Normandy, the wife of Antoine Primot, had better luck. According to an anecdote reported by Dollier de Casson, the Iroquois surprised *la bonne femme Primot* within two rifle shots of the palisade and wanted to take her alive. She cried out and two or three of the aggressors overpowered her: all she had to defend herself with were her feet and hands. An Iroquois jumped on her to scalp her, but she immediately came to her senses. "More furious than ever, she grabbed the cruel attacker with such violence in a place that decency prevents me from naming that he was barely able to escape; he hit her on the head with his hatchet, but she held out until once again she fell unconscious on the ground, and in falling she gave the Iroquois an opportunity to flee as fast as he could, which was the only thing he was thinking of doing at the time."

Clearly, Dollier had not lost the taste for spicy stories that he had developed in the guards! He goes on to tell us that this episode concluded with "something quite humorous." Some French settlers ran to the scene and one of them leaned over and embraced Madame Primot "as a sign of friendship and compassion." She came to again and slapped him in the face. When people asked her why she did that, she answered, "*Parmanda*, I thought he wanted to kiss me!"

The *Montréalistes* kept up their guard so successfully that the Iroquois got tired of prowling around Ville-Marie and turned their attention to the settlement at Trois-Rivières instead.

We can imagine how impatiently Jeanne Mance waited for news of Maisonneuve. In 1652, to get information about the outcome of his voyage at the earliest possible moment, she had Closse take her to Trois-Rivières, hoping that the commander there would escort her to Québec. She made the voyage early in the season; this was a good thing, for had there been much delay, she would have been captured by some of the 600 Iroquois who blockaded Trois-Rivières. On August 19, Governor Duplessis-Kerbodot of Trois-Rivières and fourteen of his men were ambushed. The governor was killed, and all the others were either killed or taken prisoner. Life on the St. Lawrence in those days took courage!

The Recruits of 1653 Save Ville-Marie

───────────── ➤❮ ─────────────

The ships did not bring Maisonneuve back to New France in 1652. The first ship ran aground at Île aux Coudres. Michel Leneuf du Hérisson, a brother of the governor of Trois-Rivières, must have been on board, for according to Dollier de Casson it was he – coming on the first ship – who brought Jeanne Mance the news that Maisonneuve would come later with a hundred men. It is not hard to imagine Mance's joy, and she asked the governor to relay the news to the *Montréalistes*. The governor sent out a launch bound for Ville-Marie, but it was delayed by unfavourable winds. On the way, people told the crew about the Iroquois blockade of Trois-Rivières. The launch had to turn back.

In 1652 as in 1651, the *Montréalistes* lived under threat and waited for reinforcements. On October 14 the dogs, sent out as scouts, started to bark furiously. Lambert Closse boldly came out of the fort with twenty-four men and the fight began, but the French were outnumbered. One of the settlers, Louis Prudhomme, had taken refuge in a small shack; Prudhomme cried out to Closse, warning him that he would be surrounded and inviting him to take refuge in the shack as well.

Closse and his men joined Prudhomme and they quickly began to open loopholes in the walls. The walls did not offer much protection: a bullet got through and cut down the soldier Étienne Thibault *dit* La Lochetière. Brisk fire finished off several Iroquois, but the *Montréalistes* could see that they were running out of ammunition. The soldier Baston, known to be a fast runner, offered to go to the fort under the cover of a brisk volley to replenish their supplies. He came back with ten more men. The Iroquois, seeing that the French were "not as paltry a group as they were before Baston arrived, judged it more prudent to withdraw than to draw further on our good nature." The French did not know how many Iroquois had been killed, for they quickly took away their dead, but they learned from other Iroquois that thirty-seven of them had been "completely incapacitated."

Another anecdote illustrates just how serious the danger to Ville-Marie was. In the spring of 1653, the governor sent a boat to Ville-Marie with a stern warning to the captain: don't get off the boat without some greeting from the little population of the settlement. If the Iroquois had taken Ville-Marie, they would probably be waiting in ambush for the first visitors. The boat anchored in the river, in front of the fort. The *Montréalistes* could see the boat's silhouette in the mist, but they could not identify it. They lay low behind the ramparts, and the captain decided to return to Québec without going ashore.

In France during these months, Maisonneuve was busy recruiting new settlers to save Ville-Marie. Crucial to his endeavour was the collaboration of La Dauversière, who had completely recovered his strength. Once more, the Société de Notre-Dame de Montréal had wavered; now it came to life again, and Maisonneuve and La Dauversière found subscribers to finance the venture, most notably the always-generous Marquise de Bullion. The amount of money they collected in this way is estimated at 75,000 livres.

Historians have carefully analysed the sixty-five agreements signed between March 23 and May 17, 1653. All except two bear the signature of Maisonneuve, La Dauversière or both. One was signed by La Dauversière's son, and one by his brother. These precious documents, preserved at the Hôtel-Dieu in La Flèche, cover 119 people, of whom seventy-one were from La Flèche and its immediate vicinity. The new settlers, who all at once would double the population of Ville-Marie, worked at a variety of trades: joiner, carpenter, shoemaker, digger, ploughman, lumberjack, cooper, woodcutter, gunsmith, miller, cutler, baker, farrier, brewer, mason, roofer, weaver, gunsmith-locksmith, tailor, gardener, well-sinker, hatter, pastry-cook. There were even two surgeons among them: Étienne Bouchard, a Parisian who lived in Épernon, near Chartres, and Gilles Fricquet, from La Flèche. Bouchard, who signed on for five years, started a family in New

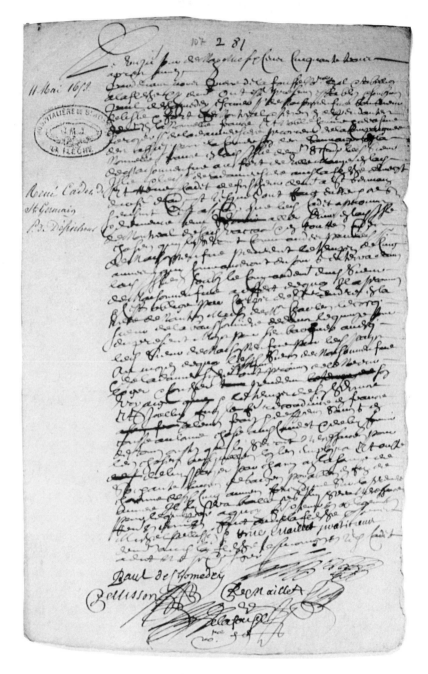

One of the contracts preserved at the Hôtel-Dieu in La Flèche. The signatures of Paul de Chomedey (Maisonneuve) and Jérôme Le Royer (La Dauversière) can be seen. René Cadet, a settler from Saint-Germain-du-Val, contracts to work in Ville-Marie for five years for wages of sixty livres.

In the Hôtel-Dieu in La Flèche, this file containing the contracts signed by the recruits of 1653 lies right beside an ornamented box containing a relic of Jérôme Le Royer de La Dauversière.

France, while Fricquet appears to have returned to France after three years, the period for which his services were contracted.

According to the historian Abbé Faillon, 154 men contracted to go to Ville-Marie at that time, of whom only 113 actually sailed, and eight of those died at sea. In other words, the number exceeded the minimum of 100 recruits established by Maisonneuve when he left for France. But there were still a number of obstacles to overcome. Some of the recruits defaulted despite the contract they had signed. The whole group boarded the *Saint-Nicolas* off Saint-Nazaire on June 20, 1653, but according to Marguerite Bourgeoys the ship's hull was rotten. They thought they would be able to caulk it at sea, but 350 leagues out the captain realized that this improvised refitting would not hold up and they sailed back to port.

While they waited to find another ship, Maisonneuve had everyone go ashore on an island from which, as Bourgeoys wrote, "it was impossible to escape, for otherwise not one of them would have stayed." According to Faillon some of them, feeling that they were being led to perdition, jumped

This stele identifies the old harbour of Luneau in La Flèche, from which many pioneers left for Ville-Marie. Unveiled in 1954 by the Canadian ambassador to France, Jean Désy, it evokes all the departures from this point between 1640 and 1659.

into the water. They did not sail again until July 20. The crossing would take two months.

Another Fruit of Champagne

In the spring of 1653, Jeanne Mance again went to Québec to wait for Maisonneuve. The ship did not arrive until September 22. As a result of poor seamanship, it rammed so far into the edge of a rock that it could not be dislodged even at high tide and eventually had to be burned where it stood. Even if New France breathed more easily as it welcomed its reinforcements, Maisonneuve had a very hard time getting enough boats to carry all his recruits to Ville-Marie. He probably didn't want to transport them in stages for fear that the governor would keep them in Québec. It was only on November 16 that everybody reached Montréal Island.

However, the delay allowed Maisonneuve to be present at the conclusion of a new peace treaty. In August, the Iroquois had captured and tortured a Jesuit, Joseph-Antoine Poncet de La Rivière, and his companion, Mathurin Franchetot. Franchetot died in the flames after the torturers had burned the index finger on each of his hands in their pipes. By comparison, Father Poncet was more fortunate. An old woman adopted him, sparing his life and making him do menial tasks instead. The Iroquois knew that some of their warriors had been captured during the blockade of Trois-Rivières and that the exchange value of the Jesuit would be high. They took him to the Dutch, who nursed him and fitted him out in clothes, and then they set out for Québec via the St. Lawrence.

The missionary and his feathered companions reached Montréal on October 24 and Québec on November 5. There the Iroquois ambassadors exchanged gifts with the French. Thus, Father Poncet reported, "on a Sunday night, eighty-one days after I was captured, the great business of peace, so much desired, was completed." But it was not peace with all the Iroquois nations, so the palavers with Governor de Lauzon continued until the first signs of winter. The Iroquois had both a gift for symbolism and practical sense, and it is unfortunate that space does not permit us to discuss the significance of all the gifts that were exchanged. One of the presents was a meal offered to the governor "so that having eaten, he would hear the words of peace more easily, as long speeches are not pleasant for someone who is hungry." Or as an old French saying has it, *ventre affamé n'a pas d'oreilles* – a hungry stomach has no ears.

Maisonneuve brought a devoted companion for Jeanne Mance. While he was in France he had visited his family in Champagne. In addition to the sister mentioned earlier, Jacqueline, Maisonneuve had another sister, Louise, a nun in the convent of the Congrégation de Notre-Dame in Troyes, Champagne's principal city. It was no doubt through Louise that Maisonneuve met a noncloistered member of the congregation, Marguerite Bourgeoys.

Sister Louise suggested that she and several companions should go to Ville-Marie with Maisonneuve, but he refused her offer. He probably thought that the presence of a community of women in such an exposed outpost was premature. He did, however, agree to take Bourgeoys herself, who had unsuccessfully tried to gain admission to the Carmelites and other orders. As a member of the external wing of the Congrégation de

Two choirboys lay a bunch of flowers in front of Saint-Jean church in Troyes on November 5, 1982, in a ceremony marking the canonization of Marguerite Bourgeoys, which had taken place less than a week earlier. The plaque identifies Bourgeoys as the "founder of education in Montréal, apostle of French culture in Canada."

Notre-Dame, she was very well disposed to the idea of following Maisonneuve so that she could take charge of educating the young daughters of pioneer couples.

Maisonneuve had already told the *Montréalistes* that the young woman

This high relief on Le Royer Street near St. Lawrence Boulevard indicates the place where Marguerite Bourgeoys opened the first school in a stable.

from Troyes would be coming. "I am bringing a splendid girl who will be of great help to Montréal," he had written. "Moreover, she is another fruit of Champagne, which appears to want to give more to this place than all the other provinces combined." This testimonial can be found engraved on a plaque on the façade of Saint-Jean church in Troyes, where Bourgeoys, a future saint (she was beatified in 1950 and canonized in 1982), was baptized in 1620.

While he was in Paris, Maisonneuve had met the Marquise de Bullion, even though he was not supposed to know the identity of Ville-Marie's rich benefactor. He wanted to talk to her about the settlement, and he resorted to a pretext, taking advantage of the fact that one of his sisters "had legal proceedings against her." This was most likely the incorrigibly litigious Jacqueline de Chomedey, who spent a disproportionate amount of time in court. Maisonneuve offered to accompany his sister to the private mansion on Rue Plâtrière, and as one thing led to another, the marquise wondered whether he wasn't in fact the governor of Montréal. Maisonneuve said he was indeed, and the marquise asked him questions and received him several times. The result was that she turned another 20,000 livres over to the Société de Notre-Dame de Montréal to use for recruiting settlers, in addition to the 22,000 livres mentioned earlier.

Marguerite Bourgeoys tended to the many people who were laid low by illness during the crossing. She continued to take care of them in Québec while waiting for the boats that would take the recruits to Ville-Marie.

It would not be until five years later that Bourgeoys would open her first school: when she first arrived, there were no pupils. In the meantime, she went from house to house helping settlers' wives, helped Mance with her patients, and worked on teaching the pioneers. The cross that had been erected on top of the mountain in 1642 had fallen into disrepair, and Bourgeoys raised it again. She also thought that the *Montréalistes* should have a chapel. Maisonneuve gave her a piece of land 400 paces from the fort for that purpose, and the settlers endeavoured to prepare the wood for the frame. In this way, the plan for a chapel dedicated to Notre-Dame de Bonsecours took shape.

Having come back to Ville-Marie with a fine crew of workers, Maisonneuve decided that the time was ripe to build a real hospital, next to *la maison de Mlle Mance*. He also decided that it should have a chapel that would serve as a parish church: the facilities inside the fort had become too cramped, especially with the arrival of the new settlers.

"For Montréal Owes Him Its Life"

Joyfully, New France sent out the news of a new peace treaty on a ship bound for the mother country. But the peace was a very fragile one – all the more so because despite Iroquois efforts to destroy their nation, the Hurons were now making agreements with the Iroquois, no doubt in the hope of being spared. "They kill each other," noted the Jesuit *Relations*, "they massacre each other, they plunder, they burn, say on a Wednesday; then on Thursday they exchange gifts and visit each other as if they were friends." Negotiations began again in February 1654. It was a period of respite for the *Montréalistes*, during which the new recruits were able to get settled and work on the hospital progressed.

Also in 1654, a Parisian named Jean-Jacques Moyen, his wife Élisabeth Lebret, and their three children, thirteen-year-old Élisabeth, ten-year-old Jean-Baptiste and seven-year-old Marie, settled on Île aux Oies, in the St. Lawrence off Montmagny below Québec City. The next year, on the feast of Corpus Christi, the Iroquois killed the parents and captured the two girls along with eight-year-old Marie Macard and her six-year-old sister Geneviève, the daughters of a Company of One Hundred Associates agent in Québec who appear to have been visiting the Moyens. Young Jean-Baptiste Moyen managed to get away, but he would be mortally wounded by the Iroquois at Ville-Marie six years later.

Charles Le Moyne was passing through Québec at the time, and he returned to Ville-Marie with the sad news. A little later, during a skirmish, Lambert Closse captured an Iroquois who had some influence in his community. The Iroquois – whom they called La Barrique (The Barrel) because he was fat – had been wounded by a direct hit with large musket slugs, and the French took such good care of him that his anger turned to gentleness. His brother, thinking that he had been killed, prowled around the fort looking for an opportunity to avenge his death. The French took La Barrique outside and he told his brother, "You want to kill my best friends." The brother quickly came to him, swore that he would work for peace, and endeavoured to bring back all the French whom the Iroquois were holding in their villages.

Soon afterward another group of Iroquois were outside Ville-Marie looking for scalps. Through the efforts of Le Moyne and Closse several of them were captured. One of these, La Plume (The Feather), offered to approach the Mohawk chief La Grand'Armée, who he said was leading a party of Mohawks towards Ville-Marie, and propose an exchange of prisoners. And so the Moyen and Macard girls, along with three Frenchmen who had not been heard from, were brought to Ville-Marie.

It might be tempting here to say all's well that ends well, but we are not yet at the end of the story. Two years later, on August 12, 1657, Lambert Closse married Élisabeth Moyen. Three honorable citizens acted as witnesses: Pierre Gadois, Montréal's first *habitant*; Nicolas Godé, who unfortunately would be killed by the Iroquois two and a half months later; and the treasurer Gilbert Barbier.

Two daughters were born of the marriage: Élisabeth, who lived only one day, and Jeanne Cécile, who would marry Jacques Bizard when she was eighteen. Bizard would follow in his father-in-law's footsteps and serve as Montréal's military commander from 1677 to 1692. Governor Buade de Frontenac granted him the island in the Rivière des Prairies that became known as Île Bizard. Unfortunately, the marriage of Lambert Closse and Élisabeth Moyen would be brutally ended by the Iroquois.

For the most part, 1655 was a quiet year. In the fall, Maisonneuve went to France again, leaving Closse in command. The purpose of his voyage this time was not to recruit new settlers but rather to find priests to take on the pastoral role that the Jesuits were no longer able to fulfil because of the growing scale of their evangelization work.

In 1657 the Iroquois went on the warpath again. On October 25, the notary Jean de Saint-Père and a servant, Jacques Noël, were helping Nicolas Godé build a house when a group of Oneidas appeared. Since they were at peace, the *Montréalistes* had no reason to be suspicious of the natives: they greeted them and even offered them food. Then they went back up on the roof. This was what the Iroquois had been waiting for, and they killed the three settlers. Dollier de Casson mourned their loss at the hands of raiders who "after eating their bread, surprised them when they were unarmed and shot them down like sparrows." The Oneidas scalped Godé and Noël and cut off de Saint-Père's head so that they could later lift off his fine head of hair without spoiling it. The story was told that as long as they kept the head it spoke in a vengeful voice, reproaching them for their cruelty.

Lambert Closse wanted to settle on his own land. He had acquired a thirty-arpent tract in 1652, and six years later Maisonneuve granted him 100 arpents "bounded on one side by Jacques Archambault, on the other by Sieur bouchart surgeon, starting at a distance of ten perches [about five metres] from the great river."

After the battle of Long-Sault in 1660, described further on, the Iroquois adopted a more circumspect attitude towards Ville-Marie. The settlement became consolidated and its population grew. But the Iroquois still prowled nearby. On February 6, 1662, Closse went out of the fort to go help some settlers who were engaged with a party of raiders. He led twenty-six men against some 200 Iroquois. The battle began early in the morning, and in mid-afternoon, with the enemy threatening from every side, his Flemish

This deed of concession of 100 arpents of land to Lambert Closse, dated February 2, 1658, contains an excellent specimen of Paul de Chomedey's signature.

The section of St. Lawrence Boulevard between Craig (Saint-Antoine) and Notre-Dame streets used to be called Côte Saint-Lambert. This plaque explains: "This place used to be called Côte Saint-Lambert in honour of the military commander Lambert Closse (1630-1662), acting commandant of Ville-Marie in the absence of M. de Maisonneuve, who was killed near here in combat with the Iroquois."

domestic servant abandoned him. Three settlers had already been killed. Closse defended himself with an energy born of despair, but his pistols jammed and he too fell. The next day the victims were buried: Simon Leroy, a *habitant* from the La Flèche region; Jean Lecomte, from Orléans, a servant of Closse's; and Louis Grisson, a labourer from La Rochelle, along with Closse.

Closse's legendary bravery has been universally recognized. "We owe his memory this eulogy," said the Jesuit *Relations*, "for Montréal owes him its life."

Montréal's First Parish Clergy

The Jesuits had served Ville-Marie since it was founded, but their presence was increasingly required at their missions. Maisonneuve again left for France in the fall of 1655 to see Jean-Jacques Olier and ask him to send priests who would become Montréal's first parish clergy.

Olier had founded a seminary in Vaugirard, in Saint-Sulpice parish, to train young clerics for missionary work. One of his first assistants was Gabriel de Thubières de Queylus, who became a priest in 1645. Within ten years, de Queylus founded four Sulpician seminaries: at Rodez, Nantes, Viviers-sur-Rhône and Clermont. The *ancienne maîtrise* at Viviers, where he opened his seminary, is still standing. De Queylus had also been a member of the Société de Notre-Dame de Montréal since 1646, and to Olier he seemed to be the person to fulfil Maisonneuve's request.

The members of the society wanted a bishop to be appointed in Canada, and de Queylus seemed to them a completely appropriate candidate. De Queylus agreed to have his name stand before the general assembly of the French clergy. The Jesuits, however, were opposed. They had been solely responsible for the fate of the little church in New France for twenty years, and they had chosen one of their former students, François de Laval. On May 17, 1657, de Queylus sailed from Saint-Nazaire with letters patent from the archbishop of Rouen naming him *grand vicaire* for all of New France. Accompanying him were two priests, Dominique Galinier and Gabriel Souart, and a deacon, Antoine d'Allet. Unfortunately, Father Olier died six weeks before the departure of these first Sulpicians bound for New France. Vincent de Paul, the future saint, attended to him as he breathed his last.

Maisonneuve returned along with the four Sulpicians. On July 29, the ship anchored in front of Québec, and the Jesuit superior, Father Jean de Quen, greeted the new arrivals. Dollier de Casson wrote that "M. l'abbé Kelus was complimented on his letters as *grand vicaire*," but it is doubtful that the satisfaction was universal: on April 30, 1649, the archbishop of Rouen had granted similar letters patent to the Jesuit superior. The result was a jurisdictional conflict, of which even a brief summary is beyond the scope of this book.

De Queylus spent the winter in Québec in his role as pastor. In

On board the *Saint-André,* in the harbour at La Rochelle, La Dauversière bids fare-well to the first hospital nuns leaving for Ville-Marie.

Ville-Marie, the Sulpicians chose to live in *la maison de Mlle Mance* while their seminary was being built. But Mance was in a bad way. In late January 1657 she slipped on the ice, breaking two bones in her right forearm and dislocating her wrist. The surgeon Étienne Bouchard was able to set the broken bones, but the dislocated wrist eluded him. It was difficult for Mance to take care of the hospital without the use of her arm, so she decided the time had come for her to cross the Atlantic and go to La Flèche to recruit hospital nuns. De Queylus sent two sisters from the Hôtel-Dieu in Québec to take charge of the hospital. They were greeted with very understandable coolness. With some justice, Mance wondered whether de Queylus wanted to place the Ville-Marie hospital under the authority of the Hôtel-Dieu in

This stained-glass window in Hôtel-Dieu in Montréal shows Maisonneuve greeting the hospital nuns. One can only imagine his joy.

Québec, and indeed this was probably the case. The annals of the Hôtel-Dieu are very clear, reporting that de Queylus believed "it would be an advantage for us and for the whole country if there were only a single Institute at Québec and at Ville-Marie." According to the same source, "It was believed that this should be kept in the utmost secrecy until those on whom the foundation depended had been won over." De Queylus, it should be remembered, was a member of the Société de Notre-Dame de Montréal.

In late September 1658, Mance left for France along with Marguerite Bourgeoys, who was looking for women to help her, as five months earlier Maisonneuve had put a shed at her disposal to use as a school. Their fellow passengers included Huguenots "who chanted their prayers evening and morning against the ordinances of the king." From La Rochelle Mance was carried on a litter to La Flèche, where La Dauversière greeted her in a fatherly way. In 1643 La Dauversière had obtained from the bishop of

Angers, Claude de Rueil, the canonical establishment of the Congrégation des Filles Hospitalières de Saint-Joseph. What he wanted most was to have nuns from the Hôtel-Dieu in La Flèche establish the Hôtel-Dieu in Ville-Marie. But the new bishop, Henri Arnauld, at first categorically refused his request to send hospital nuns to the far-off colony.

Mance went to Paris and visited the new superior of the Sulpicians, Alexandre Le Ragois, Sieur de Bretonvilliers. He kept Olier's heart in a reliquary and gave it to her for a few moments. She pressed it to her crippled arm, "all packed as it was in many and various bandages attached with a multitude of pins," and she was immediately cured.

At her request, the Société de Notre-Dame de Montréal wrote to Bishop Arnauld and obtained the authorization it wanted. But his previous misgivings turned out to be justified. When the first three nuns missioned to the Ville-Marie hospital came out of the convent to board their ship, a rumour had spread that they were being taken to Canada against their will and a path had to be cleared for them with drawn swords. At the beginning of July 1659, the *Saint-André* weighed anchor at La Rochelle with Mance and the three hospital nuns – Judith Moreau de Brésoles, the superior, Catherine Macé and Marie Maillet – on board. Also on board were two Sulpicians, Jacques Lemaître and Guillaume Vignal, who not long afterward were burned by the Iroquois.

The Sacrifice of the Seventeen

————————— >< —————————

In 1660, there were rumours in New France that the Iroquois were preparing a major offensive against the French settlements. The Jesuit *Relations* noted that it would be easy for a thousand Iroquois to surprise all the French *habitations* on both banks of the St. Lawrence and massacre their occupants, "except for Québec, which is in a state of defence, but which nevertheless would no longer be anything but a prison, from which people could not go out safely and where they would die of hunger if the whole countryside was ruined."

In Québec in mid-May, an Iroquois (who would be burned by the Algonquins "according to their customary justice," as Marie de l'Incarnation would write to her son) revealed that a horde of between 900 and 1,200

This bas-relief on the Dollard des Ormeaux monument in Lafontaine Park shows Dollard leaving Ville-Marie.

Iroquois was gathering to attack the little town and capture *Ontario*, as they called the new governor, Voyer d'Argenson. Did the settlers at Ville-Marie know that a general offensive was being prepared against the French? Opinions are divided on this question. But if they didn't know, how can the sacrifice of Dollard des Ormeaux and his companions be explained?

In 1659, Father Jérôme Lalemant wrote to his provincial in France that the Iroquois were getting ready to "flood" the country with an army the next spring. It is also clear that the Iroquois had cut off one of the major fur trade routes, the Ottawa River. In any case, Dollard des Ormeaux asked Maisonneuve for authorization to lead an expedition against the Iroquois upstream from Montréal. Little is known about Dollard's ancestry. Dollier de Casson wrote that he was "a boy of good heart and family who had had a command in the armies of France." The governor would have refused Dollard's request if he had not considered the young man trustworthy. At the same time, he was commander of the garrison and was well liked: his signature as a witness can be found on several notarized contracts drawn up

Dollard and his companions are brought down by the numerical strength of their attackers. (Bas-relief, Maisonneuve monument, Place d'Armes)

before Bénigne Basset. And a few months earlier, he had been the godfather of Lambert Closse's firstborn daughter.

But if the settlers at Ville-Marie knew that the Iroquois were preparing a general offensive, why did three prominent *Montréalistes* – Charles Le Moyne, Pierre Picoté and Lambert Closse himself – say that they were ready to take part in the expedition if it were put off until after seeding time? Dollier de Casson explains that Dollard des Ormeaux refused because "he would not have had the honour of commanding it" and "it would have been very convenient for him to distinguish himself in this way, so that it could help him with some business that it was said had arisen in France." Was this a slander against him? Some sixty years ago, Dollard des Ormeaux's motives came under highly publicized scrutiny by historians. It is not easy to probe Dollard's thoughts solely on the basis of the documents of the time. What no one has ever questioned is his bravery.

With sixteen men, all of them bachelors, Dollard headed out of Ville-Marie towards Long-Sault. Each of them had made out a will before leaving. Eight of the men had been among the recruits of 1653. Jacques Brassier was twenty-five years old; François Crusson *dit* Pilote was twenty-four; René Doucin, a woodcutter, was thirty; Nicolas Josselin, from Solesmes near the northern tip of France, was twenty-five; the digger Jean Lecomte, twenty-six; Étienne Robin *dit* Desforges, twenty-seven; the gunsmith Jean Tavernier *dit* Laforêt, twenty-eight; and the ploughman Jean Valets, twenty-seven.

The remaining eight men had come to Ville-Marie more recently. Christophe Augier *dit* Desjardins was twenty-six; Jacques Boisseau *dit* Cognac was twenty-three; the lime-burner Alonié Delestre (whose name Abbé Lionel Groulx would one day use as a pseudonym) was thirty-one; Simon Grenet, twenty-five; Roland Hébert *dit* Larivière, twenty-seven; Robert Jurie, twenty-four; the ploughman Louis Martin, twenty-one; and the locksmith Nicolas Tiblemont, twenty-five. Jurie was the only one who survived the adventure, as the Iroquois spared his life so that they could torture him. He managed to escape, and with the help of the Dutch he returned to France.

In a rickety fort made of stakes at Long-Sault, Dollard des Ormeaux and his companions dug themselves in along with four Algonquins and some forty Hurons whose chief, Anontaha, remained loyal to the French to the end even when the other natives defected. They had barely had time to take refuge there when 300 Iroquois appeared on the river. After several futile attacks, the Iroquois sent messengers to ask for help from the five hundred others who were at the mouth of the Richelieu waiting for the horde that was to ravage the French settlements on the St. Lawrence to be fully assembled.

The besieged defenders held out for three days, until a desperate Dollard wanted to throw a large musket loaded to the muzzle over the palisade. Unfortunately the missile, held back by a branch, exploded in the fort. It was the end. With a sword in his right hand and a knife in his left, each of the survivors defended himself until he fell.

Whatever the goal of the Seventeen – as Dollard and his companions came to be known – had been, the result of their action was to save Ville-Marie and possibly New France. Once they saw that seventeen Frenchmen holed up in such a simple shelter had been able to push back 800 warriors so many times, the Iroquois no longer considered destroying Montréal and Québec such a simple matter.

A monument to Dollard des Ormeaux, the work of the sculptor Alfred Laliberté, was erected in Montréal's Lafontaine Park in 1920. In 1968, near its Carillon dam, Hydro-Québec built a huge mausoleum made up of as many monoliths of reinforced concrete as there were courageous

Le 3.me de Juin 660

Nous auons sceu nouuelles par Vn huron qui s'estoit
sauué d'entre les mains des Jroquois qui l'auoient pris
prisonier au combat qui s'estoit fait 8 iours auparauant
entre lesd. Jroquois qui estoient au nombre de huit
cent Et dix sept francois de cette habitation et quatre
Algonkins et enuiron quarante hurons au pied du
long sault. que treize de nos d. francois auoient esté
tuez sur la place. et quatre emmenez prisoniers
lesquels du depuis nous auons appris par 4 autres hurons
qui se sont sauuez aussi este actuellement bruslez par
lesd. Jroquois en leur pays. Or les noms des d. francois
morts estoient.
Adam Daulat commendant aagé de 25 ans.
Jacques Brassier 25 ans
Jean Tauerinier dit La Lochetiere armurier 28 ans
Nicolas Tiblemont serrurier 25 ans.
Laurent hebert dit La Rauiere 27 ans.
Alonie de l'estre chausournier 31 ans.
Nicolas Josselin 25 ans.
Robert Jurie 24 ans. N'o auons appris qu'il s'est sauué par les
hollandois et retourné en france.
Jacques Boisseau 23 ans
Louys Martin 21 ans.
Christophe Augier dit des Jardins 26 ans
Estienne Robin dit des forges 27 ans.
Jean Valets 27 ans.
René Douain 30 ans.
Jean Le Compte 26 ans
Simon Grenet 25 ans.
francois Cruffon dit Pilote 24 ans.

The death certificate of Dollard des Ormeaux and his companions in the Notre-Dame de Montréal parish register. There is a note beside the name of the sole survivor, Robert Jurie: "We have learned that he was saved by the dutch and returned to france."

Frenchmen who fought the Iroquois in May 1660. The mausoleum was conceived by the architect Jacques Folch-Ribas and the ceramic artist Jordi Bonet.

Institutions Take Root

Thanks to the inexhaustible energy of a handful of leading figures, the institutions the *Montréalistes* needed for their well-being put down deep roots. The devotion of the three hospital nuns brought over from La Flèche in 1659 made it possible for Jeanne Mance to save her Hôtel-Dieu, although great sacrifices were required to achieve this end. The nuns lived in such destitution that to be properly outfitted they had to repair their robes using dresses from Madame d'Ailleboust.

In 1662 Mance made her last voyage to France. The Société de Notre-Dame de Montréal had been floundering since the death of La Dauversière on November 6, 1659, and care had to be taken to ensure that its work would continue. Mance returned to Ville-Marie in 1664 and continued her own work until early 1673. She died on June 18 of that year. In 1659, as noted earlier, Marguerite Bourgeoys had gone to France along with Mance. She too was looking for assistants, and she found three – Edmé Châtel, Marie Raisin and Anne Riou – along with a "strong girl" who would do menial work.

In 1663, at the instigation of his minister Jean-Baptiste Colbert, Louis XIV ended the sterile regime of the companies in New France and took the colony under his own wing. This was the beginning of a new era in several respects. To increase the population, young orphan girls in French religious institutions were recruited as *"filles du Roy"* to marry the bachelors of New France. The industrious Madame Bourdon went to France several times to choose girls for this purpose. Marguerite Bourgeoys was in charge of receiving the girls who decided to settle in Ville-Marie, and it was to her that a *Montréaliste* in search of a wife would go.

In 1662, Maisonneuve granted Bourgeoys sixty arpents of land in Point Saint-Charles, and six years later she enlarged this holding by buying a neighbouring piece of land that belonged to François Le Ber. There was a house on this piece of land, and Bourgeoys used it to house a charity

Saint-Gabriel house remains one of the jewels of Montréal's heritage.

workshop she had founded in 1663. The house burned down in 1693, but five years later, on the same site, work was begun on the construction of Saint-Gabriel house, which remains one of the jewels of Montréal's heritage, with its long beams of squared timber, its rafters with wooden pegs and its huge halls.

Everyone was completely satisfied with the way Bourgeoys carried out her tasks of teaching girls and receiving the *filles du Roy*, and in 1667, at an *assemblée d'habitants*, it was decided to petition the royal court to issue letters patent officially recognizing the *filles de la Congrégation*, a term that was already being used for her embryonic community. Two years later, Bishop Laval endorsed the work of the teachers in Ville-Marie and even gave them permission to open schools anywhere in New France that people expressed a desire for their services.

In 1670 Bourgeoys left for France, confident of success at court. New France's astute intendant, Jean Talon, had made Colbert aware of the existence of this "Congregation of a sort" that taught "letters, writing and small handicrafts" to young girls. "We should use our interest to set this up," Colbert wrote in the margin of Talon's letter. Nothing more was needed for the king to issue the letters patent that the *Montréalistes* had requested, and the Congrégation de Notre-Dame formally came into existence. Bourgeoys returned to Ville-Marie with three nieces from Troyes, the Soumillard

This plaque, unveiled by Mayor Jean Drapeau in 1962, summarizes the rich history of Saint-Gabriel house. The inscription reads: "In 1662 Marguerite Bourgeoys established her first farm in Point Saint-Charles. In 1668, another house was built on this site to house the '*filles du Roy*.' This house was destroyed by fire in 1693 and was rebuilt in 1698 on the same foundation. Here Marguerite Bourgeoys opened her first school in Point Saint-Charles."

sisters. Two of them, Catherine and Marguerite, became nuns. The third married a settler of Breton origin, François Fortin *dit* Ploermel.

Bourgeoys was also concerned with the education of young native girls, and she welcomed them in her school and later in the Mission de la Montagne, where the teachers received them in cabins made of bark and later in stone towers, two of which still exist, along Sherbrooke Street in front of the Grand Séminaire. The education of settlers' daughters had begun in a converted shed in April 1658. At first, boys were not so fortunate. Eventually, however, the Sulpicians took charge of their education, and they carried out this responsibility with extraordinary devotion, to which historians have perhaps not done justice.

The first four Sulpicians who arrived in Ville-Marie in 1657 worked both as parish priests and as missionaries. With his responsibilities as *grand vicaire*, their superior, Father de Queylus, had little time to help his

This stained-glass window in Notre-Dame Basilica commemorates the arrival of the first Sulpicians (centre). On the left, Dollier de Casson looks over the plans for the first parish church, while the right panel shows Gabriel Souart, the first teacher.

colleagues. Father Galinier took charge of evangelizing the natives. The deacon Antoine d'Aillet served as secretary to de Queylus and returned to France in 1661.

Thus it was the fourth Sulpician, Gabriel Souart, who became the first teacher. Souart came from a rich family and Ville-Marie's institutions benefited from his generosity. He was a doctor, and it is said that the pope had authorized him to practise medicine in Montréal. As a parish priest, he had the first group of churchwardens in place within a year of his arrival. But these tasks did not exhaust his boundless energy and over the years he assumed others as well, becoming chaplain of the Congrégation de Notre-Dame and the Hôtel-Dieu and superior of the seminary. He also had a natural gift for teaching and his favourite title was that of schoolteacher. Starting in 1668, he found the time to teach young boys. A stained-glass window in Notre-Dame Church in Montréal shows him teaching children in the garden of the old seminary.

In 1663, the Sulpicians became the owners of Montréal Island, and as superior of the seminary, Souart acted as the island's first seigneur. It was a place about which he had heard much while growing up: he was a nephew of the Récollet Joseph Le Caron, who had celebrated the first mass on the banks of Rivière des Prairies in 1615.

The Sulpicians Become Seigneurs of Montréal Island

From December 1640, when the Company of One Hundred Associates granted Montréal Island to the Société de Notre-Dame de Montréal, the island belonged to the society. While the devotion of the society's members had its ups and downs over the next twenty years, given the many pressing demands on the generosity of these prestigious figures, there was always some Good Samaritan to stimulate their enthusiasm for far-off Ville-Marie each time it flagged. But with the deaths of Jean-Jacques Olier in 1657 and Jérôme Le Royer de La Dauversière in 1659, the energy that had driven this devout group was gone. The society was in the process of dissolving.

In 1662 Jeanne Mance left for Paris on what would be her last voyage to France. The situation was very serious. The assets of La Dauversière's estate were being seized – no doubt his generosity in supporting his good works had outstripped his resources. What would happen to Montréal Island, belonging as it did to a society that was wasting away, just at the time when the Sun King was about to infuse new energy into his colony on the North American continent?

Maisonneuve had wanted to go with Mance, and they arrived in Québec together on September 16, but Mance left for Paris alone. A new governor, Pierre Du Bois d'Avaugour, had replaced Voyer d'Argenson the previous year, and after a dispute with the Jesuits had revoked an edict of d'Argenson's restricting the liquor trade. In Montréal, Maisonneuve had outlawed the sale of spirits to natives. Appearing to be on the side of the clergy meant arousing the anger of the governor. D'Avaugour refused to let Maisonneuve leave and even had the merchant Jacques Le Ber, who had brought him to Québec along with Jeanne Mance, arrested. The animosity between the government of New France and the government of Montréal, of which this was one of the first instances, would gradually harden into a futile rivalry.

This was not the first time Mance had faced a daunting challenge. In

Paris, she showed the partners how tragic it would be if a venture to which so many people had dedicated themselves – notably the Marquise de Bullion, who had devoted a personal fortune to Montréal – were ruined. Her position strengthened by Maisonneuve's support, she persuaded the Société de Notre-Dame de Montréal to donate Montréal Island to the Society of Saint-Sulpice. The Sulpicians, however, hesitated to accept such a gift; indeed, how could it really be called a donation with all the conditions that were attached to it?

The contract of March 9, 1663 that formalized the grant contained eleven conditions, two of which turned out to be especially onerous. First of all, the Sulpicians agreed to assume all the debts of the Société de Notre-Dame de Montréal, which were considerable. And second, if there was a surplus, it had to be spent locally for the benefit of Ville-Marie. The reader may wonder how much these obligations amounted to. The Sulpician Pierre Boisard, who wrote the history of his congregation, established that the debts totalled 130,000 livres and that the new Sulpician superior, Alexandre Le Ragois de Bretonvilliers, paid them out of his personal fortune. When de Bretonvilliers died in 1676, it was estimated that he had devoted more than 400,000 livres to Ville-Marie. Still according to Boisard, the Sulpicians spent seven million livres in Canada in the century between their acquisition of Montréal Island in 1663 and the Treaty of Paris in 1763. The Treaty of Paris obligated all French subjects to turn their Canadian assets over to British subjects. Thus, the Sulpician seminary in Paris gave all its assets to the seminary in Montréal, which continued to administer the island until the seigneurial system was abolished in 1854.

When Mance returned to Ville-Marie in the spring of 1664, she found the atmosphere rather tense. Not only was Maisonneuve still involved in hostilities with the Iroquois, but he also had serious cause for worry about the attitude of the colonial authorities. On October 18, 1663, the new Conseil Supérieur de Québec, instituted by Louis XIV, proceeded to appoint a royal judge, a crown prosecutor and a clerk of the court "in the Seneschalship of the Island of Montréal." Did the new seigneurs not have the right to administer justice?

Five days later, Governor Augustin de Saffray de Mézy bestowed a commission on Chomedey de Maisonneuve as governor of Montréal Island "until it shall be otherwise provided by His Majesty" and gave the new owners eight months to produce their titles. Father Souart explained to the council that in 1644, by letters patent, the king had granted to the Société de Notre-Dame de Montréal "the power to name and provide for the government of the island." The rift between the colonial authorities and the administration at Ville-Marie was widening.

While Maisonneuve never hesitated to face the Iroquois when the settlement under his command was threatened, he was not a man to get involved in byzantine struggles out of a desire for personal glory. In September 1666, after Maisonneuve had returned to France for good, the wise intendant Talon, having examined all the documents in the file, issued an ordinance decreeing that "the justice of the Gentlemen of the Seminaire of Sainct-Sulpice in Paris shall be established in Montréal according to the terms of their titles and contracts." But it is not yet time to bid farewell to Sieur de Maisonneuve. Rather, let us describe the last months he spent in Ville-Marie before he left the scene for the tranquillity of a discreet retirement.

The Old Sulpician Seminary

>‹

Initially impressed with the resistance of Dollard des Ormeaux and his companions in May 1660, the Iroquois abandoned their plan to set New France aflame. The next spring, however, they once again began their depredations around Ville-Marie. On March 28, 1661, three new victims were buried: Olivier Martin *dit* Lamontagne, a native of the town of Auray in Brittany; Sébastien Dupuis, from La Rochelle; and Vincent Boutereau, from Poitou. On June 22, the *Montréalistes* learned that more French prisoners had been killed: Pierre Cauvin *dit* Le Grand Pierre, from Normandy; Pierre Martin *dit* Larivière, from Anjou; Jean Millet, from La Rochelle; and Pierre Pitre, of Dutch origin. Michel Messier, from Normandy, was mistakenly included in the list, but he reappeared. With Anne Le Moyne, Charles's sister, whom he married in 1658, he would have twelve children.

As noted earlier, the first four Sulpicians arrived in Ville-Marie in 1657. Two years later a fifth Sulpician, Jacques Lemaître, was put in charge of looking after accommodation for the others, and he undertook to build a stone house not far from the hospital. On August 29, 1661, reading his breviary as he went to Saint-Gabriel farm along with some labourers, he was attacked and killed by a group of Iroquois. Gabriel Derié, who had arrived two years earlier, was killed at the same time. Scalps clearly still served as valued trophies: the *Liber defunctorum* specifies that the bodies were buried without their heads.

Another Sulpician, Guillaume Vignal, took Lemaître's place. Vignal had already served as a priest in Québec; at de Queylus's suggestion, he had gone to Paris to do a year's novitiate at Saint-Sulpice seminary and then come back to New France, this time serving in Ville-Marie. He was appointed treasurer and continued Lemaître's work.

In late October 1661, Vignal left with thirteen labourers whom he was taking to Île à la Pierre. Maisonneuve had suggested to him that since he had gone there the day before, it would be reckless to go again so soon, especially since some people thought they had seen natives in the area. Vignal thought they were only moose. Some of the labourers stretched their legs while others got to work. According to Dollier de Casson, one of them "went to perform the functions of nature, placing himself at the edge of the enemy ambush, to which he turned his back." An Iroquois, "indignant at this insult," pricked him with a sword. Having never "felt so lively or so pointed a syringe," he ran wincing towards his companions. It was a complete surprise.

The soldier Claude de Brigeard, Maisonneuve's secretary, held off the Iroquois while the labourers retreated, but then he fell, seriously wounded. Vignal, seeking to take refuge in a canoe belonging to René Cuillerier, a settler, got the gun that was in the canoe wet. He was helpless without the gun, and the Iroquois "ran him through." Seeing him fatally wounded, they would burn him soon afterward. They nursed Brigeard back to health, then submitted him to unspeakable torture that lasted twenty-four hours. It was not until February 13 that the *Montréalistes* learned of their deaths, along with the death of Jacques Leprêtre, who had worked for the Sulpicians as a domestic servant.

Even with the loss of two treasurers, the Sulpicians appear to have moved ahead fairly quickly on the construction of their first seminary. Maisonneuve, who had gone back to France by 1665, is said to have lived there for a while. In 1672 Dollier de Casson, by then superior of the Sulpicians, designated the location of the first parish church, which would be built on Notre-Dame Street. At the same time, he outlined a plan to build a main residence linked to the church by a corridor, with the idea of establishing the seminary there. Thus, the Sulpicians were thinking of leaving their first house. In September 1693, Dollier de Casson signed a contract to rent the

The venerable Sulpician seminary, right beside Notre-Dame Basilica, is one of the most precious historic monuments in Montréal.

"house called the old Seminary" for three years to the intendant Bochart de Champigny, who converted it into "a storehouse and armoury for the king."

Dollier had big plans, and they caused some unease when they landed on the desk of the superior general in Paris, especially since at the time no Sulpician was allowed to go work in Montréal unless he could personally assume the cost of his upkeep. At the same time, Vachon de Belmont was "swallowing up" large sums of money to build the Fort de la Montagne; however, he was digging into his own pockets. De Belmont was a very talented designer and architect, and Dollier undoubtedly used his services in drawing up the plans for the seminary on Notre-Dame Street.

The Sulpician Olivier Maurault, who was president of the Société Historique de Montréal, combed the Sulpician archives to piece together the history of this beautiful building, another jewel of Montréal's heritage. Even though Paris urged caution, Dollier de Casson pushed the work forward. Thus, according to one document, in 1687 36,000 slates, 300 lead footings and 60,000,000 nails (should that be 60,000?) were shipped from La Rochelle.

A view of the courtyard of the old seminary in 1872. (Sketch appearing in *L'Opinion publique,* 1872.)

At the beginning, the Sulpicians were satisfied with putting up just the main part of the building. The wings were added later, probably in the early eighteenth century, and the clock, so familiar to passersby today, dates from the time of Vachon de Belmont. The face of the clock was engraved by the mapmaker Paul Labrosse, while the noted sculptor and goldsmith Philippe Liébert made the hands, and the sisters of the Congrégation de Notre-Dame covered them with gold.

Faced with the same circumstances as Maisonneuve, anyone else probably would have slammed the door behind him as he left Ville-Marie for good, and historians would have understood. But it was with characteristic grace that Maisonneuve left the settlement at whose founding he had presided and for which he had cared like a devoted father for twenty-three years.

When the companies of the Carignan regiment landed at Québec, there was great joy in the colony. There was every reason to believe that these battle-hardened soldiers would free the settlements from the incessant attacks that had prevented them from flourishing. Even the Iroquois were impressed. The brave Charles Le Moyne, who had long been a target of the Iroquois and whom they had captured while he was hunting, told them: "My death will be well avenged. I have often told you that a great number of French soldiers will come here, who will go to your lands and burn you in your villages: they are arriving now in Québec, I have definite news of it." These words were enough to stay the hands of the elders who for several years "had from time to time been gathering wood to burn him." Le Moyne was spared. The Onondaga chief Garakontié, the main negotiator with the French, left for Québec at the head of a delegation and brought Le Moyne back to his people.

There were things to cheer about in Ville-Marie. And yet for the *Montréalistes* New France's time of joy turned into a time of sadness.

Alexandre de Prouville de Tracy, lieutenant-general for America, landed with the Carignan regiment, accompanied by an aide-de-camp, preceded by twenty-four guards, and followed by pages, footmen and officers in fancy uniforms. The pomp of his arrival bespoke a certain arrogance. Two governors, Voyer d'Argenson and Saffray de Mézy, had picked fights with Maisonneuve, whose authority came initially from the Société de Notre-Dame de Montréal and then from the Society of Saint-Sulpice. The governors of the colony were not happy with a situation that they regarded as ambiguous and damaging to their prestige. With typical military tact, Prouville de Tracy directed Maisonneuve to return to France on leave for an indefinite period.

Dollier de Casson, who arrived in Montréal the next year, was in a position to have first-hand knowledge of the distress that overtook the little population at this news, and he expressed it in unequivocal terms. All the joy that the Sun King's decisions had aroused in the Ville-Marie pioneers "dissolved into much bitterness when they saw that M. de Maison-Neufve, their father and very dear governor, was leaving this time for good, leaving them in the hands of another from whom they would not hope to expect the same faithfulness to his word, the same love and the same fidelity."

To receive such instructions undoubtedly did not come as a surprise to Maisonneuve. The sterile rivalry between royal power in Québec and seigneurial authority in Montréal, as manifested in the bitterness and arrogance of Saffray de Mézy's attitude towards the governor of Ville-Marie, had already begun.

Maisonneuve left without the slightest indiscretion, and even the Jesuit *Relations* said nothing about his departure. Throughout his mandate, people who came in contact with him were unanimous about his qualities. It has been written of him that he was vowed to both perpetual chastity and evangelical poverty. He was a "man of great prayer," humble "like an ardent novice," and especially, "as good as an angel." In Abbé Lionel Groulx's judgement, "this layman needed only the robe and ritual investiture to be a true monk." But it is not for his religious fervour alone that Maisonneuve has been praised. We know of no historian who has had any reason to cast doubt on his honesty or on the wisdom of his decisions.

For all that, some might say, the fur trade was carried on in Ville-Marie under his administration. But trade is not harmful if it is carried out morally and legally. The fur trade was the basis of New France's economy: the court depended on it to make possible the consolidation of the colony without having to dip into its own purse. At no time did Maisonneuve benefit from the fur trade or succumb to the temptation to change furs into hard cash, "a transmutation he was not able to learn," as Dollier de Casson wrote. The same could not be said of his successor as governor of Montréal, François-Marie Perrot.

If Maisonneuve left without a fuss, it is probably because the development of New France and of "his" Ville-Marie brought the gradual decline of his mystical dream. The mustard seed he had planted twenty-three years earlier no longer had urgent need of his care to spread its leaves.

Maisonneuve retired to the house of the fathers of Christian Doctrine on Rue des Fossés-Saint-Victor on Sainte-Geneviève hill in Paris and spent the last eleven years of his life there. Today, an inscription at 73 Rue du

The monument to Chomedey de Maisonneuve by the sculptor Philippe Hébert that was unveiled in Place d'Armes in 1895 (above) is clearly more dignified than the one that was proposed in 1879 (opposite page).

Cardinal-Lemoine indicates the location of the congregation's mother house, where he died in 1676. He was buried at the nearby cemetery of Saint-Étienne-du-Mont abbey.

When consideration was being given to building a monument to

Maisonneuve in Montréal's Place d'Armes in 1879, the design that was submitted included a base consisting of a fountain with two beavers. The monument that was built was more dignified, but it was not until sixteen years
later that it was unveiled by the lieutenant-governor of Québec, Adolphe
Chapleau. It was the masterwork of the noted Québec sculptor Philippe
Hébert.

At Long Last, A Stable Peace

The arrival of the Carignan-Salières regiment gave Montréal twenty years
of peace. The Iroquois threat had hindered the evangelization of peaceful

aboriginal nations, decimated the French population of the colony and diverted part of the fur trade to the English, and Prouville de Tracy's mandate was to crush that threat once and for all.

It was through Lake Champlain and the Rivière des Iroquois (Richelieu River) that the Iroquois reached the St. Lawrence and infested the great artery of communication linking Québec, Trois-Rivières and Montréal. Prouville de Tracy immediately began to place fortifications along the Richelieu wherever rapids forced the enemy to come ashore. In July 1665 he sent four companies to begin building Fort Richelieu, Fort Saint-Louis and Fort Sainte-Thérèse. The next year he continued to put his plan into effect, beginning construction on Fort Saint-Jean, Fort Sainte-Anne and Fort Lamothe.

In December 1665, Garakontié arrived in Québec to begin peace negotiations in the name of the Onondagas, Cayugas and Senecas, and asked for some time to convince the Mohawks and Oneidas to do the same. The Iroquois had gone back on their word so many times that the lieutenant general did not trust them. He especially feared the treachery of the Mohawks, who lived in the valley of the Mohawk River, a tributary of the Hudson, and he authorized Governor Rémy de Courcelles to launch an expedition against them.

Courcelles left Québec with his detachment on January 9, but the French soldiers had not learned the tricks of skirmish warfare and were unused to the rigours of winter. By the time they arrived at Fort Richelieu, a number of them were suffering from chilblains. Algonquins were supposed to serve as scouts and guides, but they didn't arrive when they were expected, and on January 29 Courcelles got tired of waiting. He gave the soldiers their marching orders, and 600 men set out on a long walk on snowshoes, carrying their weapons and supplies on their backs. Charles Le Moyne was in charge of the vanguard, made up of *Montréalistes* who were more accustomed to a venture of this sort than their cousins newly arrived from France, who had been trained for formal battles.

It was not a glorious expedition. Without native guides, the soldiers followed false trails and suddenly found themselves in front of the Anglo-Dutch settlement of Corlaer (now Schenectady, New York). France and England had been at war for two weeks, but no one in America was yet aware of it. The soldiers saw very few Mohawks: they were several days' march from the Mohawk villages. The few Mohawks they did see took ten prisoners.

The baptism of Garakontié. (Bas-relief decorating the base of the monument to Bishop François de Laval, Québec City.)

The soldiers were worn out. A sudden thaw made Courcelles's position untenable, and he decided to go back. Harassed by the Mohawks, the small expeditionary force headed back towards Québec. This time the governor carefully assigned the rearguard to Le Moyne and his men. "He gave them the honour," Dollier de Casson wrote, "of assigning them the front on the way out and the rear on the way back, as there were few others to whom he could have entrusted these honourable and dangerous marches through the woods for which our troops were so ill-trained at that time."

Courcelles had lost a tenth of his men in an expedition that had accomplished little. The Mohawks now knew that the French could come after them into their own country, but they doubted that the French had the capacity to strike. Tracy and Courcelles hoped to reestablish the king's prestige, and 1,400 men left Fort Sainte-Anne in late September 1666 with the goal of forcing the Mohawks to submit. The expedition included 110 *Montréalistes*, again commanded by Le Moyne, with Pierre Picoté de Belestre as lieutenant. They were given the same honour as on the previous expedition, "being made to march quite far ahead until they saw the enemy villages, undergoing the greatest dangers that could be incurred." This time the venture was successful. They burned four Mohawk villages and took the

Mohawk lands in the name of the king. The *capots bleus* (blue hoods), as Courcelles liked to call the *Montréalistes*, had found another opportunity to serve New France.

This time, the five Iroquois nations asked for peace and agreed to respect the conditions laid out by the French. People sensed that a new and very promising era was beginning. It was not without hitches, but throughout his mandate Courcelles worked to maintain the Iroquois in a state of fear that made them respectful and prudent. Garakontié, the main architect of peace on the Iroquois side, devoted his efforts to making the work of the missionaries easier. A few years later he asked to be baptized, and Bishop Laval himself fulfilled his wish.

Montréal – as Maisonneuve's Ville-Marie was increasingly being called – benefited from peace and flourished as never before. In May 1667 Prouville de Tracy visited the settlement. Montréal being the farthest upstream of all the French settlements, the purpose of his visit was probably to entrench his prestige among the natives. Jean Talon also came to Montréal to do his job and meet the people. He did this, Dollier de Casson wrote, "to the edification and satisfaction of the whole public, who saw him walking from house to house along the shores of the island, to see if everyone, down to the poorest, was treated with justice and equity."

On August 28, 1667, Prouville de Tracy left Canada for good, having fully carried out his mission. He left behind the Carignan regiment, a number of whose officers would receive seigneuries bearing their names, especially along the banks of the Richelieu. The Sulpician superior, Gabriel Souart, left for France to recruit colleagues for the New France missions; now that there was peace, evangelization work could be revived.

Promising Signs of Growth

———————— >< ————————

As a result of the concern that Louis XIV showed for New France, manifested in the *conseil souverain* with which he endowed the colony, the prestigious senior administrators he appointed to run it and the successful action that was taken to end the Iroquois incursions, a propitious period of development began in Montréal.

In September 1666, the sailing ship *Moulin d'Or* brought four Sulpicians to Montréal, including Dollier de Casson, whose acquaintance we have already made, and Jean Cavelier. Father Cavelier had a brother, Robert, who was considering becoming a priest but was wracked by indecision. He was a native of Rouen, which had strong ties with Canada, and had thus heard much about the colony. Robert Cavelier landed at Québec in 1667. When he arrived in Montréal, peace had just been made, so that it was now possible to develop lands in the country some distance from Montréal proper and the Sulpicians were beginning to grant fiefs and subfiefs in these areas.

The first to benefit from such a grant was Jean Philippe Vincent de Hautmesnil, in 1665. His domain, however, was close to the fort, southeast of a small river called the Saint-Pierre. The second was Robert Cavelier. His fief was at the head of Saut Saint-Louis, the departure point for canoes heading for the Great Lakes. But he did not do much work on the land, as he dreamed of exploring the Ohio River so that "the honour of finding the way to the South Sea, and through it the way to China, should not be left to others." Dollier de Casson wrote wryly of the "renowned transmigration of *Lachine* [China] to these parts, in giving its name to one of our shores this winter in so authentic a fashion that the name has stuck." He added that it would be "a great consolation to those who come to Mount Royal when they find out that it is only three leagues from *la Chine.*"

Cavelier de La Salle, as he was known, gave his fief back to the Sulpicians so that he could go explore the continent, receiving compensation for the work that he had done. He also sold a piece of cleared land to the pioneers Charles Le Moyne and Jacques Le Ber, who finished building a house that was already under construction. That house is now at 100 La Salle Road in the city of Lachine, which opened a museum there in 1948.

As seigneurs, the Sulpicians continued to grant fiefs. In 1671, they granted one to Zacharie Dupuis, a native of Saverdun in what is now the department of Ariège in the Pyrénées. His domain was named Verdun and he became the Sieur de Verdun. Pierre Picoté de Belestre received his the same year, at the east end of Montréal Island where the parish of Pointe-aux-Trembles would develop. The next year Michel Sidrac Dugué, Sieur de Boisbriand, was granted a fief on the shores of Lac des Deux-Montagnes that became known as Senneville.

Hunched up to protect itself against the Iroquois raids for too long, Montréal was now beginning to stretch. But the Sulpicians' minds were not only on developing their great seigneury. Under their energetic superior, Dollier de Casson, they were also creating, one by one, the elements of a

Montréal's first parish church, built right in the path of Notre-Dame Street.

future city. In 1672 Dollier put Bénigne Basset in charge of laying out Montréal's first streets. Basset was a notary who had taken over from Jean de Saint-Père; the roughly 2,500 documents he signed during his career are in the National Archives of Québec. At the same time, he was a master surveyor, and he marked out Saint-Joseph, Saint-Pierre, Saint-Paul, Saint-Charles, Saint-François, du Calvaire, Saint-Lambert, Saint-Gabriel and Notre-Dame streets in what is now old Montréal.

The population was now growing rapidly and had reached 1,500. The church built fifteen years earlier next to the enlarged Hôtel-Dieu, as much for patients as for parishioners, was no longer adequate. Bishop Laval realized this and in 1669 called Montréal's residents together to suggest to them that they build their own church.

The project took shape in 1672. The Sulpicians donated the land, Dollier de Casson contributed a gift of 3,000 livres, and the master mason

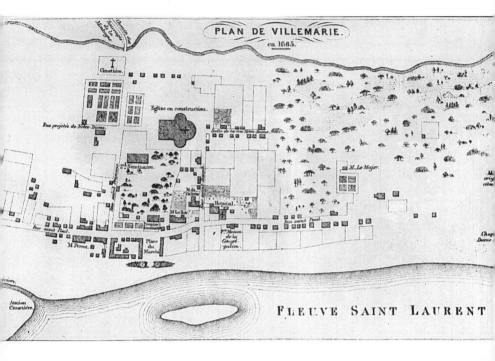

A map of Ville-Marie in 1685. The original Notre-Dame church, in the path of Notre-Dame Street, is at centre left. The planned westward extension of Notre-Dame Street is shown to the left. At the far right is the Coteau windmill. Later, the citadel would be built here. Eventually, the hill would be levelled and the old Dalhousie Station would be built on the same site. Bonsecours Chapel is at the lower right.

François Bailli began the excavation. On June 30, Dollier presided at the laying of not one but five inscribed stones, laid by Governor de Courcelles, the intendant Talon, Governor François-Marie Perrot of Montréal Island, Jeanne Mance and Dollier himself.

Work went on for thirteen years and then the *Montréalistes* were finally able to attend their parish church. To reduce costs, the old fort was partially demolished and its stones and wood were used. The church was still only a nave bisected by a transept containing two chapels; there was no façade, side naves or bell tower. It was only over a period of generations that the building was completed, primarily through additions made necessary by the growth of the population. The church had been in existence for more than a century when the traditional cock was placed on top of the bell tower.

It was not only Montréal but all of New France that enjoyed a good year in 1672, largely because of Talon's wise leadership. Until then, the seigneurial system had developed without an overall plan. It was difficult for settlers living on seigneuries that were scattered more or less at random to escape the Iroquois threat. Talon had a land register drawn up and his land-grant policy favoured the clearing of lands close to ones that were already settled.

Talon signed dozens of grants in 1672, including many to officers of the Carignan regiment who had chosen to stay in the colony. Thus, on October 29, seigneuries were granted to François Jarret de Verchères, Jacques de Chambly, Antoine Pécaudy de Contrecoeur, Pierre de Saint-Ours and Pierre de Saurel. The names of these soldiers would become the names of towns along the St. Lawrence and Richelieu rivers that would help reduce the isolation from which Montréal had suffered for so long.

A Messy Controversy

✦

François-Marie Perrot, appointed governor of Montréal by the king, had married Jean Talon's niece – a circumstance that undoubtedly had some bearing on the advantages he enjoyed. He landed at Québec in mid-August 1670, at the same time as his wife's uncle. "As he is a very distinguished and well-born gentleman," Dollier de Casson wrote, "his arrival has given all of us much cause for hope." Unfortunately, it didn't take long for the Sulpicians to become disenchanted.

Perrot's first acts as governor gave no hint of the commercial spirit that animated him. In 1671, he accompanied Governor de Courcelles to the shores of Lake Ontario in an effort to get the Iroquois to stop their attacks on tribes allied with the French and thus nip in the bud a situation that was hindering the effectiveness of the peace.

Perrot was among the new seigneurs favoured by Talon's grants of 1672: on October 29 of that year, he received the large and beautiful island west of Montréal that would bear his name. The governor of Montréal quickly understood the strategic nature of his island domain, where the Ottawas reached the St. Lawrence in their canoes laden with furs after their long journey down the river that bears their name. From that time on, Perrot devoted himself to the fur trade. When Montréal's merchants complained about this unfair competition, he abused his authority as governor to put an end to their complaints. On Île Perrot, the native trappers who were bringing the furs they had gathered to the king's factors were received by his henchman, Antoine de La Fresnaye, Sieur de Brucy.

Two Sulpicians are important to our story: François de Salignac de Lamothe-Fénelon, who arrived in 1667, and François Saturnin Lascaris d'Urfé, who arrived in 1668. Fénelon was a half-brother of the famous writer and archbishop of Cambrai of the same name, while Lascaris d'Urfé belonged to a noble family of the Forez region in central France and was related to an illustrious Greek dynasty that had once reigned in Constantinople. These important figures had renounced the advantages of their birth to devote themselves to missionary work, and since their arrival they had worked with the Iroquois near Lake Ontario.

Count Frontenac, who became governor of New France in 1672, had great respect and admiration for the two missionaries. Unfortunately, Perrot's manoeuvrings would soon complicate matters. Perrot trafficked openly with the natives on his island. While he received 3,000 livres for fulfilling his duties as governor of Montréal, Baron de La Hontan reported that he quickly accumulated 50,000 écus (150,000 livres) in this illegal business. The Sulpician Father Faillon reported that Perrot was seen personally filling barrels with spirits to trade for furs. News of such insolence inevitably reached Governor Frontenac. The governor, however, was indiscreet enough to call on Fénelon's friendship, asking him to request Perrot's presence in Québec. When Perrot arrived, Frontenac imprisoned him in the Château Saint-Louis without the formality of a trial.

Fénelon protested to the governor, but Frontenac wouldn't budge. Incensed that Frontenac should have used him so shamelessly, the Sulpician denounced the governor in thinly veiled terms from the pulpit. Frontenac would not tolerate having his pride injured in this way. He arraigned Fénelon before the Conseil Supérieur and conducted the proceedings himself, acting as both prosecutor and judge. The trial lasted five months. Frontenac ordered Perrot and Fénelon to go to France so that their behaviour could be judged there. The court upheld the governor in Perrot's case but reproached him for the criminal proceedings he had brought against Fénelon. It concluded that the Sulpician should have been turned over to his bishop or the *grand vicaire* "to punish him with ecclesiastical penalties."

Fénelon was ordered never to go back to New France. He maintained complete silence and died five years after his return to France. Such firmness of character could be described as a family trait: the archbishop of Cambrai fell into disgrace for writing *The Adventures of Telemachus*, which implicitly criticized the policies of Louis XIV.

In 1673 Frontenac had granted Fénelon the Îles de Courcelles in Lac Saint-Louis so that he could establish rudimentary schools for native youth there, and Fénelon founded a settlement that he named Gentilly. Fénelon Boulevard in nearby Dorval is named for him. Fénelon's colleague, Father Lascaris d'Urfé, became the first permanent curé of Saint-Louis du Haut-de-l'Île. According to tradition, the parish chapel was on Pointe Caron, now within the limits of the town of Baie-d'Urfé. In 1961, at Baie-d'Urfé's request, French President Charles de Gaulle sent the town some stones from the ancestral château of the Cornes d'Urfé in the department of Loire, which were to be incorporated into a monument that was planned for the fiftieth anniversary of Baie-d'Urfé's accession to municipal status.

Still on the Alert

————————— ✼ —————————

It was on the Bay of Quinte on the north shore of Lake Ontario that the Sulpicians first worked as missionaries. Father Lamothe-Fénelon founded this mission, and Father Lascaris d'Urfé served three Iroquois villages as well as isolated cabins. Some twelve years later, the Sulpicians realized that this apostolic work had not had much effect in relation to its cost. Instead, they resorted to a formula that had previously been used by the Jesuits, who had established the sedentary mission of La Prairie de la Magdeleine to receive new Iroquois converts in about 1670. This is where Kateri Tekakwitha, the "Lily of the Mohawks," would take refuge seven years later to escape persecution by her own people. Similarly, in 1676, the Sulpicians established the Fort de la Montagne, at the foot of Mount Royal.

This mission was initially very unassuming, but it took on a more distinguished air under the leadership of Vachon de Belmont, a native of Grenoble. De Belmont was very wealthy – his mother paid him an allowance of 1,000 livres – and out of his fortune and his private income he paid for the construction of a tastefully decorated chapel, a house for the missionaries, and an enclosure made of stakes, which he later replaced with four stone walls with a turret at each corner. Two of these turrets are still standing

One of the towers of the Fort de la Montagne where Marguerite Bourgeoys and her companions educated young native girls.

today along Sherbrooke Street. De Belmont later opened a mission at Sault-au-Récollet. With de Belmont's encouragement, small schools were opened in the Fort de la Montagne, where he taught native boys and Marguerite Bourgeoys taught the girls. De Belmont was also good with his hands and taught his students a variety of trades: tailor, mason, shoemaker.

Even though there was peace, the French were not completely safe from the warlike instincts of the Iroquois, some of whom wanted to capture the Fort de la Montagne. A number of defensive works had been built in the country to protect the settlers. In the area of Lachine a windmill, designed to serve as a redoubt, had been built in 1671; there was also a manor house built by the pioneer Jean Milot. The two buildings were surrounded by a

A view of the Fort de la Montagne in 1690.

palisade made of stakes, and the entire construction became known as Fort Rémy. In 1676 René Cuillerier built a trading post, Fort Cuillerier, at the head of the Lachine Rapids. In 1670, François Le Noir *dit* Rolland received a concession within what are now the Lachine city limits, and soon afterward he had a fort built to protect the settlers who would develop his land. Fort de la Présentation, built in 1674 opposite the Îles de Courcelles, completed the ring. Zacharie Dupuis, the seigneur of Verdun, had also built a small fort in his fief, at the foot of the rapids.

In 1684, Louis Hector de Callières succeeded François-Marie Perrot as governor of Montréal. Upon his arrival, Callières realized the strategic importance of the place and saw that it was pretty well open to any invasion. The old fort was in such disrepair that it was falling down. There was nowhere that residents could take refuge in case of attack. The peace with the Iroquois was fragile because of intertribal hostilities and the machinations of the English, who wanted to take as large a share as possible of the fur trade. Callières ordered all the *habitants* to supply stakes to fortify the town. The palisade of stakes was completed in 1687, but it did not last very long. In 1722 it had to be replaced with stone walls.

In 1682, with the warlike spirit of the Iroquois increasingly in evidence, Lefebvre de La Barre succeeded Frontenac as governor of New France. The king wanted to keep the peace through diplomacy. The next year, at the request of Charles Le Moyne, some fifty Iroquois chiefs came to

Québec to parley. They demanded that Cavelier de La Salle leave Fort Saint-Louis on the Illinois River. In March they attacked the fort. Although the missionaries advised against such an expedition, La Barre left for Lake Ontario with a thousand men. With his troops ravaged by illness, he did not dare attack the representatives of the Five Nations who came to meet him near Oswego, and the woebegone expedition returned to Québec. Louis XIV did not hide his disappointment at this "shameful" peace, and he recalled the governor. Despite the treaty, the Iroquois continued their depredations against the French and the tribes allied with them.

In 1685, Brisay de Denonville became governor of New France. He was faced with a dual task: governing the colony wisely and dealing firmly with the contentious question of the Iroquois threat. He would have liked to solve the Iroquois question without resorting to arms, but the English were inciting Iroquois hostility towards the French so that they could make more profit from the fur trade. Denonville even suggested to Louis XIV that he enter into negotiations with James II of England for the purchase of the colony of Manate (New York) as a way of putting an end to the English intrigues. After months of reflection, Denonville came to the conclusion that sooner or later, at a time of their choosing, the Iroquois would attack the French settlements.

In June 1687, he left for the Great Lakes at the head of an expedition of 2,000 militiamen, French soldiers and native allies. The expedition did not meet its goals: the Mohawks managed to escape, although their villages were burned. After that, Denonville concentrated on consolidating the colony's defensive works, in the constant expectation of renewed Iroquois raids. His fears turned out to be justified. On August 5, 1689, 1,500 warriors attacked Lachine, burning fifty-six houses, killing twenty-four settlers and capturing nearly a hundred other people, half of whom would never return from the Iroquois villages. New France faced another ten years of constant skirmishes.

An Eventful Decade

————————————— ✢ —————————————

In October 1689, Count Frontenac returned to New France for a second term as governor. The War of the League of Augsburg had broken out in Europe. There is no evidence that Louis XIV had shown any desire to act on

Denonville's suggestion of negotiating the purchase of New York. In any case, France and England were now at war, and hostilities in Europe always had repercussions in America.

When Frontenac returned, he rejected the idea of attacking Albany, given the risk of operations by the English colonies and the need to protect the French settlements against possible Iroquois incursions and help the native allies on the western frontier. Instead, he decided to send expeditionary forces against three English settlements: Corlaer (present-day Schenectady), Salmon Falls on the Maine coast and Fort Loyal on Casco Bay, also in Maine. The French undertook these three campaigns in midwinter, on snowshoes. The 114 *Canadiens* and ninety-six natives in charge of launching a surprise attack on Corlaer left Montréal in January 1690. The small force included three of Charles Le Moyne's sons: Sainte-Hélène, who was in command along with Nicolas d'Ailleboust de Manthet; Iberville, second in command; and Maricourt. The raid turned into a slaughter. The expeditionary force massacred sixty of the English, took thirty prisoners and left the village only after burning it. Some fifty horses were needed to carry the booty. The other two targets met with the same fate.

The three expeditions raised morale throughout New France, but they also galvanized a desire for reprisals in the English colonies. The English conceived a major two-pronged operation: an attack on Montréal by land and a naval expedition against Québec. The operation against Montréal was abandoned, apparently because of an outbreak of smallpox among the militia, but the plan to attack Québec was carried through. Frontenac was in Montréal when the Québec town commandant brought him the news that a large fleet had left Boston. The rest is well known. The commander of the fleet, Admiral William Phips, laid siege to Québec. About ten days later, the enemy withdrew after trying to establish a beachhead at Beauport.

We can imagine that people in Montréal breathed a sigh of relief. It seemed to them that the last decade of the century was starting on a promising note. The promise, however, was not fulfilled. Unable to defeat the French colony, the English relied on the Iroquois to keep it on the alert and on the defensive. Frontenac was in a similar position, with forces that were not sufficient to carry the war into enemy territory, and so he resorted to the same tactic. Montréal was the farthest French outpost, and so its governor, Callières, and military commander, Rigaud de Vaudreuil, were put in charge of these raids. Experienced skirmish-fighters that they were, the *Canadiens* played a conspicuous role in this operation.

Nevertheless, in 1696, Montréal was the point of departure for more

View of Ville-Marie in 1683, reconstructed from notes by the historian Jacques Viger, the first mayor of Montréal. (Watercolour attributed to James Duncan.)

than 2,000 soldiers, militiamen and native allies, led by Courcelles and Rigaud de Vaudreuil under Frontenac's command. Frontenac was a determined man. Seventy-four years old and ill (he died two years later), he had himself carried on a litter through the woods to the country of the Onondagas. The Onondagas, however, had abandoned their villages, probably after being warned that the expedition was coming. Vaudreuil, meanwhile, pushed on to the country of the Oneidas; they too had fled into the woods. His forces burned everything, including their crops. It was not a glorious expedition, since it was conducted without striking a blow, but it broke the back of the Iroquois, whose numbers dwindled while the population of the French settlements grew. Was this perhaps the first instance of French Canada's celebrated "revenge of the cradle"?

The inconveniences of these expeditions and the Iroquois raids were not the only problems facing Montréal in the early 1690s. It was only with

The Récollet church and convent on Notre-Dame Street.

difficulty that crops could be planted, and the result was a food shortage that was not solved until supplies of flour arrived from France. But despite everything, the little town was growing. The Récollets came to Montréal in 1692 and built an initial monastery there. The Jesuits returned the same year, taking up residence on Notre-Dame Street. The indefatigable Sulpicians were constantly opening new schools. In 1696 Father Léonard Chaigneau was put in charge of the expansion of the Sulpician educational network, and in the next few years new schools were opened in Pointe-aux-Trembles, Rivière-des-Prairies, Sorel, Repentigny and Saint-Sulpice.

Montréal already had a hospital, but in 1694 the Frères Charon, a community established by a merchant, François Charon de La Barre, built a second one at Pointe à Callières in what is now Old Montréal, on land granted by the Sulpicians. The new hospital was intended for men only. Its twenty-four rooms were used by the infirm and orphans as well as the sick, and trades were taught there to young boys. At the same time, construction was begun on a new Hôtel-Dieu, more in line with the features of contemporary French hospitals than the previous one. Once the foundation was laid, the first Canadian nun of the Hôtel-Dieu, Sister Marie Morin, took charge

Although this drawing shows the Château de Longueuil and its towers in a state of advanced decay, it gives us an idea of the grand appearance this building must have had.

of the project. The hospital was opened in 1694, but tragically, it was destroyed by fire along with the old buildings three months later.

Montréal was gradually taking on the characteristics of a city. But unfortunately, its development was marked not only by achievements but by disasters as well.

The Le Moynes, a Leading Family of Great Renown

The military exploits of the most prominent family in New France in the late seventeenth century, the Le Moynes, are a fascinating story. We have chronicled the early years in Ville-Marie of the soldier and settler Charles Le Moyne, who arrived in New France in 1641. In 1654 he married Catherine Thierry, the adopted daughter of Antoine Primot. The sturdy offspring produced by this union left an indelible mark on the history of French America.

The eldest son, Charles (1656-1729), began his military career in France.

Arms of Charles Le Moyne: blue, with three gold roses, with head sewn with gules with a gold crescent surrounded by two gold stars.

When he returned to Montréal, his parents presented him with the seigneury of Longueuil. In 1687 he commanded four companies in the army raised by Brisay de Denonville against the Senecas. Three years later, he distinguished himself at Beauport with his brother, Sainte-Hélène, when Admiral Phips tried to establish a bridgehead there. He would have died from the wound he received in his side had he not been protected by his powder horn. Shortly after the turn of the century, he was made a baron by Louis XIV – the only native-born Canadian to be so honoured. His seigneury of Longueuil boasted a fort flanked by four towers, which the king acknowledged was "the only one fortified and constructed in that fashion." The honour resulted from the great contribution the fort had made to the protection of the inhabitants of the surrounding seigneuries.

Appointed military commandant of Montréal in 1706, Charles Le Moyne de Longueuil served as ambassador to the Oneidas, the Onondagas and the Cayugas, and managed to keep them on the side of the French. He had already been made a Chevalier de Saint-Louis when he was entrusted with the government of Trois-Rivières in 1720. Five years later, on the

death of Rigaud de Vaudreuil, he was put in charge of the general administration of New France. He died in 1729.

Jacques Le Moyne de Sainte-Hélène (1659-1690) had accompanied his
father on Lefebvre de La Barre's ill-fated expedition to Lake Ontario. In
1686 he fought alongside his brothers, Iberville and Maricourt, in the expedition launched by Chevalier de Troyes against the English forts on Hudson
Bay. After a difficult, three-month journey with many portages, they captured three posts, Fort Monsipi, Fort Rupert and Fort Albany, along with
a ship. Historians credit the Le Moyne brothers with the success of this
expedition. Sainte-Hélène had scarcely arrived home when he was given
command of 300 native warriors making up the advance guard of the expeditionary force that Brisay de Denonville was raising against the Senecas in
the Great Lakes region. Then he brought back English ships captured by
Iberville after a second expedition to Hudson Bay. Back in Québec in
November 1689, he put on his snowshoes and with Iberville, Maricourt and
Bienville took part in the action against the English settlement of Corlaer.

He was good at aiming cannons and Frontenac put him in charge of
the artillery when Phips came to Québec in October 1690. Tradition has it
that the first ball he fired knocked down the flag of Phips's flagship. The
Canadiens hurried to pick it up and later hung it from the vault of the cathedral. Like his older brother, he took part in the operation against the English
on the beach at Beauport. He received what appeared to be a minor wound
in his leg, but it grew worse and he died on December 3. The Jesuit historian Pierre-François-Xavier de Charlevoix later wrote that the colony had
lost "one of the bravest men it had ever had."

The third son, Pierre (1661-1706), who took the additional name of
Iberville, went to Hudson Bay in 1686 in the company of Sainte-Hélène
and de Maricourt, and to Corlaer four years later. In 1690 Frontenac put
him in command of the French posts on Hudson Bay. In the years that followed he tried to recapture the posts that had been taken from the English
and lost again, but these efforts met with indifferent success because the
resources he was allotted either were insufficient or arrived after the close of
the brief navigation season. He also sailed along the coasts of Newfoundland
and New England during this period.

In 1694 Iberville, in command of the *Poly*, and his brother Sérigny, in
command of the *Salamandre*, set sail from La Rochelle for Québec. From
there, accompanied by their brother Maricourt, they left for Hudson Bay.
Without much difficulty they took Fort York, the wealthiest of the English

This plaque on Saint-Sulpice Street in Montréal reads: "Pierre Le Moyne, Sieur d'Iberville, born on this site on July 20, 1661; died on board the *Juste*; buried in the cathedral at Havana on July 9, 1706. The greatest warrior produced by New France."

posts, and renamed it Fort Bourbon. In 1696, a new campaign was mounted along the coastlines of Acadia and Newfoundland. The following year, Iberville won a memorable battle on board the *Pélican* against three English sailing ships and retook Fort York, which the English had in the meantime occupied again.

In 1698, at the prompting of Louis XIV's minister of marine, Comte de Pontchartrain, this indomitable *Canadien* turned his energies towards the Gulf of Mexico and the West Indies. In 1702 he founded Mobile with the help of his brothers Bienville and Assigny. When he returned to the seigneury of Ardillières in the Aunis region of western France that he had purchased in 1700, he was suffering from malaria. In 1706 he attacked Nevis in the West Indies and claimed everything there for himself, including twenty-five sailing ships anchored in the harbour, a prize worth more than fourteen million livres. That was his last exploit. He died in 1706 in the arms of his brother Sérigny, on board the *Juste*, and was buried in Havana.

Paul Le Moyne de Maricourt (1663-1704) accompanied Iberville and Sainte-Hélène in 1686 on the expedition led by Chevalier de Troyes. In later years, he distinguished himself for his bravery and endurance at Hudson Bay and was wounded during an engagement there, but recovered fairly quickly. In 1689, he took over command of the posts in the region when Iberville returned to Québec with the ships captured from the English. In 1690, he served brilliantly in the defence of Québec with his brothers Sainte-Hélène and Longueuil. Later he was given various military duties, an indication of the esteem in which he was held by the colony's authorities. In 1696 Frontenac asked him to raise a militia for Iberville, who was going to sail to Newfoundland, and that same year Frontenac gave him command of a native detachment in his expedition against the Iroquois.

In later years Maricourt did not often leave Montréal, where he had interests in a trading firm and was a captain in the garrison. Colonial authorities relied on his prestige among the natives, especially among the Onondagas, who regarded him as a son. His career ended with a great diplomatic success: he was the main force behind the peace of 1701, signed in Montréal. More about this later.

The fifth son, François (1666-1691), took the surname of Bienville. Unfortunately, he did not live long enough to win as much fame as the four older sons. In early 1690 he fought at Corlaer, with Iberville and Maricourt. In June of the following year, under Vaudreuil's orders, he chased a band of Oneidas from the Pointe-aux-Trembles area. The Oneidas spent the night at an abandoned house at Repentigny. Some took refuge inside, but their pursuers did not give up. They waited until dark to fall on them and quickly massacred those who were sleeping outside. The noise of the slaughter, however, awakened the others, who defended themselves with a strength born of despair. In the course of the battle, Bienville received a fatal gunshot wound. He was buried in Montréal on June 7. His brother Jean-Baptiste, the future founder of Louisiana, took the name Bienville in his place.

The name Sérigny, adopted by the sixth son, Joseph Le Moyne (1668-1734), undoubtedly comes from the town of that name in Aunis. The town, which still exists, is northeast of La Rochelle. Joseph Le Moyne de Sérigny joined the navy at nearby Rochefort. He was promoted to lieutenant in 1692 and for the next seven years devoted all his time to Iberville's expeditions to Hudson Bay. In 1694 the two brothers took back Fort York from the English, but unfortunately lost another family member, Louis Le Moyne de Châteauguay, who was Sérigny's ensign on the *Salamandre*.

In 1697 Iberville and Sérigny had to retake Fort York, which the English had occupied again. Sérigny then took over command of the installations in the region. He did not return to La Rochelle until November 1698. Later, he accompanied Iberville on his expeditions to the West Indies and Louisiana. After the death of his brother, he was suspected of fraud and seemed for a time to have lost the confidence of the authorities, but the matter was resolved. He commanded Louisiana jointly with his brother Bienville, and in 1719 he seized the Spanish post of Pensacola. He became governor of Rochefort in 1723 and died there eleven years later.

The sixth son, François-Marie, died prematurely in 1687 at the age of seventeen and did not have time to make a name for himself on the honour rolls of New France.

Had the seventh son, Louis Le Moyne de Châteauguay (1676-1694), not died so young, he would undoubtedly have had as brilliant a career as his brothers. He had already gained valuable experience with Iberville at Hudson Bay. In 1693, his brother solicited a midshipman's commission on his behalf, saying he "was capable of sailing a ship by himself with respect to piloting and commanding it." And he was only seventeen! But, as we said, fate decided otherwise; he died the following year at Fort York. His younger brother Antoine, then eleven years old, took his name of Châteauguay.

It was the eighth son, Jean-Baptiste (1680-1767), who had the longest career. He took the name of Bienville, which his brother François had used until his death in 1691. Jean-Baptiste had already taken part in Iberville's expeditions to Hudson Bay and the shores of Newfoundland and New England when Iberville was asked to search for the mouth of the Mississippi in 1698. This was the beginning of Bienville's more than three decades of service in that part of America, and especially in Louisiana.

He was made commander at Biloxi in 1701 and presided in an enlightened manner over Louisiana's development for ten years. This was a difficult decade because there was considerable envy and hostility towards the Le Moynes. Investigations into Bienville's conduct continued for another decade. He was accused of inflexibility towards the French, condescension towards the natives, dissolute behaviour and other deficiencies.

Nothing was ever proved against him. Meanwhile in 1714 he was given the military command of the Mississippi and in 1717 he was made a Chevalier de Saint-Louis.

To save Louisiana in 1732, the king turned to Bienville and appointed him governor. He remained in this post until 1742 when he decided to retire. He moved to Paris, where in 1763 he learned with sadness of the signing of the Treaty of Paris by which France ceded both Canada and Louisiana. On March 7, 1767, he died there at the age of eighty-seven. A sign at 17 Rue Vivienne in Paris indicates where Bienville died. In Louisiana's largest city, New Orleans, which Bienville founded, a statute was erected in his memory.

Charles Le Moyne's last two sons did not serve in Canada. Gabriel, Sieur d'Assigny (1681-1701), probably accompanied Iberville and Sérigny to Santo Domingo in November 1701, for that is where he died shortly afterwards. The youngest son, Antoine (1683-1742), who took the name of Châteauguay after his brother Louis was killed at Fort York in 1694, became a midshipman at Rochefort in 1699, then was made lieutenant and later captain. He commanded the troops of Louisiana for ten years (1717-1727) and died at Rochefort in 1742.

The Le Moynes were an impressive family. No other family had such an illustrious name or performed such outstanding deeds in the defence, development and consolidation of France's empire in America. In Montréal, at the corner of Saint-Sulpice and Saint-Paul streets, three bronze plaques honour the memory of Charles Le Moyne and two of his sons: Le Moyne d'Iberville, "the greatest military man produced by New France," and Le Moyne de Longueuil, the only Canadian-born baron.

The New Century Gets Off to a Good Start

The eighteenth century opened in Montréal with a stunning diplomatic coup. During the summer of 1700, Onondaga and Seneca chiefs told Governor de Callières that they wanted to make peace and asked him to send representatives to their villages to open discussions. Two factors lay behind this move. On the one hand the western tribes, who were allies of the French, would not stop harassing the Iroquois; on the other hand, the

Iroquois were being told by the English that they were British subjects. The governor agreed to their request and asked three representatives to make the first overtures. One of them was the Montrealer Paul Le Moyne de Maricourt.

The mission was fully successful. In the fall the emissaries returned, accompanied by a score of Iroquois who agreed to work out a treaty together with representatives of the Hurons, the Abenakis and the Ottawas. It was decided that the treaty would be signed in Montréal the following summer. Accordingly in July 1701, 1,300 natives, representing some thirty tribes, assembled in Montréal, with each delegation announced by cannon fire. It is not hard to imagine how colourful the negotiations must have been.

A skilled diplomat, the governor convinced the tribes to live together in peace, to accept his services as a go-between in dealing with whatever violations might occur rather than take to the warpath, and to remain neutral in the event of a conflict between the French and the English. Callières had a right to be proud of this diplomatic success. He had just brought the Iroquois raids on New France to an end and had secured an invaluable opportunity for the colony to develop in peace.

About the same time, the adventurer Antoine Laumet *dit* Lamothe-Cadillac, founded a colony that would eventually be called Détroit, on the river joining Lake St. Clair and Lake Erie. The city of Detroit has often been called Montréal's eldest daughter. Lamothe-Cadillac, a native of Gascony, first served in Acadia and then took part in the expeditions of Lefebvre de La Barre and Brisay de Denonville against the Iroquois. In 1691 he was in Québec, where Frontenac planned to use his knowledge of the Atlantic coast. The following year, he accompanied the cartographer Franquelin on a voyage along the New England coast.

It was probably following his appointment as commander of the strategic post of Michillimakinac, located between Lake Huron and Lake Michigan, that he settled in Montréal. A plaque on Notre-Dame Street at the corner of St. Lawrence Boulevard shows where he lived. His efforts to mediate with the local tribes of the region may not have borne fruit, but the same cannot be said of his talents as a trader; when he returned to Montréal four years later, he led a flotilla of canoes transporting 80,000 kilograms of beaver pelts.

Assigned the task of delivering the mail for the colonial authorities to France in 1698, he took the opportunity to approach Comte de Pontchartrain with a project that had interested him for several years: to establish not just a trading post but a real colony along the banks of the Détroit River, right at the entrance to the area where the Iroquois lived. And so, during the summer of 1701, while the peace treaty was being signed in Montréal, Cadillac arrived on the banks of the Détroit with a hundred men ready to carry out his plans.

There was soon open conflict with Governor Rigaud de Vaudreuil, for Cadillac would have preferred to have this colony under direct French rule rather than being governed from Québec. He had even suggested to the court that he be elevated to the rank of marquis. He made a few grants of land, and by 1708 the settlement already had a population of 300. Following an investigation into his administration and his competence, he lost the confidence of the court and in 1710 he was appointed governor of Louisiana. A statue of Cadillac has been placed in a niche on the façade of Detroit's city hall.

The twenty-five canoes bearing the founders of Détroit left from Montréal in 1701. In a single day, May 27, the notary Antoine Adhémar had countersigned the documents of forty-four men who engaged to live in the new settlement, including a dozen Montrealers bearing names that by this time were fairly comumon: Renault, Cusson, Lemire, Guay, Chauvin, Latour, Vaudry, Richard – all pioneer inhabitants of a city that was to become the capital of the automobile industry. One of the most prestigious cars manufactured in Detroit would one day bear the name of its founder.

While Courcelles was making peace with the Iroquois, Cadillac was founding Détroit, and Iberville and Bienville were laying the foundations of Louisiana. From Montréal, the influence of France was radiating outward to the Great Lakes and the Gulf of Mexico.

A New Governor, Claude de Ramezay

————————— >‹ —————————

Dollier de Casson, the superior of the Sulpicians, was a man of action. His superior general in Paris, Monsieur Tronson, often worried about the projects Dollier de Casson submitted to him, because Dollier sometimes did not wait for permission before starting them.

In 1670, Lamothe-Fénelon had said that it would be a good idea to have a canal between Montréal and Lachine so that goods bound for the Great

Lakes region would not have to be transported overland to avoid the
Lachine Rapids. Ten years later, Dollier began to think about carrying out
the project, reasoning that the canal could also help supply the flour mills.
However, construction of the parish church was not yet finished, and the
response from Paris was negative. In 1689, the intendant Bochart de Champigny took up the idea again; the Iroquois massacre at Lachine unfortunately prevented the plan from being carried out.

But Dollier de Casson would not easily be stopped. In October 1700 the
surveyor Gédéon de Catalogne, who also had a knowledge of engineering,
signed a notarized contract for the excavation of a canal, three and two-
thirds metres wide and two and three-quarters metres deep. The Sulpicians
provided the tools and paid him 13,000 livres as the work progressed. But
Dollier died the following year, when the canal was only two-thirds completed. The project was abandoned and attempts to revive it in 1703, 1706
and 1732 were unsuccessful. Much later, the famous North West Company
may have extended the canal as far as Lac Saint-Louis, for it seems that the
sturdy canoes of its voyageurs took the canal as far as Montréal. A real canal
was not begun until 1821 and took three years to complete.

In 1701, as we have mentioned, Governor de Callières signed a peace
treaty with the aboriginal nations. On that occasion, Montrealers attended
the funeral of an old Huron chief that was as remarkable as it was picturesque. The chief was Kondiaronk, known as The Rat, who was renowned
for his wisdom and had taken active part in the negotiations. On August 1,
he participated for the last time, his voice growing ever more faint. He was
carried in his armchair to the Hôtel-Dieu where he died during the night.
He lay in state and a sword was placed beside him, for he had been made a
captain in recognition of the services he had rendered to France.

Six grand chiefs were the pallbearers, preceded by an escort of sixty soldiers and sixteen Huron warriors, their faces blackened as a sign of mourning. Members of the clergy and Philippe de Rigaud de Vaudreuil, governor
of Montréal, brought up the rear, accompanied by staff officers. The dead
chief was buried in the church, in recognition of the great esteem in which
he was held.

Montréal soon had a new governor. In May 1703, while attending high
mass in the Québec cathedral, Governor de Callières suffered a hemor-
rhage. He died on May 26, leaving behind the admiration and sorrow of
everyone who had been in a position to appreciate his administration.
Rigaud de Vaudreuil, who had been quite disappointed not to be appointed

ICI VÉCUT, À PARTIR DE 1689,
GÉDÉON DE CATALOGNE, INGÉNIEUR,
OFFICIER ET ANNALISTE, QUI
TRAVAILLA AUX FORTIFICATIONS
DE QUÉBEC, DES TROIS-RIVIÈRES
ET DE LOUISBOURG.

COMMISSION DES MONUMENTS HISTORIQUES

This inscription, attached to the wall of the old courthouse on the west side of Saint-Vincent Street, reads: "From 1689 on, here lived Gédéon de Catalogne, engineer, officer and diarist, who worked on the fortifications of Québec, Trois-Rivières and Louisbourg."

after Frontenac died, had his heart's desire realized this time: Pontchartrain, the minister of marine, named him governor. This was a very wise appointment, for Vaudreuil had shown determination in Montréal and had earned the confidence of the native tribes. Moreover, he became the first governor to marry a Canadian-born woman, Louise Élisabeth de Joybert de Marson, who was herself the daughter of Canadian-born parents. Their son, Pierre, would be the first and only governor of New France to be born in the colony.

Vaudreuil was succeeded by Claude de Ramezay, who had been governor of Trois-Rivières and then commander of the Canadian troops and had been decorated with the Croix de Saint-Louis. He loved comfort, surrounded himself with prominent friends and led an active social life. Thus, it was not surprising to find him on April 27, 1705, in the offices of the notary Adhémar together with the "master mason and architect" Pierre Couturier, to whom he entrusted the construction of his future manor

The Château de Ramezay, built in 1705. The tower on the far left of the façade is not original. (Engraving by J. Walker, 1864.)

house: "sixty-six feet long on the outside with an exterior of stone and lime and sand with three stories, the cellars and kitchen included and the attic floor not included."

This is none other than that noble residence known as the Château de Ramezay, one of the jewels of Montréal's heritage, which now houses a well-stocked museum run by the Société d'Archéologie et de Numismatique de Montréal. Montréal almost lost the building when plans were afoot to extend Gosford Street beyond Notre-Dame Street. Some city councillors suggested that that "tumbledown cabin" be demolished and the "pots, rags and scrap iron" be moved to the former Viger residence if people really wanted to keep them. The councillor and journalist Léon Trépanier spearheaded the opposition and it is in large part to him that we owe the preservation of this historic monument.

While Claude de Ramezay was building this opulent residence, however, Montréal was facing a famine. The War of the Spanish Succession had been raging since 1701. New France and Acadia were automatically at war against New England and Virginia. Montréal was not attacked during that period, but the city did not escape the repercussions of the naval encounters. Thus, in 1704, Virginian ships captured the *Seine*, a store ship that was bringing a variety of provisions valued at a million livres to Canada. Staples especially were hard to come by in Montréal and their cost became prohibitive. It is said, however, that every misfortune has its good side.

There was another factor aggravating the situation. The market for furs in France was saturated and the colony's economy was based on beaver pelts. The settlers were deprived of a large part of their income just when the price of cloth was rising. When they sought to grow more hemp for weaving, the king, realizing that they would be competing with the cloth manufacturers of metropolitan France, refused to send weavers out to the colony, reminding the settlers that one of the main goals of establishing colonies was "the utility of the countries that form them." However, faced with the crisis in New France, he authorized the manufacture of cloth and fabric.

Mention was made earlier of Jean de Saint-Père, the first notary of Ville-Marie, who was killed by the Iroquois in 1657. He left a daughter, Agathe, who married Pierre Legardeur, Sieur de Repentigny, in 1685. A dynamic woman, she had looms set up in her house on Saint-Joseph Street and employed English weavers familiar with this type of work, whom she had ransomed from the natives who had captured them during their raids. When these workers were able to return to Boston, she replaced them with workers trained on the job. Her spirit of initiative not only made it possible for the city's inhabitants to procure the clothes they needed so desperately but also led to the introduction of manufacturing and dyeing techniques that aroused a great deal of interest in France.

By the end of the first decade of the eighteenth century, Montréal, with its 3,500 inhabitants, had the appearance of a small city. However, a new threat was looming on the horizon.

Two False Alarms

When conflict arose between France and England, Acadia was more at risk than New France because of its geographical situation. The enemy had sea access to Acadia's fortified settlements. In any expedition against Québec, however, English ships ran the risk of being intercepted as they sailed up the St. Lawrence. As for Montréal, a land invasion was the only feasible strategy. Only a combined sea and land attack had any real chance of success, especially since troops that could come to the defence of Québec were kept in Montréal.

In 1709 the War of Spanish Succession was still raging. On March 1, London ordered the invasion of Canada by sea and by land. Francis Nicholson, who had governed Virginia for fifteen years and had acquired valuable experience in colonial matters, agreed to lead troops up the Hudson towards Montréal, while Samuel Vetch would lead others from Boston towards Québec. Towards the end of July, Nicholson's forces reached Lake Champlain and stopped there while awaiting reports on the progress of Vetch's units. They built three forts and some small craft in preparation for the time when the expedition would again get underway.

When Rigaud de Vaudreuil learned that enemy forces were on the march towards Montréal, he ordered the governor of Montréal, Claude de Ramezay, to take 1,500 men and meet those forces at the Richelieu River. Ramezay was instructed to avoid any encounters involving loss of life and to be content with destroying the boats and damaging the weapons of the English.

Meanwhile the English secretary of state, Sunderland, had to come immediately to the assistance of Portugal and decided it was vital to turn the ships that were supposed to bring the troops to the city of Québec back to Europe. Nicholson, seeing that he was being left in the lurch, held a war council and decided that there was nothing to do but beat a retreat. Montréal had had a false alarm, but it was not to be the last one. The following year, Nicholson captured the fort Port-Royal in Acadia when Auger de Subercase surrendered.

Nicholson's initiatives convinced the authorities of Montréal that it was becoming essential to rebuild Fort Chambly, which had been destroyed by fire in 1702. The decision was made to build it in stone this time. With the support of Governor Rigaud de Vaudreuil the joint intendants, Jacques Raudot and his son Antoine-Denis, ordered the settlers living in the jurisdiction of Montréal "each to donate eight days' labour and to bring limestone, stone, squared beams and the wood that was needed to the Fort as soon as possible." The materials were brought in during the winter, and in the spring of 1711 a military engineer, Boisberthelot de Beaucours, was put in charge of the work. Rumours of another invasion attempt became increasingly persistent that spring. The work was rushed and by September the fortress was finished. Built entirely by *Canadiens*, it is the only fortification dating from the French Regime in Canada (the impressive fortress that stands at Louisbourg in Cape Breton is not a restoration but a reconstruction).

The rumours were true. Rigaud de Vaudreuil was so certain of them that he brought Boisberthelot de Beaucours on an urgent mission to Québec to prepare the city for a siege. His engineer told him it was too late to think of building new fortifications and that there was nothing they could do but ready their swords.

In late June, a British fleet arrived in Boston, carrying more than 5,000 soldiers and 6,000 sailors. On July 30, nine warships and some sixty ships transporting troops and supplies, under the orders of Admiral Hovenden Walker, left Boston and sailed up the coast towards the Gulf of St. Lawrence. Nicholson, whose expedition against Montréal had had to retreat two years earlier, commanded a corps that was supposed to take the city. The second attempt failed, just like the first, and for good reason: part of Walker's fleet sank off the reefs of Île aux Oeufs. At least eight large transport ships had their bottoms torn out, and after sailing around the area for two days the admiral decided to go home. On October 1, François Margane de Lavaltrie, on his way to Fort Pontchartrain, saw the wrecked enemy ships and counted more than 1,500 bodies thrown up by the sea.

Nicholson waited at Lake Champlain for news of Walker before proceeding towards Montréal. His anger can be imagined when he learned of the catastrophe that had befallen the admiral and his decision to turn back. It is reported that he fell into such a rage that he snatched off his wig and stamped on it. Once again, Montréal had escaped the fearsome threat of Britain's dreams of conquest. Unfortunately, however, things would be different in 1760.

The War of the Spanish Succession ended in 1713 with the Treaty of Utrecht. In addition to Acadia and Newfoundland, Louis XIV ceded Hudson Bay to England. The area drained by Hudson Bay was a major source of beaver pelts, and Montréal felt the impact from the resulting decline in the fur trade. For many years, its trading posts had been the busiest in New France. Charlevoix wrote in 1721 that "there are still now and then companies or rather flotillas of Indians arriving at Montréal, but nothing in comparison of what used to resort hither in time past." Small trading posts had been established near native settlements to collect the valuable beaver pelts close to their source.

Montréal Expands and Builds a Barricade

———————————— >< ————————————

The rural parishes in the Sulpicians' seigneury had grown substantially by the early 1720s. In 1721 Governor de Vaudreuil and Intendant de Meulles asked Benoît-Mathieu Collet, procurator general of the Conseil Supérieur, to visit both sides of the river to meet with the priests and their parishioners. He was to prepare a report on their wishes and grievances regarding the location of churches in relation to the territorial distribution of the population.

After visiting Île Jésus, Collet and his clerk, Nicolas-Gaspard Boucault, crossed onto Montréal Island at the parish of Saint-Joseph de la Rivière-des-Prairies, founded in 1687. Abbé François Julien, a missionary from the Montréal seminary, was the priest in that parish and the neighbouring village of Saint-Léonard. The parish itself consisted of fifty-four families, while Saint-Léonard had thirty-three. Collet travelled across the island to the parish of l'Enfant-Jésus de la Pointe-aux-Trembles, established in 1674. Abbé Charles de la Goudalie, *grand vicaire* of the bishop of Québec, was there. Côte de la Pointe-aux-Trembles numbered sixty-three households, and Côte de la Longue-Pointe, which belonged to the same parish, had thirty-two.

At the Montréal seminary, it was Vachon de Belmont, superior of the Sulpicians and curé of *Nostre Dame de Villemarie*, who welcomed the investigators, giving them information about the heads of households living along the byways of that parish. Thirteen households along the Côte de la Longue-Pointe belonged to Notre-Dame. Along the other parish roads, the households were distributed as follows: Côte Saint-Martin, thirteen; Côte Sainte-Marie, nineteen; Côte Argoulets or Verdun, fifteen; Côte de la Visitation, four; Côte Sainte-Catherine, four; Côte Nôtre-Dame des Neiges, eighteen; Côte Saint-Pierre, twenty-eight; Côte Saint-Paul, seven. To this census must be added four concession holders, including the sisters of the Congrégation de Notre-Dame and the Frères Charon, installed in Point Saint-Charles, ten properties under cultivation, including the Saint-Gabriel farm, Île Saint-Paul, with two households, and Île aux Hérons, with one.

The parish of Saint-Laurent had been founded recently (1720). Its curé was another priest from the Montréal seminary, François Seré. It had a total of eighty-three households: Côte Saint-Laurent, twenty-nine; Côte Notre-Dame-des-Vertus, twenty-six; Côte Saint-Michel, twenty-seven; Côte Notre-Dame-de-Liesse, one. There were also fifty-three concessions farmed by nonresidents and thirty-two others that had not yet been put under cultivation.

The curé of the older parish of Saints-Anges de Lachine (dating from 1675) was the Sulpician Jacques Le Tessier, a native of the diocese of Angers. This parish counted seventy-seven households: Côte de Lachine or Côte du Saut Saint-Louis, fifty-eight; Côte Saint-Pierre, eight; Côte Saint-Paul, eleven (plus three uninhabited concessions). The inhabitants of Lachine had apparently not forgotten the massacre of 1689; the families of Côte Saint-Pierre told Collet they wanted to belong to the parish of Notre-Dame de Montréal because to go to the church in Lachine they had to cross a wood forty arpents wide. The women and children could not go to church without an escort "because of the savages."

The next parish in Collet's report was Saint-Joachim de Pointe-Claire. This parish, which had been established four years earlier, had just welcomed a new curé, the Sulpician Jean-Baptiste Breul, and had settlers along two of the ranges: Côte Pointe-Claire, with seventeen families and eleven concessions cultivated by nonresidents, and Côte Saint-Rémi or Côte des Sources, with five households. Ten families from Île Perrot also belonged to that parish, as well as four concessions farmed by nonresidents.

Collet concluded his survey with the parish of Sainte-Anne du Bout-de-l'Île (now Sainte-Anne de Bellevue), established in 1672. It had only one *côte*, with thirty-two houses. A delegation of nine inhabitants of Île Perrot hoped for a chapel. Until one was built, they preferred to attend Sainte-Anne church, because to reach Saint-Joachim de Pointe-Claire church they had "one and a half leagues to cross on lac de St. Louis which was very difficult in bad weather."

This parish census illustrates the benefits secured by the peace treaty with the Iroquois signed twenty years earlier. From that time on, the seigneurs had found it easier to find takers for their concessions and the city had spread broadly into the countryside.

There was no longer any fear of attacks by the natives, but as we have seen Montréal was not safe from attacks from the English colonies. Twice, in 1709 and in 1711, Francis Nicholson had commanded forces which were supposed to capture the city but had turned back after reaching Lake

Champlain. On both occasions the fleet that was to besiege Québec had not been able to reach its goal. It appears that the Montrealers were not very worried about this threat. There was some talk of building fortifications, but once calm had been restored none of the projects was completed. In 1716, however, the court finally ordered construction of stone walls to proceed, at a cost of 6,000 livres. A third of this cost was to be assumed by the seigneurs – the Sulpician seminary – and the other two thirds by the other religious communities and the inhabitants. No exceptions were allowed. Six years were to pass, however, before the work was begun.

In 1716, the engineer Gaspard-Joseph Chaussegros de Léry had come to Québec to prepare plans for the fortifications and decide what needed to be done to secure the city against attack. In 1722 in Montréal, he began building an enclosure of rough stone, five and a half metres high, more than a metre thick at the base and almost a metre thick at the top. It enclosed an area of more than a hundred arpents in all. It was provided with barbicans and thirteen bastions were spaced along the walls, armed with cannons and pierced with gates and posterns. The whole project cost fully 300,000 livres. The king bore half the cost and advanced the money for the other half – one third was to be repaid by the seminary and the rest by the inhabitants.

No attack was ever launched against these fortifications, and they were torn down in the early nineteenth century. From time to time, traces have been found in the course of various excavations, notably under the asphalt covering the Champ-de-Mars in 1986. The area it enclosed by and large corresponded to the rectangle now described by Berri, Commune, McGill and Saint-Antoine streets. The Ruelle des Fortifications is a reminder of these fortifications.

The First Great Fire

While Collet was making the rounds of the parishes on Montréal Island in 1721, another visitor who had already travelled in New France returned with an unusual assignment: to take a close look at the claims that there was a western sea separating the New World from the Orient. The Jesuit Pierre-François-Xavier de Charlevoix, whose *Histoire et description générale de la*

Nouvelle France (History and General Description of New France) would be published in Paris in 1744, reached Montréal by *carriole*, a horse-drawn sleigh, on March 14. "The city of Montréal," he wrote, "has a very pleasing aspect, and is besides conveniently situated, the streets well laid out, and the houses well built. The beauty of the country round it, and of its prospects inspire a certain cheerfulness of which every body is perfectly sensible."

Charlevoix noted that the city had not yet been fortified, "only a simple palisade, with bastions, and in very indifferent condition with a sorry redoubt." The reason, he said, was that the Montrealers were brave and "are fully persuaded that their own courage is more than sufficient to defend their city against all invaders." Then he described the city and mentioned the main buildings: the Jesuit church, which was large and well built; the spacious Récollet convent; the seminary, "solid and commodious [rather] than magnificent"; the parish church, "more the air of a cathedral than that of Québec"; the house of the daughters of the Congrégation de Notre-Dame, one of the largest; and the Hôtel-Dieu, which gave no indication that the nuns who served there were poor, for their poverty "neither appears in their hall, or yards, which are spacious, well-furnished, and extremely well provided with beds; nor in their church, which is handsome, and exceedingly richly ornamented."

Unfortunately, the Hôtel-Dieu was the starting point of a great fire that very year. In those days, Pentecost was celebrated with some pomp. On June 19, as the procession was leaving the chapel, the garrison wanted to greet the passage of the Holy Sacrament as usual, with a salvo. One of the musketeers aimed his weapon by mistake towards the cedar-covered roof of the hospital. It caught fire immediately. The alarm bell summoned the citizens to help, but the fire was out of control and spread from house to house as far as the river. When the terrible blaze was finally extinguished, 138 houses had been levelled. It was the largest fire suffered by the city during the eighteenth century, but it was not to be the last.

On April 10, 1734, Marie Josèphe Angélique, a black slave in the service of Thérèse de Couagne, widow of François Poulin de Francheville (the founder of the Saint-Maurice Forges), set fire to her mistress's house, hoping to distract her mistress's attention so that she could flee with her lover. The blaze spread like wildfire and burned down not just the Hôtel-Dieu but another forty-six houses as well. This was the third time the hospital had burned down. In 1685, a fire had reduced the main hospital and the old buildings to ashes. On that occasion, the nuns placed furniture and instruments in the snow in the middle of the night to save them from the fire. Unfortunately, the morning after, they did not find all the things they had put outside: a great quantity had been stolen.

The year 1721 saw the beginnings of an ambitious project. At that time, letters and other mail shipped among Québec, Trois-Rivières and Montréal travelled by canoe. Nicolas Lanouillier de Boisclerc, agent of the general treasurers of the marine in Québec, petitioned the authorities for an exclusive licence to link these cities by a public coach system that would transport mail and travellers, as in France.

Since mail by canoe often suffered delays that were sometimes inadvertent and sometimes deliberate but were in any case substantial enough to be "harmful to public welfare and trade in the colonies," Governor de Vaudreuil and Intendant Bégon signed an order granting the licence. The entrepreneur was optimistic about the success of his venture: at the same time he obtained an authorization to build and manage ferries for all the rivers, large enough to carry cattle, horses, wagons and other vehicles. The tolls would go to him. However, his project was premature, and he did not register his patent with the Conseil Supérieur. It was his half-brother, Jean-Eustache, roadmaster of New France, who would complete the first land route between Québec City and Montréal thirteen years later.

In the field of education, the Sulpician Gabriel Souart, despite his duties as first curé and later as superior of the seminary, found the time to educate the youth of Montréal. In that task he had the assistance of Marguerite Bourgeoys who, at the beginning, did not confine herself to the education of little girls. When the Frères Charon opened their Hôpital Général, they were also interested in the education of the young. In 1718, they obtained a contribution of 3,000 livres from the court to hire and maintain eight schoolmasters. Four years later the Conseil Supérieur intervened because part of that money, which was paid annually, had been used for the hospital: from then on, it was decreed that every teacher would get 375 livres and the schools would be free, "without asking anything from the parents," but also "without restricting any charities that the inhabitants of Canada might wish to make with respect to the instruction of their children." That year, ten additional schoolmasters arrived from France, and two years later six more crossed the Atlantic to assist them.

Philippe de Rigaud, Marquis de Vaudreuil. This portrait is kept in the Château de Ramezay.

Another Troubled Period

Philippe de Rigaud de Vaudreuil, who had wanted to be governor of the colony on the death of Frontenac, finally achieved his goal after the death of Callières. He had been living in New France for more than fifteen years and

This plaque on St. Lawrence Boulevard, near Saint-Paul Street, indicates the location of the Château de Vaudreuil.

had earned valuable experience both as troop commander and governor of Montréal.

He was almost eighty and he knew he would soon have to retire after so many years in a leading position in the colony's government. He undoubtedly intended to end his days in Montréal, especially since he could live nearer the seigneury of Pointe aux Tourtes that he had obtained from Callières in 1702, which had four leagues of river frontage and stretched back a league and a half.

Thus in 1723 Vaudreuil decided to have a manor house built for him in Montréal, next to the one belonging to Claude de Ramezay. There was no Place Jacques-Cartier at that time: Saint-Charles Street ran where the *place* now ends. In 1721 he purchased the rectangular piece of property that ran west from Saint-Charles to the line of properties formed by the houses facing on Saint-Vincent Street, between Notre-Dame and Saint-Paul. The façade of what would later be called the Château de Vaudreuil faced the river and the garden was situated in the back, on Notre-Dame Street, more or less across from the Jesuits' garden.

The old Château de Vaudreuil on Notre-Dame Street, which became the home of the Collège de Montréal in 1773.

The work began in 1723, but by the time the manor house was finished in 1726, Vaudreuil was no longer alive. He had died the previous year before he could retire, which explains why the inventory of his property was taken at the Château Saint-Louis in Québec. His heirs leased the building to the government of the colony for 1,500 livres a year, and it became the residence of the governors general of the colony and staff officers when they stayed at Montréal. Governors La Galissonnière and La Jonquière, as well as Montcalm and Lévis, stayed there on various occasions.

The Château de Vaudreuil had been standing for half a century when in 1773 the churchwardens of the parish of Notre-Dame decided to purchase it for 19,500 livres for a Latin School, which became the Collège de Montréal under the direction of Curatteau de la Blaiserie, a Sulpician schoolmaster. This was the only school in the whole region where the classical course of study was offered. Twenty years later, a fire levelled the building and spread to some thirty houses. That was when the market, which up until that time had been located on Place Royale, moved to more spacious quarters on the other *place*, Place Jacques-Cartier.

There had been peace between the French and the aboriginal nations of the colony since 1701, but the treaty that was signed did not include the Fox, the Sauteux and the Illinois, who lived farther south. Coureurs de bois coming from the St. Lawrence valley traversed these regions.

In 1715 the Fox went on the warpath. As acting governor of New France, Claude de Ramezay sent Constant Le Marchand de Lignery at the head of a large detachment to Michillimakinac to quell them. However, problems arose, notably a delay in forwarding the required provisions, and the expedition was cut short. The Fox continued their incursions. Eventually Lignery managed to sign two treaties with them, but these did not protect the Illinois, so the skirmishes resumed.

Following the death of Rigaud de Vaudreuil, Charles Le Moyne de Longueuil had asked to be appointed his successor. He would have been well suited for this position, but the court decided that the governor of the colony should have no ties with *Canadien* families and so Charles de Beauharnois was appointed. He arrived in Québec in August 1726 and sought to impose his authority on the aboriginal nations. In 1728 a small army of 450 Frenchmen with a contingent of more than 1,000 native braves left Montréal under Lignery's command to attack the Fox. Numerically speaking, it was the largest military expedition ever to penetrate so far into the west. But the Fox knew how to hide from his advancing troops and Lignery's forces had to be content with burning villages and destroying the harvests.

Although Montréal was now safe from the Iroquois threat, epidemics posed another threat that was more insidious and no less devastating. In 1733, an epidemic of smallpox broke out. The sickness spread like wildfire. Some writers speak of 900 deaths in the jurisdiction of Montréal alone. That figure may be exaggerated, but the mother parish of Notre-Dame nevertheless reported 278 burials during the first four months of the year, compared with fifty over the same period in the preceding year. One of the first victims was the governor of Montréal himself. Jean-Baptiste Bouillet de La Chassaigne died on January 29 and was buried two days later. He had married Marie-Anne Le Moyne, daughter of the elder Charles Le Moyne, in 1699. La Chassaigne was thus a brother-in-law of the famous Le Moyne brothers whose achievements we have chronicled. He had been military commandant of Québec and governor of Trois-Rivières.

The year after the Hôtel-Dieu fire, the nuns were living in the house of Jacques de Montigny near the Bonsecours Chapel, having taken refuge there while waiting for the hospital to be rebuilt. They took in a soldier who had landed in Québec shortly before and had come from a sailing ship where a malignant fever was raging. Nine hospital nuns died of the contagion. Their coffins were carefully leaded and people avoided passing in front of the house. The bishop of Québec ordered the nuns to divide into two groups. Only those who were absolutely necessary for the care of the sick were to remain. They obeyed, according to the community's chronicler, "some to go to the grave and others to avoid it." Thanks to all the precautions that were taken, the epidemic was confined to the hospital.

Sewers and Firefighters

———————— >‹ ————————

Even the epidemics could not hold back progress, and in 1734 the first highway in New France was opened. In 1709 the intendant Jacques Raudot said it was necessary to "mark out a road" between Québec and Montréal and ordered the *habitants* living along the north shore of the river to set out markers for this purpose in front of their dwellings "in the most convenient places."

In 1721 Nicolas Lanoullier de Boisclerc had obtained an exclusive licence to establish a public coach service between the two cities, undoubtedly to try to join these sections together. As already noted, it was his half-brother who took up the challenge. His name was Jean-Eustache and he became chief roadmaster of the colony in 1730. His first concern was to build bridges where the rivers were narrow enough. He then undertook to standardize the dimensions and specifications of the road: it would be twenty-four feet wide and would run between fences. Those living along the road were to dig ditches wherever good drainage was needed. After that, he arranged for ferry service wherever it was too hard to build bridges.

Between August 9 and September 10, the chief roadmaster did not sign any reports. There was a reason for this: he was busy becoming the first person ever to go from Québec to Montréal without setting foot in a canoe. He made the distance in four and a half days in a sedan chair, a sort of armchair suspended between two shafts. In so doing, he opened the way to future coach travel. There is a bronze plaque on Saint-Jean gate in Québec City, commemorating the departure of the chief roadmaster in August 1734 to inaugurate what would become the *Chemin du Roy*.

After the great fire of 1721, the intendant had placed the engineer

This bronze plaque on Saint-Jean gate in Québec City commemorates the opening of the *Chemin du Roy* between Québec and Montréal.

Chaussegros de Léry in charge of inspecting the devastated portions of the city and making recommendations to make sure, insofar as it was possible, that the disaster would not be repeated. On July 8, an ordinance concerning reconstruction of the houses was issued.

The engineer realigned the streets because they were not wide or straight enough. There would be no more houses built of wood or half-timbering; houses would have two storeys and be made of stone. It was forbidden to use large roof frames; instead horizontal beams supporting the rafters

The old Notre Dame de Bonsecours Chapel, destroyed by fire in 1754.

were to be used, which made it possible to pop off the cover in case of fire. There would be no more mansard roofs to make the attics more spacious. Attic floors were to be covered with tiles or brick with three or four inches of mortar. It was henceforth forbidden to cover the roofs with shingles; until supplies of tiles or slates came in, two rows of planks were to be used.

These regulations did not prevent another great fire from breaking out thirteen years later. On this occasion, the intendant Gilles Hocquart gave Montréal its first firefighters' brigade. The ordinance provided for the manufacture of 280 buckets, eighty to be made of leather and the rest of wood; 100 axes and the same number of shovels; twenty-four iron hooks or jointed poles with chains and cords that could be used to pop off the rafters; twelve long ladders; and twelve hand battering rams, probably to knock down walls. All these instruments were marked with a fleur-de-lys, presumably to avoid the possibility that heedless residents might walk off with them.

The equipment was to be stored in four places: at the guardhouse and with the Sulpicians, the Récollets and the Jesuits. Notwithstanding the "overabundance of precautions," citizens were supposed to provide themselves with an axe and a bucket. Since some people had not brought along their equipment during recent fires on the pretext that it might be stolen, any person found guilty of failing to bring equipment would be punished with a fifty-livre fine and the stocks.

Chimney-sweeping was made mandatory, and every chimney was to have a ladder that could easily reach the chimney though an appropriate opening. The attic of every house was to be provided with two battering rams long enough to reach the ridgepole. The lieutenant general of the city was to draw up a list of carpenters, masons and roofers who were to be divided into two squads, each under the direction of a master worker. The members of these squads were to be the first on the scene of a fire, on penalty of a six-livre fine. The intendant thought that because of their trades these workers would be the most experienced in fighting fires.

By this ordinance, dated July 12, 1734, Intendant Hocquart gave Montréal its first fire brigade. Five years later, Hocquart rewarded a master carpenter, Louis Trudeau, for the public-spiritedness he had shown during various fires. He dispensed him from the obligation to billet the military and paid him an annual bonus of thirty livres to inspect the buckets periodically and report to the police officers. All these precautions seem to have been useful, because with the exception of the fire of 1754, which levelled the Bonsecours Chapel and several surrounding houses, Montréal had no more real conflagrations before the end of the French regime.

The Women of Montréal

In 1749 New France welcomed a learned naturalist, Peter Kalm, a Swedish professor and a member of the Royal Academy of Stockholm. Governor Barrin de La Galissonnière, informed of his arrival, gave him a warm

reception. He came in July after spending a year examining the flora of the
English provinces of New Jersey and New York. His memoirs were published in Stockholm under the title *Resa till Norra America* (Travels into
North America) a few years later, and since he cannot be suspected of chau-
vinism it is interesting to see his impressions of Montréal.

"Montréal," he wrote, "is the second town in Canada, in regard to size
and wealth; but it is the first on account of its fine situation and mild climate." He goes on to describe the city. "The town has a quadrangular form,
or rather it is a rectangular parallelogram, the long and eastern side of which
extends along the great branch of the river. On the other side it is surrounded with excellent corn-fields, charming meadows and delightful
woods."

After pointing out that the city took its name from Mount Royal, he
noted that its system of defence was vulnerable: "It is pretty well fortified,
and surrounded with a high and thick wall. On the east side, it has the river
St. Lawrence, and on all the other sides a deep ditch filled with water, which
secures the inhabitants against all danger from the sudden incursions of the
enemy's troops. However, it cannot long stand a regular siege, because it
requires a great garrison, on account of its extent; and because it consists
chiefly of wooden houses."

That last comment seems to indicate that the ordinance issued by Intendant Hocquart fifteen years earlier had not been respected. Kalm returned
to the subject, pointing out that "some of the houses in the town are built of
stone, but most of them are of timber, though very neatly built." Often, he
noted, the houses have a door towards the street, with a seat on each side of
it, "for amusement and recreation in the morning and evening."

Kalm noted significant differences in the climate of the two main cities:
"The wind and the weather of Montréal are often entirely different from
what they are at Québec. The winter there is not near so cold as in the last
place. Several sorts of fine pears will grow near Montréal; but are far from
succeeding at Québec, where frequently the frost kills them. Québec generally has more rainy weather, spring begins later, and winter sooner than at
Montréal, where all sorts of fruits ripen a week or two earlier than at
Québec." He also noted a difference in the taste of meat: "The beef and veal
at Québec is reckoned fatter and more palatable than at Montréal. Some
look upon the salty pastures below Québec as the cause of this difference."
He was referring here to pastures that were covered at high tide twice a day.

Peter Kalm's observant gaze fell on every aspect of his surroundings. He
noted that "the ladies in Canada are generally of two kinds: some come over

A Montréal beauty who frequented the salons at the time of Peter Kalm's visit, Marie-Élisabeth Rocbert de la Morandière, daughter of a king's storekeeper in Montréal, was the widow of Claude-Michel Bégon, who had been governor of Trois-Rivières.

from France, and the rest natives. The former possess the politeness peculiar to the French nation. As for the second group, another distinction must be drawn, this time between the ladies of Québec and those of Montréal."

The ladies of Québec, he continued, "are equal to the French ladies in good breeding, having the advantage of frequently conversing with the French gentlemen and ladies, who come every summer with the king's ships, and stay several weeks at Québec, but seldom go to Montréal. The ladies of this last place are accused by the French of partaking too much of the pride of the Indians, and of being much wanting in French good breeding."

Kalm wrote that "the ladies in Canada, and especially at Montréal, are very ready to laugh at any blunders strangers make in speaking. In Canada nobody ever hears the French language spoken by any but Frenchmen, for strangers seldom come thither." The Swede's accent must have caused some derisive laughter. Perhaps wishing to be pardoned for this minor slur, he made a smooth recovery: "There are some differences between the ladies of Québec, and those of Montréal; those of the last place seemed to be generally handsomer than those of the former."

The naturalist found the behaviour of the ladies in Montréal "more of a becoming modesty." The ladies of Québec, "especially the unmarried ones lead a fairly lazy and frivolous life," he wrote. The ladies of Montréal are more industrious. "They are always at their needlework, or doing some necessary business in the home. They are likewise cheerful and content; and nobody can say that they want either wit or charms. Their fault is that they think too well of themselves."

The daughters of people of all ranks, Kalm notes in their praise, go to market and carry home what they have bought. They rise as early and go to bed as late as any of the people in the house. However, "the girls at Montréal are much displeased that those in Québec get husbands sooner than they. The reason of this is, that many young gentlemen who come over from France with the ships are captivated by the ladies at Québec, and marry them; but as these gentlemen seldom go up to Montréal, the girls there are not often so happy as those of the former place." Fortunately, travelling up the St. Lawrence is not so difficult nowadays as it was in 1749.

A Social Whirl

Québec, of course, would remain the seat of government, but over the decades Montréal took on undisputed importance. In addition to the advantages of a milder climate, it enjoyed an exceptional geographical situation, at the junction of the main roadways into the interior of the continent: the Ottawa River, the Richelieu River, and the St. Lawrence River. From Montréal one could reach the very heart of North America. The governor general of New France had his official residence in Québec, but he often came to Montréal and generally spent the winter there. We learn this from Peter Kalm. "It is easier to stay in Québec in the summer because of the frequent arrivals of the king's ships, which bring the governor correspondence to which he must reply," wrote the naturalist, but he added that the Marquis de La Galissonnière preferred Montréal to Québec: "In fact, the situation of the former is a lot more agreeable than that of the latter."

In the past, Québec had held a monopoly on good society and refined salons while the former Ville-Marie was carving out a place for itself in the wilderness. But as Montréal developed, it slowly acquired a social life rivalling Québec's in sensibility and delicacy, and in gossip and intrigue as well.

The intendant Bigot, indefatigable and haughty but a prodigal and inveterate gambler, was no stranger to these changes. It has been written that he incarnated the elegant and refined vices of his century. He surrounded himself with pomp and apparently took his silver service with him wherever he went. In 1749 he brought it to Montréal where he planned to spend some time. He had himself taken from Québec in comfortable sleighs along the frozen river. Party after party was held at a dizzying pace. Every day the company would take their seats at table towards six o'clock for dinner. They would not get up until about eleven and then dance until six o'clock in the morning. The next day it was the same story. On one Saturday that lingered on into the next morning, Bigot even sent a message to the curé to ask him to delay mass. The messenger came back with a formal refusal, injuring Bigot's vanity.

At the end of February 1753, another gastronomical "expedition" excited the gossips. This time, it was Governor General Duquesne de Menneville who had decided to take a large company off to feast at the

Sulpician mission in Oka. In a procession, more than twenty carriages left Montréal on February 26. Among the party were Intendant Bigot, the engineer Louis Franquet, five beautiful ladies of high social rank and, naturally, the superior of the Sulpicians, Monsieur Louis Normant de Fara-don, who acted as host, perhaps more out of a sense of duty than by choice. The governor general had earlier had his entire "kitchen" transported to Oka and lent it to the Sulpicians for the preparation of the banquet. Fran-quet later reported that they ate "nobly," but that the excursion on the Lac des Deux-Montagnes was unpleasant because of the intense cold that was accompanied by a snowstorm, both going and coming back.

To get a flavour of Montréal society at that period, there is no better source than the letters written in 1748 and 1749 by Madame Claude-Michel Bégon to her son-in-law, Michel de La Rouvillière, commissioner-director in Louisiana. Madame Bégon had come back to Montréal to live in her house on Saint-Paul Street, where Bonsecours Market now stands, after the death of her husband. Her correspondence reads like a diary recording the city's pulse.

"Dear Son, Yesterday there was a splendid party at Monsieur de Lantag-nac's," she wrote on December 18, 1748. "It consisted of Monsieur de Longueuil, Noyan, Céloron and Lantagnac. They sat down to lunch at noon and stayed there until eleven at night; they sang so well that passersby stopped to listen." On December 27, she wrote that many townspeople were getting ready for the balls: "It is safe to say that Monsieur Bigot is caus-ing a great deal of expense, for there are not enough dancing masters for all those who want to learn how to dance."

So far there was nothing very reprehensible, but on January 21 she reported an event that must have occasioned much talk: "There were some great drinking bouts yesterday at dinner with Monsieur de Lantagnac. I was told that they were all having trouble dancing the minuet. Then it was decided that they would go to Deschambault's for onion soup. A great deal more wine was drunk, in particular five bottles between Monsieur de Noyan and St. Luc who, as you might expect, stayed there. They wrapped Noyan up and put him in a *carriole* and took him home." This "scapegrace" de Lantagnac – Gaspard Adhémar de Lantagnac, to call him by his full name – was the king's lieutenant in Montréal and was sixty-seven years old at the time! He lived for eight more years.

The day after Christmas, there was a violent outburst from the curé of Notre-Dame, who said that the balls and country parties were vile and that the mothers who took their daughters to them were adulteresses, taking advantage of these nocturnal pleasures to conceal their immodesty and fornication. "And then after that," he added, "they think they can come ask permission to eat meat in Lent!" Le Moyne de Longueuil hastened to congratulate the preacher, assuring him that he would not organize any more balls for his daughters. "You should know," wrote Madame Bégon, "that while this hypocrite was speaking, his daughters were all having a fine old time with a settler from Rivière des Prairies."

There was mention earlier of a visit to Montréal by Intendant Bigot in early 1749. "He brings all his silverplate here, under the care of his butler and his housekeeper, a line of sleighs stretching from Longue-Pointe to here," wrote Madame Bégon on February 2. It was during that stay that Intendant Bigot leased Madame Bégon's house for 1,500 livres a year to use as his residence when business or pleasure took him to Montréal. On March 1, Madame Bégon wrote to her son that the intendant was leaving in the morning. "I confess," she said, "that I am not at all sorry, given the fears that his presence has caused me. So many people staying in two houses, so many fires lit in every room, so much light all night long, it was more than enough to give me a great deal of worry. I think that the priests are no less happy than I to see him go, for they regard him as a destroyer of religion in Canada." Madame Bégon mentioned two houses: the other house was the Château de Vaudreuil, where Governor General Barrin de la Galissonnière was living.

The intendant left Montréal on March 2, and Madame Bégon wrote to her son, with some exaggeration, "He left this morning with, I believe, a thousand sleighs. You don't often see a procession like that; he must have carriages for all his mirrors and trinkets. If Monsieur Hocquart saw that, I think he would die of distress." Gilles Hocquart had preceded Bigot as intendant, and had tried to put finances and administrative methods on a sound footing.

The social whirl went at even merrier pace when thousands of soldiers, whose officers were fond of social events, arrived in New France. Montréal became a sort of staging area for the military operations that were entrusted to the Marquis de Montcalm under the authority of Governor Pierre de Rigaud de Vaudreuil. High society fluttered back and forth among three manor houses: the old Château de Vaudreuil, the official residence of the governor general; the Château de Ramezay, residence of the governor of the city; and the house that Madame Bégon had rented to Bigot as a pied-à-terre for the Intendant.

A Staging Area for Military Operations

—————————— ✄ ——————————

In 1755 the English government sent two regiments to America, which were added to the regular and colonial troops. The same year, France took a similar step and sent 3,000 men to Canada, under the command of Baron de Dieskau. Once more, clouds were gathering over Europe. The two traditional enemies would face off once again.

During 1755, England opened hostilities by methodically capturing French trading vessels. It was learned that an army commanded by Col. William Johnson was on the move, with Montréal as its target. Dieskau advanced in haste, but unfortunately fell into enemy hands. In January 1756, Marquis de Montcalm succeeded Dieskau, with the rank of captain-general. The new commander-in-chief had Brigadier-General François-Gaston de Lévis as his second in command and a gifted young man, Louis-Antoine de Bougainville, as his aide-de-camp. They set sail for Québec with 1,200 officers and men.

Montcalm spent only twelve days in Québec. He went upstream to Montréal to meet up with the governor general who was preparing a campaign to capture Fort Oswego, an English post on the south side of Lake Ontario across from Fort Frontenac, which was held by the French. Lévis met them in mid-June. After inspecting Fort Carillon (now Ticonderoga, New York), Montcalm left Montréal in July. The venture was successful: Fort Oswego surrendered and 1,700 prisoners were taken, along with armed ships and large amounts of supplies.

On August 28, the troops that had taken part in the expedition returned to Montréal, where they were readied for departure to Carillon. With the fall of Oswego, the French had taken control of the entire Lake Ontario region. There were now plans to prepare a campaign for the following year to keep the English at arm's length to the south of Montréal, which required continuing the work begun at Carillon.

Montcalm and Bougainville spent the winter in Montréal. Bougainville had been chosen to announce the capture of Oswego to the Montrealers. The governor went off to spend the holidays at Québec. On the way back, he fell seriously ill in Trois-Rivières. Montcalm and Bougainville went to his bedside and brought him back to Montréal. A few days later, eight English prisoners captured during a skirmish near Fort Carillon were brought in. Bougainville questioned them and on the basis of their responses drew up plans of Fort George and Fort Lydius, on the shores of Lac Saint-Sacrement (now Lake George in New York State).

Thus it was in Montréal that winter that plans were made for an expedition to attack the English positions south of Lake Champlain in order to forestall any attack from that direction. The French could count on the neutrality of the Iroquois. On September 8, 1756, the Iroquois had sent a 180-man delegation to Montréal to hold a "sort of congress," as Lévis reported, in the course of which they assured the French of their neutrality: "It was all that we could hope for from a people hemmed in on all sides by English settlements."

It was about that time that an unfortunate rift developed between the governor general and the commander-in-chief. The rift was so deep that Vaudreuil took to issuing orders without consulting or even informing Montcalm. Bougainville wrote about Montcalm's representations: "His speeches are meeting with the fate of Cassandra's predictions, and no one does him the honour of consulting him. For the most part, it has been through the public that he has learned of the war operations decided on by Marquis de Vaudreuil." When Montcalm wanted an explanation concerning an expedition that Vaudreuil was thinking of launching in the middle of February against Fort George, the governor finally invited him to dinner. Over a muzzle of moose, they exchanged information but not, as Bougainville said, "without creating new grounds of dissension between the two chiefs."

Despite the painful situation, they could smile politely at each other when they met in society, but according to Montcalm, Marquis and Marquise de Vaudreuil maintained a reserved attitude towards the festivities. It would have been otherwise if their taste had not been "turned towards devotion and if it had not been necessary to be careful about the tone given in a country where there is a mixture of Italian-style devotion that does not exclude gallantry." But they did not let themselves become bored in Montréal. "M. le Chevalier de Lévis, reported Montcalm, gave a very fine ball for all the ladies in the town. There were lavish refreshments and a great deal of care was taken in the attentions paid to them."

In the spring of 1757, Montréal offered a really picturesque appearance. Swarms of canoes filled with natives appeared. Some represented nations such as the Iowa who had never been seen before in those parts. On the *place*, beautiful ladies wore elegant clothes from Paris while squaws wrapped in blankets carried papooses on their back. Bewigged functionaries with

The heart of Montréal in 1760. From left to right, the Récollet convent, the parish church, the Hôtel-Dieu, the Jesuit college (with its four steeples), the Château de Vaudreuil (in front of the Jesuit college), and finally the citadel, already under the British flag. (Engraving by B. Cole, *The Royal Magazine,* London, September 1760.)

gleaming swords exchanged words with warriors wearing plumes, scalps hanging from their waists. In the middle of this menagerie, coureurs de bois, recognizable by their style of dress, loaded and unloaded bundles of furs.

Plans for the summer campaign were ready. Lévis left Montréal on July 3, 1757, and reached Carillon on July 7. The remaining staff officers set out on July 12. Two days later, at the Saut Saint-Louis mission, the Iroquois "adopted" Bougainville and gave him the name of Garoniatsigoa (Big-Sky-in-Anger). On his arrival at Carillon, Montcalm took command of 6,200 soldiers and militia and 1,800 braves. On August 3, he laid siege to Fort George (also called Fort William Henry). The commander refused Montcalm's invitation to surrender. Six days later, after Montcalm opened fire with eight cannons, the white flag was raised above the fortifications. Bougainville negotiated the surrender, and once again he was asked to take the good news to Montréal. He arrived there on August 11.

Autumn began with an indescribable orgy of violence. During the taking of Fort George, it had been agreed that the prisoners would be taken to another English post to protect them from the natives' bloodthirsty attentions, but the natives managed to carry off some prisoners. They massacred many of them on the spot and took the others, for whom they were planning the same fate, to Montréal. Attempts to negotiate their release were unsuccessful. Bougainville reported that "in the presence of the entire city, they killed one of them, put him in a pot and forced his unfortunate compatriots to eat him."

There were no soldiers in the city; the troops sent to Lake George had not yet returned. What could be done? To ransom the prisoners as quickly as possible, they offered the natives an exchange: two kegs of brandy for each prisoner. Some agreements were made, but as Bougainville again reported, "the English who were kept in the cabins died a hundred deaths every day," which gives some indication of the unbelievable tortures they suffered. "My soul more than once shuddered with the sights witnessed by my eyes," he added.

With the coming of autumn, the army was packed off to winter quarters. The militia, who were mainly *Canadiens*, were sent off to bring in the harvest. But famine loomed, for there had not been enough people left to cultivate the land. The Béarn regiment had to spend the winter in Montréal and its four battalions were installed in their quarters on November 1. Provisions had to be rationed. The soldiers in the garrison were reduced to a half pound of bread, three quarters of a pound of beef, a quarter-pound of codfish and a quarter-pound of peas. The Béarn regiment submitted to this regime without complaint, but the regular troops refused these rations. Lévis had to intervene: he explained the reasons behind the action and threatened to hang the first man who did not draw his ration on the spot.

Next, the regular soldiers and townspeople urged the Béarn regiment to mutiny. Lévis called four grenadiers together and told them that the troops should think of themselves as serving a city under siege with no reinforcements. Since the grenadiers should set an example, he would see that they were punished if the troops showed a lack of discipline in that respect. To avoid criticism, the officers were put on "short rations" – they were forbidden to have more than "a large bourgeois dinner at a single sitting." Montcalm cancelled all festivities: "It was my opinion that there should be no balls, violins, parties or assemblies throughout the winter."

The people also suffered from the famine. On December 1, they found themselves without bread, which the authorities wanted to replace with beef and horsemeat. In Montréal, the women assembled in front of Vaudreuil's princely residence, demanding bread. The governor invited four of them in, told them there was not any to be had and that they could have beef and horsemeat. When they said that the horse was the friend of man, that religion forbade killing horses and that they did not want to eat them, he lost patience and told them that if they rioted again, he would have them all thrown in prison and half of them hanged.

A few days later, the soldiers were also put on horsemeat. The Béarn regiment wanted to protest. Lévis hurried in, called the battalions together and had horsemeat served to himself and the brigadier-generals. He forced them to eat the horsemeat and said that the first among them to refuse would be strung up and hanged. Montcalm spent the first weeks of the winter in Québec, then left for Montréal where he arrived at the end of February to talk to the scouts who were going to "sniff" around the English forts and prepare for the next campaign. By spring, there was no more food for the troops in Québec. They were sent off immediately to Carillon where the provisions taken the year before from Fort George were kept.

The campaign of 1758 was to be the most brilliant of all Montcalm's campaigns. At Lac Saint-Sacrement, Major-General James Abercromby was in command of the largest army ever assembled in North America: 6,000 regular soldiers and 9,000 militia. Space does not permit us to dwell on the famous French victory at Carillon. When the English columns advanced towards the inextricable confusion of tree trunks and branches that Montcalm had positioned in front of the fort on July 8, he had scarcely more than 3,600 men at his disposal. Volleys of shots greeted wave after wave of English troops, and Abercromby's army finally took to its heels, leaving more than 2,000 men dead on the battlefield.

This brilliant victory obviously dampened the ardour of the English, but it became increasingly clear that the French would soon succumb to the sheer numerical superiority of the enemy. The situation was so desperate that at autumn's end Montcalm sent Bougainville to the court in France to request reinforcements. These were refused, as France was in dire straits itself. Bougainville returned in the spring of 1759 with nothing but a promotion to troop colonel.

Montcalm spent the winter in Québec while Lévis stayed in Montréal. Bougainville told Montcalm that the English were mounting a huge offensive. Lévis received representatives of the Iroquois nations who were well informed of the enemy's preparations. Food was growing scarce. It had been thought that the region under Montréal's jurisdiction would produce 30,000 minots of wheat, but only 8,000 were obtained. "We scarcely have enough to keep our armies for one month in the field if they had to go," wrote Lévis sadly. In Acadia, Louisbourg had surrendered. On the Great Lakes, the English had taken Fort Frontenac (Kingston). And the French army was confined to quarters. In Québec, the soldiers and militia all had to be marched off to Carillon because there were no supplies to feed them

The year 1759 was marked by the fateful battle on the Plains of Abraham, where Montcalm was mortally wounded on September 13. Lévis did not take any part in the engagement: Montcalm had sent him to Lake Ontario, for it appeared certain that the English would march on Montréal. After Québec surrendered, the remnants of the French army regrouped at the Jacques-Cartier River. Vaudreuil and Lévis returned to Montréal. Lévis had automatically taken over command of the troops after Montcalm's death and he spent the winter preparing an expedition to dislodge the English from Québec.

On April 20, 1760 Lévis' army in Montréal, numbering 6,910 combatants (officers, men and militia), began to move. These troops were accompanied by sixteen surgeons and 307 servants. On April 28, Lévis won a brilliant but unfortunately useless victory in the battle of Sainte-Foy. It was useless because the fate of New France would depend on the first sail to appear at the end of Île d'Orléans once the ice broke up on the St. Lawrence. The first sail was English. Lévis, who was besieging Québec, had no choice but to withdraw.

Three English armies converged at Montréal, whose fate was already sealed. On September 6, General Amherst's army had reached Lachine, General Murray's army was breaking through the outlying neighbourhoods to the east and Brigadier-General Haviland's army was at Chambly, awaiting orders for the final assault. Vaudreuil convened a war council. All he could do, Vaudreuil said, was to seek to surrender with honour by proposing articles of capitulation to the enemy.

Lévis protested. "We are asking," he wrote to Vaudreuil, "to break off all negotiations with the English General now and resolve ourselves to conduct the most vigorous defence possible under our present position. We are occupying the city of Montréal which, although in very poor shape and in no condition to withstand a siege, is safe from a surprise attack and cannot be taken without cannon. It would be unheard of to surrender to such harsh and humiliating terms for the troops without having been shelled." Amherst refused to grant the French the usual honours of war.

"Furthermore," Lévis continued, "we still have sufficient arms to sustain a combat if the enemy wishes to attack us sword in hand and to deliver combat, if M. de Vaudreuil wishes to try his luck, although the forces are extremely disproportionate and there is little hope of success." He ended on a note of great nobility: "If, for political reasons, M. le Marquis de Vaudreuil thinks he must now surrender the colony to the English, we will ask his permission to withdraw with our troops to St. Helen's Island to uphold the honour of the king's arms in our name."

He was refused this last satisfaction. "I order M. le chevalier de Lévis," replied Vaudreuil, "to comply with the surrender and to order the troops to put down their arms." Lévis had no choice but to submit, and he ordered the regiments to burn their flags. And so the curtain fell on the French regime.

Three Years of Military Government

————————— >< —————————

"I have received via Mr Abercromby the Letter which Your Excellency has deigned to send me. I have remitted to the commander the articles of capitulation which I signed. Kindly send me a double sign from you. In accordance with the capitulation order Your Excellency may take possession of the posts and gates which Your Excellency considers most appropriate. If Col. Haldimand is your choice, that is fine with me. I am greatly flattered by the courtesy with which Your Excellency has honoured me. I have the honour to be, with highest consideration, Monsieur, the most humble and obedient servant of Your Excellency. Vaudreuil."

This letter, dated at Montréal on September 8, 1760, sounded the death knell for New France. Twenty thousand soldiers with powerful artillery surrounded the town. The next day, the English troops posted sentinels at the gates and entered the town. The French soldiers laid down their arms in Place d'Armes. The curtain rose on the English regime. As soon as he received the letter from Governor de Vaudreuil, General Jeffrey Amherst, commander-in-chief of the English forces, prepared to take possession of the provisional capital of the country.

While Lévis reviewed his troops, nine battalions with only 2,132 men, officers and soldiers, the enemy prepared to savour its victory. When the French battalions were handing over to their conquerors the English flags captured during the battles, it might be supposed that some of Amherst's officers regretted that he had refused to grant war honours to the vanquished, since they had beaten the French only as a result of superior numbers. The French battalions burned their own flags rather than surrender them.

On September 11, Amherst paraded his troops to Place d'Armes, in front of the parish church. He was to meet with Governor de Vaudreuil, the last episode in the often courteous relations that had been established between the two camps throughout the hostilities. Both sides had brought the gentlemanly conduct of lace-cuff wars to America.

At that time, receiving news depended on favourable winds, and ships could take three months to cross the Atlantic if they were becalmed for long periods. When the Kirke brothers occupied Québec in 1629, peace had been in effect for several weeks. This is perhaps what motivated the governor to insert a conditional clause in the articles of capitulation.

"If before, or after, the embarkation of the Marquis de Vaudreuil," he included in the proposed articles, "news of peace should arrive, and by treaty Canada should remain to his most Christian Majesty, the Marquis de Vaudreuil shall return to Québec or Montréal, everything shall return to its former state under the dominion of his most Christian Majesty, and the present capitulation shall become null and of no effect." Amherst contented himself with writing in the margin, "Whatever the King may have done, on this subject, shall be obeyed."

Then the regiments that had distinguished themselves during the death throes of French America set sail: the regiments of Languedoc and Berry and the regular soldiers on September 14, Royal-Roussillon, La Sarre and Guyenne the next day; La Reine and Béarn on September 16. Lévis left for Québec with his second-in-command, François-Charles de Bourlamaque, on September 17. Rigaud de Vaudreuil left on September 20 and the intendant Bigot the day after.

New masters took over the direction of affairs, but time did not stop for all that. On September 22, Amherst announced the formation of a provisional military government and the institution of three districts, Montréal, Québec and Trois-Rivières, with a governor for each. Thomas Gage was placed in charge of Montréal, following a rather undistinguished military career. Amherst had in fact given him command of the rearguard of the forces that advanced on Montréal. The commander-in-chief recognized his valuable administrative experience, however, and rightly so. Gage presided for three years over the development of the government of Montréal; took care not to upset the population; won the friendship of the seigneurs, sometimes to the detriment of the *habitants*; tried to keep to the substance of the police ordinances issued by the former intendants; and even set up a court where militia captains handed down judgement on grievances presented by individuals. He kept the clergy at a distance, believing that it had remained loyal to France and was therefore suspect. Also, he foresaw a time when trade would not be limited to furs but would extend to other commodities and be a further source of prosperity.

In 1761, the governors of the three districts were asked to report on the size of the population under their jurisdiction. The following figures resulted: Québec, 30,211 inhabitants; Montréal, 24,957; and Trois-Rivières, 6,612. We do not know how this census was carried out, and Canada had almost 15,000 other inhabitants who were not accounted for. In any case, the *Canadiens* were vastly outnumbered by the people of the English colonies to the south, who at that time numbered well over a million.

While the military government of Montréal was entrusted to Gage, Ralph Burton was put in charge of the government of Trois-Rivières. At the battle of the Plains of Abraham, it was Burton who received from the dying General Wolfe the order to cut off the retreat of the French forces. In 1763 Gage left for England and Burton succeeded him in Montréal. The following year, he became commander-in-chief of the troops of the northern department, whose seat was located in Montréal and not at Québec. This could doubtless be explained by the strategic position of the town, since this military region extended to the Great Lakes outposts and thus included Michillimakinac and Detroit.

It is certain that the French in Montréal could not have withstood a long siege in September 1760. Not only did they have just a tenth of the enemy's manpower, but Montréal's defences also left a great deal to be desired. Lieutenant John Knox, who had taken part in the battle of the Plains of Abraham and the battle of Sainte-Foy, was in Montréal for the surrender. In notes that he signed a few years later in London, Knox wrote that the fortifications had been "designed to inspire fear in the Indian tribes rather than withstand the attacks of well-equipped forces." He added: "The breastworks are no more than twenty inches thick, which shows that they sought protection only from arrows and light arms."

In the fall of 1763, a proclamation by the British government reestablished civil administration and united the three districts of Québec, Montréal and Trois-Rivières into a single province, which the British named Québec.

That same year, 1763, Benjamin Franklin, who ten years earlier had been appointed His Majesty's Postmaster General in the British colonies of North America, opened offices in the three main cities in the province of Québec. Riders on horseback took about thirty hours to get from Québec City to Montréal. Franklin also set up a mail service between Montréal and New

York. He would return to Montréal several years later to encourage the Canadians to support the cause of the American colonies seeking their independence.

John Knox, who was so unimpressed with Montréal's defences, was struck by the good humour and elegance of the society. "The inhabitants," he wrote, "are gay and sprightly, much more attached to dress and finery than those of Québec, between whom there seems an emulation in this respect; and from the number of silk robes, laced coats, and powdered heads of both sexes and almost of all ages that are perambulating in the streets from morning to night a stranger would be induced to believe Montréal is entirely inhabited by people of independent and plentiful fortunes."

General Gage, for his part, emphasized the harmony that reigned between the Montrealers and the occupying troops. They had, he said, only two worries: that their paper money might lose its value and that another religion besides theirs might be introduced. Only the soldiers and the administrators of the king of France had left the city. Gage did not anticipate any emigration at the time the peace treaty was signed.

The Protestant Religion Puts Down Roots

><

We have noted that Thomas Gage, the first governor of the district of Montréal under the new government, believed that one of the main concerns of the Montrealers after the surrender was that another religion might be introduced.

Anglican priests accompanied Amherst's troops. One of them, Rev. John Ogilvie, was the chaplain of the Royal American Regiment. He had assisted the soldiers during the siege of Québec. Amherst made him responsible for the spiritual well-being of the Anglicans who were now in Montréal, and on September 14, 1760, six days after the surrender, he celebrated the first Protestant service in the chapel of the Hôtel-Dieu.

The hospital was full of wounded soldiers, and the nuns devoted equal attention to soldiers from both sides. Amherst greatly appreciated this and complimented them on their courtesy and devotion. They offered the general several bottles of maple syrup and fruits and vegetables from their garden. The superior, Sister Catherine Martel, received an immediate response, accompanied by a well-filled purse. "I dare to entreat you to be kind enough to allow me to present the community," he wrote, "with a couple of hundred écus, and two dozen bottles of Madeira wine. These are only tokens of my good wishes for a society as respectable as that of the Monastère de Saint-Joseph of the Hôtel-Dieu of Montréal, which can count on the British nation for the same protection that it enjoyed under French rule." The welcome the nuns gave Rev. Ogilvie followed the example set by the Ursuline sisters of Québec. The first Anglican service in celebration of the English victory was held on September 27, 1759, fourteen days after the battle of the Plains of Abraham, in the Ursulines' chapel.

In Montréal, beginning in June 1761 the Anglican congregation met in the Récollet church. Rev. Ogilvie was appointed minister of Trinity Church in New York City in 1764. The same year Governor James Murray of the province of Quebec issued an ordinance on Sunday observance: "All owners of public houses in Quebec City, Montreal and Trois Rivieres must close their doors during divine service. Any one over 12 years of age who is absent for more than three months from religious services shall pay a fine of 5 shillings."

In 1765, the Anglican Church decided to appoint French-speaking ministers in the three cities – in the hope, it was said, of bringing the French closer to the Crown. In Montréal, the incumbent minister, Samuel Bennet, was replaced by Rev. David Chabrand Delisle, who served for twenty-eight years. But this practice was unpopular; some considered it a use of religion for political ends.

So far we have only referred to the Anglicans. Other Protestant denominations did not become established in Montréal until later. In Québec City, the first Presbyterian minister was the regimental chaplain of the Fraser's Highlanders, Rev. Robert Macpherson. In 1759 he conducted a service following the fall of Québec, and then one of his colleagues, the Rev. George Henry, founded a congregation that met in the Jesuit college. The Presbyterians of Montréal waited twenty years for their first minister: Rev. John Bethune settled there in 1786. The following year he was succeeded by Rev. John Young, from the United States, who preached at the Récollet church. The Récollets refused any financial compensation, and the minister brought them two casks of Spanish wine and a box of candles as a sign of gratitude. In 1792, the Presbyterians opened their own church on Saint-Gabriel Street.

The Methodists had no real congregation in Montréal until the early nineteenth century when Rev. Joseph Sawyer held the first meetings on

Saint-Sulpice Street in the shadow of Notre-Dame Church. In 1821, the Methodists opened their own church, on Saint-Jacques Street, and the original chapel became a reading room. Three other churches were opened during the next twenty years.

The first Congregational church in Montréal was opened in 1833 on Saint-Maurice Street. It was the result of efforts undertaken by the Canada Education and Home Missionary Society, founded four years earlier by Henry Wilkes. Montréal had seven churches belonging to that denomination, but most of them joined the Unitarians. An initial attempt to establish a Unitarian congregation was made in 1832, but it failed to get off the ground because of the terrible epidemic of that year and later because of the rebellion of 1837-38. A second attempt in 1841 was more successful. The congregation soon had its own church on Beaver Hall Hill, where the manor house of Benjamin Frobisher, one of the magnates of the famous North West Company, had once stood.

The Baptist presence in Montréal dates from 1820. Beginning in that year, several members of that denomination began to meet at the house of Ebenezer Muir "to pray to God and for mutual edification." This continued until 1831, when the twenty-five members of the congregation opened their first church on Sainte-Hélène Street, under the spiritual leadership of Rev. John Gilmour, from Aberdeen, Scotland. It should be pointed out that a member of the Baptist congregation, T.J. Claxton, later played a central role in giving Montréal a Young Men's Christian Association, the first in North America. This movement was founded in England in June 1844 by George Williams, later Sir George, whose name was borne by a well-known Montréal college until it was incorporated into Concordia University.

Montréal Is Still Burning!

Montréal had had several fires before, notably the fire of 1721, which destroyed 138 houses, and 1734, which levelled forty-six. The Hôtel-Dieu was destroyed on both occasions. In the early years of the British regime, the city fell victim to two more fires, one after the other.

Mère d'Youville recited the *Te Deum* at the height of the fire that reduced her hospital to ashes.

A man named Levington, who lived at the corner of Saint-François-Xavier and Saint-Sacrement Streets, had the thrifty but unfortunate habit of carrying ashes from his hearth up to his attic, where he sometimes used them for making soap. Unluckily, the ashes he took up to his attic on May 18, 1765, were still hot and flames broke out. In no time flat, the house became a blazing tinderbox spewing forth burning embers that were carried by gusts of wind to the adjacent rooftops. At that time, the Hôpital Général, directed by Sister Marguerite d'Youville, was located near the square that now bears her name. The Mother Superior thought that the stone walls of the fortifications would protect her institution, so she sent the nuns under her direction to the fire to help save what could be saved from the houses. But she had not counted on the wind, and the burning brands soon set fire to the roof of the institution.

Back at the hospital, the nuns barely had enough time to gather together the patients, the poor and the orphans in their care in an enclosure – 118 needy people in all. Once the fire was out, it was found that 108 houses had been destroyed, throwing 215 families out into the street. During the worst of the disaster and in the hours following, the population was kept on the alert by successive explosions of some twenty powder kegs, according to d'Youville. A quarter of the city was destroyed, and it was estimated that the buildings that had been levelled represented a third of the combined value of all buildings. Total losses were calculated at nearly £88,000 sterling, including merchandise and furniture that had been reduced to ashes.

There was consternation in London at the news of the catastrophe, and at the initiative of the philanthropist Jonas Hanway a pamphlet was even printed to launch an appeal. King George III donated £500. Hanway was able to give Montréal about £9,000 in aid, and at the same time he gave the city two fire pumps and a bust of the king, which Montrealers hastened to put up in Place d'Armes. The many occasions on which Hanway demonstrated his generosity earned him a monument in 1788 in the north transept of Westminster Abbey.

Reconstruction of the houses that had been destroyed went ahead bravely, but while people were consoling themselves with the thought that the new buildings were an improvement over the old ones, a fire broke out on the property of one of those who had been victimized in the first fire. On April 11, 1768, towards ten in the evening, flames attacked a stable located near the St. Lawrence gate, facing the river. By a cruel twist of fate, the building belonged to a man named Tison, which means "firebrand." The fire spread to the neighbouring houses and raged until five in the morning, levelling more than a hundred houses, a school and two churches, including the chapel of the Congrégation de Notre-Dame.

Meanwhile Bonsecours Chapel, which Marguerite Bourgeoys had begun in 1674 with the help of appeals and the contributions and labour of her fellow residents of Montréal, had been destroyed by fire in 1754 along with several neighbouring houses and had not been raised from its ashes. The keystone for a new chapel was laid in 1771. This is the present-day

A view of the present Notre Dame de Bonsecours Chapel in 1872.

chapel, which underwent various transformations over the years, especially between 1886 and 1894 and later between 1900 and 1910. The statue overlooking the port was blessed in September 1894.

The Seigneurs of the Island of Montréal

Mention was made of the extent of the debts and obligations undertaken by the Sulpician seminary in Paris when it took over Montréal Island from the Société de Notre-Dame de Montréal in 1663, and the energy that the new seigneurs put into the development of the island and the establishment of essential services. Their success was due not only to careful management of the taxes and rents collected from the *habitants* but also to the generosity of a number of priests who did not hesitate to dig deep into their family fortunes to pay for projects directly in keeping with the objectives of Jean-Jacques Olier. Olier's successor, Monsieur Le Ragois de Bretonvilliers, who died in 1676, was especially generous: it is estimated that he gave more than 400,000 livres to Ville-Marie.

Until the Conquest, the Gentlemen of the Seminary of Saint-Sulpice in Paris were the seigneurs of Montréal Island. Thus, in 1731 when the register of land holdings was being prepared for the seigneury, the superior of the Montréal seminary, Louis Normant de Faradon, acted as the agent of the superior general in Paris, Charles-Maurice Le Pelletier. In addition to giving us the names of the tenants or *habitants*, this precious document shows that there were 1,211 houses on the island, of which 266 were made of stone. The seigneurs always had to ensure that there were one or more mills where the tenants could bring their wheat or their oats to be ground. These were common-use mills. The tenants were required to use these mills and pay fees, and the honesty of the millers was closely watched.

There was a windmill on a hill near the gate known as du Coteau, at the east end of the fortified perimeter. In 1689, the seminary leased it to a certain Jean Lumineau. The following year, it was proved that this man had appropriated nearly a hundred minots of flour belonging to the inhabitants of Ville-Marie. The forces of justice did not see the humour in his lack of tact: the man was sentenced to strangulation and hanging "until death should ensue." The Conseil Souverain was more merciful in reviewing the judgement: the sentence was amended to "a scourging of the shoulders and branding with a fleur-de-lys upon the right shoulder."

Mgr. Olivier Maurault, himself a Sulpician and the former president of the Montréal Historical Society, has found evidence in the seminary's archives of the construction or purchase by the Sulpicians of no fewer than thirty-six mills between the late seventeenth and early nineteenth centuries: mills for grinding wheat or oat flour, carding and fulling mills, sawmills, nail mills and oil presses. This illustrates the care taken by the seigneurs in recruiting tenants and looking after their welfare.

The 1760 articles of capitulation contained no particular provisions regarding the property of the Sulpicians, but London decreed that the priests should become British subjects if they wished to keep their property or else sell it to British subjects.

The Hôpital Général of Montréal in 1844. Founded by the Frères Charon, it was taken over by Mère d'Youville. (Drawing by James Duncan, Archives of the Seminary of Québec.)

From 1759 on, the Montréal seminary had an exceptional man as its superior. Étienne Montgolfier – uncle of the brothers of that name who became the pioneers of ballooning – had come over in 1751 and had been appointed vicar general for the Montréal region of the diocese of Québec. After the battle of the Plains of Abraham the bishop, Mgr. de Pontbriand, had retired to Montréal. He died at the seminary on June 8, 1760, and his remains now lie in the small Sulpician cemetery located under the Grand Séminaire on Sherbrooke Street.

Feeling his time approaching, and no doubt pessimistic about the outcome of the military campaign (New France would capitulate three months after his death), Bishop de Pontbriand wrote to his canons recommending that after he died the mandate of his two vicars, Montgolfier and the canon for the Québec region, J.O. Briand, be extended. On September 15, 1760, with the king of France no longer exercising any authority over his former colony, the chapter unanimously appointed Montgolfier to succeed the late bishop. It was thought that the concordat between the kings of France and the popes would no longer apply in a country placed under a Protestant prince and that consequently the church would recover its former prerogatives.

Two weeks later, Montgolfier set sail for England, preceded by a letter from Governor James Murray, who expressed the opinion that "if a priest

The religious school built by the Sulpicians in 1806 on Saint-Paul Street, near McGill Street.

who is haughty and imperious and well known in France is placed at the head of that Church, he may later cause much unpleasantness if he finds a suitable opportunity to exercise his malice and bitterness." The Sulpician had committed the imprudent act of counselling a former Récollet to leave his lady friend, acknowledge his errors and rejoin the ranks of the Roman Catholic Church. This man, who had worked in Montréal as a priest, had thrown his cassock aside to run off with a widow and become the *Protestant* chaplain of a regiment that later took part in the battles of the Plains of Abraham and Sainte-Foy. Finally, Murray suspected the *grand vicaire* of having the remains of the English soldiers who had been buried in consecrated ground exhumed. Montgolfier did not press the point, and so it was his colleague, J.O. Briand, who became bishop of Québec.

From London, Montgolfier went to France to discuss the fate of the Montréal seminary with the superior general. It was decided that the seminary's property would pass to those Sulpicians who agreed to become British subjects. Twenty-eight of them decided to become British and, on January 31, 1765, the property was transferred from the Paris seminary to the Montréal seminary.

Montgolfier remained superior until 1789, and he must have regained the esteem of the governors because in 1785 London suggested that he be appointed coadjutor to the bishop of Québec, a position he refused on account of his advanced age. Over the years he actively protected the

The Longue-Pointe presbytery where the Sulpician priest Curatteau de La Blaiserie opened his Latin School, Montréal's first *collège*. (Water colour by Wilhem Berczy *fils*, c. 1827.)

religious communities of Montréal, persuading the nuns of the Hôtel-Dieu who thought of returning to France to stay, supporting the nuns of the Congrégation de Notre-Dame after their convent burned down in 1768, and drawing up the rule and constitution for the future community of the Grey Nuns, who became the administrators of the Hôpital Général.

It was also under his direction in 1773 that the churchwardens and parishioners of Notre-Dame purchased the Château de Vaudreuil, located on present-day Place Jacques-Cartier, to found the Collège Saint-Raphaël. Seven years earlier another Sulpician, Jean-Baptiste Curatteau de La Blaiserie, curé of the parish of Longue-Pointe, had founded the Latin School. Soon the youth of Montréal and the surrounding region no longer had to go to Québec City for their classical studies.

Attendance at the curé's small school was soon so high that he had to find larger premises. Accordingly, Collège Saint-Raphaël was opened and Curatteau was placed in charge. In 1789, courses in philosophy and the English language were offered. This was how the institution that became the Collège de Montréal was founded. After the fire in the old Château de

Vaudreuil in 1803, the college moved to a new building in Faubourg des Récollets, near McGill Street, but the military authorities purchased the building in 1861 to billet their troops, and it was moved to the mountain in 1862.

If there is any question about the scope of the contribution of the Sulpicians to Montréal under the French regime, it should be pointed out that between the time they arrived in Montréal and 1763, it is estimated that they invested more than seven million livres in nonprofit undertakings. This commitment to Montréal's welfare did not change under the new regime.

The Passing of an American Dream

———————— ✦ ————————

In 1774, London passed the Quebec Act, which put an end to the provisional regime that had replaced the military government following the Conquest, and gave the now-British colony its first constitution. For several years, both the English merchants who had settled in Montréal and Québec and the *Canadiens*, the former subjects of the king of France who had stayed after the surrender, had been asking London to give the country a new form of government. The English merchants naturally wanted a house of assembly completely controlled by themselves, while the *Canadiens* wanted redress for a number of grievances, and the restoration of French law.

There was already unrest in the thirteen colonies to the south wishing to shake off the British yoke. It was not a good time for London to upset the *Canadiens* who, it was feared, would rally to the American cause. After acrimonious debate, the House of Commons passed the Quebec Act on June 18, 1774, by a vote of fifty-six to twenty, and the House of Lords followed suit four days later by a vote of twenty-six to seven. The new constitution fixed the boundaries of the province of Québec, reestablished French civil law, maintained English criminal law, abolished the test oath and ensured freedom of religion. Such "liberality" could not fail to arouse indignation in certain quarters, and a public petition was presented to George III whose contents can be summarized in a single outcry: "No Popery!"

This protest was echoed in Montréal. After the fire of 1765, a bust of George III had been placed on Place d'Armes because the king had contributed to a fund for victims of the disaster. On March 8, 1775, it was noted with surprise that the face of the bust had been painted black, a sort of mitre had been placed on its head with a garland of potatoes around its neck, all accompanied by a sign reading: "Behold the Pope of Canada and the English fool!" The authorities offered a reward to anyone who would reveal who was responsible for this act, with a promise of pardon if the informer were an accomplice. The promised reward was augmented by 100 louis collected by the merchants and fifty guineas offered by the officers of the 26th Regiment, who announced their reward with a drum roll.

It was all for nothing. The guilty parties were never found and the commander of the garrison had the traces of this reparable act of contempt removed. Perhaps the English merchants of the city had wanted to protest in this manner against royal assent to the Quebec Act. Or perhaps this "desecration" was the work of spies, which Montréal had been harbouring since the Continental Congress in Philadelphia had flooded the province with manifestos inviting the Canadians to join in supporting its fight for independence.

Events unfolded. The rebels from the south captured Fort Carillon, Fort Saint-Frédéric and Fort Saint-Jean. Governor Guy Carleton, who had succeeded Murray in 1768, hastened to Montréal, proclaimed martial law and raised a militia. Major-General Philip John Schuyler, commander of the province of New York, had been assigned to take Montréal. Brigadier-General Richard Montgomery was his adjutant. When Schuyler's troops crossed into the province of Québec, a number of settlers, especially in the Richelieu valley, displayed increasing sympathy with the rebels. In mid-September 1775 Schuyler returned to New York, turning his command over to Montgomery.

Ethan Allen, one of the most enthusiastic supporters of the pro-Congress cause in what later became the state of Vermont, had taken Fort Carillon without firing a shot. Montgomery sent him to the mouth of the Richelieu to sound out the people, and he talked himself into believing that he could take Montréal as easily as he had taken Fort Carillon. He probably thought that the people would welcome him as their liberator with open arms.

He went up the St. Lawrence to Longueuil with his 150 men and crossed the river during the night of September 24-25, camping at Longue-Pointe. The governor, who was in Montréal at the time, immediately dispatched 300 soldiers to meet the rebels. Allen and thirty-five of his men were captured, and the schooner *Gaspé* took them in irons to England. Allen was left to meditate in the dungeons of Castle Pendennis in Falmouth on his mistaken belief that the Montrealers would have let their town of 8,000 be taken by a handful of Vermonters. Ironically, thirty-six years later, Allen's daughter Frances, who was born two years before the death of her father, took her vows at the Hôtel-Dieu convent in Montréal.

The easy victory over Allen's party did not fill the governor with optimism. Carleton had already written off Montréal since he could not adequately defend it. He barely escaped capture himself. He had boats carrying provisions and arms taken from Fort Saint-Jean and the baggage of the garrison that had abandoned the fort, all of which he wanted to bring to Québec City. Carleton waited to the last minute before sounding the retreat. After the fall of Fort Chambly, he finally made his decision and took to the river on November 11 with 130 soldiers on eleven small vessels, three of them armed. Across from Sorel, the rebels attacked the fleet. The only ones to escape were the governor; his aide-de-camp, Charles-Louis Tarieu de La Naudière; and one or two officers. They had taken their places in a lifeboat and rowed with the current without making a sound. At one time, the boat was so close to the shore that it was being guided by hand. The governor had another lucky escape at Trois-Rivières. He did not reach Québec City until November 19.

On November 11, the day Carleton left Montréal, Montgomery landed troops on Nuns' Island. The next day, he received a committee of citizens, including James McGill, an influential merchant, and Pierre-Méru Panet, whom Carleton had asked to raise militia companies. Montgomery did not want to upset either the Congress sympathizers, who were fairly numerous, or the loyalists, and he did not demand a surrender. On behalf of the sympathizers, the lawyer Valentin Jautard, who would soon be one of Montréal's first journalists, welcomed the general and his troops. Montgomery entered the city on November 13 and shortly afterwards received a delegation from Trois-Rivières whose members assured him of their benevolent neutrality.

British resistance literally crumbled all along the river, but Québec City, in its eagle's nest, was still defying the invader. Montgomery thought that it was essential to take the city, and he left Montréal with 300 men, while an army of more than a thousand men that had left Massachusetts in September under the command of Benedict Arnold was making for the same destination. The forces came together on the outskirts of Pointe-aux-Trembles (Neuville). Arnold had lost almost a third of his forces, and the situation would have been even more difficult if the local inhabitants had not fed the 600 starving soldiers who had crossed the St. Lawrence.

The siege of Québec began early in December, but it ended in failure.

Montgomery met death at the foot of the cliff of Cap-aux-Diamants during the night of December 30-31. Arnold maintained the blockade, but he became disheartened and left to take command of the troops at Montréal. Meanwhile, the Congress had decided to send a commission to Montréal to persuade the *Canadiens* to support the rebels' cause. The commission was led by Benjamin Franklin and included Samuel Chase, another member of the Congress, and Charles Carroll of Carrollton, Maryland, who was probably chosen because he was a Catholic. He was accompanied by his cousin, John Carroll, a Jesuit and the future archbishop of Baltimore. His mission was doubtless to indoctrinate the clergy whose leaders had remained completely loyal to the crown. Sulpicians and Jesuits alike gave him a rather chilly reception.

Carleton waited for reinforcements to chase the rebels out of the province. Their arrival and the smallpox that decimated the besieging party reversed the situation. David Wooster, who had succeeded Arnold in Québec City, came to replace him in Montréal. The new commander was more rigid and took arbitrary decisions that slowly cooled the ardour of the sympathizers. Carleton had asked London for reinforcements. In May 1777, General John Burgoyne assumed command of operations with 10,000 men. One by one, he took back the posts that had fallen to the rebels. When the British troops camped at Laprairie, the occupiers of Montréal had fled, as had Franklin and his commissioners. The thirteen colonies' American dream of winning the spontaneous support of the province of Québec by persuasion and armed force disappeared without a trace.

The Dawn of a Promising Era

If the American occupation of the city had deeply perturbed the existence of its citizens, then it would be correct to say that normal life resumed its course. But apart from Wooster's brusque changes of mood and some arbitrary decisions concerning some of Montréal's leading citizens, people had gone about their business in peace.

Since the Quebec Act of 1774, the Legislative Council in Québec City had administered municipal affairs. In 1777 Carleton and his council issued an ordinance for the prevention of fires, and appointed inspectors in

The Spanish and Portuguese synagogue built at the corner of Chenneville and La Gauchetière streets was the first synagogue in British North America.

Québec, Montréal and Trois-Rivières to be responsible for various tasks, especially for ensuring that citizens cleaned their chimneys at least once a month. The same year, another ordinance gave commissioners of the peace jurisdiction over police matters in Montréal and Québec.

It was also in 1777 that some of the Jewish residents of Montréal built a synagogue. Shortly after the Conquest, some Jewish settlers arrived in Montréal; nearly all were descended from Jews who had fled Spain and Portugal. In 1768, they founded the congregation Shearith Israel. Lazarus David, Uriel Moresco, Abraham Franks, Simon Levy and Fernandez du Tosco were the founders. Other Jews joined the original group, and the community built the first synagogue in Canada on property donated by David David, son of Lazarus David, at the corner of Notre-Dame and Saint-Jacques streets. It should be noted that, by an act voted in 1831 and given royal assent in London the following year, the essentially French-speaking province of Lower Canada became the first territory in the British Empire to grant Jews full political rights.

In 1778, Montréal saw the birth of its first newspaper, thanks to a printer whom Benjamin Franklin had brought along with him. Fleury Mesplet came with his printing press: his mission was to produce propaganda pamphlets under the sponsorship of the Continental Congress, which hoped to win Canadians to its cause in this way. Franklin, who had become the owner

N°. I. (1) (1778.)

GAZETTE
DU COM  MERCE
ET LITTE. RAIRE,
Pour la Ville & Diſtriȼt de MONTREAL.

MERCREDI, 3 Juin 1778.

AUX CITOYENS.

MESSIEURS,

JE me félicite de vous avoir propoſé l'é-tabliſſement d'un Papier Périodique, non pas tant par rapport à moi-même, que par quelques perſonnes, mais bien à d'autres, la Semaine ſuivante, celui qui n'eût pas daigné jetter un coup d'œil ſur le Papier précédent, ſaiſira avec avidité le ſuivant, parce qu'il flattera ſon caractere, ou ſera plus à la portée de ſes connoiſſances, les ſujets lui ſeront plus familiers, les objets peints de maniere qu'il

En-tête du premier numéro du journal fondé par Fleury Mesplets.

The masthead of the first issue of the newspaper founded by Fleury Mesplet.

of the Pennsylvania *Gazette* in 1730, was no stranger to journalism. He per-suaded Mesplet, who had settled in London, to come live in Philadelphia instead, and the printer became an early supporter of the rebel cause. In 1774, he was asked to print a handbill, a sixteen-page brochure entitled "To the inhabitants of the Province of Québec."

In 1775 Mesplet came to Montréal. Had he been entrusted with some mission, or was he looking for clients? He was welcomed rather coldly, it was said, because of his republican convictions, which did not prevent the Sulpicians from giving him a forty-page booklet to print, entitled *"Règle-ment de la Confrèrerie de l'Adoration perpétuelle du Saint-Sacrement et de la Bonne Mort."* This confraternity had been established at Notre-Dame in 1732 by the Sulpician Antoine Deat, confessor to the sisters of the Congrégation de Notre-Dame.

When the rebels withdrew from Montréal, Mesplet remained. He was thrown in prison without a trial. Once released, he returned to his press and thought about starting a periodical. Charles Berger, a friend who had lent him a large sum of money when he settled in the city, offered him financial aid once again. An associate, Valentin Jautard, joined the two. And thus it was that on June 3, 1778, the first issue of the *Gazette du Commerce et Littéraire pour la Ville et District de Montréal* was printed.

"The establishment of a periodical paper," as the publisher explained,

This bronze plaque on Capitale Street commemorates Montréal's first printer.

"appeared to me and a number of others as a project deserving of your attention in every respect." This initiative, he added, would facilitate commerce and the progress of the arts, and bring people together. "The advantages are no less with regard to individual interests: the ease of informing the public at any time of sales of merchandise, furniture or property, of finding personal property that one had thought lost and of capturing runaway Negroes; of announcing one's need for a clerk or a domestic and a number of others which will develop from the commodity offered by this project."

Some may find the allusion to runaway Negroes surprising. Slavery still existed at this time. Article 47 of the capitulation of 1760 clearly stipulated that "Negroes and Panis of both sexes shall retain their status as slaves in the possession of the French and Canadians to whom they belong; these shall be free to keep them in their service in the Colony or to sell them."

Mesplet was doubtless counting on advertising as well as on subscriptions to support his paper, but there is reason to believe that he wanted to make the paper a vehicle for the "revolutionary" opinions that he shared with a number of friends, including Valentin Jautard, who became editor-in-chief. Under the pen-name "Spectateur tranquille," Jautard was the propagandist for an academy that he and Mesplet established in 1778 in honour of Voltaire.

In early June 1779, Governor Frederick Haldimand, who had succeeded Carleton, closed down the paper and sent Mesplet and Jautard to prison. There is a bronze plaque to Mesplet's memory on Capitale Street in Old Montréal. A tablet was unveiled on Mercière Street in Lyon in 1985 to mark the location of the workshop where Mesplet learned the rudiments of printing from his father. There are those who believe that Mesplet was born in that city but, in a letter signed in 1789 and carefully preserved by the library of McGill University, Mesplet wrote that he was "born at Marseille, on January 10, 1734, the son of Jean-Baptiste Mesplet, printer, born at Agen, in Guyenne, who died in Lyon in 1760."

Montréal's elite was influenced by a current of "free thought" in the late eighteenth century. One of those who encouraged it was a rich merchant named Pierre du Calvet. His house is one of the most interesting heritage buildings in Old Montréal. Calvet had left France "for religious reasons" and had established a prosperous export business that shipped cargoes of wheat, peas and pelts to England and Spain. His business concerns did not prevent him from taking an interest in local affairs, and he did not hesitate to denounce the abuses that were tarnishing the administration of justice. Since he held a commission as justice of the peace, he was in a position to reveal the dishonesty of some of his colleagues. In 1770 he had even sent a memorandum on the operation of the justice system in the province of Québec to the secretary of state for the American colonies in London.

As might be expected, Pierre du Calvet soon joined the Academy of Montréal. He, Mesplet and Jautard were not born in Canada but rather in France, and this was enough to make them suspect in the eyes of the British authorities. They were already known to be sympathetic to republican ideals. Furthermore, they made no secret of their proselytizing activities on behalf of basic freedoms, and their sympathy for Voltaire's ideas earned them the hatred of the religious authorities.

Like Mesplet and Jautard, Calvet got a taste of prison, even though his uncompromising analysis of the conduct of representatives of the judicial system had brought him compliments, for he had taken the two judges of the court of common pleas to task. So that he could be put in jail, he was accused of having plotted with the rebels during the occupation of the city. He remained behind bars from 1780 to 1783, although no charges were ever laid. Once released, he left for London where he published his "Appeal to the Justice of the State," denouncing Haldimand's despotism and demanding respect for human rights in Canada.

For the *Canadiens*, the Mesplet-Jautard-Calvet threesome represented the beginning of a transition between the ultraconservative spirit of the old regime and the search for greater individual liberty. This transition eventually led to the troubled period of 1837-38.

Despite all these disruptions in their existence, Montrealers were seeing changes for the better in their parishes and in trade. They had waited patiently for a century before construction work was completed on their church, whose five cornerstones had been laid in 1672. Because it had to be enlarged and side aisles added, erection of the tower was postponed. In 1723, the engineer Chaussegros de Léry had given it a beautiful façade of cut stone in the baroque style of Jesuit churches. Next the tower was erected, but construction of the steeple had to be delayed for lack of funds. Work resumed in 1771. The steeple was decorated with two elegant lanterns, but had to wait until 1782 for the traditional gilded copper rooster. The church by then was already more than a century old.

Thanks to its geographical situation, Montréal had undergone some development since the end of the French regime as a result of the fur trade and the famous North West Company, which would give it a new lease on life before the end of the eighteenth century. This powerful syndicate of traders had chosen to enter into competition with the venerable Hudson's Bay Company, which claimed exclusive trading rights. It held a royal charter, but in 1627 Louis XIII had granted the right to exploit the same territory to the Company of One Hundred Associates. Later, by the Treaty of Ryswick (1697), which put an end to the War of the League of Augsburg, the entire Hudson Bay region had been ceded to France. Finally, under the Treaty of Paris (1763), France had returned this region, not to the Hudson's Bay Company but to Britain.

It was mainly on the basis of these agreements that several ambitious traders decided to launch their venture. The names of the promoters and their first associates are worthy of note, because some of them played an

Simon McTavish died in 1804 and was buried on his estate on the mountain. His nephews, William and Duncan McGillivray, raised a monumemt to his memory that survived winter storms until fifty years ago. Nowadays, it has been replaced by a modest pillar at the upper end of Peel Street. (Drawing by James Duncan.)

important role in founding the institutions and services that would make Montréal a metropolis. They are Benjamin and Joseph Frobisher, Simon McTavish, William McGillivray, Roderick McKenzie, Alexander McLeod, John Gregory, Angus Shaw and William Thornburn. The North West Company tried to recruit a Canadian workforce from the outset, since the natives had long been more accustomed to trading with French coureurs de bois. It hired foremen, voyageurs, workers, guides and interpreters in the districts of Montréal and Trois-Rivières. Some of them soon became *bourgeois*, or associates of the promoters.

It did not take the North West Company long to set up a number of trading posts, establishing a communications network across North America. Trading strategies were worked out in Montréal, under the smoky beams of the Beaver Club. The famous Lachine canoes or *canots de maître*, which could transport five tons of merchandise and were powered by eight to ten men, would leave in the spring for the west or up the Ottawa River, not to return until weighted down with furs. McTavish soon had his country residence on the slopes of Mount Royal and became the seigneur of Terrebonne. Prosperity took root in the city. Even John Jacob Astor, the famous New York capitalist and future philanthropist, came to Montréal to purchase the furs he needed in his business and kept a warehouse there. The carousing at the Beaver Club and the curious rituals engaged in by the members became legendary.

The presence in Montréal of the *bourgeois* from the North West Company gave the city a valuable commercial and financial boost, for these fur magnates invested their profits in various enterprises that made the wheels of commerce turn. Simon McTavish ruled with an iron hand, so much so that in 1795, some businessmen established a parallel syndicate as the Forsyth, Richardson Company. Forsyth and Richardson were two very active promoters who along with several others had been behind a project to establish a bank in Montréal, about which more later.

Of the many businessmen who settled in the city in the late eighteenth century, there is one whose name has survived into our own time: John Molson, a native of Lincolnshire who crossed the Atlantic in 1782. He was already in contact with Thomas Loid, the owner of a malt brewery established at the foot of St. Mary's current. He soon became Loid's partner, and when Loid could not honour his obligations, Molson bought the business at an auction. On July 28, 1786, he noted in his diary, "Today bought eight bushels of barley: my beginning in the world's great game." A joke, undoubtedly, but one marking the start of a career that kept pace with the city's growth: first bank, first steam engine, first railway and so on.

The presence of British troops who had come to repel the American invasion had fuelled the city's economy as Montréal became the principal base for supplies destined for the defence forces to the east and west. Their withdrawal would have been followed by a recession, had their place not been taken by commerce, and especially the fur trade. The annual yield to the North West Company from trading was 100,000 beaver skins, 50,000 marten, 12,000 buffalo and nearly 20,000 of a variety of other species. When the traders returned to the head of the Lachine Rapids in late summer or early fall, each carried a forty-kilogram bundle of these precious pelts, which were stored in warehouses on Saint-Paul Street and not moved until they were shipped to Europe.

It is said that Montréal grew like a mushroom, and the dynamic contribution of merchants of Scottish origin was a major factor in its growth. Just as remarkable as these merchants' leading role in the development of Montréal is the lack of friction between Scots and French Canadians. There are undoubtedly historical factors that explain why they got along so well. In wars between France and England, the Scots often fought side by side with the French. As the joke ran, the Scots and *Canadiens* had the same "stepmother country."

Reference was made earlier to the desire of Mesplet, Jautard and Calvet for more liberal institutions. As though the powers of darkness had wanted to protest their initiatives, Montréal lived through the year of the "great darkness" in 1785. On October 15, in the middle of the day, thick clouds accompanied by thunder covered the sky, and Montrealers grew fearful. The day after, the same thing happened again. Thinking their last hour had arrived, the faithful took refuge in Notre-Dame Church and Bonsecours Chapel. Some hastened to visit Madame d'Eschambault, whose piety was legendary. She lived like a recluse in the handsome residence left her by her husband, Joseph de Fleury d'Eschambault. His position as agent general of the East India Company had enabled him to buy the Château de Vaudreuil. Madame d'Eschambault followed the group to Bonsecours and prayed with them. Then the veil covering the sky broke open and the sun reappeared. Montrealers were to live through similar experiences in 1819 and in 1829.

Britain waited twenty-four years after the Treaty of Paris before sending a member of the royal family to Canada. On August 14, 1787, Prince William Henry, son of George III, arrived in Québec City on board the frigate *Pegasus*. The three ships from Commodore Sawyer's fleet that preceded him made an impressive escort: *Leander*, with the commodore aboard and 700 guns, the *Resource* and the *Ariadne*. Late in the morning of Monday, September 3, Lord Dorchester (Guy Carleton) left Québec for Montréal to make preparations to welcome His Highness. Following a stopover at Trois-Rivières, the prince arrived on September 7. The governor general and a number of staff officers went to greet him at Pointe-aux-Trembles.

The bishop's coadjutor, other clerical dignitaries, members of the

Legislative Council residing in the city, judicial officers and members of the nobility awaited him at "Faubourg Québec." He was led between two rows of soldiers to the old Château de Vaudreuil for an official reception. On September 13, the Brothers of Canada (a Masonic Lodge) gave a dinner for the prince in their lodge. Before leaving, he visited Fort Chambly, then went to Sorel where the authorities gave his name to their city. Fortunately, William-Henry later reacquired its very handsome French name, which commemorates an officer in the Carignan regiment.

Prince William Henry was a future king of England. George III reigned until 1820, although from 1811 on the king's mental illness made it necessary for his son George to act as regent. George succeeded to the throne as George IV on his father's death and reigned for ten years. When he died in 1830, his brother William Henry, now the Duke of Clarence, became King William IV. He reigned until his death seven years later, when Queen Victoria came to the throne.

The Commercial Centre of the Two Canadas

———————————— ✥ ————————————

By the early 1790s, Montréal was already starting to look like a city. The population of the district of Montréal was 18,000, compared to 14,000 for the district of Québec. With the independence of the colonies as the United States of America, there was an influx of Loyalists into the province of Quebec, leading to an increase in the number of Protestants from several hundred to approximately 15,000. Some settled in Montréal, but most chose the upper St. Lawrence region, west of Montréal, or the territory south of the seigneuries fronting on the south shore of the St. Lawrence, which became known as the Eastern Townships.

In Loyalist circles, France was suspected of harbouring designs on the territory it had lost. After all, General Lafayette had been given command of an army to invade the province of Quebec during the American War of Independence. The expedition had halted at Albany, where the fiery champion of liberty had been warmly welcomed by Hurons and Iroquois who gave him the name of Kayewa-la (fearsome horseman). His dearest dream was to retake Canada. "Our hearts are perched on snowshoes and gliding along Lake Champlain," he wrote to Admiral d'Estaing, whose preference would have been to attack the English at Halifax. One can only speculate as to what might have been the attitude of the *Canadiens*, some of whom were already in sympathy with the rebel cause, had they encountered an army commanded by a French general.

Two Frenchmen, both of whom could have left us a description of Montréal, were refused entry into Lower Canada (as the French-speaking eastern part of the province of Quebec had become) in 1795. Frenchmen could not visit their Canadian "cousins" who had become British subjects. The Duc de La Rouchefoucault-Liancourt toured Upper Canada, but when he wanted to go from Niagara to Montréal and Québec City, he was stopped. "This English flag under which I am sailing over lakes where the French flag was so long displayed," he wrote, "these forts, these guns, the spoils of France, this constant obvious proof of our former weakness and of our misfortunes, all are a burden to me, a source of pain, shame and embarrassment that I find difficult to disentangle and even more difficult to explain."

The heroic commander Aristide-Aubert Dupetit-Thouars was also refused permission to visit Montréal and Québec City after he had admired Niagara Falls. "I do not know why I am beginning to find myself so ill at ease in a place where grandeur and nobility are combined with the most attentive hospitality," he noted in his travel diary. "Is it the oppression of the English atmosphere on a Frenchman's lungs? Is it the sadness of seeing these beautiful lakes – these lakes where the first ships worthy of their great size were French ships – now under the same flag that also flies over Pondicherry and our strongholds in the West Indies? Is it the pain I must conceal in seeing the *Canadiens* in subjection to their proud conquerors?" Three years later, at the battle of Aboukir in Egypt, Dupetit-Thouars lost his legs to a cannonball while commanding the *Tonnant*. He died ordering his men not to strike their colours.

In 1774, London had passed the Quebec Act to bind its new Canadian subjects to Britain in view of the ferment in the American colonies. But the mass arrival of the Loyalists, and especially their settlement in the Great Lakes region, created a new political situation, which led to the birth of representative government and the provinces of Upper and Lower Canada in 1791. On February 25, 1791, British Prime Minister William Pitt read out a royal message: "His Majesty deems it fitting to inform the House of Commons that the interests of his subjects in the province of Quebec appear to him to require the division of that province into two separate provinces, to be called the province of Upper Canada and the province of Lower Canada." A few weeks later, the contents of the accompanying bill were made known. They included maintenance of all guarantees enacted in the Quebec Act and institution of a parliamentary system.

The bill gave Canada a constitution similar to that of Britain, but two factors had to be taken into account. First of all, "In doing this," said Lord Wyndham Grenville, "a considerable degree of attention is due to the prejudices and habits of the community, and every degree of caution should be used to continue to them the enjoyment of those civil and religious Rights which were secured to them by the Capitulation of the Province." Lord Sydney, secretary of state for the Home Department, addressed the second factor: "The most considerable part of the disbanded Troops and Loyalists who have become Settlers in the Province since the late War, have been placed upon Lands in that part of it which lie to the Westward of the Cedars ... as these People are said to be of the number desirous of the Establishment of the British Laws, It has been in Contemplation to propose to Parliament a division of the Province."

The new constitution gave Canada as a whole a governor general and each province a lieutenant-governor. But the two provinces were quite unequal in population: 146,000 inhabitants in Lower Canada as against a mere 10,000 inhabitants in Upper Canada. Under the Quebec Act the Legislative Council had administered municipal affairs. With the entry into force of the new Constitutional Act, this responsibility was transferred to justices of the peace appointed by the Executive Council.

Montréal's merchants were having a number of difficulties in carrying on their businesses. There was a shortage of money in circulation, and furthermore the coins that were in use were very diverse. In 1792, three companies planned to found a bank that would print paper money: Phyn, Ellice & Inglis of London and Todd, McGill & Co. and Forsyth, Richardson & Co. of Montréal. Their efforts were unsuccessful. Other attempts were made, but all were to no avail until 1817 when the Bank of Montreal was established. We will return to this subject.

There was another obstacle to commerce: the slowness of mail service with Britain. In winter, ocean-going ships that crossed the Atlantic to Canada had to moor at Halifax. In 1792 Canada and the United States signed their first postal agreement. Mail coming by boat from Falmouth to New York was given to a courier who brought it to Burlington, Vermont, where

RAN AWAY

FROM the Subfcriber on Thurfday t
12th Auguft laft, a Negro man named T I G H T ; about twen
eight years of age, about 5 feet 8 inches high, fpeaks Englifh and a
tle German ; he went away in company with a Negro man belongin
Capt. Laforce named Snow, tall and flender, who fpeaks Englifh
French. They were feen croffing the River St. Lawrence from
South fide to L'Affomption about the firft inftant, and are fuppofed
have gone towards the Lake behind Montreal. Whoever will apprehe
the firft mentioned Negro named Tight, and fecure him fo tightly that his mafter m
have him again, fhall have *Forty Shillings* reward, and all reafonable charges, paid by
Chrifty Cramer, Merchant in Montreal, or the Subfcriber in Quebec.

Quebec, 7th September, 1784.   JOHN SAUL.

a Canadian courier collected it and took it to Montréal. This new fort-
nightly service began on December 20, 1792. But it was not until 1797 that
weekly mail service was established between Montréal and New York on a
year-round basis.

Lower Canada was subdivided into counties, and the major cities into
wards. The first elections took place in June 1792. In Montréal James
McGill and J.-B. Durocher were elected to represent the west ward, Joseph
Frobisher and John Richardson to represent the east ward, and Joseph
Papineau and James Walker to represent the county.

It was mentioned earlier that one of the Articles of Capitulation of 1760
guaranteed the inhabitants property rights over their slaves. This provision
was still in effect at the turn of the nineteenth century and a reward was generally offered to anyone who captured a runaway slave. For example, on
September 7, 1784, the *Gazette de Québec* advertised that Christy Cramer, a
merchant of Montréal, would pay fifty shillings to whoever might capture
Tight, a Negro belonging to him who spoke English and a little German
and who had run away with another Negro, Snow, the property of Captain
Laforce.

Slaves were routinely advertised as merchandise. One advertisement featured a Negro woman and a mulatto baby boy, nine months old; she had
formerly been the property of General Murray and made butter to perfection. Another featured a Negro who understood waiting on a gentleman
and looked well in livery. In still another, a stout, healthy young Panis

---

A VENDRE,

UNE NEGRESSE qui est présentement en ville. L'on pourra s'adresser à Madame PERRAULT pour le prix.

A VENDRE,

UN NÉGRE, agé d'environ 25 Ans, qui à eu la Petite Verole.
Pour plus amples informations il faut s'adresser à l'IMPRIMEUR.

TO BE SOLD,

A Healthy NEGRO LAD, who has had the Small-Pox, and
is about 25 Years of Age.
For more ample information apply to the PRINTER.

TO   BE   SOLD,

A STOUT, healthy, young Panis Girl, about
12 years of age, has had the small-pox, speaks French and English, and is perfectly honest and sober. For further particulars enquire of
                          MELVIN, WILLS & BURNS.

TO BE SOLD, at Public Vendue, on Friday
the 16th Instant, a Negro Woman, aged 25 Years, with a Mulatto Male Child,
9 Months old. She can be well recommended for a good House Servant.—Likewise a
Negro Man, aged 23 Years, a very good House Servant, and understands a good deal
of Cookery.   tt

AS MILES PRENTIES, Tavern-keeper in the
Lower-Town of Quebec, intends leaving the Province, he requests all Persons
who have any Demands upon him, to give in their Accounts; and he also requests all
Persons who are indebted to him, to make speedy Payment, so as he may be the better able
to pay off his just Debts.——
    Mr. Prenties has to sell a Negro Woman, aged 25 Years, with a Mulatto Male Child,
9 Months old; she was formerly the Property of General MURRAY; she can be well
recommended for a good House-servant, handles Milk well, and makes Butter to Perfection: Likewise a Negro Man, aged 23 Years, a very good House-servant, understands
waiting upon a Gentleman, and looks well in Livery.

(native) girl, about twelve years of age, was offered for sale, the fact that she
had had smallpox being carefully noted. This detail was often mentioned,
because it indicated that the slave was immune to the disease.

The sale of slaves before a notary continued under the English regime.
Thus, in 1778, Hector-Théophile Cramahé, lieutenant-governor of the
province, bought the mulatto Isabella from the butcher George Hipps, to
whom she had been sold at auction. The price was £50, equivalent to 200

Spanish piastres. The following year, Cramahé sold Isabella before the same notary, Jean-Claude Panet, for £45 to ship's captain Pierre Napier. In 1795 the merchant John Young purchased a sixteen-year old Negro from the innkeeper Dennis Daly for £70, the Halifax rate. Two years later, the purchaser signed a notarized contract promising to emancipate his slave after seven years if he had faithfully served his master in the meantime.

Often the slaveowners were prominent citizens. In 1797 the owner of the *Herald*, Richard Dillon, accepted a mulatto woman named Ledy, aged twenty-six, as security for a loan. Slaves took the religion of their owners, Catholic or Protestant. Thomas Gage, the governor of Montréal; James McGill, founder of McGill University; Rev. David Chabrand Delisle, an Anglican priest; bishops of Québec; members of the clergy; and even religious communities owned slaves. Some merchants apparently traded in slaves. In 1734, Charles-Augustin Rhéaume, of Île Jesus, sold a total of five slaves to a *bourgeois* of Québec City. The historian Marcel Trudel states that the Le Moyne family of Longueuil owned at least forty slaves over the generations.

On one occasion a family of slaves was even shared out *inter vivos*. The elder Charles Le Moyne owned a couple, Charles and Élisabeth, who had five children baptized as François, Marie-Élisabeth, Marie-Charlotte, Joseph and Charles. In 1729, two of the patriarch's sons, the Baron de Longueuil and the Chevalier de Longueuil, divided up the members of the family: the baron took two children, François and Marie-Élisabeth, while the chevalier took the parents and two other children, Marie-Charlotte and Charles. As Joseph is not mentioned, he may have died. Since the shares were unequal, the chevalier gave the baron two Panis slaves, Gabriel and Marie-Joseph. Panis were so called after Pawnees, natives living west of the Mississippi who were often sold to the French when they were captured by the Fox Indians. At least in these circumstances they were not killed.

It is estimated that in 1784 there were more than 200 black slaves in the district of Montréal. The slaves had their own cemetery in Montréal, at the corner of Saint-Jacques and Saint-Pierre Streets, the site of the later Mechanics' Institute. There is reason to believe that the slaves were generally well treated. The conditions under which they lived cannot be equated with those experienced by some slaves in the cotton fields of the south. Slavery was a widely practised social phenomenon, but fortunately the conscience of society was finally alerted.

In 1793, a movement to put an end to slavery took shape in the two Canadas. In July of that year, bringing new slaves into Lower Canada was outlawed. No contract of ownership could be extended for more than nine years from that time, and children of slaves were to be freed when they reached the age of twenty-five. The slaves early sought to cast off their yoke. In 1798 Charlotte, who belonged to Jane Cook, gave her mistress the slip and refused to return. She was put in prison, but she obtained a writ of habeas corpus, the provision that ensures freedom of the person under English law. No guarantees were required of her to ensure her subsequent appearance before the Court of King's Bench. That same year Jude, a Negro woman belonging to Montréal businessman Elias Smith, was exonerated of the charge that she had refused to return to her master's service. He had bought her three years earlier in Albany.

An initial attempt at abolishing slavery had failed in 1793. Six years later Joseph Papineau, member of the Assembly for Montréal's east ward, put the question back on the order paper, but did not get enough votes: a petition signed by the citizens of Montréal demanded that masters' rights over their slaves be maintained. People don't give up property rights lightly. Subsequent attempts failed in 1800, 1801 and 1803. It was only in 1833 that slavery was definitively abolished by an act of the British Parliament.

By the end of the century, Montréal could boast of being the main commercial centre of the two Canadas. The Richelieu River and Lake Champlain provided direct access to the United States. Thanks to the St. Lawrence, all traffic from Upper Canada and beyond was channelled through Montréal. The city had long since spread beyond the fortifications and was now surrounded by outlying neighbourhoods. Public buildings stood on Notre-Dame Street, while Saint-Paul Street with its warehouses and stores served as the main commercial artery. The slopes of the mountain were dotted with woods and orchards.

Travellers noted that relations among residents were warmer in Montréal than in Québec. Isaac Weld, who travelled through Lower Canada in 1796, wrote that Montrealers "kept up such a constant and friendly intercourse with each other that it seems then as if the town were inhabited by one large family."

Communications between Montréal and Québec were as good as could be expected considering the times, as Weld also noted: "In no part of North America can a traveller proceed so commodiously as along this road between Québec and Montréal." No fewer than twenty-nine post-houses were spread out along its length and sixteen rivers had to be crossed. Each postmaster was obliged to have four *calèches* and the same number of *carrioles*,

Montréal seen from the mountain about 1812. The fortifications are still standing; a little to the right of centre the steeple of the first Notre-Dame church can be seen clearly; and at the far left is the hill on which stood the small citadel, which has now disappeared. (Drawing by Thomas Davies.)

with the horses needed to pull them. The trip took three or four days. In 1800 four stagecoaches were added to the coach service. Four horses were hitched to the vehicle, which could carry six travellers. But most transportation took place by water, on small boats with four oarsmen and small 400-ton sailing ships that could sail upstream as far as St. Mary's current.

Although Montrealers were primarily French-speaking, commerce was generally in the hands of the Scots, the English and the Irish. Weld noted that while it was very rare to find a Francophone who could speak English, "the English inhabitants are, for the most part, well acquainted with the French language." He could not have made such a notation in his diary a century later.

There's No Stopping Progress

––––––––––––––– ✦✦ –––––––––––––––

Civic progress requires constant improvement in public services. In 1799, an ordinance established two districts for the maintenance of roads and bridges, Québec City and Montréal. The justices of the peace were supposed to appoint inspectors, decide how to collect the funds needed to carry out the work and to establish an assessment roll for purposes of taxation. The following year, an inspector was appointed for Montréal and, interestingly enough, his jurisdiction extended beyond the fortifications. The result was that Montréal's two main arteries, Notre-Dame and Saint-Paul streets, were soon paved and new streets were opened.

At the same time, construction was begun on a courthouse on Notre-Dame Street on a piece of land that had belonged to the Jesuits. The legislature had voted £5,000 sterling for that purpose. The building served until 1844, when it was destroyed by fire. The devotion of the sheriff, the clerks and the lawyers was highly praised because they managed to save the files and hundreds of books from the library as well. A certain Carolus Lepage was found guilty of having set fire to the building and sentenced to prison. He later admitted that he had screwed a sharp cutting blade into the heel of his boots, and while appearing to help the firefighters he was actually cutting through the hoses by walking on them!

Beginning in 1802, the Court of Common Pleas held assizes in Montréal. Once the Place Jacques-Cartier market was built, a pillory was erected across from the courthouse, as the purpose of that device was to expose shady characters to public opprobrium. The head of the person sentenced to the pillory was held by a wooden collar, and it was the target not only of jokes but frequently also of tomatoes and whatever other projectiles littered the market's paths. Use of the pillory was not abolished until 1841.

Downtown Montréal was hemmed in by the fortifications – which, incidentally, had never been used. The city had twice surrendered without a shot being fired: once in 1760 to the British, who could have gobbled it up in a single mouthful, and again in 1775 to the representative of the Continental Congress, General Montgomery, and his army. There was no point in keeping these walls, which by that time would have harmed defence operations more than they would have helped them. The authorities decided on demolition and gave the work to three commissioners, James

Montréal's first courthouse was built on Notre-Dame Street in the early nineteenth century.

McGill, John Richardson and Jean-Marie Mondelet. The job took several years: in 1820 the so-called Québec Gate, then situated at the eastern end of Saint-Paul Street, still existed. Commune Street (formerly Commissioners Street) and Ruelle des Fortifications now run where the old walls stood two centuries ago.

Although the population of the city proper was approximately 9,000 by the early nineteenth century, Montrealers did not yet enjoy the convenience of running water. They had to get their water either from the river or from wells. The main wells were located at Place d'Armes, the market and the Jesuits' property. This system was not only very inconvenient but also played havoc with the efforts of the volunteer firefighters.

Joseph Frobisher, one of the founders of the North West Company, had retired from business in 1798 and must have had some capital to invest. On April 8, 1801, he and his partners formed the Montreal Water Works Company, which undertook to give the city running water in exchange for exclusive rights for five years. Work began immediately with the installation of wood pipes made from tree trunks with holes bored from end to end, and water was obtained from springs at the top of the western part of Mount Royal. This was the first waterworks, and it was undoubtedly appreciated as the franchise was renewed for thirty-five years. However, the amount of water was soon insufficient for the needs of the townspeople, and in 1815 water had to be obtained from the river.

As early as 1803, it was realized that the original water works would not allow for effective firefighting when a fire destroyed the Collège Saint-Raphaël (the former Château de Vaudreuil), the Jesuit convent, part of the jail and a score of houses. The following year, an English company specializing in fire insurance, the Phoenix, established an agency in Montréal, the first in Canada. It was not until 1818 that the first Lower Canadian business of this sort, the Quebec Fire Insurance Company, was founded. By this time, the Fire Insurance Association of Halifax had been founded in that city. Then two American companies began doing business in Lower Canada: Aetna in 1821 and the Hartford in 1836.

Across the river from Montréal, Longueuil was growing. South shore residents who wanted to do business in Montréal went to Longueuil to cross the river. Mère d'Youville was said to have begun operating a ferry between the two towns in 1740 to earn money for her hospital, but it is not known how long this service was in operation. In the spring of 1801, an enterprising man named Alexis Patenaude operated a regular run between the two shores. It was thanks to the biceps of sturdy oarsmen that passengers crossed the St. Lawrence. This service lasted more than twenty years, until in 1826 a certain Captain White began operating "horse boats" just below St. Mary's current. These boats had paddlewheels powered by horses walking around in a circle, hitched to a shaft – a sort of floating winch. It was not long before steam power was introduced.

With the passage of time and the dredging of the St. Lawrence, Montréal would become a seaport situated farther inland than any other, but that lay in the future. Only light craft could sail upstream to the foot of St. Mary's current. However, the first Montréal shipyard dates from the early nineteenth century. It was the industrialist David Nunn who took the initiative in 1806. He later went into partnership with another leading businessman, Robert Hunter. Three-hundred-ton hulls slipped down to the river from their launching pads: they were vessels designed for the coastal trade, but the shipwrights also grew confident enough to build a 600-tonner, the *Earl of Buckinghamshire*.

For relaxation, the British businessmen who settled in Montréal and worked in trade and industry brought various sports with them from their native land. Curling was perhaps the first sport practised by the occupation troops after their arrival. They used the frozen rivers and lakes, and old engravings show us Scottish soldiers curling on the St. Lawrence. It was not until the early nineteenth century that curling clubs were started. The first one, the Royal Montreal, was established in 1807 under the presidency of

The Fils de la Liberté were founded at the Hotel Nelson, on Place Jacques-Cartier, in the shadow of the column erected in honour of Admiral Nelson.

C.T. Hare. The first match was played on the ice of the St. Lawrence on April 11 of that year.

Before the conventional granite stones were used in Canada, curlers used pieces of metal in the shape of teapots, weighing about thirty kilograms. As the saying went, it was a sport for strong biceps. Perhaps that was why the first women's club was not founded until 1894, under the presidency of Mrs. W.L. Jamieson. It also was called the Royal Montreal. The Canadian clubs were affiliated directly with the Royal Caledonian Curling Club of Scotland until a branch of the organization was established in Ontario in 1874.

Markets have always played an important role in the daily lives of city dwellers the world over. Montréal's market was no longer large enough, as a growing number of farmers came there to sell their products. In 1803, after Collège Saint-Raphaël burned down, it was decided not to rebuild it but to use its vast terrain for a new market, and the Place Jacques-Cartier Market was built as a result. In 1807 a sum of £2,500 sterling was voted for that purpose, but it was not enough and a new ordinance the following year authorized forty temporary stalls until the necessary funds were found. The "new market" built in this way was enlarged in 1821. The whole thing was torn down when Bonsecours Market was opened, and the space freed up was turned into a public square.

New regulations for the management of markets were adopted in 1810. Slaughtering animals in markets was forbidden, and only fish, meats, sugar, tobacco, cloth and shoes brought in by farmers could be sold there. Fruits and vegetables could be sold in the streets, however. At the foot of the new marketplace, a space was provided to tie up the boats used to bring in the provisions.

In December 1805, while Montréal society was amusing itself at the Exchange Coffee House on Saint-Paul Street, a messenger came bearing sad news: Admiral Nelson, the hero of Trafalgar, had just died. The ladies began to weep, and the organizers of the evening decided to end the festivities immediately as a sign of mourning. One man suggested that a monument be erected to the memory of the deceased. A public subscription was opened, and on August 17, 1809, the cornerstone was laid for the imposing Nelson Column. This was the third monument erected in Montréal: the bust of George III, installed in Place d'Armes after the fire of 1765, was the first, and the McTavish Pillar was the second. The pillory – where robbers were put who were sentenced to be whipped with a cat o' nine tails or branded on their palms with an iron heated in the fire for as long as it took to say "Vive le roi!" or "God save the King!" three times, depending on one's cultural allegiance – was placed under the gaze of the famous admiral.

In 1807, Robert Fulton built the first steamboat that could actually be used for practical purposes. The *Clermont* made the trip up the Hudson River between New York and Albany. This inspired John Molson to emulate the famous inventor. Two men arrived in Montréal in the fall of 1808 to help him: John Jackson, an engineer, and John Bruce, a ship's carpenter. On June 5, 1809, the three Johns concluded a partnership agreement. The keel had been laid in late March, and the hull was finished in June. Fulton had ordered his engine from England, but Molson had confidence in the

Launching of the *Accommodation,* the first Canadian steamship. With his top hat in his hand and standing next to his wife, John Molson presides over the ceremony. (Painting by Adam Sherriff Scott.)

Saint-Maurice Forges. Its artisans were accustomed to making boilers, stoves, cauldrons and weapons and must have had a fairly advanced knowledge of metallurgy to perform such precision work. On August 19, the first Canadian steamship was launched.

The *Accommodation*, as the ship was called, left Montréal for Québec on November 1 and arrived three days later. Euphoria reigned. An era full of promise for transportation had begun. "Neither winds nor tides can stop it," said the *Mercury*. "The great advantage of a boat built in this manner, is that one can calculate with certainty the time it takes and the hour of arrival, which is impossible in the case of a sailboat."

The *Accommodation* had a keel twenty-three metres long and its bridge was twenty-five metres long. There were some twenty bunks. There was an excursion on November 5, and the *Gazette de Québec* thought that the steam engine left something to be desired. "The wind was high and the tide unfavourable," reported the newspaper, "so that its course was slow. It is obvious in its present state the machinery is not strong enough for the river. It would be a loss for the public if the owners became discouraged and abandoned the undertaking." No one who knew John Molson would imagine

Another steamship belonging to John Molson, probably the *Malsham*.

that he would give in to defeatism. The steam era was not going to end before it even began, even if this "smoke boat," as some called the prototype, had a rather disastrous four-and-a-half-month season in 1810: expenses were £4,000 but revenues only £2,000.

Molson consulted Fulton. According to Fulton, a steamship that could take an average of fifty passengers and make a return trip every week between Montréal and Québec for a six-month season would generate gross revenues equal to twice the outlay. Satisfied, the entrepreneur left for England to procure a Bourton & Watt engine, for he had decided to build another steamship. In 1812, the *Swiftsure* began operations after the governor, Sir George Prevost, had broken the customary bottle over its bow. In May 1813 it made the distance between Montréal and Québec in less than twenty-four hours. The ship was forty metres long at its keel and 42.7 metres long at the bridge.

Molson sought a fifteen-year exclusive operating licence for steam navigation on the St. Lawrence, but other businessmen wanted to profit from his experience. Thus in 1819, the *Malsham*, the *Québec*, the *Car of Commerce*, the *Lady Sherbrooke*, the *Telegraph* and the *Caledonian* plied the waters between Montréal and Québec, in addition to the *Swiftsure*.

In an overview of the high points of Montréal's history, it is impossible to recount the history of every newspaper, or even every one that made headlines itself. Nevertheless, the founding of the Montreal *Herald* in 1811 by two Scots, William Gray and Mungo Kay, is worth noting. The paper changed its name three or four times and was published until 1957, after switching to a tabloid format in 1944. In 1910, the daily became a sensational news item in its own right when its premises were destroyed by fire: a reservoir on the roof caved in at the height of the fire, killing thirty-two people.

Salaberry Saves Montréal

————————— ❧ —————————

The big traders' importing business provided them with numerous contacts in the United States and Britain, and these commercial ties often yielded useful political information. Thus on June 24, 1812, the Montréal firm of Forsyth, Richardson & Co. informed Herman Witsius Ryland, secretary of the Executive Council of Lower Canada, that the United States had just declared war on Britain. The following day the governor general, George Prevost, sent a dispatch to that effect to the colonial secretary in London, Lord Liverpool.

The young republic was looking to swallow Canada in one bite. "The acquisition of Canada as far as the suburbs of Québec City, this year, will just take a single march," wrote former president Thomas Jefferson. The secretary of war, William Eustis, was no less optimistic. "We can take the two Canadas without soldiers," he said. "We only have to send some officers to the provinces and the people, disaffected from its government, will rally around our flag."

Of course, there was a great disparity in size between the two countries. The United States already had six million people (not counting slaves), while the Canadas had almost a half million. The republic had 6,500 men in arms, but Congress had decided to add 50,000 volunteers and 100,000 militiamen to that number. The two provinces would be defended by some 12,000 soldiers, half of whom belonged to the British regular army and the other half to six colonial battalions, including the Canadian Voltigeurs under the command of Charles-Michel d'Irumberry de Salaberry.

In 1812, the United States met with setbacks in the vicinity of Detroit and on Lake Champlain, but their naval victories over British ships stiffened

Congress's faltering resolve. Upper Canada was the more exposed of the two provinces, for the St. Lawrence, Lake Ontario, the Niagara River and Lake Erie formed a common area between Upper Canada and the enemy. By contrast, an area covered with forests and broken up by rivers separated the United States from Lower Canada. Furthermore, the border states of Maine and Vermont were very cool towards the war. Early in 1813, hostilities were launched against Upper Canada. In the fall, Congress decided to turn its attention to Lower Canada. The objective was the principal city: Montréal.

A 10,000-man army commanded by General James Wilkinson, headed downstream from the shores of Lake Ontario towards Lac Saint-Louis. There it was to meet up with a second army, consisting of 5,500 soldiers and militiamen led by General Wade Hampton, which left Lake Champlain at the same time and planned to reach the rendezvous point via Châteauguay. From there the generals thought they would crush Montréal.

Salaberry was given the job of closing off Hampton's route. Everywhere Hampton found the roads covered with trees. He took Odelltown, but when his soldiers ventured into the abatis of fallen branches and became entangled in it, companies of riflemen, militiamen and even native warriors were waiting for them. Hampton tried to evade these pitfalls. He evacuated Odelltown and decided to use the Châteauguay River to reach the St. Lawrence. This may have been a trap set for him by Salaberry; in any event, Salaberry chose his terrain well, just as Montcalm had at Carillon.

Salaberry had four rows of abatis erected to check the rush of the infantry. These were lines of defence that the enemy would have to take one after the other. Behind his positions there was a ford at which his assailants might be tempted to cross the river in the hope of taking them from behind. He had trenches dug. When Hampton's troops appeared on October 26, Salaberry was waiting for them at the head of his Voltigeurs and the 300-strong Fencibles battalion. Six hundred militiamen waited as a rearguard to be sent towards the most exposed point. Here and there in the woods, other soldiers held themselves at the ready to sound their trumpets at the right moment to make it appear that there were sizable forces.

Towards 10 o'clock, Salaberry gave the signal to fire by shooting a cavalry officer. The enemy mounted an assault on the abatis but failed to breach it. Piercing trumpet calls rang out from all over. Behind their sturdy rampart of tree trunks, the Canadians fired at Hampton's men for four hours. In vain the general tried to cross the ford: Salaberry had sent several companies of militiamen who crossed the river themselves and routed the enemy. In the midst of this confusion, Hampton decided to withdraw his troops who were pointlessly trying to breach the abatis. In the disorder of the retreat, the soldiers abandoned their drums, guns, knapsacks and supplies.

General Wilkinson, who had had a terrible experience of his own at Chrysler's Farm, received news of Hampton's defeat on November 12. He crossed the St. Lawrence and set up his troops in winter quarters at Malone, New York, while Hampton did the same at nearby Plattsburgh. The two Canadas had been saved. This time, Montréal had been spared enemy occupation. The Treaty of Ghent, signed on December 24, 1814, put an end to the war, but the news did not reach Washington until mid-February and took three more weeks to reach Montréal. In the middle of winter, communications were still difficult. Once again, it was said, the city's merchants were the first to hear the news.

The Good Old Days in the City

———————————— ✢ ————————————

Montréal's citadel has been all but forgotten, and compared to the imposing one in Québec City it was hardly worthy of the name. Nevertheless, there was once a citadel on a natural elevation that at the time blocked Notre-Dame Street to the east. When the engineer Chaussegros de Léry was rebuilding the fortifications, he decided to put the powder house and a battery of guns there, and from then on it was called Citadel Hill. It was only twenty metres high. This modest defence work had never been fired on when it was decided to dismantle it. Montrealers had become used to hearing the cannon firing morning and noon, faithfully marking the passage of time.

The city needed a drill ground for the garrison. The ground being used for that purpose was unsanitary, since the Saint-Martin rivulet (which flowed along present-day Saint-Antoine Street) ran along the north side, and people threw their garbage into it. The authorities decided to kill two birds with one stone: level Citadel Hill and move the dirt to the drill ground. The present-day Champ-de-Mars is the result. The work began in 1814 and the soldiers of the garrison were given an opportunity to put their muscles to work. But part of the elevation remained, and a reservoir was dug in it for the waterworks. In 1821, however, Governor General Lord

Dalhousie decided to level the rest of Citadel Hill. In this way, it became possible to extend Notre-Dame Street, fill in a swamp and make a public square that was named Dalhousie Square after the governor general.

In 1801, the Montreal Water Works Company had given the city its first network of pipes to bring water from the springs of Mount Royal. The company's franchise was later renewed. However, it was soon found that the quantity of water was insufficient, and in 1815 Montreal Water Works sold its installations to another business that planned to get water from the river using steam pumps and replace the wooden pipes with metal cast ones. Reservoirs holding a million litres were installed on the top floor of a building on Notre-Dame Street. The city council rented the ground floor for its meetings, but one day a reservoir broke and the mayor and councillors barely escaped drowning.

Until 1815, someone who wanted to go out at night had to carry a lantern because the streets were unlit. Montréal's first street lights may have been installed because of a break-and-enter. Robbers got into the Alexander Hart & Co. store through the cellar that year. They broke down the door of the accounting section and cracked the vault, taking off with £1,196 sterling. The Herald's reporter used the occasion to point out that it was high time for Montréal to light its streets and have them patrolled by guardians of the peace. Perhaps this was what prompted some enterprising citizens to install lamps on Saint-Paul Street. There were twenty-two lamps eighteen metres apart, and they burned a nauseating, smoky whale oil. Apparently the results were satisfactory, for similar equipment was installed on Notre-Dame Street the following year. Initially, the cost of this service was borne by private citizens, but the authorities agreed to assume responsibility for it in 1818.

A committee was asked to estimate the cost. The manufacture and installation of 100 lamps would cost £150 sterling, and the annual outlay would be £86 for the purchase of 375 gallons of oil and £36 for wages for two men to light and clean the lamps. Incidentally, the little cross in the upper portion of decorative lampposts used nowadays for gardens is a reminder of the past: lamplighters needed something to lean their ladders against! Gas lighting was not installed in Montréal until 1837.

We may owe the introduction of a police force in 1815 to the same robbers. The Herald, as we have seen, had called for guardians of the peace. There was still no municipal government; thus, it was the legislature that responded to the wishes of the townspeople. The police force numbered some thirty officers and was also responsible for lighting and extinguishing the street lamps. Armed with a blue stick and a lantern hooked to his belt, the policeman did his rounds carrying a bell to ask for help if the need arose.

How did Montréal appear to visitors back then? People used to the cleanliness and comfort we enjoy today would find it hard to believe that Montrealers could have been happy with their city in the early nineteenth century. For want of paving, most streets turned into mud puddles when it rained, and when it was sunny there were clouds of dust. There were no sidewalks and no drains to carry off dirty water. As for household garbage, most people just threw theirs into the sluggish waters of the Saint-Martin rivulet. Running water was available only downtown and, at that, only at street level. It was brought from the St. Lawrence where the ships had discharged whatever was left in their bilges. The vehicles in use were either carts for the transport of goods or open carriages, with double seats resting on leather traces. There were only two four-wheeled carriages, one belonging to the wealthy merchant John Forsyth and the other to Lady Bowes, the daughter of Sir John Johnson, the superintendent general for Indian affairs.

There was only one fire pump and it weighed so little that it took only one man to bring it to the foot of a burning building. Every head of family was supposed to bring two leather buckets to the fire at a run as soon as the bell of Notre-Dame sounded the alarm. Montrealers would line up in two rows between the river and the fire and pass the buckets from hand to hand down one row to the river and then pass them up the second row filled with water.

Animals ran loose in the streets. Any Montrealer capturing a runaway pig was supposed to report it to the town crier, who would make an announcement in front of the church the following Sunday. If no one claimed the pig it became the property of the holder, who was then at liberty to turn it into bacon. Ah, the good old days!

New Signs of Progress

——————————— ⇥⇤ ———————————

In 1813, as we have seen, Salaberry succeeded in blocking General Hampton's advance towards Châteauguay. This was a good thing because Montréal had no defence works worthy of the name. The city could not have withstood a siege with its few sections of wall still standing and its piti-ful citadel. The imperial authorities were concerned about this state of affairs. Any enemy coming from the south via St. Helen's Island would have occupied a very favourable position. London therefore decided to purchase that island in 1818.

It belonged at the time to the Baroness de Longueuil, the wife of David Alexander Grant, and was quite a charming piece of land. In his *Topographical Description of the Province of Lower Canada* (1815), Joseph Bouchette offered a vivid depiction. The island, he wrote, "being fairly elevated, offers a very advantageous view of the city; it is reserved as a domain, very fertile, extremely well cultivated and has beautiful stands of wood for building. The Baroness de Longueuil lives on the south side, in a lovely house surrounded by nice gardens and walks; on the other side are the enormous mills called Grant's Mills, which belong to the family; there are no other inhabitants on this superb little property." Historians estimate that there was only one mill on the island. During the French regime, it ground flour for export. It was probably because the baroness's husband substantially improved the mill that it was given his name.

The British government became the owner of the island at a cost of £15,000 sterling, which it raised from the sale of three properties located in Montréal and its suburbs. It built arsenals between 1820 and 1822 and then completed the works with barracks, powder magazines and storehouses. What is left of these buildings is used nowadays for recreational and cultural purposes. For example, the powder magazine in the centre of the island became a summer theatre known as La Poudrière, and the Macdonald-Stewart Museum was opened in the barracks near the Jacques-Cartier Bridge.

Although medicine was still in its infancy in the early nineteenth cen-tury, vaccination was introduced to Montréal in 1817. Everyone knows how the smallpox brought to America by the white settlers had continually ravaged the natives. But the French were not spared either. In 1757, for example, more than 2,000 of Montcalm's soldiers came down with small-pox, and a fifth of them died. André Doreil, a wartime ordnance officer, said at the time that if New France ever surrendered, smallpox would be as much the cause as the English. Inoculation was introduced in Canada towards 1764, and Col. Landman, an officer in the garrison at Québec City, used vaccine around 1802. As soon as the procedure had proved itself, civilians were invited to use it, but they were reluctant. As a result of campaigns to promote its use, Montréal had a vaccination institute in 1817.

The second headquarters of the Bank of Montreal on Saint-Jacques Street, across from Place d'Armes.

In 1792 commercial firms had unsuccessfully attempted to found a bank whose first task would be to print paper money. After the War of 1812-14, during which the ease of using army vouchers was appreciated, the idea resurfaced. The Legislative Assembly of Lower Canada considered draft legislation but without immediate results.

Private initiative won the day. On May 19, 1817, the city's merchants gave their final approval to articles of association to form the Bank of Montreal. The principles on which it was based were fairly close to the ones Alexander Hamilton, the first secretary of the treasury of the republic to the south, had incorporated in the charter of the Bank of the United States, founded in 1791. The nine founders could not immediately obtain incorporation and they called on capitalists from the United States, who put up almost half of the capital. When the charter was issued in 1822, however, 85 per cent of the shares were held by Canadians.

The Bank of Montreal, the first bank in Canada, opened its doors on November 3, 1817, in a building on Saint-Paul Street. It opened with a capital stock of $1 million, of which $150,000 had been paid up by that time. This institution made a noteworthy contribution to commerce. It gave the country its first sound currency in the form of bank notes redeemable in specie at any time.

At that time, exchange operations were not performed by telegraphic transfers or other means, and cash was moved by rudimentary vehicles that

Burnside, the estate of James McGill, graced the lower slopes of Mount Royal.

were quite unlike the armoured trucks of our time. In 1818, in the middle of winter, the Bank of Montreal wanted to deliver 130,000 Spanish dollars destined for the China trade to Boston. The three tons of metal coins were entrusted to a convoy that took a week to reach its destination over snowy New England roads. However, cash did not flow in one direction only: during the first eleven years of its operations, the Bank of Montreal imported more than $2 million in cash from the United States. Less than two years after it opened, the Bank of Montreal left the premises it had leased on Saint-Paul Street and set up its offices in a new building on Saint-Jacques Street across from Place d'Armes.

In 1801, the Lower Canada Assembly considered a bill that eventually led to the establishment of the Royal Institution for the Advancement of Learning. One of the Assembly's most prominent members at the time was James McGill, a prosperous merchant whom we have already referred to as one of the magnates of the fur trade. He was a partner in the North West Company, devoting his efforts to preventing American traders from siphoning off pelts from what is now western Canada, and the Russians from dominating trade along the Pacific coast. James McGill thus accumulated a handsome fortune. His eighteen-hectare property, Burnside, stretched up the slopes of Mount Royal. When McGill died on December 19, 1813, he left his vast property and £10,000 to endow a college bearing his name to be founded in the following ten years. McGill College received its charter on

March 21, 1821, but it did not open its doors until seventeen years later. Within five years it had three faculties – arts, medicine and law – and McGill University was born.

In the early nineteenth century Montréal had a population of 15,000 and had become by far the largest commercial centre in the country. Its port, however, was hardly worthy of the name because of its shoals, its backwashes, its small size and the narrowness of the channel leading to it. The strength of St. Mary's current often made it necessary for vessels to stop two or three kilometres below the docks to unload their cargoes. They frequently had to be towed by oxen. Sometimes even steamships had to dock in that manner.

In 1819 the Lachine Canal Company was founded to carry out the project suggested by its name. Unfortunately, it could not garner the necessary capital and lost its charter. Sensitive to the project's importance, the government of Lower Canada took it over two years later and appointed commissioners to supervise the works under the presidency of businessman J. Richardson. The Bank of Montreal advanced funds. The first shovelful of dirt was dug on July 19, 1821. The work took four years, approximately four hundred diggers were employed, and the total cost was £109,601 sterling (approximately $440,000). When it was completed, the canal measured some thirteen kilometres in length and had seven locks.

Probably because they were buoyed up by that achievement, Montréal's merchants turned once again to Lower Canada's parliament in the hope of having a channel dredged in the St. Lawrence, as boats of more than 250 tons could not reach the port. That project, however, had to wait another twenty years.

The First Cathedral

In 1820 it was decided that the time had come for Montréal and its region to become a diocese, and a Sulpician priest was chosen to head it. Jean-Jacques Lartigue was born in Montréal. Ordained a priest in 1800 by Bishop Pierre Denaut of Québec, whom he served as secretary, he entered the Sulpician order in 1806. When the seminary was facing the confiscation of its property in 1819, he went to England to argue the case for his fellow Sulpicians.

On his return to Montréal in 1820, Lartigue was considered for the see of Detroit, but instead was appointed suffragan and auxiliary to the bishop of Québec for the Montréal region. He became the first bishop of Montréal in 1836.

A cousin of Lartigue's, Denis-Benjamin Viger, offered a huge plot of land at the corner of Saint-Denis and Sainte-Catherine streets for the construction of the first cathedral. The project represented a major challenge, especially since the seminary began building the new Notre-Dame Church, with its enormous nave (still an object of admiration today) at the same time.

On May 22, 1823, the first stone of the cathedral was blessed. A gold sovereign bearing the likeness of George IV and a medal from that monarch's coronation donated by Jacques Viger, who would become the city's first mayor, were placed in it. Montréal's first cathedral, named Saint-Jacques-le-Majeur, was opened on September 22, 1825. If the contemporary historian and journalist Michel Bibaud is to be believed, it was a beautiful building. It could hold 3,000 worshippers, and it was fifty metres long and twenty-two wide. Its curved vault rested on Corinthian columns on a gallery that rested on another series of Ionic columns. Great crystal candelabra hung from the vault and two side altars were placed at each end of the transept.

The principal façade, decorated with pilasters, had no particularly noteworthy features. There was a proposal to give it towers that would have corresponded to the ends of the transept, top them with belfrys and spires, and join them above the steps on the front with a portico of Ionic columns. Unfortunately, the necessary funds had not even been gathered before the whole thing had to be rebuilt as a result of a fire.

Right at the corner of Saint-Denis and Sainte-Catherine, a small bishop's palace was built for Mgr. Lartigue, and he lived there until his death in 1840. Ignace Bourget succeeded him and thought it would be a good idea to build a large palace, in view of the increase in diocesan work. In keeping with the prevailing ultramontane philosophy, the new incumbent wanted a building in the baroque style evoking the Vatican, and he called on the eminent architect John Ostell, who designed so many of Montréal's buildings. Rectangular in shape and with a portico of Ionic columns, the palace might have appeared quite austere had it not been surmounted by a proud dome – one more reminiscent, however, of St. Paul's Cathedral in London than of St. Peter's basilica in Rome.

We are speaking in the past tense, because the cathedral and episcopal palace burned down in 1852, along with more than a thousand houses.

A portico with Ionic columns embellished the bishop's palace built for Mgr. Bourget.

Bishop Bourget may have been disappointed, but there was a consolation. In 1856 it was decided to build a new cathedral reminiscent of St. Peter's, the largest Christian church in the world, near the Windsor Hotel. We will come back to the fire and the new cathedral later. In the meantime, the *fabrique* (board of trustees) of Notre-Dame parish agreed to rebuild Saint-Jacques. The church would become a branch of the mother parish, since Saint-Denis, as the neighbourhood was called, had a large population. The new church had scarcely been finished when a second fire reduced the interior to ashes. Only the outer walls remained. Reconstruction was entrusted to the architect Victor Bourgeau in 1859. He clearly had the bishop's confidence, because two years later Bourget sent him to Rome to make a careful study of St. Peter's with a view to building a new cathedral in the near future.

The new Saint-Jacques church lasted for more than a century. In 1972, Archbishop Paul Grégoire of Montréal agreed to sell the land the church was on to the Université de Québec à Montréal. This decision relieved the administrators of a financial burden and made it possible to carry out a major university project. But the archbishop invited designers of future university buildings to retain architectural elements of the church and integrate them into the buildings as representative of the neighbourhood's heritage. In our time, the spire of Saint-Jacques dominates the university buildings. The main door on Saint-Denis Street and the great rose window on Sainte-Catherine Street recall this corner's history – meeting place of Montréal's aristocracy for many years and scene of student pranks when the presence of an earlier French-language university, the city's first, had made the area Montréal's "Latin Quarter."

Mens Sana in Corpore Sano

———————— ➤❮ ————————

Despite the city's growth, Montréal's inhabitants, who now numbered 20,000, had no hospitals other than the Hôtel-Dieu, with thirty beds, and the Hôpital Général. In January 1819, Lower Canada's Legislative Assembly was asked to build a new hospital, but the proposal was not taken up. An appeal was launched among the townspeople.

The French population had had charitable organizations for a long time, and the English, whose numbers had increased substantially, understood the need for such organizations as well. Immigration had stopped during the war of 1812-14, but it started up with renewed vigour after the conflict. Every summer brought a new wave of impoverished peasants from England, Scotland and Ireland, in poor physical shape after an exhausting voyage and lacking resources for the coming winter. Accordingly, the Female Benevolent Society was founded in 1816. It soon rented a small four-bedroom house to house the sick. In its third year, the society welcomed thirty-seven patients. At that point it sought government support, hoping to build a new 200-bed hospital. Its request was turned down, but in the same year, 1819, donations from the public and wealthy business people made it possible for the society to set up its embryonic institution in a building on Craig Street (now Saint-Antoine Street) that could hold twenty-four beds. The society called the building the Montreal General Hospital.

But the society still wanted to build its planned hospital and tapped even greater resources of generosity to do it. On June 6, 1821, the cornerstone of the new building was laid on Dorchester Street. It opened on May 1, 1822, and could house eighty patients. The cost of construction was £5,856 sterling. Montrealers donated £2,167 while the rest was a debt assumed

The first stone of the Montreal General Hospital was laid in 1821. This engraving dates from 1831.

personally by John Richardson in 1823. This philanthropist had been appointed president of the commissioners responsible for digging the Lachine Canal in 1821.

The founding of the Montreal General Hospital also marked an important step in the teaching of medicine. The first four members of the institution's medical staff wanted a school where clinical work with patients would be part of the students' training, as was done in Edinburgh. Among these physicians was Dr. Andrew Fernando Holmes, who would thus become the founder of the first school of medicine in Canada (1823), and later the first dean of the Faculty of Medicine at McGill University. He had done his apprenticeship with the famous Dr. Daniel Arnoldi, who had a profound influence on the practice of medicine and in 1841 became the first president of the province's College of Physicians.

In 1825 John Molson, by now a brewery owner, director of a steamship company, and one of the barons of Montréal's business world, entered another field of endeavour: hotels. He built the Mansion House Hotel on Saint-Paul Street, which became a meeting place for the elegant and affluent. The Beaver Club held its meetings in the Mansion House. Molson soon decided to add a theatre to his hotel. Plays had long been staged in Montréal, of course, but in makeshift theatres. The soldiers of the British garrison loved theatrical events. The French-speaking population was just as interested and had enjoyed the offerings of theatrical troupes made up of local talent. Around 1789, for example, the Théâtre de la Société presented works by the playwright and composer Joseph Quesnel – notably his operetta *Colas et Colinette*, which it staged in 1790.

The Théâtre Royal that Molson built at a cost of £7,500 was the first building in Montréal specifically designed for the presentation of dramatic works. It was a product of Montrealers' enthusiasm for the dramatic arts; the initial capital was raised by subscription to the tune of 200 shares at £25 apiece. Molson held forty-four shares. The building, which was located where the east wing of the Bonsecours Market now stands, was ornamented by a main entrance in the Doric mode and measured approximately twenty metres by thirty, not counting backstage and wings. It opened on December 21, 1825, and the next summer the great English tragedian, Edmund Kean, played the leading roles in *Richard II*, *The Merchant of Venice*, *Othello* and *King Lear*. Kean's interpretations of the great Shakespearean characters made him the most famous English actor of the Romantic era. It was a theatrical feast for Montréal.

Another noteworthy event of 1826 was the birth of a new newspaper, *La Minerve*, in a sense the successor to Québec City's *Le Canadien*, founded twenty years earlier by Pierre Bédard and François Blanchet to uphold the political ideology of the French-speaking professional classes against the propaganda of the Quebec *Mercury*. At that time freedom of the press was still only a dream, and the government's authority was not flouted with impunity. In mid-March 1810, the Executive Council seized *Le Canadien*'s presses and type and had the two founders and one of their editors, Jean-Thomas Taschereau, arrested. This did not prevent Taschereau from being elected to the Assembly as a representative for Dorchester two years later.

Le Canadien reappeared in 1817 and was published sporadically for the next eight years. After suspending publication in 1819, it resumed the good fight in 1820, only to suspend publication again in 1825 because of financial difficulties. A final attempt at publication lasted only a few weeks.

La Minerve owed its existence to the initiative of a twenty-three-year-old law student, Augustin-Norbert Morin, who would play an important political role in the Union period. In its very first issue, the newspaper announced its position, declaring itself "ardent in supporting the interests of the *Canadiens*." It promised to "teach them to resist any usurpation of their rights as we try to teach them to appreciate and cherish the good deeds and the government of our mother country."

After undergoing a difficult period of several months and suspending publication, *La Minerve* reappeared in February 1827 with Morin as political director and Ludger Duvernay as owner. Duvernay was imprisoned for libel three times in the next ten years. The paper was banned in November 1837, but it resurfaced later thanks to the financial support of Denis-Benjamin Viger and bookstore owner Édouard-Raymond Fabre. *La Minerve* continued to appear until 1899. Its issues constitute an excellent source of documentation for anyone wishing to take the pulse of Montréal's life in the nineteenth century.

Montréal continued to grow. While the city proper huddled in a rectangle bounded by present-day Bonsecours, Saint-Jacques and McGill streets and the river, it was extended by outlying neighbourhoods or *faubourgs*. The neighbourhood to the east, near the Molson Brewery, was called Faubourg Québec because the road to Québec City passed through it and high society lived there; to the north and east were farmers who brought their goods to market along Papineau Road. Faubourg Saint-Laurent began at Saint-Martin rivulet, which flowed where Craig Street would later run and extended north to present-day Ontario Street. This was the most densely populated of the faubourgs. Faubourg Saint-Antoine was to the west of McGill Street and its buildings stretched all the way to Rue de la Montagne. Faubourg Sainte-Anne lay to the southwest and was crossed by Lachine Road.

For a long time, some Montrealers claimed that Rue de la Montagne should be called *Mountain,* arguing that its name came from the Anglican bishop Jehoshaphat Mountain. In fact, the *chemin de la Montagne* leading to Mount Royal was already in existence a century earlier, which should settle the matter. The name "Mountain Street" probably originated with a directory of the city's merchants, traders and landlords, published by a Montrealer named Doige who in his "respect" for place names translated everything. One example among many: under his pen, Rue des Enfants-Trouvés became "Foundling Street."

The rapid growth of Montréal's population, which reached 25,000 in 1820, put a strain on the parish church. The first Notre-Dame church took a century to build and was not finished until 1782 because over the years it had been necessary to enlarge it repeatedly. Thus the nave was lengthened and the side aisles and rood loft were added. Even so, in the second half of the eighteenth century many worshippers were forced to hear mass on the front steps or even out in the street.

In 1789 the bishop of Québec had presented the case for a new church to

This engraving by the water colourist Robert Sproule, which dates from 1830, shows us the first parish church in front of the new church, whose towers do not yet dominate the façade.

the churchwardens, who argued in vain for using the Bonsecours Chapel as the basis of a second parish. In 1822 a committee formed to study the situation came out in favour of building a new church. This was a highly sensitive decision in several respects, especially in light of the need to build a cathedral for Mgr. Lartigue, who had become the auxiliary bishop of Québec for the district of Montréal the year before.

The new church would be erected across from Place d'Armes, adjacent to the seminary, which would serve as a residence, and near the old church, which would be demolished, making it possible to extend Notre-Dame Street to the west. The cost was estimated at £30,000; it was hoped to obtain a third of this amount by popular subscription, with the balance to be a debt to be paid from parish revenues. The committee also had to choose an architect. There was no lack of architects at the time, especially in France, but most relied on Greek and Roman monuments for their inspiration. In the end, the committee hired James O'Donnell, an Irish Protestant who had studied with the best European masters, had practised in New York for twelve years, and was known for his great professional integrity. He later became a Catholic and when he died in Montréal in 1830 his remains were interred under the church.

The epitaph of the architect James O'Donnell, inscribed on a masonry pillar under Notre-Dame Basilica, reads: "Here lies James O'Donnell, Esq., Architect, Born in Ireland and died in this City on January 28, 1830, at the age of 56. For five years he worked on this church, for which he drew up the plan and directed the construction with zeal and intelligence. Then he embraced the Catholic faith and wanted his ashes to rest in this place. His unselfishness, talent and integrity won him the esteem of this parish. And the Churchwardens have devoted this Monument to his Memory. May he rest in peace."

On September 1, 1823, the cornerstone was laid in the presence of a brass band and the soldiers of the garrison. By 1824 the foundations were in place, and the following year the walls of the immense nave had reached a height of six and a half metres. They were built of cut stones from the quarries of the Tanneries, as the Saint-Henri neighbourhood was then called. This was a colossal undertaking for the time and there would be numerous problems, notably in obtaining materials. Thus, the beams and timbers

The new Notre-Dame church before the towers were built. Of the old church, only the steeple is still standing. (Drawing by W.H. Bartlett, 1839.)

required for the work were brought to Montréal in huge rafts. In 1826, customs officials in Coteau-du-Lac seized a large number of these rafts as a result of a dispute among suppliers.

There was talk that year of suspending the work for lack of money, but it was a false alarm, and the walls were built to the height of the cornice. By 1827 consideration could be given to installing the framework for the roof and the cover, and in 1828 the façade was built to the height of the parapet. The church was finally open for mass. Its two towers, however, scarcely rose above the crenellated parapet, and would not be finished for another twelve years.

Times of Change

————————— ✣ —————————

The year 1832 marked the beginning of a period of great change. It was in 1832 that Montréal was granted its first charter. Submitted to London for approval the previous year, the charter received royal assent on April 12 and

Jacques Viger, the first mayor of Montréal. (Watercolour miniature attributed to James Duncan.)

was proclaimed by the governor general on June 5. It divided the city of Montréal into eight wards: Montréal East, Montréal West, Sainte-Anne, Saint-Joseph, Saint-Antoine, Saint-Laurent, Saint-Louis and Sainte-Marie. Each ward was to elect two councillors, for a total of sixteen, and seven councillors were needed for a quorum.

All powers that had been exercised up to that time by magistrates –

administration of city streets, markets, lighting, policing, sanitation, public works, and the like – were transferred to the council, which was also given the authority to raise taxes for these purposes. An election was to be held each year on the first Monday in June, with half the council seats at stake. All male citizens twenty-one years of age and older who were property owners and had been residents of the city for the previous twelve months were eligible to vote. Each year, the council would chose a new mayor from among its ranks.

On June 5 of the following year, the council held its first meeting and elected Montréal's first mayor, Jacques Viger, an industrious and learned man. Viger had helped to defend the borders of Upper and Lower Canada during the War of 1812-14, and in 1829 had been given the rank of lieuten-ant-colonel and command of the Sixth Battalion of the County of Montreal militia. Along with Louis Guy, Viger had completed a census of Montréal Island in 1825. A model civil servant, he was appointed commissioner of public works seven times and returning officer eight times.

It is not surprising then that the council appointed Viger as mayor in 1833 and again in 1834 and 1835. In spite of his public duties Viger, called the *bénédictin du Canada*, still found time to devote to research, and at his death he left a rich archival legacy: the *Saberdache* composed of twenty-eight volumes *in-quarto* and a collection *in-octavo*.

Interestingly, Montréal's articles of incorporation lapsed after three years and were only reinstated after the 1837-38 rebellions, but more of this later.

In May 1832, the first election riot in Montréal's history broke out. The previous month, a by-election had been called in Montréal's west ward when one of its seats in the Legislative Assembly had become vacant. Two candidates came forward: Stanley Bagg, a prominent Protestant business-man of American origin, and Daniel Tracey, the Irish Catholic editor of the *Vindicator*, the paper of the French-speaking majority in the Legislative Assembly. Tracey and Ludger Duvernay, the editor of *La Minerve*, had been jailed on charges of libelling members of the Legislative Council. On their release, they were led through the streets of Montréal on a triumphal tour and even presented with gold medals bearing a commemorative inscrip-tion.

At this time, each electoral ward had only one or two polls, which remained open until an hour had elapsed since the last ballot was cast. Fight-ing broke out almost immediately, as both sides tried to rally voters to their cause and make sure that the one-hour limit did not take effect. Tracey led by a narrow margin until, on the fourteenth day, he and Bagg were tied with

633 votes. On the eighteenth day, Tracey and Bagg were again tied, with 658 votes each. Tensions ran very high and the two candidates' supporters had resorted to using their fists and sticks. It was said that Jos Monferrand – the mighty Jos Monferrand whose heel had left a mark on the ceiling of a tavern in the Gatineau – had thrown his weight behind Tracey.

Tracey's supporters pushed Bagg's men towards the Place d'Armes, where the fighting degenerated into an all-out brawl. When police constables were unable to regain control of the crowd, the magistrates called in the troops. A magistrate read the Riot Act and, as stones rained down on the soldiers, they opened fire. Three men, Billet, Languedoc and Chauvin, were killed. Chauvin, a printer from *La Minerve*, had been a staunch supporter of the Patriote cause. Louis-Joseph Papineau attended the funeral and every session of the inquiry set up to establish the circumstances in which the army had opened fire. Criminal charges were laid against two officers, Colonel Macintosh and Captain Temple, but the grand jury withdrew the case. The turmoil surrounding the election did not subside.

On May 22, it was officially announced that Daniel Tracey had won the by-election by a margin of four votes. Tracey's success, however, was short-lived. Before he could take his seat in the Legislative Assembly, he died of cholera. Having decimated Europe, the contagion was now spreading through Québec, claiming many lives. The sailing vessel *Carrick's*, which had left Dublin with 192 passengers, stopped at Grosse Île on June 8. Fifty-nine passengers had died during the crossing. The survivors were transferred to *Le Voyageur*, and at least two more had died by the time the little vessel reached Montréal.

The epidemic spread like wildfire. Between mid-June and late September, 1,904 people died. On June 19 alone, 149 burials were recorded. It is estimated that the epidemic claimed 4,500 lives. Almost every household was affected. The clergy were overwhelmed, and in many cases church services were dispensed with and the victims transported directly to the cemetery. There were even instances of victims, catatonic from doses of opium, being buried alive. The cholera epidemic took its toll on the Montréal's social and economic life as well. The diary of an immigrant who arrived in the city that year provides a vivid description of daily life. She wrote of church bells tolling incessantly, funeral parlour windows displaying mass-produced coffins and, everywhere, advertisements for funeral services provided "on short notice, at the lowest prices."

The devotion of the city's clergy was matched by that of its physicians. For one, the epidemic provided a unique business opportunity. Dr. Stephen

Ayers offered for sale a "miraculous" ointment made of lard, maple sugar and maple wood ash. The ointment was rubbed into the skin of the invalid who perspired copiously, fell into a deep sleep and awoke completely cured – or so Ayers claimed. When the epidemic spread to Kahnawake, the Iroquois believed that Dr. Ayers' ointment saved a hundred lives. To express their gratitude, they took the place of Dr. Ayers' ox and pulled his cart back to Montréal themselves. Rumours circulated about the physician's powers. Some thought that he was St. Anthony returned to earth; others thought that he was a quack. In any event, when he asked the Legislative Assembly to recognize his public service officially, he was rebuffed. Shortly thereafter, he disappeared without a trace.

To find homes for children orphaned by the epidemic, the women of Montréal established the Dames de l'Asile des Orphelins Catholiques Romains (Ladies of the Asylum for Roman Catholic Orphans). The orphanage was lodged in the former Récollet monastery, where the women were already providing refuge for destitute elderly women. The children became known as the Récollet Orphans.

The epidemic ended as quickly as it had broken out, and in September the sighting of a whale in the harbour provided a welcome diversion. Fourteen metres long and two metres in diameter, the whale had been unable to find its way back to the ocean and was trapped. A week later, a tugboat operator harpooned it and dragged it onto the shore. An enterprising citizen put the carcass on display in a hangar at the foot of the Sainte-Marie current.

(After the dredging of the river channel, whales were sighted in Montréal harbour in 1901 and again in 1979. The 1901 sighting was a great curiosity. Louis Payette, manager of the Grand Central Theatre on Commissioners Street, harpooned a whale and sold it to George Kennedy, a hockey promoter, for $1,000. Kennedy displayed the carcass in a tent in Longueuil. Apparently, a Montréal taxidermist stuffed the whale and put it on display. It was later shipped by rail to Québec City. In 1979, a small whale measuring eight metres was sighted. Its throat had been slit, no doubt by the propeller of a passing ship.)

By 1832, Montréal had a population of 30,000. The city was faced with an inadequate supply of drinking water, and a syndicate was formed to refurbish the aqueduct with the addition of a pump driven by a forty-horsepower steam engine to fill two reservoirs with a capacity of more than a million litres. The man responsible for this improvement was businessman Moses Judah Hayes, who later built a hotel and a theatre which he named

Montreal Water Works, 1839.

after himself. Hayes was the chief of police from 1845 until his death in 1861.

Even though the reservoirs, which were only nine metres above Notre-Dame Street, produced very weak pressure and water carriers were still needed, they were a source of great pride. "With the exception of Philadelphia, Montréal has the best water supply of any city on the continent," wrote Newton Bosworth in *Hochelaga Depicta* in 1839. Responsibility for the city's drinking water supply was not transferred to municipal authorities until 1845.

The founding of Canada's first medical school was mentioned in relation to the construction of Montreal General Hospital. However, the school did not have university status and anyone who wanted to practise medicine had to leave the country to study. In 1831, the hospital's faculty wrote to Lord Aylmer, governor general of Upper and Lower Canada, requesting that McGill College be authorized to grant diplomas to students on satisfactory completion of a program of study and examination. Medical students, they wrote, were forced to study in Europe, which was often prohibitively expensive, or in the United States, "where they are exposed to ideals that run counter to our government and our institutions." Their letter touched a nerve. In 1832 the statutes, bylaws and ordinances of the Faculty of Medicine of McGill University received royal assent, and the first degree was granted to W. Logie on May 24, 1833.

The *Royal William* under construction, Cap-aux-Diamants, Québec City. (Painting by J.D. Kelly, Confederation Life Collection.)

That same year, ships in the shipyards of Montréal and Québec City were dressed from bow to stern to celebrate the launching of a ship that was to become the first to cross the Atlantic under steam power. The *Royal William*, whose keel had been laid in 1830 at Anse aux Foulons, just below Cap aux Diamants, was a three-masted, square-rigged schooner equipped with 200-horsepower steam engines built by Bennett & Henderson of Montréal. Her hull, fifty-eight metres in length and 14.5 metres on the beam, was of 1,370 tons burden. On August 5, 1833, the *Royal William* began a voyage famous in marine history. She encountered severe storms, but her captain, John McDougall, managed to maintain control and keep the engines running.

The *Royal William* became famous on a number of other counts as well. She was the first steam vessel to enter an American port flying the British colours. She became Portugal's first steam-powered cargo vessel and, later, Spain's first steam vessel and the first to fire a cannon under steam. On May 5, 1836, now renamed the *Isabella Secunda* and wearing the colours of Commodore Henry, she fired her cannon in the Bay of San Sebastian while under way. In 1891, when testimony about the *Royal William* was being collected, James Goudie, who had laid her keel, and a man by the name of Henry, who had made the moulds for her engine, were among those who provided sworn statements.

Mention has already been made of Ludger Duvernay, under whose leadership *La Minerve* became one of the most influential papers in Lower Canada. From his printing shop at the corner of Saint-Paul and Saint-Gabriel, Duvernay provided printing services to businessmen and professionals. *La Minerve* became the paper of those members of Parliament who denounced the oligarchy and called for reform. These people became known as *Patriotes*. Duvernay and his fellow reform journalist Daniel Tracey had been jailed in 1832 on charges of libelling members of the Legislative Council. On his release, Duvernay was given a medal on which was inscribed, "La liberté de la presse est le palladium du peuple" (Freedom of the press is the palladium of the people).

Not surprisingly, Duvernay wanted to create a national holiday for French Canadians that would appeal to their sense of patriotism and lend credence to their demands. On June 24, 1834, he organized a large garden party at the home of lawyer John Bélestre-MacDonell, which stood at the present site of Windsor Station. This was the beginning of the Société Saint-Jean-Baptiste. (The previous March 17, the Irish had founded their own group, the St. Patrick's Society.)

Mayor Jacques Viger presided over the banquet, attended by sixty or so people, including Georges-Étienne Cartier and others who would later play key roles in the rebellion. The political sympathies of the guests were expressed in toasts drunk to Louis-Joseph Papineau, leader of the Patriotes, Daniel O'Connell, the Irish reformer, and Elzéar Bédard, who had presented his ninety-two resolutions the previous February. The guests also raised their cups to the government of the United States, the liberal members of the clergy and the reformers of Upper Canada. The national society of French Canadians had been born. The Patriotes met again over the course of the next three years, but during the 1837-38 rebellion, annual meetings were suspended.

As we have seen, the first Anglican priests arrived in Québec City and Montréal with the British army after the Conquest. By 1836, Montréal's

Rasco's Hotel, Montréal's first large hotel, opened on Saint-Paul Street in 1837.

Anglican community had grown sufficiently large to warrant the appointment of a bishop. Jacob Mountain, the first bishop of Québec City, was appointed before the end of the eighteenth century, and the cathedral in Upper Town was built under his leadership. When Mountain died in 1825, he left a son, George Jehoshaphat Mountain. On February 14, 1836, Mountain's successor, Bishop Charles James Stewart, named George Jehoshaphat Mountain his coadjutor and the first bishop of Montréal.

Shortly thereafter, Jehoshaphat Mountain succeeded Stewart as bishop of the diocese of Québec City. In 1850, Montréal became a diocese in its own right, and Francis Fulford became its bishop. Christ Church was elevated to the rank of a cathedral, only to be destroyed by fire in 1856. It was decided that a new cathedral should be built on Sainte-Catherine Street, where it still stands. We will come back to the cathedral later.

Montréal's most popular innkeeper at the time was a man named François Rasco. Originally from Lombardy, Rasco began as a merchant, selling groceries and sweets. Later he became an innkeeper, then managed the Masonic Hall, a small hotel that was expanded to include a dance hall and renamed the British American Hotel. The hotel, which enjoyed an excellent reputation, belonged to John Molson. When the hotel burned down and Rasco found himself out of a job, he decided to build his own hotel. On May 1, 1836, Rasco's Hotel opened on Saint-Paul Street. It could accommodate eighty people and had several large rooms including a concert hall, a conservatory and a restaurant. Although Rasco's Hotel was

DONEGANA'S HOTEL, MONTREAL, DESTROYED BY FIRE ON AUGUST 16.

Donegana's Hotel, at the corner of Bonsecours and Notre-Dame streets, was said to rival the hotels of New York and Boston.

ravaged by a fire in 1977, the façade was saved and restored and is now part of the heritage of Old Montréal.

One of the factors that made Montréal an excellent commercial and industrial centre was its location, due north of New York City. However, it was only by water that goods could be transported between Montréal and New York, and boats travelling north from New York up the Richelieu River were unable to navigate the rapids at Chambly – it was not until 1843 that a canal was built. Goods from Montréal on their way to New York City had to be taken by ferry to the south shore, then moved across land to the landing station at Chambly. The idea of building a "portage" railway to connect the St. Lawrence River to Lake Champlain was proposed as early as 1824, although it was only six years later that the proposal was taken seriously by promoters. At that time, there were only three railways in North America: the Granite Road in Massachusetts, the Carbondale & Honesdale in Pennsylvania and the Baltimore & Ohio in Maryland.

Plans for horse-drawn carriages on rails were quickly replaced by plans for steam engines. One newspaper advocated raising the tracks to overcome the problem of drifting snow; it suggested laying the tracks in such a way as to take full advantage of the prevailing winds, enabling the trains to reach speeds of sixteen to twenty-six kilometres per hour. Some members of the

Canada's first railway, from Laprairie to Saint-Jean, was a "portage" line. (Painting by J.D. Kelly, Confederation Life Collection.)

Legislative Assembly felt that the government should take the project in hand. Louis-Joseph Papineau was in favour of a privately-funded railway, and it was this plan that prevailed.

Seventy-two businessmen contributed a total of £50,000 sterling, mortgaging their personal property to purchase a locomotive. On July 21, 1836, the railway linking Laprairie and Saint-Jean, a distance of 23.33 kilometres, was officially opened. The wooden tracks were sheathed in iron. The *Dorchester*, pulling cars carrying a precious cargo of passengers, left the platform in Laprairie at 12:30 and arrived in Saint-Jean at 1:29 p.m. Canada's first railway was now in operation.

The Eye of the Storm

The 1837-38 rebellion began in Montréal. For a number of years, tension in Upper and Lower Canada had been mounting. When Lord John Russell in London authorized the governor general, Lord Gosford, to use £150,000 sterling from the provincial treasury to meet the government's administrative expenses, the Legislative Assembly refused to give its approval.

There were vehement protests on both sides of the Atlantic. In the House of Commons in London, Sir William Molesworth stated that English colonial policy with regard to the people of Canada had, for many years, been extremely unjust and oppressive, subjecting the nation to the despotic rule of irresponsible councillors, incompetent governors, drunken magistrates and a horde of speculators and petty tyrants. Fox stated that when freedom was trampled underfoot in one country, the cause of humanity suffered everywhere, and that every movement of the Canadian people would be echoed among the people of Britain.

Although the French Canadian population of Lower Canada numbered half a million, compared to an English Canadian population of only 75,000, French Canadians made up a very small minority in the judiciary and the legislature. Of the thirty judges appointed between 1800 and 1830, only eleven were French Canadians. In 1835, only fifty-four of the 126 members of the civil service were French Canadians. French Canadians were also paid less. Civil servants of British origin received 58,000 livres, compared to 28,000 livres for their French-speaking counterparts; for judges, the figures were 13,500 livres and 8,000 livres respectively.

There were many other reasons for the mounting discontent. On May 7, 1837, a thousand people attended a protest meeting in Saint-Ours at which Wolfred Nelson was the main speaker. A number of resolutions were enthusiastically passed, including one that denounced Lord Russell's actions. Another resolution attacked the government and deemed it unworthy of the people's respect or even obedience because it had used force to curtail their rights. Yet another called on the people of Lower Canada to boycott imported goods and to purchase only those made locally. Nelson declared that just as Ireland had rallied around O'Connell, Lower Canada had to rally around a political leader, someone who "was blessed with incomparable intelligence and eloquence, a hatred of oppression and an unshakeable love of his country that neither promises nor threats could diminish." His audience quickly understood whom Nelson was referring to: Louis-Joseph Papineau.

Gosford was indignant. In mid-June, he issued a proclamation exhorting the public not to attend "seditious" meetings. Instead of having a calming effect, his proclamation stirred up antigovernment sentiments. In this heavily charged atmosphere, two new groups, the Fils de la Liberté (Sons of Liberty) and the Doric Club, were founded in Montréal.

The founding of the Fils de la Liberté took place at the Nelson Hotel on Place Jacques-Cartier on September 5, 1837, within sight of the monument to the famous English admiral. Its members included young men who burned with a desire "to show their support for the national cause." Laurent-Olivier David summed up the spirit of the group when he wrote that the Fils de la Liberté, which was both a civilian and a military organization, had chosen as its motto: *En avant!* (Forward march!) Most of its members dressed in simple, homespun clothes, in keeping with one of the resolutions passed at the protest meeting at Saint-Ours. The Doric Club was said to be a secret society. Its members had but one objective: to defend the British constitution and honour.

On October 23, a meeting was called in Saint-Charles. It was referred to as the meeting of the six counties because it brought together citizens from the rural districts of Richelieu, Saint-Hyacinthe, Rouville, Chambly, Verchères and L'Acadie. More than 5,000 people gathered to hear their idol, Louis-Joseph Papineau, speak. Their response was overwhelming.

The leaders of the Patriote movement were in attendance. "All those who would later prove their love for their country and freedom on the battlefields and in the prisons and on the scaffolds were there," wrote David. A company of militiamen stood around a column erected to honour the leader of the Patriotes, lending a military tone to the assembly presided over by Dr. Wolfred Nelson. Nelson denounced Lord Russell and Lord Gosford and called on the people to meet violence with violence. Papineau, whose eloquence was deeply moving, was more cautious than usual. While he denounced the attitude of those in power, he believed that the solution lay in constitutional reform. Nelson had other plans. "I beg to differ with you," he cried. "The time has come for us to melt our spoons into bullets." This was to be the largest public meeting before the rebellion broke out. Alarmed, the authorities decided to issue warrants for the arrest of all of the Patriote leaders in the Montréal area.

The Fils de la Liberté planned to hold a public protest on Saint-Jacques Street on November 6. The Doric Club posted an announcement that club members and sympathizers would also meet on November 6 in Place d'Armes to nip the rebellion in the bud.

On Saint-Jacques Street, there were a number of speeches, including one in which the Fils de la Liberté were told that they would soon be the Fils de la Victoire – the Sons of Victory. Shortly thereafter, the meeting broke up. Two or three hundred people were still gathered when they were attacked with stones. The Dorics had thrown down the gauntlet. Those in front, wielding sticks, headed for Place d'Armes, pushing any protesters out of their way. Then, mercifully, the crowd dispersed, for the army and militia – no doubt alerted by the Dorics, who wanted their adversaries to be held responsible for the incident – had arrived on the scene to quell the "riot." When this plan went sour, the Dorics vented their frustration by breaking the windows of Papineau's house and destroying the presses of the *Vindicator*, which had courageously taken up the Patriote cause.

In issuing warrants for the arrest of the Patriotes, Gosford committed a strategic blunder. The Patriotes were now galvanized into action; they wanted to protect their leaders and were prepared to take up arms to do so. Even Joseph-Vincent Quiblier, the superior of the Sulpicians and a man who had little sympathy for the Patriote cause, wrote in his memoirs that two magistrates had asked the king's attorney for permission to arrest Papineau, one promising to carve out his heart with a knife and the other promising to burn his brain.

The first instance of the use of arms in the Patriote cause was a protest over two arrest warrants. Rewards had been offered for the capture of Dr. Joseph-François Davignon and Pierre-Paul Desmarais. On the night of November 16, soldiers arrived in Saint-Jean, pulled the two men from their beds, handcuffed them and departed for Montréal. News of their arrest

spread quickly throughout the region, and Bonaventure Viger, a close rela-
tive of Montréal's first mayor, Jacques Viger, quickly called a meeting of the
men of Boucherville, Longueuil and Chambly to prepare an ambush. As
the military convoy approached, shots rang out. The soldiers were caught
completely off guard and handed over their prisoners. The Patriotes took
them to a blacksmith who removed their irons. These can still be seen at the
Château de Ramezay museum.

There followed bloody confrontations in Saint-Denis and Saint-Charles
on the banks of the Richelieu and in Saint-Eustache in Deux-Montagnes
County.

On November 22, Colonel Sir Charles Gore, an old soldier who had
been decorated for his actions at Waterloo, left Montréal for Sorel aboard
the steamer St. George with five companies. That evening, he left Sorel with
a detachment of Royal Artillery and a twelve-pounder howitzer. Gore's
instructions were to take Saint-Charles and to join up with the companies
that had left Chambly under the command of a young lieutenant by the
name of Wetherall, and his mission was to arrest the Patriotes. He was
accompanied by a magistrate with warrants in hand.

Louis-Joseph Papineau and Dr. Edmund Bailey O'Callaghan, the fiery
journalist who had taken Tracey's place at the Vindicator, took refuge in
Saint-Denis with Dr. Timothée Kimber. In Saint-Denis, Gore's men were
met by the Patriotes. Gore had not counted on the determination of the
Patriotes, who under the command of Wolfred Nelson repelled the attack.
Twelve Patriotes lost their lives and eight more were wounded. It was
estimated that thirty redcoats were killed and thirty more wounded.

The seigneur of Saint-Charles, Pierre-Dominique Debartzch, had been
sympathetic to the Patriote cause; however, that year he had become a
member of the Executive Council, a move that cost him the trust of many
Patriotes. They convinced him to abandon his manor and take refuge in
Montréal, then took up their places around the manor house to await the
arrival of Wetherall's men. This proved to be a fatal mistake, for the house
offered little protection and no cover in the event of a retreat. Although
Colonel Wetherall had 400 well-armed men, the fighting lasted two hours.
Wetherall gave the Patriotes time to surrender before launching an assault,
but the 200 Patriotes, armed with old hunting rifles, scythes and two rusty
cannons, stood their ground, perhaps emboldened by the success of the
ambush at Saint-Denis. After shelling the Patriote positions, Wetherall
ordered his men to charge with their bayonets. The battle was over. Among

the Patriotes, there were forty dead, thirty wounded and another thirty taken prisoner.

Patriotes to the north of Montréal, in Deux-Montagnes County, were also preparing for a military expedition. On December 14, lookouts posted south of the Rivière des Mille-Îles rushed back to Saint-Eustache with the news that they had seen a detachment, with bayonets flashing in the morning sun, advancing towards the village. The detachment consisted of eighty men who had volunteered to join the two thousand troops under Colborne, with nine guns, 120 horses, and carts loaded with arms and munitions.

As the tocsin sounded in Saint Eustache, the Patriotes placed themselves under the command of Dr. Jean-Olivier Chénier. With only 250 men and not enough arms to go around, Chénier told those who did not have arms, "There will be wounded, take their arms!" Old Firebrand, as Colborne was known, quickly entered the village and pointed his guns at the church, the presbytery and the convent. The soldiers succeeded in gaining entry to the church and set fire to the altar. The flames quickly spread to the ceiling. Chénier and his men took refuge in the cemetery. By four in the afternoon, seventy Patriotes had lost their lives and seventy more had managed to flee. Roughly a hundred, now in chains, thought seriously about the price of freedom.

On December 5, Gosford had proclaimed martial law in Montréal, authorizing Colborne to arrest and put to death or otherwise punish anyone who took part in or supported the insurrection. Scores of men were arrested and put behind bars each day. Efforts were stepped up to finish the new prison, located on Route de la Longue-Pointe, which became known as Pied-du-Courant Prison. Soon all the cells were filled and the old prison on Notre-Dame Street, opposite Place Jacques-Cartier, and an old building at Pointe à Callières were pressed into service. When martial law was lifted in April 1838, 500 people who had been incarcerated in Montréal were released.

It is not difficult to imagine the atmosphere of tension that reigned in Montréal between November 1837 and April 1838 as 112 Patriotes were brought before a military tribunal. Twelve were acquitted, thirty released on bail, fifty-eight exiled and twelve put to death.

Those sentenced to death were taken to Pied-du-Courant for hanging. On December 21, 1838, a notary named Joseph-Narcisse Cardinal and a law student named Joseph Duquet were led to the scaffold. Cardinal died

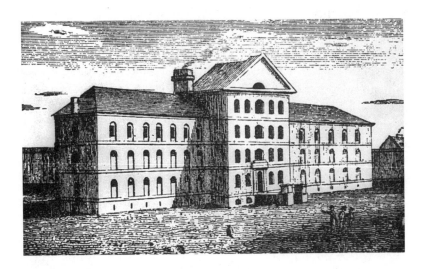

The new prison at Pied–du–Courant. Twelve Patriotes were hanged in front of the prison.

quickly but it took the hangman two attempts to hang Duquet, despite appeals for clemency. On January 18, 1839, another notary by the name of Pierre-Théophile Decoigne and four farmers were hanged, and on February 15, five more men were put to death: François-Marie-Thomas Chevalier de Lorimier, a notary, François Nicolas, a teacher, Pierre-Rémi Narbonne, a painter, Amable Daunais, a farmer, and a young Frenchman named Charles Hindelang. Hindelang had come up from the United States to join the Patriotes. As the noose was placed around his neck, he cried, "Death is nothing for a Frenchman. Long Live Freedom!" Perhaps this is why the Rue Lafayette in Paris was chosen as the site for a plaque in Hindelang's honour in November 1990. Visitors to Paris may view the plaque at 70 Rue Lafayette.

On July 2, 1837, eight prisoners in manacles were taken to the steamer *Canada*, moored at Pied-du-Courant, then taken to Québec City, where they were transferred to a warship, the *Vestale*. The *Vestale* transported the prisoners to Bermuda for indefinite exile. The following year, sixty-four more Patriotes were exiled, this time to Australia.

The names of these men are engraved on plaques at the base of a monument erected in their memory by the Institut Canadien of Montréal in the Côte-des-Neiges cemetery in 1858. The monument also bears the names of the Patriotes who fell at Saint-Denis, Saint-Charles, Saint-Eustache and Odelltown where, on November 7, 1838, they fought loyalist volunteers for

Five Patriotes about to be hanged.

two hours until British regulars arrived. Another monument, at the corner of De Lorimier and Notre-Dame Streets, is the work of sculptor Alfred Laliberté. It was unveiled on June 24, 1926 by the lieutenant-governor of Québec. At his side was a very old woman, Madame Marion, the daughter of Joseph-Narcisse Cardinal, one of the first men hanged at Pied-du-Courant.

Some historians argue that the events that took place in 1837-38 were not, in fact, a popular rebellion. If there had been a rebellion, they maintain, the Patriotes could have obtained arms from the United States, instead of using pitchforks, scythes and flails when they could not find hunting rifles. In his famous report, Lord Durham wrote that the English precipitated an inevitable revolt, for fear that stalling would give the French Canadians time to prepare.

According to historian Félix Desrochers, the Patriotes' greatest error was to have lost. We owe the freedom we enjoy today to these *"fous sublimes"* (sublime fools), he continues, for until the rebellion England had always resisted giving its colonies their own constitutional system.

The Aftermath of the Rebellion

———————— >< ————————

The charter granted to the city of Montréal in 1832 was not renewed when it expired three years later. Perhaps the administrators of Lower Canada felt that the political situation had deteriorated to such an extent that allowing the Corporation to continue would be dangerous. During the 1837-38 rebellion, Montréal was placed under military control. When calm was restored, the special council that handled the province's affairs issued a decree authorizing the lieutenant-governor to appoint a superintendent of police, whose powers were later transferred to an organization called the Société du Feu.

Made up of approximately 100 magistrates, the organization had an annual budget of £6,000 provided by the government. Among other duties, the magistrates were authorized to arrest any individual who caused a nuisance, refused to lend assistance to firefighters or engaged in looting after the outbreak of a fire. Later, when city council was reconvened, the powers of the Société du Feu were transferred to it.

Kerosene had already replaced whale oil as the chief source of lamp fuel when, in 1837, the streets of Montréal were equipped with gas lamps. The previous year, a company whose main shareholders were two prominent businessmen, A. Furniss and John Ostell, had founded Montréal's first gas company with capital of £15,000. Some stores subscribed to the new service immediately and the first gas lamps were lit on November 23, 1837. Once the problems presented by the cold winter months were resolved, gas lamps appeared in the streets. Gas lighting enjoyed great favour with the public, even after the advent of electricity. At the beginning of the twentieth century, a third of Montréal's 2,000 street lamps were still lit by gas.

In 1840, Montréal received its second charter under the corporate name "Le Maire, les échevins et citoyens de la cité de Montréal." As might be expected, the governor general, Charles Poulett Thomson, later Baron Sydenham, chose the members of the first council from among the English-speaking elite. Peter McGill became the first mayor under the new administration. At the end of its first two-year term, a new council was elected, and French-speakers won a majority of the seats. As Montréal's new mayor, lawyer Joseph Bourret embarked on what was to be a long and fruitful political career.

Gas lamps first appeared on the streets of Montréal in 1838.

Montréal had a population of slightly more than 40,000. It was divided into six wards, each of which elected two councillors. In addition to choosing a mayor from among their ranks, the councillors selected six other members of the community to become aldermen. In 1844, the city was divided into nine wards that elected twenty-one councillors: three from each of three city wards and two from each of six suburban wards.

In 1840, Montréal's first diocesan seminary was built. As early as 1825, Montréal's first bishop, J.J. Lartigue, had asked the Sulpicians to train seminarians. Initially the Sulpicians had been reticent, because they were being threatened with confiscation of their property. However, they received assurances that this would not happen and, on November 7, 1840, signed an agreement with Lartigue's successor, Ignace Bourget, giving them responsibility for training seminarians for the diocese forever.

The Sulpicians maintained a religious school on Saint-Paul Street, built in 1806. Those admitted as seminarians lived in one wing of the building. Their numbers quickly grew as young men arrived from the United States, especially the diocese of Boston. Between 1840 and 1857, 338 young men entered the seminary, of whom 239 completed their training and became priests. And of these, eight received the rank of bishop. Eventually, having two schools under one roof was no longer manageable, and in 1854 work began on the Grand Séminaire on Sherbrooke Street.

Bourget, who had been Lartigue's coadjutor, was appointed bishop after Lartigue died on April 19, 1840. Later that year, Bishop Bourget invited one of France's greatest religious orators to speak. Msgr Charles-Auguste-Marie-Joseph, Comte de Forbin-Janson, bishop of Nancy and Toul and primate of Lorraine, came to Montréal to preach missions.

Comte de Forbin-Janson had become bishop of Nancy in 1824. Six years later, when France experienced major upheavals that culminated in an insurrection and the institution of the July Monarchy under Louis-Philippe, he left his post and appointed a coadjutor to replace him. In 1839, he travelled to the United States and preached retreats in many dioceses. His first stop in Canada was Québec City and, one night in early December 1840, he arrived by boat in Montréal harbour. In his haste, he got off the boat as it advanced slowly towards the shore through pans of ice, which in the moonlight appeared to be a single solid sheet. He fell through the ice and nearly drowned.

A few days later, he preached a retreat at Notre-Dame Basilica. The prelate's great eloquence and the splendour of the preparations made for his stay attracted large numbers of people. The newspapers reported that 10,000 people, one quarter of the city's population, gathered to hear him speak. In the months that followed, Bishop de Forbin-Janson toured the countryside, preaching in churches filled to capacity. Before leaving Lower Canada, he blessed the Calvary at Saint-Hilaire in the presence of 30,000 people.

On May 3, 1841, Bishop Bourget left on a voyage to Rome. En route to New York, he stopped at Burlington, where he was greeted by many Patriotes, including Ludger Duvernay, who had taken refuge there. In New York, he met with Bishop de Forbin-Janson. Moved by the plight of the Patriotes, Bishop de Forbin-Janson decided to visit them and he and his entourage stayed with Duvernay. During a visit to France in December, Bishop de Forbin-Janson went to London to plead for the Patriotes in exile. In 1843, he founded a religious movement, l'Oeuvre de la Sainte-Enfance.

In 1841, Lachine was a stopping point on a voyage around the world by Sir George Simpson, remembered in history books as the governor of the Hudson's Bay Company and governor of Rupert's Land. Simpson left London on March 2, 1841, and travelled to Halifax and Boston before reaching Montréal. In Lachine, he hired the services of Nor'westers, known for their experience and endurance. Together with Count Caledon and Count Mulgrave, who were travelling to the Red River to hunt bison, Simpson left Lachine by canoe on May 2. He travelled up the Ottawa River, crossing Georgian Bay and Lake Superior, and stopped at Fort William, Fort Garry and Fort Edmonton. After crossing the Rocky Mountains and visiting Vancouver and Sitka, he travelled down the west coast to California. He returned to Sitka, then headed for London via Siberia and Tobolsk. The account of this hardy world traveller's voyage, which lasted nineteen months and twenty-six days, was published in 1846. He died in Lachine in September 1860.

When Notre-Dame Basilica was consecrated in 1829, it did not have the towers we see today. In 1840, it was decided that a collection should be taken up to fund completion of the basilica. An architect named John Ostell was hired to supervise construction of the towers. Ostell designed many buildings in Montréal: the seminary on Sherbrooke Street, the second Saint-Jacques Church, Notre-Dame-de-Grâces Church, the Arts Building of McGill University and the Old Court House on the north side of Notre-Dame Street. Work was completed on the western tower, the Tour de la Persévérance, and it was consecrated by Bishop de Forbin-Janson on November 4, 1841. It was only when the eastern tower, the Tour de la Tempérance, was completed two years later that the basilica took on the appearance we know today.

During his trip to Rome in 1841, Bishop Bourget hoped to attract religious communities to his diocese. For this purpose, he stopped in Marseille to meet Abbé Eugène de Mazenod. Fifteen years earlier, the order founded by Abbé de Mazenod had been officially sanctioned by Pope Leo XII under the name of the Society of Oblate Missionaries of Mary Immaculate. Following Bishop Bourget's visit, six Oblates arrived in Montréal on December 2. In 1842, the first Canadian, Father Damase Dandurand, entered the order, embarking on what was to be a long and fruitful career in the western territories. The work of the Oblates, particularly in Canada's far north, deserves the highest praise.

In 1841, the quintessential Montréal businessman was, without a doubt, Peter McGill. A merchant and politician, McGill sat on the boards of many banks and businesses. Born Peter McCutcheon, he changed his surname to McGill when his uncle, John McGill, died childless and left his fortune to his nephew on the condition that Peter take his name. Elected president of the Bank of Montreal in 1834, McGill was a partner in a company that imported goods from Britain and the Caribbean and owned a fleet of six freighters and steamers. McGill became the first president of Canada's first railway and later played a key role in the construction of rail links to the Atlantic provinces and Portland, Maine.

Mindful of the need for businessmen to join forces to protect their interests, McGill chaired a meeting on April 6, 1841, that led to the creation of the Montreal Board of Trade. Under the leadership of Augustin Cuvillier, who was to become a member of Parliament of the new Province of Canada established by the Act of Union, a committee was set up to obtain articles of incorporation, and on March 19, 1842, the Board of Trade received its charter.

The city council elected in 1840 quickly introduced changes that spurred Montréal's growth. In 1841, it introduced bylaws regulating the operation of public markets and began ambitious projects to widen and extend public roadways. In the space of two years, close to $250,000 was spent on civic improvements, a considerable sum of money at the time. The council also defined the duties of municipal assessment officers, for a new taxation system was inevitable. Until that time, taxes had been paid solely by property owners on the basis of the value of their land. Under the new system, tenants were also required to contribute to the municipal coffers and a business tax was introduced.

The Special Council and the Union of the Two Canadas

—————————— ➤< ——————————

Early in 1838, Queen Victoria gave royal assent to a law suspending the constitution and establishing "temporary measures" for the administration of Lower Canada. Because of the upheaval of recent months, it was decided that the province could not be governed in accordance with the Constitutional Act of 1791, and a special council was set up to assist the governor in designing and implementing laws and ordinances to restore peace, welfare and good government.

John Colborne, who had quelled the uprising in Saint-Eustache, replaced Lord Gosford as administrator of Lower Canada. Colborne then appointed a special council, which met in Montréal in mid-April for seventeen days. The council passed twenty-six ordinances, one of which suspended the Habeas Corpus Act. "Miss Vic," as the Queen of England was called by the Patriotes, quickly appointed Lord Durham governor general of Canada and commissioned him to investigate the political situation and make recommendations for a constitution. Upon his arrival, Durham had to deal with the problem of Lower Canada's jails, now filled to overflowing. His answer was to wield both carrot and stick.

On June 28, 1838, Durham dismissed Colborne's special council and appointed a new council of five members, none of whom spoke French or were from Lower Canada. The council was made up of military and naval officers and members of his own staff. At its first meeting, that same day, the council adopted an ordinance designed to "restore security in Lower Canada." Eight prisoners were exiled to Bermuda and were to be executed if they returned without the governor's permission. Fourteen others who had fled the country and for whom warrants had been issued on charges of high treason ran the risk of execution if they attempted to return. Among them were Papineau, O'Callaghan, Duvernay and Georges-Étienne Cartier. Full amnesty was granted to all other detainees and fugitives. Clearly, Durham was attempting to ease the tension and to resolve a complex issue through efforts at clemency. His efforts were well received, even by some Patriotes.

In early November, Durham left for London to report his findings and present his recommendations. Colborne resumed his administrative duties and reconvened his special council, which met in Montréal from November 9 to 21. As the council was passing fifteen ordinances, a second uprising led by Patriotes who had taken refuge in the United States was crushed. In January 1839, Colborne became governor of Lower Canada. The special council reconvened on February 14, the day before five Patriotes were scheduled to be executed. During the session, which lasted until April 13, the council members passed sixty-seven ordinances on subjects ranging from the regulation of inns to confirmation of the Sulpicians' title as the seigneurs of Montréal Island.

While the council deliberated on legislative issues in Montréal, preparations were underway in London for legislation to determine Canada's constitutional future; it was generally agreed that the Constitutional Act of 1791, which had divided the territory into two provinces, could not be reinstated. On March 23, 1840, Lord John Russell introduced a bill at Westminster uniting the two Canadas, which was passed on July 23, 1840. The debates that accompanied the bill are too lengthy to recount here. Suffice it to say that Lower Canada had a population of 650,000 people, while Upper Canada had a population of 450,000, but each was to elect forty-two members to an assembly. Equally unfair was the fact that the new province was saddled with the debts of the former provinces, although Upper Canada's annual deficit was greater than its total revenue and it was incapable of paying even the interest on its debt. In fact, Upper Canada's indebtedness was twelve times that of Lower Canada.

On February 10, 1841, the new governor, Edward Poulett Thomson, announced that Upper and Lower Canada were now a single province, and so they were to remain until Confederation in 1867.

Life Returns to Normal

———————————— >< ————————————

In anticipation of Montréal's bicentenary, it was decided that bonds would be issued to raise the funds necessary for a rapid improvement in public services.

Following the union of the two Canadas, Montréal received its second charter and embarked on an ambitious public works program to improve its roads, markets and water supply. To do so, however, the city needed money. Even though the Bank of Montreal had loaned the city £10,000 in 1840, albeit on a relatively short-term promissory note, attempts to borrow from the bank a second time were in vain. This time, the city needed only £2,000. It resorted to issuing bonds, and has continued to use this formula ever since.

Through the efforts of Bishop Bourget, the bicentenary celebrations coincided with the return to Québec of the Jesuits, who had directed the religious life of Ville-Marie in its earliest days. Reestablished by Pope Pius VII in 1814, the order provided education services in France that were widely admired. French Jesuits had been teaching at St. Mary's College in Kentucky since 1831, and Bourget may have felt a certain understandable envy towards the bishop there.

Father Pierre Chazelle, the superior, and eight other Jesuits arrived in Montréal on May 31, 1842. Relations were not altogether smooth at first. The Jesuits were more interested in converting native populations living in the northern part of what had been Upper Canada than in establishing an institute of learning in Montréal. Furthermore, the French priests believed that the French language and culture were doomed in Canada. It is important to remember that at this time Montréal had an English-speaking majority. The Jesuits founded Collège Sainte-Marie in 1848. The general superiors of the order had wanted the college to be an English-language institution but its first two rectors, sensitive to Bishop Bourget's plans, managed to overrule them. And so it was that Montréal acquired a college that was to train generations of young men, many of whom became distinguished thinkers.

Mention has already been made of the Théâtre Royal, which opened in 1825, and its importance to the officers of the garrison, who became regular theatregoers. In 1842, they were honoured by a visit from Charles Dickens, who although barely thirty was at the time England's most popular playwright. Dickens remains one of the most widely read authors in the English-speaking world. Dickens had not come to Montréal to direct a play; he was thinking over an invitation to direct the officers' theatrical troupe. According to Dickens' biographers, his success at the Théâtre Royal on the evening of May 28 marked a turning point in his career. He played three roles in three different plays. Attendance at an evening performance three days earlier was by invitation only: the female roles were played by ladies of good families who would perform only before a select audience.

Despite Montréal's English-speaking majority (57 per cent in 1844), there were performances by French artists. In August 1843, for example, Théâtre Royal audiences were treated to a performance of *Les diamants de la couronne et du chalet* by the French Opera, a troupe of eight singers that included two prima donnas from the Opéra-Comique de Paris. The performance was given a highly favourable review by *La Minerve*.

Critical acclaim is never a sure thing, however, and one note falsely played can have disastrous results. On completion of the first of Notre-Dame Basilica's two towers in 1841, the churchwardens hired the firm of White Chapel in England to produce a carillon of eleven bells, including a great bell weighing 7,000 kilograms. Two years later, as work on the second tower neared completion, the carillon arrived from England. *Grande Marie*, as the great bell was named, was considerably heavier than originally planned, weighing 7,420 kilograms. On October 20, 1843, *Grande Marie*, decorated with flags, was carried from the harbour to the entrance of the church where ten smaller bells that had arrived earlier rang out a welcome.

The great bell sat at the foot of the tower for a week before being hoisted to what should have been its final resting place in the tower. Alas, the following year, on the eve of Saint-Jean-Baptiste Day, the bell put forth a false note. On examination, it was found to have a large crack. It was shipped back to White Chapel's in 177 large pieces and five cases of small pieces. The churchwardens decided that *Grande Marie*'s replacement should be even

The dome of Bonsecours Market was supported by a circle of Doric columns.

heavier. The new bell, *Jean Baptiste*, weighed 11,100 kilograms. It arrived in Montréal in September 1847, but a year passed before it was hoisted into place. On holidays and days of mourning, *Jean Baptiste*'s solemn voice can still be heard.

In 1844, the city's municipal offices were moved to the Montreal Water Works Building, which the city had purchased from Moses Judah Hayes, until such time as a permanent home for a city hall could be built. The market on Place Jacques-Cartier also needed a permanent home. A solution to both problems was found with the construction of Bonsecours Market. The east wing was built on land purchased from John Molson after the British American Hotel was destroyed by fire. A contract for the foundation work was awarded in May 1844, and work began above ground in September.

Two different architects worked on the design. The city councillors announced a competition and selected the drawings of William Footner. Footner provided the general plans for the building; however, for the market's silver dome, a more experienced architect, George Browne, was called in. Browne produced a design that placed the dome on a circle of columns in the Grecian Doric style of architecture. Construction took place over a period of eight years, and it was not until January 1852 that city council met in its new chambers, still incomplete, for the first time. Some taxpayers complained that the building was too large, but it contained four halls, including a concert hall with a capacity of 3,000 people.

Bonsecours Market has been ravaged by fire many times and renovated as many times. In August 1976, a crane was used to remove the dome so that the circle of columns, badly damaged by a fire the previous month, could be restored.

Montréal businessmen deplored the fact that when the water level fell, vessels of more than 300 tons burden were unable to reach Montréal's piers. As early as 1826, they had submitted an application for the dredging of a channel to the Legislative Assembly. There were those who thought that such an undertaking would be a waste of time, particularly in Lac Saint-Pierre, which would begin filling with sand and clay as soon as it was dredged. Barge operators also feared the end of a lucrative source of income. The petition went unanswered for many years. In 1838, the issue of a channel was again raised and the Assembly voted to fund a study. There were conflicting views on the route that the channel should take. Some wanted the lake's natural channel to be widened and deepened. Others felt that it should be dug in a straight line. The second view prevailed.

Work began in May 1844 and went on for many months. Finally, after three years, it ground to a halt altogether, the cost having become prohibitive. The project had swallowed up £70,000 and it was estimated that an additional £30,000 would be needed to complete it. The Quebec *Mercury* wrote that the channel had become an infatuation and that suspending work on it would avoid throwing good money after bad. But when the *City of Manchester*, a vessel that drew 4.25 metres, moored in the harbour in 1851, people realized that the channel had not been an infatuation after all and that it was critical to Montréal's economic prosperity. Montréal was to become one of the world's largest inland seaports.

Montréal, Capital of the Province of Canada

———————— >‹— ————————

When the notion of uniting Upper and Lower Canada was presented to Upper Canada, it declared that it was in favour of union provided certain conditions were met, notably that one of its cities be made the capital of the new province. In London, the response was that sessions could be held in Toronto, Kingston, or even Bytown, as Ottawa was then known. There was no mention of Montréal. The 1837-38 rebellion had probably left too many scars for Montréal to be chosen as the new capital despite its status as Canada's largest city, and the new constitution made no provision for a capital city.

Governor Charles Poulett Thomson decided that the first Assembly of the united province of Canada would meet in Kingston. The session lasted from June 14 to September 18, 1841. The next day, the governor died of complications after falling from his horse. His successor, Sir Charles Bagot, called a second session for September 8 of the following year. It lasted barely a month, ending on October 12. Kingston was no more than a large village and the honourable members must have found the breaks between the sessions interminably long. In a resolution that carried by a vote of forty to twenty, they found Kingston unfit to be Canada's capital.

When Bagot became gravely ill in March 1843, he handed the reins of power to Sir Charles Metcalfe. Bagot died on May 19. The Assembly reconvened on September 28 and one of the first issues was location. The imperial government had refused to rule on the issue, since it did not know the opinion of the legislature. Forced to make a choice, the ministry chose Montréal. The only member of the cabinet to resign over the issue was J.B. Harrison, the honourable member from Kingston. His supporters would not have forgiven him had he endorsed such a decision. A bill was passed by the Assembly and the Legislative Council and given royal assent.

Still, there was considerable opposition to the selection of Montréal as capital of the Union. Some felt that transferring the capital to what had been Lower Canada would run counter to one of the objectives of the new constitution: the assimilation of the French Canadians. The speaker of the Legislative Council, Robert S. Jameson, resigned his seat and thirteen of his colleagues left their seats in protest. One of the two members from Montréal, a merchant named George Moffatt, resigned his seat rather than vote in favour of the ministry's choice.

When the Assembly was prorogued on December 9, the ministry had just resigned in protest over the governor's behaviour. Accustomed to handling public affairs in British colonies in which responsible government had not yet been introduced, Governor Metcalfe had made appointments without consulting the Ministry.

Thoughts now turned to the problem of finding suitable lodgings for the Assembly. Sainte-Anne Market, located between McGill and Saint-Pierre streets, seemed a logical choice. Built of cut stone by enterprising citizens around 1830, the market was 104 metres in length. On either side of a central hall, two wings accommodated numerous stalls, thirty-two of which

were reserved for the sale of meat while other stalls displayed poultry, produce and fish. The Saint-Pierre, a little creek that flowed under the long
building, was channelled and covered, and underground storage areas were
built on either side of the channel. The upper storey over the central hall
contained a very large room.

The city purchased Sainte-Anne Market in 1842 for £15,600. The owners had authorized three businessmen to handle the sale. The most prominent of these was George Moffatt, who had far-reaching business interests
and had been elected to the Legislative Assembly the previous year. It was
thus that Sainte-Anne Market became the new home of the government.

A place of residence had to be found for the governor general as well. At
this time, affluent Montréal families had country homes. This was the case
of James Monk, chief justice of the District of Montréal, who had served
repeatedly as speaker of the Legislative Council of Lower Canada. Monk
had acquired a large tract of land which he named Monklands. The manor
house stood at the end of a long treed avenue – what is now Brillon Avenue,
an extension of Monkland Avenue running east from Décarie Boulevard.
The manor house, which was to become the central building of Villa
Maria Convent, was rented by the government for the governor general.
Visitors admired its isolation, hardly an exaggeration when we consider that
Lord Elgin used snowshoes when snowdrifts prevented him from travelling
to Montréal by sleigh.

When the first session of the new Assembly opened in the newly renovated market building on November 28, 1844, one of the first bills approved
was an appeal to the queen for amnesty for the rebels of 1837-38, a measure
that would not be implemented for another five years. The Assembly also
unanimously approved an address to the queen to repeal the clause in the
Act of Union that forbade the legislative use of French. The sum of
£40,000 was set aside to indemnify citizens of Upper Canada for losses suffered during the rebellion, and it was decided that a commission would be
set up to assess losses suffered by people in Lower Canada. Finally, the members approved the establishment of a company to build a railway between
Montréal and Halifax. The session lasted four months.

Governor Metcalfe was forced to resign because of ill health. He left
Canada in late November 1845 and died less than a year later. Lord Cathcart,
commander in chief of the British troops, replaced him on an acting basis
and was appointed governor general in March 1846.

The next session opened on March 20 and ended on June 9. Measures
were passed to indemnify citizens of Québec City for losses suffered in the

fire that had swept through Saint-Roch the previous May, engulfing 1,630 homes in flames and destroying a third of the city. More than half a million pounds was earmarked for completion of the Welland Canal. Improvements to the canals of the upper St. Lawrence River (£283,500) and the dredging of Lac Saint-Pierre (£9,500) were also approved. Thus, almost all of the capital project funding was allocated to Upper Canada, even though the economic prosperity of Montréal, the country's largest city, depended on development of the St. Lawrence.

The members of the Assembly unanimously approved a bill reorganizing and consolidating the militia in response to the tension between the United States and Britain over the Oregon boundary. Another bill was passed to encourage parents to send their children to school: parents now had to make a monthly contribution whether or not their children attended. The Assembly also approved an address to the Queen for the delivery of mail to Canada twice a month instead of once a month. A report was submitted concerning losses suffered during the 1837-38 rebellion, but measures to provide compensation were not proposed.

Once the Oregon boundary dispute with the United States was resolved, there was no further reason why a military man should be responsible for civil administration of the country. Cathcart was replaced by a new governor general, James Bruce, Lord Elgin, on January 30, 1847. Lord Elgin had years of administrative experience. On his arrival in Canada, he reaffirmed his belief in responsible government; however, in the speech from the throne that opened the session on June 2, he made no mention of the country's political problems. Perhaps he wanted an opportunity to test the ministry. He noted that the ministers did not have adequate public support and that Francophones were underrepresented.

While the session did not produce any major changes, it did provide for the creation of three notarial offices, the establishment of a college of physicians, help for Irish immigrants decimated by an epidemic, and the incorporation of companies to establish telegraph links among Canada's major centres and between Canada and the United States. Deciding that this lacklustre performance indicated a weak ministry, the governor decided to dissolve the Assembly in early December. The reformers won a decisive victory in the subsequent election, and several respected figures won seats. When Lord Elgin reconvened the Assembly in February 1848, the new cabinet was formed by Lafontaine and Baldwin. The session was very short, as the governor wanted to give the new ministry time to draft legislation, a task that took up the remainder of the year.

This period of political calm was followed by a session so tumultuous that Montréal lost its title as the capital of Canada. It began peacefully enough on January 18, 1849. The governor announced – in elegant French – that he was repealing the proscription of French in legislative texts. He also announced that London was prepared to grant a general amnesty to French Canadians who had been involved in the rebellion. The session was to be a very busy one: amendments to laws governing the school system, the judiciary and municipal government; the repeal of English laws denying access to the St. Lawrence to foreign vessels; continuation of work on the canal systems; an increase in the number of parliamentary seats; amendments to various electoral acts and measures for the construction of railway lines.

The debates pitted two equally respected politicians against each other: Louis-Joseph Papineau and Louis-Hippolyte Lafontaine. The recent period of calm seemed to have had an adverse effect on Papineau, who enjoyed the cut and thrust of debate. He complained about the lamentable torpor that had descended over most of the province. However, his malaise was short-lived. Lafontaine condemned Papineau for proclaiming, no doubt in a flight of oratory, "Better that the country should perish, than a principle!" To which Lafontaine responded, "May I die that my country might be saved!"

A bill passed by a large majority in both houses to compensate citizens who had suffered losses during the rebellion ended the period of calm. Some English-speakers felt that the bill made no distinction between "rebels" and "loyalists" and rewarded those who had committed treason. They wanted Lord Elgin to deny royal sanction. Well aware that a similar bill had been passed for Upper Canada, Elgin felt that the Union could not achieve political freedom if he rejected a law passed by the majority of the members. He signed.

As he prepared to leave the Parliament building, he was pelted with eggs and beat a quick retreat to Monklands. That evening at around 8 o'clock, protesters gathered on the Champ-de-Mars to listen to appeals for an address to the queen for the governor general's recall. Suddenly, there was the sound of bells and cries of "Fire! Fire!" Members of the volunteer fire brigades arrived carrying torches. "The Parliament building is on fire!"

The crowd rushed towards the Parliament building. A ladder truck arrived and the longest ladder was used to break down the heavy doors. A chandelier fell and the gas immediately burst into flame, igniting the ceiling. A tall Scot managed to save a large portrait of the Queen: it was Sandford Fleming, who later became president of the Royal Society. Soon, the entire

Sainte-Anne Market before and during the fire set by rioters in 1849.

building was engulfed in flames. The Hôtel-Dieu was also in danger but the firefighters, intimidated by the rioters, dared not intervene. The rioters reassured them and two brigades, the "Héros" and the "Voltigeurs," saved the hospital from destruction.

By midnight, all that remained of the Parliament building was smouldering ruins. The government archives and libraries containing 22,000 volumes, including a collection of rare works on the new world, were completely destroyed. The following day, the Assembly reconvened at Bonsecours Market under the watchful eye of soldiers carrying bayonets. The rioters continued to wreak havoc, and despite a military escort Lord Elgin was greeted with a shower of stones when he returned to the Assembly. There were even attacks on the governor's wife.

Thus Montréal lost its title as capital of the Union. The Assembly voted thirty-three to twenty-five to ask the governor general to hold sessions alternately in Toronto and Québec City. For the two years remaining before the next election, Parliament convened in Toronto. It was agreed that Québec City would be the capital for the next four-year period and this arrangement was followed right up to Confederation.

Typhus — Montréal's Prosperity Suffers a Setback

Canada's first bank, the Bank of Montreal, was founded in 1817. It was only a matter of time, however, before it lost its monopoly. As the city grew, other institutions sprang up. In 1835, Viger, De Witt et Compagnie was founded by Louis-Michel Viger, Jacob De Witt and a dozen merchants who supported the Patriote cause. They accused the Bank of Montreal of exercising a monopoly over lending in Lower Canada. Their goal was to promote commerce and industry within the French Canadian community.

Louis-Michel Viger was the member of Parliament for Chambly and a staunch supporter of his cousin, Louis-Joseph Papineau. He did not hesitate to attend Patriote meetings. Born in Connecticut, De Witt had arrived in Montréal as an adolescent. As his hardware business prospered, he began buying up land. Like Viger he was a member of Parliament, serving as the member for Beauharnois. Although he was not an outright Patriote, he did support the cause of reform.

The bank's clients were mainly artisans and farmers who wanted to borrow money. This is probably why Viger, De Witt et Compagnie was popularly known as the "banque du peuple." During the rebellion of 1837-38, the colonial authorities suspected that the bank was lending money to the rebels. In mid-November 1837, Viger was arrested for high treason and spent nine months behind bars. A year later, on the eve of the second insurrection, he spent another forty days in prison.

The bank survived these troubled times, no doubt because of De Witt's able leadership, then began to prosper. In September 1843, Viger and De Witt together with their ten partners applied to have the bank incorporated as the Banque du Peuple. The following year, their application was granted. At the time of its dissolution, the bank was lodged in a building with a magnificent façade at 57 Saint-Jacques Street. Luckily, the building has survived and has been transformed into an office building.

In 1845, Henry Morgan and David Smith founded a retail business that would grow with the expansion of Montréal. When Henry Morgan & Co. opened on Notre-Dame, it employed nine clerks. Six years later, Smith left for Chicago and one of Henry's brothers, James, left a business career in Glasgow, Scotland, to join the firm. The business was so successful that a second store was opened on McGill Street. The Morgan brothers later moved the business into its own building on Saint-Jacques Street, opposite Victoria Square. In 1889, land was purchased on Sainte-Catherine Street between Union and Aylmer for the construction of what was to be Canada's largest store at a cost of $400,000. It opened to the public in 1891.

In 1847, the Legislative Assembly granted a charter to the College of Physicians and Surgeons of Lower Canada. The bill carried the signatures of 141 practitioners in three districts: Montréal, Trois-Rivières and Québec City. Dr. Daniel Arnoldi was its first president.

That year another Montréal physician, Dr. Horace Nelson, conducted experiments on dogs to test the effectiveness of ether as an anaesthetic. A few weeks later Nelson tested his method on a human subject, while his father Dr. Wolfred Nelson, the famous Patriote of 1837, removed a tumour. Then, on March 11, 1847, Dr. E.D. Worthington used Dr. Nelson's method to amputate a patient's leg in Sherbrooke. Worthington placed the ether in an animal bladder hooked up to a mask with an old umbrella handle. In the months that followed, the use of chloroform as an anaesthetic was investigated.

It will be recalled that Canada's first railway, linking Laprairie and Saint-Jean, was built in 1836. It was called a "portage line" because the rapids at Chambly made it impossible for boats to travel up the Richelieu to the St. Lawrence. It was not long before the idea of a railway between Montréal and Lachine was proposed so that people travelling to the Great Lakes could avoid the many locks at Lachine. Carriages were no longer able to keep up with the growth in river traffic. It was James Ferrier, the Scottish mayor of Montréal, who suggested the idea and so the Montreal and Lachine Rail Road was born. The company was granted a charter to provide rail service

Montréal seen from Mount Royal, circa 1845, with the towers of Notre-Dame Basilica visible in the middle distance. (Painting by James Duncan.)

between Montréal and Lachine and boat service on the St. Lawrence and Ottawa rivers.

Work on the railway began on May 1, 1847, and proceeded apace, even though one section of the line had to be shored up as it passed over swampland along the banks of the Saint-Pierre River. By mid-November the line was completed. As the two locomotives and eight passenger cars manufactured by a firm in Dundee, Scotland, had not yet arrived, a locomotive purchased in Philadelphia was used for the inauguration on November 19. To the delight of onlookers, the locomotive, which weighed eighteen tons and had 1.52-metre wheels and thirty-seven-centimetre pistons, was paraded up and down Saint-Antoine Street. The governor general, Lord Elgin, and his wife boarded the 4-4-0, as the locomotive was called, for its maiden voyage, during which it reached a speed of forty kilometres an hour.

It was also in 1847 that the first messages were sent by telegraph in Canada. Three years earlier, Samuel Morse had succeeded in establishing a telegraph link between Washington and Baltimore. Morse invented an international code that came to be known as the Morse Code. In 1846, the Montreal Board of Trade established a committee to study the possibility of a link between Montréal and Toronto. The Montreal and Toronto Magnetic Telegraph Company was established in July 1847 and on August 3, a network linking Québec City, Montréal and Toronto went into service.

That same year, the first telegraphic message between New York and Montréal was sent, and in 1848 the company paid out its first dividends. The company's chief officer, O.S. Wood, had been Morse's first student. The company did so well that by 1875, it had 40,000 kilometres of telegraph lines, 1,400 offices and 2,000 employees. It sent two million messages each year, not counting dispatches to newspapers.

It was also in 1847 that typhus decimated the population of Québec, claiming more than 10,000 victims, at least half of them in Montréal. The epidemic broke out on vessels bringing Irish immigrants to the New World. In late May, thirty or so vessels stopped at Grosse Île. Of the original 12,519 passengers, 777 had died during the voyage. According to official reports, of 70,000 immigrants, 8,000 perished at sea and another 5,424 died in quarantine. However, quarantine measures did not prevent the contagion from spreading to the city. By July 22, 3,500 people lay dying in lazarets built on Pointe Saint-Charles to contain the disease. Six thousand people died during the epidemic.

At the height of the epidemic on July 7, the temperature reached 44 degrees Celsius and the population called for the lazarets to be moved to St. Helen's Island or the islands off Boucherville. All commercial and social activity ground to a halt. When members of the clergy tending to the sick were struck down by the disease, priests from the countryside took their place. In Montréal death was everywhere. Many leading citizens, unable to abandon their civic duties, succumbed to the disease. Montréal Mayor John Easton Mills, who had been appointed commissioner of immigration, was among those who died. During construction of the Victoria Bridge in 1859, a boulder taken from the riverbed was used to mark the cemetery in which some 6,000 immigrants had been buried in 1847 and 1848.

In 1847, Saint Patrick's Basilica was finally completed. At first, the Irish community had worshipped at Notre-Dame-de-Bon-Secours Chapel, then had celebrated Sunday mass at the Récollet church. The generosity of the Sulpicians and the enterprising spirit of their superior, Joseph Quiblier, were instrumental in the construction of Saint Patrick's. The first seven stones were blessed in September 1841 and construction of the church took place over six years. With its seventy-metre spire, the new church was remarkable.

When the Théâtre Royal founded by John Molson and his associates burned down and Montréal found itself without a theatre, Moses Judah Hayes came to the rescue. A man of remarkable energy with a great sense of civic duty, Hayes had built the Montreal Water Works and made many other remarkable contributions to the city, including the gas company and banking services. Through his involvement in public affairs, Hayes helped Canadian Jews obtain the right to hold public office and was himself chief of police.

After selling the Montreal Water Works to the city, Hayes built a large hotel and spacious theatre on Dalhousie Square, where the hill of the citadel had been levelled. Hayes House was a four-storey hotel; the theatre located behind the hotel had three balconies, loges and even baths. The curtain, painted by the Italian artist Martanni, cost $6,000.

The theatre opened on July 10, 1847, with a play by Shakespeare. A mime troupe, Ravel and Martini, played there for three months. Among the 126 artists were sixty Viennese dancers who were accompanied by an orchestra of thirty-eight German musicians. Five years later, the hotel and theatre were completely destroyed in a fire that swept through a hundred establishments.

The year 1848 began with a general election. Lord Elgin had dismissed the Assembly the previous December because the Executive Council did not have a sufficient majority to administer the province. At that time, Montréal was a Conservative stronghold, and the election was marked by much unrest, culminating in a riot at the Royal Oak Inn. Feeling threatened by the rise in the popularity of the Reformers, the Conservative elements called in a group of Orangemen, popularly known as the Glengarries.

They took over a polling station located near Molson's brewery. In anticipation of just such an eventuality, the Reformers had their own strongmen. Led by lawyer and journalist Euclide Roy, and future mayor Charles-Joseph Coursol, both on horseback, they made their way to the Royal Oak Inn, where they were greeted by gunfire. Pistols in hand, they made their way to the inn. Two Glengarries were killed and several others were injured. The Reformers won the election by an overwhelming majority. Lord Elgin, who was in favour of reform, was not displeased.

In 1849, the Montreal Bar was established. After the Conquest, French Canadian lawyers could practise only in courts of common law; however, Brigadier James Murray, who became military governor of Québec soon after Wolfe's victory, realized that none of the English-speaking lawyers could speak French, and from 1766 on, all lawyers who were "Canadian subjects of His Majesty" were given access to the other courts.

With the Quebec Act of 1774, which restored the French Civil Code, the number of lawyers increased, and any individual who obtained a commission from the governor could practise law. This led to many instances of abuse. Later, a decree stipulated that a person could practise law only after serving as a legal clerk for five years, undergoing an examination and being deemed fit to practise. When the Law Society of Lower Canada was formed in 1849, it was composed of a general council and three divisions: Montréal, Québec City and Trois-Rivières. Its first meeting was held on July 24, 1849.

Progress in Education

Mention has already been made of the vital role in education played by the parish of Notre-Dame and the Sulpicians in the early days of Ville-Marie and by two pioneers in education, Marguerite Bourgeoys and Gabriel Souart, Montréal's first teachers. Far from relinquishing their role in primary education after founding the "Latin School" at Longue-Pointe and later Collège Saint-Raphaël, the Sulpicians continued to fund French-language education in Montréal from the time of the Conquest to the establishment in 1845 of the Montreal Catholic School Commission and beyond.

In 1833, they founded the Académie de la Visitation at the corner of Visitation and Craig streets, and the Congrégation de Notre-Dame took responsibility for its operation. The academy was rebuilt after the great fire of 1852 and when it came time to expand, a member of the Sulpician order, Adam Charles Gustave Desmazures, provided the necessary funding. In 1836 the Sulpician seminary established the Académie Saint-Joseph in

Saint-Joseph parish, again under the aegis of the Congrégation de Notre-Dame, and assumed the costs of the Academy for more than forty years.

The superior of the seminary, Joseph-Vincent Quiblier, enlisted the help of the Christian Brothers of France. Four members of the order arrived in Montréal in November 1837, and a few weeks later more than 200 children were enrolled in classes to begin before the end of January. The Sulpicians not only accommodated the Christian Brothers under their own roof but also assumed the cost of building a huge school on Côté Street that was to serve as the cradle of the Christian Brothers in North America. In 1869, forty-two priests trained 4,500 pupils in schools belonging to and subsidized by the seminary.

We should perhaps mention some of the other schools made possible by the generosity of the Sulpicians: École Bonsecours, a school for boys of Irish descent (1838); École Saint-Laurent on Côté Street, where the Christian Brothers taught upon their arrival in Montréal (1840); a school for girls, also named École Saint-Laurent, on Sainte-Catherine (1843); École Saint-Jacques at the corner of Saint-Denis and Sainte-Catherine (1843); École Sainte-Brigide (1845); Académie du Plateau established on Côté Street (1853), later moved to Sainte-Catherine near Saint-Urbain; Académie Sainte-Anne in the parish of the same name (1857); Académie Saint-Denis on Saint-Denis Street (1861); École Saint-Joseph in the basement of Saint-Joseph church (1863); Académie Marchand (1869), which opened on Saint-Dominique Street and moved in 1910 to the corner of Berri and Dorchester; and Académie Saint-Ignace on Saint-Hubert Street (1871). There were many other schools, but we will mention only two more, no doubt still remembered by older Montrealers: École Saint-Stanislas, founded in 1903 by the rector of Saint-Jacques church at the corner of Sanguinet and Ontario streets, and Académie Montcalm.

Teacher training was provided by Montréal's two normal schools, Jacques-Cartier and McGill, founded in 1857.

Good Times and Bad

————————— >‹ —————————

Near Place Royale is a statue of one of Montréal's finest citizens, John Young, who earned the title of "Father of the Port of Montréal." As early as

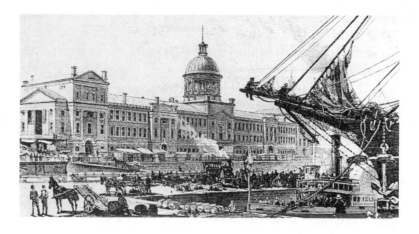

The deepening of the St. Lawrence made Montréal Canada's most important port. Here, a sailing vessel and a steamer at the pier below Bonsecours Market.

1826, Montréal merchants had urged the Assembly to improve harbour facilities and dredge the St. Lawrence, particularly in the stretch below Montréal known as Lac Saint-Pierre. Four years later, three commissioners were appointed to address these problems, but it was not until 1850, with the nomination of John Young, that the Harbour Commission began dredging operations in earnest. Young was appointed Chief Commissioner two years later and held the position for twenty-five years.

Young, one of the many Scots who helped make Montréal a "flourishing emporium" in the nineteenth century, arrived in Canada at the age of fifteen. He began his initiation into the world of commerce by working for wholesalers, then founded his own shipping company with a partner, Harrison Stephens. Young later took on another partner, a former clerk with the Bank of Montreal named Benjamin Holmes. Young did not lack ambition. To further increase profits from the canals of the upper St. Lawrence, he campaigned tirelessly to have a canal dug from Kahnawake to Lake Champlain. Needless to say, the Montréal business community was less than enthusiastic, since the canal would have enabled steamers from the Great Lakes to bypass Montréal and proceed directly to New York.

The advent of rail transportation fascinated Young, who in 1845 was a partner in the St. Lawrence and Atlantic Railroad Company, which received a charter to build a railway connecting Montréal with Portland, Maine. Five years later, Young was a strong supporter of the Intercolonial, a project to link Montréal and the Atlantic provinces by rail. With such an enterprising advocate of free trade at the helm, the Harbour Commission was destined to prosper.

In 1851, dredging of the St. Lawrence resumed. This time, however, the natural channel of the river's clay bed was followed, and four and a half months later a twenty-five-metre-wide channel had been dredged over a distance of six and a half kilometres. On November 8, the steamer *City of Manchester*, which drew 4.25 metres, steered a clear course among the shoals of Lac Saint-Pierre on its maiden voyage.

The following year, the dredging operation resumed. Nine metres wide and 4.57 metres long, the harrows were triangular in shape; each was equipped with 250 ten-centimetre-long teeth. The harrows were pulled on chains of adjustable length behind a boat with a 150-horsepower steam engine. Dredgers equipped with chains and buckets removed the clay that was dredged. In 1855, the Harbour Commission was authorized to charge any vessel drawing more than eleven feet (3.35 metres) the sum of one shilling (approximately twenty cents) per ton.

The founding of the Harbour Commission in 1850 was critical to Montréal's status as an important seaport. That year, another event captured the imaginations of Montréal's citizens. Many thought of it only as a fascinating experiment, but it was probably the first aeronautical event in the history of the city. Hot-air balloons were the rage in Europe and it was not long before they reached the United States. On September 12, 1850, the citizens of Montréal watched a balloon rise up over the magnificent trees of Monklands. Six years later, a second balloon – this one proudly bearing the name *Canada* – was flown over Griffintown.

In 1851, the first North American chapter of the Young Men's Christian Association opened in Montréal. The YMCA had been founded in London in 1844 by a young merchant, George Williams, who was later knighted. A well-known college in Montréal was named after him; Sir George Williams College later became a university and eventually merged with Loyola College to become Concordia University. In November 1851, a committee was struck at the Baptist church on Sainte-Hélène Street to approach other religious denominations about the possibility of introducing the YMCA in Montréal. The response was favourable, and a room was rented on Saint-Jacques Street where the chapter was founded. Five years later, the North American convention of the YMCA was held in Montréal. It was also in Montréal that the Young Women's Christian Association was founded.

Montréal's charter was amended in 1851. Instead of being chosen by the councillors from among their ranks, the mayor would now be elected by the

The bishop's palace following the great fire.

people. Like the city wards, the suburban wards would now elect three councillors, bringing the total to twenty-seven. They were to meet at least four times a year, but the mayor could call special meetings. The first mayor under the new system was Charles Wilson, a hardware store owner from Coteau-du-Lac. However, in the first election the people of Montréal did not have an opportunity to put the new system into practice: Wilson became mayor by acclamation.

On June 26, 1851, Mayor Wilson opened a reservoir at the top of Côte à Baron, the section of Saint-Denis between Sherbrooke and Ontario. The new reservoir was built in response not only to Montréal's growing population but also to the city's inability to respond quickly to fires. Little did those present at the inauguration of the reservoir realize that ten days later a fire would destroy 1,100 homes. Tragically, the new reservoir had been drained so that water mains could be installed.

The fire broke out at around 9 o'clock on July 8 on Sainte-Catherine Street between Saint-Laurent and Saint-Dominique. Twenty-four hours later, with the help of a gusting westerly wind, the fire had reached Pied-du-Courant (De Lorimier Street). All that was left of the neighbour-hoods of Saint-Jacques, Saint-Louis, Sainte-Marie and part of Montréal East – roughly one quarter of the city – was smoking ruins. The basilica, the bishop's palace, Molson's Brewery and the Hayes Hotel were among the buildings destroyed. Ten thousand people were left homeless and tents were erected for those who were unable to find shelter with family members or friends. The damage caused by the fire was estimated at $2.5 million.

Following this catastrophe, city council decided that Montréal needed a new aqueduct. Plans were drawn up without further delay to pump water from the Lachine Rapids to the McTavish Street reservoir, which could hold twenty-three million litres. Contracts for the construction of the aqueduct were signed in December 1852; construction lasted three years and cost close to £300,000 sterling. When the new aqueduct went into service in the fall of 1856, the old facilities were completely abandoned; however, during the winter months, the new aqueduct sometimes became blocked with ice, cutting off the water supply.

Mention has already been made of the construction of two railways, one linking Laprairie and Saint-Jean in 1836 and the other linking Montréal and Lachine in 1847. In 1850, the two companies were merged as the Chemin de Fer de Montréal et New York, and construction began on a line from Kahnawake to the United States border, where it linked up with an American line. The line went into service on September 20, 1852. Motor works in Manchester, New Hampshire, built four locomotives, the *New York* and the *Caughnawaga*, to haul passenger cars and the *Saint-Rémi* and the *Hemmingford* for freighters. The following year, the *Iroquois*, a paddlewheeler forty-five metres long and ten metres on the beam, began plying the waters of the St. Lawrence between Lachine and Kahnawake. It was the only one in Canada to provide year-round service.

In 1852, the American philosopher Ralph Waldo Emerson visited Montréal on a speaking tour. Emerson had such a great reputation as a speaker that the concert hall at Bonsecours Market was reserved for his address. Emerson, who had crossed the St. Lawrence on April 17 just hours before the ice broke up, described the scene for his audience: "From the pier, I saw acres and acres of ice pans, colliding with one another. Suddenly, the smooth path by which I had crossed the river shifted and broke into blocks, which turned over and over like porpoises." The founder of transcendentalism, a religious and philosophical movement, Emerson wanted American society to break with European traditions. In 1837, Emerson had delivered a speech at Harvard University that was considered the American declaration of intellectual independence. One journalist who heard Emerson speak described him as a Yankee philosopher with his feet planted firmly on the ground and his head in the stars.

The appearance the next year of another celebrated lecturer produced a very different response. Alessandro Gavazzi was a defrocked Italian monk who had been a chaplain with the revolutionary troops in Italy and had been involved in the rebellion against papal authority. When papal forces captured Rome, he fled to Britain where he began lecturing on the "Errors of Popery." While on a lecture tour in the United States in 1853, Gavazzi decided to take his crusade to Canada. He was driven out of Québec City by the Irish and in Montréal he was prevented from speaking in the great hall of Bonsecours Market. On June 9, 1853, he delivered his diatribe at the Congregational Church of Zion at the hay market, now Victoria Square.

A hundred Irishmen attacked the church, but the citizens inside had prepared themselves to repel any attack. Seventy policemen were unable to quell the riot that ensued. Mayor Wilson called in a company of Scottish infantrymen who had arrived at the garrison the previous day and read the Riot Act. According to one account, the troops fired just as the crowd began to disperse peacefully. Eleven people died and thirty were wounded. During the investigation, which lasted twenty-two days, more than a hundred witnesses were heard, yet it was impossible to determine who had given the order to fire. Some people blamed the mayor and went so far as to deface his portrait hanging in the municipal chambers at Bonsecours Market.

During the riot, Gavazzi took refuge at St. Lawrence Hall at the corner of Saint-Jacques and Saint-François-Xavier Streets. This hotel, which had opened in 1850, had a great reputation and had received many illustrious visitors, including the Prince of Wales (the future King Edward VII), who visited Montréal in 1860; John Wilkes Booth, who later assassinated Abraham Lincoln; the famous Italian soprano Adelina Patti; and General Tom Thumb, the famous dwarf of P.T. Barnum's circus who had entertained the Royal Court of England. Throughout its long history, St. Lawrence Hall received many political leaders as well. Political parties held their banquets there and sometimes even their caucuses.

Montréal now had a population of 60,000. One of the results of this phenomenal development was better contact with the outside world. In 1853, the Canadian Steam Navigation Company received a charter to provide regular steamship service between Montréal and England. That year, the first propeller-driven steamer to navigate the St. Lawrence arrived in Montréal. Two years later, Hugh and Andrew Allan founded the Montreal Ocean Steamship Company and obtained a grant of £25,000 sterling to provide mail service between England and Montréal using four steamers.

When four more steamers were added to their fleet in 1858, weekly service began. Rail links were also expanded. In June 1853, the line between Montréal and Portland went into service. The following month, work began on the Victoria Bridge. Three years later, in November, rail service between Montréal and Toronto was inaugurated.

Unfortunately, progress in medicine did not keep pace with developments in engineering. In 1854, a cholera epidemic broke out in Montréal once again and in the space of two months claimed more than a thousand lives. That year, the wardens of Notre-Dame acquired land that in 1855 became the new Côte-des-Neiges cemetery.

By the mid-nineteenth century, Montréal had made its reputation as a major industrial centre, and it was the subject of a major exhibit at the 1851 London fair. The *Illustrated London News* had been on hand the previous fall when items to be included in the exhibit were brought together at Bonsecours Market. The wide variety of items displayed was testimony to the skills of Montréal's artisans: articles of furniture, silverware, printing presses, lithographs, engravings on leather and wood, model locomotives, carts and other farm equipment, summer and winter carriages, and even a model cannon. When the fair opened in London, crowds of visitors gathered to see a fire-engine that had won first prize in Montréal. A group of Montréal citizens who wanted to promote the quality of local craftsmanship had paid for it to be shipped to the London fair. On the fire-engine were depicted many of the city's most famous buildings, as well as scenes from one of the great fires that had ravaged the city.

Five years later, in March 1855, another competition was held in the concert hall at Bonsecours Market for items to be displayed the following year at the Palais de l'Industrie in Paris. On August 18, 1855, the Parisian paper *L'Avenir* mentioned the great variety of products displayed and congratulated the Canadian government for opening the St. Lawrence to ships of all nationalities, adding that France's former colony was ready to trade its raw materials and resources for French luxury items and that the citizens of Montréal still preferred beautifully crafted products from Paris to less elegant articles produced in England. Following the success of Montréal's exhibit at the Paris fair, where according to the *Illustrated London News* Canadian products had been admired by everyone including Emperor Napoleon III, space was set aside in London's Crystal Palace for a permanent exhibit of Canadian products.

Now that the St. Lawrence was open to vessels from every country, the French government decided to send one of its corvettes, the *Capricieuse*, to

Montréal to renew contact with the former French colony. Some official circles in Paris disapproved, fearing that because France had abandoned Canada, such a visit would reopen an old wound and rekindle feelings of animosity in the French Canadian population. Nothing could have been further from the truth. The corvette's captain, Henri de Belvèze, and his crew were given a tumultuous welcome.

On July 13, 1855, the *Capricieuse* entered the harbour at Québec City, escorted by the steamer *Admiral*. Three ministers sent by the governor general stood on the *Admiral*'s bridge. As the vessels mounted the St. Lawrence, they were greeted with cheers and musket fire by crowds on either shore. The captain and his crew were wined and dined for two weeks. English-speaking Montrealers were particularly welcoming. Although relations between France and Britain had previously been strained, a new spirit had been inaugurated in 1854. When Napoleon III and Empress Eugénie visited London, Queen Victoria and Prince Albert reciprocated with a visit to the world's fair in Paris.

On July 30, it was learned that the *Admiral* was off Lanoraie, with Captain de Belvèze and members of his crew. Five vessels, their bridges packed with well-wishers, immediately set off to meet them. The *Aigle* and the *Cultivateur* were positioned on either side of the *Admiral*. Beam on beam, the *Jacques Cartier*, the *Verchères* and the *Castor* took their places astern.

When the steamers reached the port, every bell in Montréal was ringing. Mayor Wolfred Nelson, one of the leaders of the 1837 rebellion, and members of the town council greeted the visitors in an atmosphere of euphoria. At noon the following day, a large reception was held at St. Lawrence Hall with John Young, president of the Board of Trade, acting as host. The mayor gave a speech, stressing that the arrival of the *Capricieuse* paved the way for increased international trade. Young could only approve. No doubt, France also wanted to rebuild cultural ties with Canada. The Institut Canadien, which played a key role in the city's intellectual development, received a gift of books and works of art for its library from Captain de Belvèze. French Canadians, he told the reception, were the only group in North America that had always claimed to have a distinct nationality and had put up a valiant struggle to protect it. French Canadians rightfully believed that the destiny of a people is not entirely a matter of material perfection but is reflected in spiritual and intellectual accomplishments as well.

On Monday, July 30, the French party toured Mount Royal and the city, seeing many reminders of the French regime. The following day, the party was taken to Sainte-Anne-de-Bellevue aboard the steamer *Beaver* to see the iron bridge that the Grand Trunk Railway was building. They crossed the river at Kahnawake to attend an Iroquois reception, then returned to Montréal by way of the Lachine Rapids, an experience that thrilled the French sailors. On the evening of July 31, the day before the French visitors were scheduled to leave Montréal, a festival was organized on the Champ-de-Mars. More than 10,000 people gathered to pay tribute to Captain de Belvèze and his officers. After rousing speeches, there was a display of fireworks.

While naturally delighted at the warm reception given the *Capricieuse* and her men, France wanted to make it clear that it did not have fresh designs on Canada. On August 18, in the Parisian daily *L'Univers*, columnist C. de Laroche-Héron reminded his readers that Canada was now like a grown son at the head of his own family. The ties were no less strong than when the son was an infant, but the father was content to see that his son had achieved autonomy.

In October 1855, Molson's Bank was founded. It was to play a critical role in Montréal's economic development. The first board members were William Molson, president, John Molson, vice-president, Thomas and John H.R. Molson and E. Hudon, directors. Eleven years later, Molson's Bank moved into its new headquarters designed by George Browne, which can still be seen at 288 Saint-Jacques Street. Its perfectly symmetrical façade has an elegant portico of columns that still bears the name of the bank, even though Molson's Bank became part of the Bank of Montreal in 1924. At the time of the acquisition, Molson's Bank had more than a hundred branches.

In 1856, the Treaty of Paris ended the Crimean War between Russia and the allied powers of Turkey, England and France. The 39th Regiment, which was part of the Montréal garrison, returned home in July 1856 on two steamers, the *John Munn* and the *Quebec*. The newly elected mayor, Henry Starnes, officially welcomed the regiment at a banquet in the concert hall of Bonsecours Market. The regiment marched through the streets of Montréal under garlands of ribbons.

In June 1856, the boiler aboard the steamer that provided ferry service between Montréal and Longueuil exploded just as the ferry was preparing to leave Longueuil. Its decks were crowded with passengers who had travelled by train to Longueuil. Fifty people died in the explosion, including some who were standing in the baggage shed on the quay.

The founding of the Grand Trunk Railway in 1852 marked the beginning of a new era in rail travel. The railway's first objective was to build a line linking Montréal and Toronto. Georges-Étienne Cartier had often said that the key to Montréal's prosperity was its geographical location. Montréal would be acting against its own best interests, he stated, if it turned down an opportunity to become the destination for goods from western Canada. With £3 million sterling, the Grand Trunk began work on the first section of what was to become a transcontinental railway. On October 27, 1856, the first passenger train left Montréal for Toronto, a tangible symbol of the union of the two Canadas fifteen years earlier. The occasion was marked by a parade of torches and a feast for 4,000 people gathered at Point Saint-Charles.

That year, there were celebrations marking another event. On May 1, the new court house was opened. To avoid any confusion, it should be pointed out that this is the court house that can still be seen on the north side of Notre-Dame. The building was acquired by the city in February 1972. Designed by the brilliant architect John Ostell, it had a hexagonal portico in the Grecian Ionic style. What is now the top floor of the building and the dome were added shortly before the turn of the century. For many years, the ground floor of the building housed the archives and the chief archivist was É.-Z. Massicotte. Years ago, the author had many enlightening conversations with him in his office on the Champ-de-Mars. This venerable edifice became known as the Old Court House, to distinguish it from the new court house designed by Ernest Cormier and built on the south side of Notre-Dame in 1923. In turn, the Cormier building became the Old Court House when the aluminum and glass cube at Notre-Dame and Saint-Laurent was built.

Tragedy struck again in 1857 when a steamer caught fire about twenty kilometres above Québec City. The *Montreal* was carrying more than 400 passengers, 256 of whom had come to the New World from the Clyde Estuary in Scotland aboard the *John McKenzie*. The steamer *Napoléon* came as close as it could to the burning vessel and lowered lifeboats into the water, but the panic-stricken victims capsized them. The newspapers carried chilling accounts of the tragedy, which claimed 253 lives. The *Illustrated London News* paid homage to a man named Lamontagne, a sous-chef aboard the *Montreal*. A good swimmer, Lamontagne removed a door from its hinges and used it as a ramp to evacuate eight children from the burning vessel. The *Napoléon* made for Montréal with the bodies of sixteen victims, shrouded in sailcloth, on one of its decks.

In 1857, Montréal's court house hosted the week-long convention of the American Association for the Advancement of Science. The participants were so pleased with the venue that they returned in 1882.

Changes were evident not only in Montréal's buildings but in its people as well. Since 1844, the Institut Canadien had been attracting those interested in liberal politics and philosophy. In 1858, Bishop Bourget criticized the lay thinkers of the institute for encouraging its members to delve into the books in its library. He felt that the moral worth of the institute's collection could not be vouched for, since it included the works of Voltaire, Rousseau and even some Gallican legists and contemporary authors like Michelet, Hugo and Lamartine. The church, wrote Bishop Bourget, had the inviolable right to regulate the administration of every library in the world. No doubt to stem the tide of liberalism, the Sulpicians began work that year (1858) on a spacious reading room, the Cabinet de Lecture Paroissial, at Notre-Dame and Saint-François-Xavier. The previous year, they had founded a reading circle, the Cercle Littéraire de Ville-Marie, and in 1844 they had founded the Oeuvre des Bons Livres.

It was also in 1858 that four learned men founded the Société Historique de Montréal for the purpose of "restoring to history all of its purity" through the analysis of archival documents and the publication of works. One of the founders was none other than Jacques Viger, Montréal's first mayor.

Shortly before the end of the decade, in November 1859, the new Anglican cathedral was consecrated on Sainte-Catherine Street. Work on Christ Church was still in progress when the church tower settled, leaning towards Sainte-Catherine. The resulting lawsuit went all the way to the Privy Council in London. The tower was rebuilt, only to show further signs of weakness. In 1927, it was replaced by an aluminum tower. In spite of these setbacks, Christ Church remains one of the most beautiful historic buildings in Montréal.

The Final Years of the Union

—————————— ✦ ——————————

The 1860s began with an event that made newspaper headlines throughout the world: the opening of the Victoria Bridge. Considered a marvel of modern times, the bridge marked Montréal's coming of age.

With a population of 90,000, Montréal was the tenth largest city in North America, the largest city in Canada, and the country's leading

Originally the Victoria Bridge, which opened in 1860, was completely enclosed and had only one track.

commercial centre and port. Because of its geographical situation, however, it was still somewhat insular. Trains leaving Montréal were unable to travel directly to the United States and had to be transported to the south shore by ferry. The time had come to build a bridge across the St. Lawrence. Construction of the bridge was entrusted to James Hodges, an engineer of great repute, who had played a key role in the Greenwich Railway and the Shakespeare Tunnel at Dover at a time when gunpowder was still used to blast away rock.

Hodges supervised the project from the first caisson, put in place in 1853, to the very last rivet. The bridge was more than two kilometres long, requiring 84,000 cubic metres of masonry for the piers and 8,000 tons of iron for the tubular spans supporting the roof in which openings were made to allow the exhaust from the locomotives to escape. Hodges had to use a great deal of ingenuity to resolve the many problems involved in construction of the bridge. Work on the piers could be done only between May and November, which meant that the scaffolding had to be dismantled every fall and reassembled every spring. However, the Grand Trunk Railway was prepared to pay a £60,000 bonus in the fall of 1858 if the bridge was open to railway traffic by the end of the following year.

The Crystal Palace, at the corner of Sainte-Catherine and Peel streets, was an impressive structure. It was later dismantled and reassembled at the foot of Mount Royal in Fletcher's Field, only to be destroyed by fire in the 1890s.

An impossible task – or so it was generally thought. Work had not yet begun on the central span, which would be more than a hundred metres long. With only two months in which to build the 771-ton span, Hodges decided that his crews must continue working over the winter months, with scaffolding mounted on the frozen river. They completed the bridge, but with little time to spare: when the spring thaw came, there were still pieces of scaffolding on the ice. In mid-December, the first train crossed the St. Lawrence. The project had required two and a half million rivets and the work of 3,040 men, 142 horses and four locomotives. The total cost had been $6.3 million, a colossal sum of money at the time.

Queen Victoria was asked to open the bridge and sent the young Prince

The Prince of Wales inaugurates the Victoria Bridge by lowering a commemorative stone block into place.

of Wales, the future King Edward VII, in her stead. When the prince stepped ashore on August 25, 1860, he was greeted by Mayor Charles-Séraphin Rodier. A procession formed to accompany him to the Crystal Palace on Sainte-Catherine Street at the corner of Peel, where he inaugurated an exhibition. The hall, only recently built, was a smaller version of the Crystal Palace in London. After cutting the ribbon, the prince was conducted to Bonaventure Station where he boarded a train covered in bunting for the ride to the Victoria Bridge. Here, a commemorative stone was put in place and the last spike, a silver one, was driven.

During his stay, the prince arrived at a party near Lachine in a birch bark canoe, with an honour guard of 100 Iroquois in traditional costumes, and attended a display of musket fire by 1,600 soldiers at Logan's Farm (later renamed Lafontaine Park), a concert featuring a cantata for 400 voices with Emma Lajeunesse, who was to become a world-famous soprano, and three balls.

A circular pavilion lighted by 2,000 gas lamps and capable of accommodating 10,000 guests was erected for the royal visit on the block bordered by Sainte-Catherine, Sherbrooke, Drummond and Peel streets. On August 27,

A circular pavilion was built for the visit of the Prince of Wales, then dismantled and reassembled in Boston.

the prince attended a ball there in his honour, along with more than 4,000 Montrealers. As for the pavilion, *La Minerve* announced on October 2 that it was being sold to the city of Boston where the prince would attend a ball given in his honour on October 18. Montrealers were nothing if not enterprising. In sixteen days, the pavilion was dismantled, loaded on to a convoy of trains and shipped to Boston, a distance of more than 600 kilometres, where it was reassembled. The prince must have been perplexed to note that the architectural tastes of his Bostonian hosts also ran to circular pavilions.

In 1847, a small group of artists and art lovers, including Cornelius Krieghoff, had formed the Montreal Society of Artists. It held many successful exhibitions. In 1860, a group of about eighty Montréal citizens formed the Art Association of Montreal, precursor to the Montreal Gallery of Fine Arts, under the aegis of the Anglican bishop, Francis Fulford. It was hoped that the Crystal Palace could be used for permanent exhibitions. This plan did not materialize and, awaiting a permanent home, the association held exhibitions in private homes and hotels.

Today, piers along the waterfront protect the city from the spring flood waters. It will be remembered that in 1642, a sudden rise in the water level of the St. Lawrence had threatened to flood Ville-Marie, leading the settlers to build the first cross on Mount Royal when the waters subsided. Over the years, Montréal experienced many floods, not the least of which was the flood in the spring of 1861. It happened so quickly that worshippers attending St. Stephen's Church in Dalhousie Square and the Wesleyan Chapel on

Two horses pull a tiny streetcar along Notre-Dame Street. In the background, the establishment of D.-C. Brosseau, who offered a fine selection of spices, wines, liquors and other goods.

Ottawa Street had to be rescued by boat. The flood waters covered a quarter of the city and rose so quickly that many people did not have time to remove their belongings. The St. Lawrence is said to have risen by more than seven metres. Trains arriving from the west had to wait until the flood waters subsided before entering the city.

As the city grew, so did the need for a public transportation system. Only the wealthy could afford to keep carriages, sleighs and horses, and hiring a carriage was beyond the means of most people. And so it was that the Montreal City Passenger Railway Company was born. Its shareholders, William Molson, John Ostell, William Dow, Johnston Thomson, William Macdonald, John Carter, Thomas Ryan and William E. Phillips, raised capital of $ 100,000 by issuing debentures.

In Victoria Square, an omnibus-sleigh pulled by four horses during a snowstorm.

Streetcars moving along rails set in the street were introduced in 1861. This meant that carriages coming in the opposite direction had to yield the right of way. Because the company was not allowed to use steam, the cars were drawn by horses. Service along Notre-Dame between Place d'Armes and the toll gate of Faubourg Québec was introduced in late November. Then on December 5, service was extended to Craig and Saint-Antoine streets between Papineau and Canning Square. Initially, the company had ten kilometres of tracks, four streetcars and eight horses. The cars stopped whenever someone wished to get on or off. Passengers sometimes stopped the streetcar to greet a friend or make a purchase.

By 1863, one million fares had been paid. No doubt, some passengers used the service many times a week; twenty tickets sold for a mere dollar. During the winter months, sleighs replaced the streetcars and sometimes four horses were needed to pull them through the deep snow. Straw covered the floor of the sleighs so that passengers could stay warm.

In mid-September 1861, Montréal received two visitors from France. Prince Jérôme-Napoléon, son of Jérôme Bonaparte and nephew of Emperor Napoléon I, and Maurice Sand, son of French writer George Sand, arrived at Lachine aboard the steamer *Welland*, then boarded a train for Montréal, where they were received by Mayor Rodier. Sand later wrote that it was wonderful to hear everyone speaking French as it was spoken in Normandy and Touraine. After visiting a number of cities in the United States, hearing his mother tongue was no doubt music to his ears. Suites were reserved for the illustrious guests in one of Montréal's finest hotels. The Donegana, Sand wrote, had an Indian name, but it was in fact a very French inn and a distinct improvement over the caravansaries of the United

States. Although he was mistaken over the origin of its name (the proprietor was Jean-Marie Donegana), Sand was not mistaken about the hotel's appointments: real candles in the place of gas lamps, sash windows and servants awaiting the guests' every need. The margin of his journal contains an interesting commentary on his stay at the Donegana: "Make these improvements at home."

Paying tribute to the liberal spirit of its members, the prince made a gift of books worth $2,000 to the Institut Canadien, and on his return to France sent the institute a number of works of art. The prince's visit aroused great interest among French Canadians, no doubt proud to receive a noble personage of French blood following the visit of the Prince of Wales.

One of the main attractions for visitors from other countries was the St. Lawrence River. One such visitor, writer and journalist Émile Chevalier, lived in Montréal from 1852 to 1860. His stay provided him with ample opportunity to visit the city and its environs. In his account entitled *Les derniers Iroquois*, Chevalier wrote that there were a hundred different scenes on the river to provide instruction, reflection, pleasure and delight to the eye. Sailing ships and steamships, barquentines and schooners, birch bark canoes and warships, vessels from every nation anchored in inlets along the river. The waters of the mighty river flowed towards the sea, slowing as they passed St. Helen's Island, which rose like a basket of greenery out of the water. On the far shore were fields as far as the eye could see.

The people of Montréal spent the year 1862 in a state of suspense. Even though the United States was preoccupied with its Civil War, it almost got involved in a conflict with Britain, and Montréal would have been at the centre of the conflict. An American captain illegally arrested two Confederate delegates aboard a British steamer. Threats were exchanged and regiments dispatched from Britain. A guard was mounted at the Victoria Bridge to protect against attempts to blow it up. Calm was restored when the Confederates, who should have been immune from arrest aboard the British steamer, escaped.

In 1862, the Société d'Archéologie et de Numismatique de Montréal was founded; it still exists, as does the Société Historique de Montréal, which was founded even earlier. In 1895, the Château de Ramezay was handed over to the Archaeological Society, which has looked after it ever since. Now a heritage monument, the Château de Ramezay contains an ethnographic museum that continues to delight visitors with exhibitions of furniture, paintings and costumes from the eighteenth and nineteenth centuries.

Steam replaced musclepower in the latest in firefighting equipment, shown in
L'Opinion publique in 1873.

The city relied on volunteer fire brigades until 1862, when a professional
fire department was established. The department had twenty-seven officers
and firefighters, who had to provide their own uniforms. In the event of a
fire, the department could also count on assistance from three companies of
thirteen volunteers and six supernumeraries. When they were not battling
flames, the firefighters were employed keeping down the dust on Montréal's
streets and tending the city's street lamps. The department had six hand
pumps and although there was talk of acquiring a steam-driven pump, this
only happened nine years later. Linked to the city's water system were
thirty-five fire hydrants to which could be attached 1,830 metres of leather
hose. In 1863, a telegraph alarm system went into service, enabling the fire
department to respond more quickly.

With the St. Lawrence open to vessels from all countries, Montréal's
reputation as a seaport grew. In mid-June 1863, for example, eighty-six vessels, including a Norwegian corvette, were moored in the harbour. The
captain and crew of the corvette received an official welcome from the city.

The division of Notre-Dame parish reflected the city's steady growth.
The diocese of Montréal now had 130 parishes, but the mother parish of
Notre-Dame had remained a single entity. On December 22, 1865, Bishop
Bourget received a decree authorizing him to form other parishes out of

Notre-Dame to better meet the spiritual needs of the community. The new parishes would remain attached to Notre-Dame until they were officially recognized, as happened in 1873. Notre-Dame remains the mother church and its curé has precedence over the curés of the splinter parishes. Each year on the Day of Purification, the parishes make a gift of a candle weighing one pound to the archdiocese, a rather feudal way of recognizing their subordination.

The Irish who emigrated to the United States to flee the potato famine of 1846-47 brought not only disease with them but also the Irish nationalist movement for Home Rule. When the Civil War ended, they decided that the time had come to support their compatriots in their struggle against England by taking up arms against Canada. In 1858, Irish Americans formed a republican secret society, the Fenians, named after the ancient Irish legendary warrior band of the Fianna. In 1866 the Fenians threatened to invade Canada. Within twenty-four hours, 14,000 volunteers had responded to an appeal to defend Canada's borders. The 100th Regiment of the Prince of Wales, founded in 1858, immediately left Montréal with a battery of artillery. Canada was on alert for only twenty days, but the threat of a Fenian raid was not over.

Confederation

——————————— >< ———————————

Ever since the British Conquest in 1760, some Canadians had been in favour of annexation to the United States. In the late 1840s, a group of businessmen founded the Montreal Annexation Association and signed an annexation manifesto. By and large, however, Canadian politicians were in favour of maintaining ties with the crown, and many viewed bringing together and consolidating the British colonies as a good way of ensuring that the efforts of the annexationists would not bear fruit.

In 1864, the legislatures of Nova Scotia, New Brunswick and Prince Edward Island decided to hold a conference in Charlottetown to study the possibility of union. Meanwhile, politicians in the Province of Canada were examining the possibility of amending the Act of Union of 1841. Some of the ministers who favoured a general confederation of the British provinces saw the Maritime initiative as an excellent opportunity to put forward their plan, so the Canadian government sent a delegation of eight men to attend the Charlottetown conference. The delegation included Georges-Étienne Cartier, who had travelled to England with two members of his cabinet in 1858 to personally present a proposal to transform the union of the two Canadas into a single confederation that would include the Atlantic provinces.

At Charlottetown, the original proposal for a Maritime union was quickly set aside in favour of a proposal for the union of all of Britain's North American provinces. "We have a population of three and a half million people," Cartier declared, "and that is enough to found a nation." A second conference attended by thirty-three delegates was held in Québec City in October. During sixteen days of heated debates, seventy-two resolutions were passed. The issue that prevented the delegates from agreeing to a legislative union was the distinctiveness of Lower Canada.

As early as 1864, two conflicting tendencies emerged that are still a source of tension more than a century later: the notion of a strong central authority and that of an association of sovereign states. The issue was very complex indeed. Voters in Montréal East had the benefit of hearing both sides of the story from two prominent political figures who represented the constituency in Parliament: Cartier and Antoine-Aimé Dorion, who had run against each other in the 1863 election.

In November 1864 Dorion signed a manifesto in Montréal opposing the plan adopted in Québec City, which he felt would not result in confederation. For there to be a confederation, he wrote, states join a union to serve certain mutual interests but must remain autonomous in their internal government. Dorion wondered what powers the provinces would retain under the proposed constitution. The central government would exercise sovereign authority not only over matters of mutual interest but also over most questions of internal governance. In addition, it would have direct control over all acts of local governments. Today's advocates of sovereignty-association would have agreed with Dorion when he wrote that what the people of Canada were being offered was not confederation but a disguised form of legislative union, in which the provinces would retain only a semblance of government with no authority other than that which the central government saw fit to give them.

The resolutions passed at the Québec conference were favourably received by London. The last session of the Canadian legislature under the Act of Union ended on August 15, 1866, and on July 1, 1867, the British North America Act became law by royal proclamation. Noting that the provinces on the Gulf of St. Lawrence marked Canada's eastern boundary, Cartier predicted that the Hudson's Bay and Red River territories and British Columbia would soon join Confederation so that Canada would stretch from the Atlantic to the Pacific, as it had when it was discovered by the Europeans. Georges-Étienne Cartier's house still stands at the corner of Notre-Dame and Berri streets. It was here that Cartier lived in 1849 when rioters, who had just set fire to the Parliament building, smashed the windows of his house. The house is now operated by the Government of Canada as a museum.

During the meetings leading up to Confederation, the oratorical skills of many great statesmen were tested. That same year, skills of a very different nature were put to the test. Mention has already been made of the origins of curling. In 1867, it was suggested that the native Canadian game of lacrosse or *bagattawayo* be recognized as Canada's national sport. Montrealers had begun developing a new version of the game in the 1840s but it was played by a relatively small number of people until the visit of the Prince of Wales in 1860. The prince attended a lacrosse match between two teams with twenty-five players each, one made up of native Canadians from the Kahnawake and St. Regis reserves and the other an all-star team consisting of the best players from two clubs, the Montreals and the Beavers.

The prince expressed such interest in the "new" sport that it rapidly became popular. In 1867, Dr. George W. Beers wrote a book of rules and the National Lacrosse Association was born. Competition was so fierce that some events attracted 5,000 spectators, an impressive number for the time. However, lacrosse had to compete for spectators' attention with cricket, tennis and soccer, considered elite sports, and with baseball, which was considered less brutal than lacrosse, although some felt that it was an unwelcome intrusion from our neighbours to the south.

French Canadians, who had not played a major role in shaping Montréal's business ventures, gradually began to carve out a place for themselves in commerce and industry. One notable French-Canadian-owned establishment was a store that opened in 1868 at the corner of Sainte-Catherine and Amherst streets. It later moved three blocks over to the corner of Saint-André Street and became an east-end equivalent to the large English-Canadian-owned stores on Sainte-Catherine Street West. Nazaire Dupuis, originally from the small town of Saint-Jacques-L'Achigan, had only a cow when he arrived in Montréal. He sold the cow's milk to survive. Working as a clerk for a wholesaler, Dupuis learned the rudiments of commerce. When

Dupuis Frères' first store at Sainte-Catherine and Amherst streets.

he opened his tiny shop, he asked his four brothers, Louis, Odilon, Alexis and Joseph-Narcisse, to help him.

A century later, Dupuis Frères had a total of 2,500 employees. It was the first large store to become unionized. During the 1950s and 1960s, it went into a period of decline marked by employee unrest. At one point, mice were let loose in the store to scare off customers. Shortly thereafter the business collapsed.

On April 13, 1868, one of the Fathers of Confederation, Thomas D'Arcy McGee, was buried in Montréal after meeting a tragic and untimely death. After founding newspapers in New York, Boston and Buffalo, D'Arcy McGee started the *New Era* in Montréal on May 25, 1857, in which he advocated political and cultural nationalism and Canadian independence. He became the minister of agriculture and attended the conferences in Charlottetown and Québec City in 1864. When the Fenian movement gained momentum, D'Arcy McGee publicly criticized its plans to invade Britain's North American colony. As a result, he gradually lost the support of his Irish constituents and was even banished from the St. Patrick's Society.

It was past midnight on April 7, 1868, when the House of Commons adjourned for the Easter holidays. D'Arcy McGee was preparing to return home, looking forward to being with his family in Montréal once again, when a young Fenian emerged from the shadows and shot him, making him "the first martyr of confederate Canada." Funeral services were held at St. Patrick's Church, and the parish priest's eulogy received thunderous applause, which was highly unusual at the time. There was a *Libera* and a sermon in French at Notre-Dame, after which his body was laid to rest in the Côte-des-Neiges Cemetery.

It was also in 1868 that the first contingent of Canadian Zouaves departed for Italy. For a number of years, the Vatican had feared an invasion of the Papal States by Garibaldi's nationalist movement, which aimed to unify Italy. Bishop Bourget of Montréal launched an appeal to young Catholic men to come to the aid of Pope Pius IX.

On February 18, 1868, 137 young men met at Notre-Dame Basilica. The following day they set sail from Montréal to defend "the first flag of the world." By the end of the year, 507 volunteers had joined the crusade. In 1870, the Zouaves returned to Montréal, leaving behind eight men who had died in Rome and were buried in the cemetery of Saint-Laurent-hors-les-Murs. Louis Veuillot wrote that the young men would return home as they had departed, pious and pure, worthy of the embraces of their mothers and sisters, having earned the public acclaim that awaited them.

Until 1868, the city of Montréal was allowed to borrow money only for specific purposes. Its total debt was close to $5 million. When the new Québec legislature was created at Confederation, the city was authorized to consolidate its debt; the following year, the legislature authorized the city to increase its debt by $350,000 to acquire land for a park on Mount Royal. Although it was several years before work on the project was begun, the councillors who came up with the idea deserve our congratulations. In 1850 and 1853, both the Protestants and the Catholics had acquired large tracts of land on Mount Royal to use as cemeteries. Had the council not intervened, Mount Royal might have become totally off-limits to the living. Finally, in 1871, the city's attorney received instructions to expropriate land.

On January 16, 1869, the first edition of the *Evening Star* appeared. As the *Montreal Daily Star*, it became one of the most important daily newspapers in the country.

At the age of fifteen, a young man named Hugh Graham from Atholstan, Huntingdon County, Québec, became an apprentice to his uncle, Edmund Parsons, publisher of the *Commercial Advertiser* of Montréal.

Place d'Armes in 1870. Two newspapers, *L'Opinion publique* and the *Canadian Illustrated News,* were published where the National Bank of Canada building stands today.

Within months, Graham took over management of the paper, then began working for the Montréal *Gazette* where he became friends with twenty-two-year-old George T. Lanigan. With only $300 between them, they founded the *Evening Star*. In 1872, Graham and Lanigan had a falling out. Lanigan, who was in favour of annexation, left Canada for the United States. Graham continued to publish the *Star* until his death in 1938. Under his leadership, the *Montreal Daily Star*, as it was renamed in 1877, became one of the leading papers in the western world, not only for the quality of its writing but also for its use of modern technology. The *Star* ceased publication in 1979. In 1917, Graham received the title of Lord Atholstan.

In 1869, Georges-É. Desbarats founded a weekly newspaper which he called the *Canadian Illustrated News*. It was the first paper in Canada to illustrate its pages with lithographs. Desbarats' associate, William Leggo, had patented a process that he called "leggotype," which made it possible to produce a wide spectrum of light and dark shades by alternating very fine lines. With its many engravings and family content, the *Illustrated News* was more like a magazine than a newspaper. On the cover of the first issue, published on October 30, 1869, was the first commercial halftone engraving.

Shortly thereafter, on January 1, 1870, the first issue of *L'Opinion publique* appeared. It was printed in the same shop as the *Illustrated News* and its founders were Georges-É. Desbarats, Joseph-Alfred Mousseau and Laurent-Olivier David. The two publications, which often reproduced the same engravings, provide a wealth of pictorial information about Canada in the late nineteenth century. Unfortunately, they ceased publication at the end of 1883.

In October 1869 the third son of Queen Victoria, Prince Arthur, who had been posted to his Rifle Brigade at the Montréal garrison, arrived in Montréal aboard the steamer *Magnet*. The prince then boarded an elegant carriage pulled by four white horses and was escorted by the Rifle Brigade to Rosemount, the home of Sir John Rose on Simpson Street, where he was billeted during his stay. As England was a sports-minded nation, it will come as no surprise that His Royal Highness attended lacrosse matches and, on December 15, 1869, the inauguration of Montréal's first covered curling rink. Until that time, curling had been played outdoors; the frozen surface of the St. Lawrence was a favourite venue. The prince later returned to Canada as governor general with the title of Duke of Connaught.

While we are on the subject of sports, the 1870s marked the beginning of increased interest and participation in athletic activities. In 1870, students at McGill University introduced a form of rugby football and, four years later, played the Harvard University team in two football games in Cambridge, Massachusetts. Harvard made attendance at the games compulsory for its students. This was the first time intercollegiate rugby-style football – what later evolved into Canadian and American football – was played in the United States.

Mary Queen of Scots may have played golf in 1563, but the Royal Montreal Golf Club was not founded until 1873. Some enthusiasts were so enamoured of this outdoor sport that they played at Fletcher's Field at the foot of Mount Royal on January 1, 1878. It was a splendid day and the ground was bare – a clear indication that the winters of yesteryear were not

Victorious soldiers returning to Montréal from the border skirmishes with the Fenians in 1869. Captured enemy weapons are displayed in a cart.

always as rough as the old-timers would have us believe. At around this time, yachts made their first appearance on the St. Lawrence. The first oval-shaped race tracks also appeared.

We have already mentioned the first threat of a Fenian raid, which was directed at New Brunswick in 1866. The Fenians' determination did not wane, and four years later wild rumours circulated in Montréal that the city would be sacked and its banks pillaged. An invasion was impending. Troops were quickly dispatched to the Huntingdon area. Prince Arthur learned of the Fenian movements while attending a ball in his honour. His conduct was considered "exemplary": he left immediately to prepare to leave for the border with his Rifle Brigade. The threat of a raid ended on May 25 at Cook's Corners after a brief skirmish in which ten Fenians died and thirteen were wounded.

The streets of Montréal were covered with dust thrown up by the wheels of passing vehicles in dry weather; when it rained, they were transformed into rivers of mud. So, in 1870, the city borrowed $200,000 to pave the streets. It was decided that tarmac would be used instead of asphalt, since the land acquired by the city for a park on Mount Royal provided an unlimited supply of the raw materials needed.

In 1852, the cathedral of Montréal at the corner of Saint-Denis and

Under the leadership of Bishop Bourget, the first stone of the new cathedral was laid in 1870. The project was made possible by donations from both Montrealers and more than a hundred rural parishes within the diocese.

Sainte-Catherine streets had been destroyed by fire. The nerve centre of the city was moving westward, and Bishop Bourget, hoping to keep pace with this shift, had the new bishop's palace and a temporary cathedral built on La Gauchetière Street in 1855. He then left for Europe to study the architecture of various cathedrals. His eye finally came to rest on St. Peter's basilica in Rome. Two years later, architect Victor Bourgeau visited Rome to study the design of the basilica and prepare plans for a scaled-down replica. On August 28, 1870, the first stone was laid in place. *La Minerve* reported the next day that three bands had filled the air with their joyous sounds as flags fluttered in the breeze. Work on the cathedral lasted more than fourteen years and it was not until March 24, 1894, that Bishop Édouard Fabre consecrated what is now Mary Queen of the World Cathedral.

The site chosen for the new cathedral was Saint-Antoine Cemetery, which had fallen into disuse after the opening of the Côte-des-Neiges Cemetery. In 1870, the city purchased cemetery land not required for the cathedral to create a public park, Dominion Square, now called Place du Canada. When workers began removing the remains of those buried in Saint-Antoine Cemetery the following year, there was a public outcry. Some said that the desecration of the surface site led to the desecration of the

Exhumation of coffins from Saint-Antoine cemetery.

mortal remains. The *Canadian Illustrated News* accused the workers of transporting those who had large tombstones and rich families to a more spacious final resting place, and of throwing whatever fragments remained into an old straw basket. The paper went on to wonder whether coffin boards removed from the ground were not being dried and sold for firewood, perhaps to the families of the dearly departed.

The tone of these lines gives an indication of public sentiment about the project. The *Illustrated News* acknowledged that, as the city grew, the dead should be moved to make room for the living. However, it felt that using them as landfill for private gardens or the north end of Victoria Square was going too far. Some Montrealers no doubt still expect to hear the trumpets of the Resurrection coming from beneath the manicured lawns of Place du Canada. In 1931, excavation work in front of the monument honouring Sir John A. Macdonald turned up the gravestone and coffin of a man named John Henry, who had died in 1851. A deeper grave was dug and his remains

"The doctors sniffed the earth and were unable to distinguish between the trenches dug for the victims of cholera and those dug for victims of typhus," read the caption under this cartoon in a Montréal newspaper.

reburied. Perhaps there is no such thing as a final resting place. Records of the earliest cemeteries in Montréal suggest that the graves of many pioneers have been moved.

Clearly, Montréal was an object of princely fascination. In early December 1871, a twenty-one-year-old member of the imperial Russian court, Grand Duke Alexis, arrived in Montréal after touring the United States. Mayor Coursol organized a ball in his honour at St. Lawrence Hall. The grand duke, who was tall and fair (6 feet 2 inches or 1.88 metres) must have broken many a Montréal maiden's heart. He even accepted an invitation to skate at the Victoria Rink. People would have killed for an opportunity to watch him skate, reported one paper. Would the ice, faced with such an honour, melt? It did not. The grand duke then waved a fond farewell and departed for New Orleans, where his frigate would take him to the Far East.

In early May 1871, a strike by Montréal's cab drivers disturbed the daily routine. In an attempt to stop drivers from taking passengers without proper authorization, it was decreed that drivers would now wear their permit numbers on their chests. The drivers refused, saying that this would reduce them to the status of dogs. For a few days, no transom cabs were to be seen on the streets of Montréal and citizens resorted to hiring horse-drawn carts.

4. L'HOSPITALITÉ À LA MODE.   5. CEUX QUI SOUFFRENT LE PLUS DE LA GRÈVE.

While horses hitched to carts struggle under the load of merchandise and travellers that have arrived by train, their fellow beasts frolic in delight as their carriages stand idle.

6. LES CHEVAUX EN VACANCE.

It was also in 1871 that the Grey Nuns moved into their new residence on Dorchester Street (now René-Lévesque Boulevard) between Guy and Saint-Mathieu. Plans for the convent had been drawn up by Victor Bourgeau. Only parts of the building – the main section and the wing on Guy – were built at that time. Bourgeau's plans for the west wing and the church were executed later. The completed building was classified as a historic monument in 1976.

In 1874, the city leased part of St. Helen's Island to create a public park. An open-air concert and picnic were organized for the fortieth anniversary of the founding of the Saint-Jean-Baptiste Society. There were celebrations everywhere. So many people flocked to Montréal that the Crystal Palace was pressed into service as a huge dormitory. The traditional parade, with fifteen floats, was more than four kilometres long. Delegations from the United States were as numerous as those from Canada. The parade passed under many triumphal arches, one of which carried a message of greeting to "our American brothers."

The same year, the concert hall of the Academy of Music was built;

The stage of the Academy of Music was so vast that horses could be used.

many people felt that this marked the beginning of the modern era of theatre in Montréal. For many years, concertgoers and theatregoers attended
performances there, including appearances by celebrated artists like Albani
(Emma Lajeunesse), Adelina Patti and the French tragic actress Sarah
Bernhardt.

The year 1875 marked the conclusion of a cause célèbre. For six years,
the Guibord affair had been a topic of heated debate. Bishop Bourget condemned the Institut Canadien for its liberal ideas, and decreed that those
who persisted in frequenting the institute would be depriving themselves of
the opportunity to receive the last rites of the church. When a member of
the institute, a printer named Joseph Guibord, died on November 18, 1869,
the church refused to allow him to be buried in his plot in Côte-des-Neiges
Cemetery. The institute brought a suit against the churchwardens of
Notre-Dame. Pending settlement of the lawsuit, Guibord's remains were
temporarily laid to rest in the Protestant cemetery. The suit lasted six long
years and went as far as the Privy Council in London, which found for the
institute and ordered Notre-Dame parish to bury Guibord in the Catholic
cemetery. Guibord was indeed buried in mid-November 1875, but Bishop
Bourget placed the grave under interdict, rendering it "morally separate
from the rest of the cemetery."

Montréal, which now had a population of 150,000, was one of the

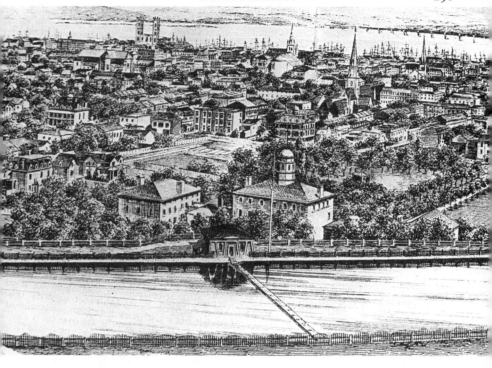

The city seen from Mount Royal in 1874. The McTavish reservoir is in the foreground.

dirtiest cities on the continent. The Saint-Martin rivulet, which flowed along what would be the course of Craig Street (now Saint-Antoine Street) and was a catchment for water running off Mount Royal, had long served as an open sewer. In 1832, the polluted waters of the St. Lawrence had been cited as one of the causes of the cholera epidemic.

Ten years later, the waterway was deepened to make it a proper sewer, but it now emptied into the St. Lawrence in two locations. In 1875, Dr. William Hingston was elected mayor. Under Hingston, the first task of the council was to approve funding for the construction of a catchment sewer under Craig Street. Work on the sewer began immediately and lasted three years, costing the city $259,000. While the new sewer eliminated a major source of pollution from the downtown area, it did not eliminate pollution altogether. The new main emptied into a tributary of the Migeon, which in turn emptied into the St. Lawrence.

The Delaware and Hudson Canal Company began offering regular train service between Montréal and New York in 1875. This may seem like a strange name for a railway company, but it had been founded for the purpose of moving coal by canal from Pennsylvania to New York. Later, when its barges were no longer equal to the task, the company built a railway. The first train reached Montréal on November 17, 1875, with many prominent businessmen and politicians on board, and the mayor was on hand to give them an official welcome. Regular service went into effect twelve days later.

Still on the subject of rail travel, July 1, 1876 marked the inauguration of another line, the Intercolonial Railway, which had been in the making for thirty years. This line was vital to the future of the country. As early as 1846, the provinces of Canada, New Brunswick and Nova Scotia had agreed on the need to link Montréal and Halifax by rail. Seven years later, work began on sections of the line, although some people believed that a Halifax-Portland line would be more profitable. At the Québec Conference in 1864, the importance of having the future federal government begin construction of the remaining sections of the line was stressed. Nine years after Confederation, Montréal was finally linked to the Atlantic by rail.

So much was written and said about the benefits of the rail travel that it may have gone to the heads of the providers of this essential service. On December 28, 1876, the engineers of the Grand Trunk Railway went on strike. One newspaper reported that in many locations, the engineers simply left the locomotives on the line. But there was no strike in the Atlantic provinces, where freight trains that had been kept in reserve in case of a snowstorm were put into service.

In terms of development and planning, Montréal presented a major problem for rail transportation. There was only one bridge across the St. Lawrence, and the Grand Trunk Railway, which owned the bridge, refused to allow other companies to use it. A group of businessmen came up with the idea of building a second bridge across the St. Lawrence, using St. Helen's Island as a stepping stone. The Royal Albert Bridge was to have six lanes on two levels, with provision for trains, streetcars and commercial and private vehicles. Plans for the bridge divided Montréal into two camps. English Montrealers felt that the bridge would promote growth in the east end at the expense of the west. The Board of Trade, whose 400 members included 130 Francophones, refused to support any application for a charter. For half a century, the plans for the Royal Albert Bridge gathered dust. Eventually, they were updated and used for the Harbour Bridge, now called the Jacques-Cartier Bridge.

In 1876 Montrealers were divided over another issue: vaccination. A smallpox epidemic broke out and the city board of health was instructed to

Customers flock to the Montreal and District Savings Bank in 1876 to withdraw their savings.

enforce a regulation making vaccination compulsory. There was considerable opposition. Four years earlier in *L'Opinion publique*, L.-O. David had criticized the medical establishment over an outbreak of chicken pox, writing that fears about the disease were heightened by concerns that the vaccine had become very dangerous. He wrote that the situation in Montréal showed the medical profession in an unfavourable light. He wondered why greater efforts had not been made to obtain a better vaccine and why doctors did not wait until a better vaccine was available to vaccinate patients.

David's remarks did little to reassure the public. There were demonstrations against the vaccination program in 1876; however, this did not prevent the regulation – which no doubt originated with the mayor himself – from being implemented. Dr. Hingston was a man of action; he also had a well-developed sense of civic duty. Journalist Léon Ledieu reported, for example, that as a surgeon, Hingston did not hesitate to reopen a patient's abdomen because he couldn't find one of the twelve sponges used during an operation. In so doing he saved a sponge – and the patient's life.

In the 1870s, there was no such thing as deposit insurance. If a bank declared bankruptcy, its customers lost their savings. When the Bank of Upper Canada faced total liquidation, there were insufficient funds in the bank's coffers to pay even the auditors hired to study the bank's financial situation.

From time to time, the population panicked. In 1848, customers rushed to the Montreal and District Savings Bank to withdraw their savings in response to a rumour that the bank was folding, but their fears were unfounded. Panic resurfaced in 1872 and again in 1876. In the space of one and a half days, the Savings Bank stoically paid out a total of $540,148. The crowd dwindled before the bank's funds did, reported one newspaper, adding that the public's confidence in the bank was now "stronger than ever."

A Decade of Achievements

————————— ➤❮ —————————

In 1877, one of the great dreams of the dynamic and popular Curé Labelle, known as the "Roi du Nord" (king of the north), came true. The curé had prayed so fervently for a Laurentian railway that he sometimes assigned railway stations for penance instead of Stations of the Cross.

The previous year, a section of the Laurentian railway went into service between Montréal and Saint-Jérôme. Work was begun to extend the line to Saint-Lin, and although only partially built, it was officially opened on August 21, 1877. Passengers left Hochelaga Station for Sainte-Thérèse, the beginning of the line, where they boarded a little train to Mascouche. They reached Saint-Lin via Sainte-Anne-des-Plaines by carriage. The main speaker at the inaugural banquet was none other than a friend of the curé's, Provincial Secretary Joseph-Adolphe Chapleau, who became premier two years later. The Montréal–Saint-Jérôme line was subsequently extended to Labelle, making the Laurentians one of the most important tourist regions in the province. Curé Labelle had, after all, predicted that the Laurentians would one day be called the Canadian Alps.

When Bishop Bourget decided to build the new cathedral west of the city centre, some said that it would be located in the sticks. However, the bishop anticipated that the heart of Montréal would lie to the west and events would soon prove him right. It was not long before the Windsor Hotel and Windsor Station were built there. In beauty, the Windsor Hotel surpassed all of its rivals. The wife of the governor general, Lady Dufferin, opened the hotel on January 28, 1878, and described it later in her diary as "gorgeous." It was indeed gorgeous, a prime example of the Victorian notion of palatial splendour and luxury and Canada's first grand hotel.

Its developers, who had invested half a million dollars, were not happy with the return on their investment and decided to risk everything by expanding the hotel. When the "divine" Sarah Bernhardt came to Montréal to perform at the Academy of Music in 1880, she stayed at the

The Windsor Hotel, Canada's first grand hotel.

Lady Dufferin surrounded by Montréal's leading families at the inauguration of the Windsor Hotel.

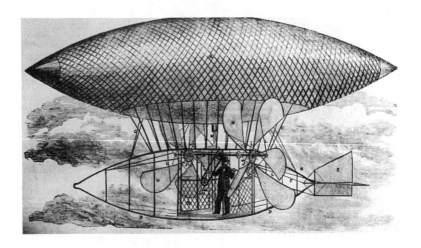

The dirigible designed by Montréal inventor Charles Pagé. As a result of an inadequate supply of lamp gas, Pagé had to strip the nacelle of its steering apparatus before the balloon would lift.

Windsor. In 1959, part of the hotel fell under the wrecker's ball, making room for an aluminum and glass skyscraper at Dorchester (now René-Lévesque) Boulevard and Peel Street. When the cupola fell, part of Montréal's rich heritage was lost.

Remembering the year 1879 provides us with an opportunity to note the career of a man who played a key role in both politics and journalism. Born in Lanoraie, he served with the French Army in Mexico in 1865, then returned to France with Napoleon III's troops. He subsequently settled in New Orleans, practising journalism for approximately ten years, before settling in Montréal. In 1879, he founded *La Patrie*. His name was Honoré Beaugrand, and his liberal views, developed on his extensive travels, did not meet with universal approval in Montréal.

Indeed, the front page of the February 17, 1894, issue of *La Patrie* gives some indication of Beaugrand's scathing criticism of the church. Here Beaugrand published his correspondence with a canon of the archdiocese on the subject of Alexandre Dumas's *Count of Monte Cristo*. "As I am a liberal," Beaugrand wrote, "I cannot say what will become of me, but I hope that the justice of the Almighty will be more equitable than the exuberance of indiscreet priests when they meddle in politics." Beaugrand ran *La Patrie* until 1897, when Henri Bourassa took over, and was mayor of Montréal in 1885 and 1886. A street and a Metro station have been named after him.

In June 1879, Montrealers were treated to an extraordinary spectacle: the first flight of an airship. The advent of the air balloon had meant the fulfilment of an age-old dream; however, air balloons were not capable of being steered or propelled. Charles Pagé, who specialized in repairing sewing machines, invented the *nacelle*, an enclosed shelter with propellers on either side that operated like paddle wheels as well as an *empennage* or tail assembly and a tiller. Handles were added so that the propellers could be made to turn – by hand.

That year, the Irish Benevolent Society was celebrating its annual holiday on June 21. Pagé decided that this was an excellent opportunity to demonstrate his flying machine. He would have liked a balloon with an elongated shape, but his sponsor had put his foot down and Pagé had to content himself with borrowing a balloon belonging to a daredevil from New York who called himself Professor Grimley.

When the time came, there was not enough lamp gas to fill the balloon, which was unable to lift the nacelle. Not wanting to disappoint the expectant crowd, Pagé removed the wheels and paddles. Grimley and a friend named Creelman climbed aboard. They had reached an altitude of 1,300 metres when a strong updraft suddenly lifted them to 3,000 metres. The balloon eventually came to rest in a freshly tilled field in Saint-Jude, some twenty-five kilometres away. In desperation, Grimley had kept the escape valve open in an attempt to land the balloon. He was overcome by the gas and it took ten minutes for Creelman to revive him.

Air travel may have been a distant dream, but in 1879 the Québec government proudly announced that passengers could now travel by train from Québec City to Ottawa via Montréal in fourteen hours. In 1875, the government acquired two railway companies, which it merged as the Quebec, Montreal, Ottawa and Occidental Railway with the goal of building a line on the north shore of the St. Lawrence through Montréal to a point in Pontiac County on the Québec side of the Ottawa River – and eventually, a bridge over the river to Ottawa. Québec received permission to build the bridge in 1879.

On February 13, 1879 *L'Opinion publique* announced that the train would leave Québec City at 8 or 9 o'clock, pick up cars from the Colonization Railway at St. Martin's Junction, then proceed to Ottawa, arriving at 11 p.m. The Colonization Railway was the line to the Laurentians, the "Curé Labelle Line."

The growth of Montréal's rail network was still being blocked by the Grand Trunk Railway, which refused to allow other companies to use the

The estate car of the governor general, the Marquis of Lorne, on the Quebec, Montreal, Ottawa and Occidental Railway.

Victoria Bridge. Longueuil was the last station for two major lines, one from Sherbrooke and the other from Portland and Boston. During the summer months ferries transported rail passengers to Montréal, but in the winter, service ground to a halt. One enterprising businessman who had been involved in railway construction, Louis-Adélard Sénécal, came up with a solution that he proposed to four partners: build a line across the ice between Hochelaga and Longueuil.

First, wooden ties varying in length from five to fifteen metres were positioned on the ice so as to distribute the weight of the train evenly over a large area. Iron rails were then anchored to the ties. On January 30, 1880, the first railway on ice went into service. The water under the track was three to ten metres deep and when the locomotive set out there were plenty of skeptics on hand to say that it would never reach its destination. However, the train did arrive at its destination, cheered on by crowds of well-wishers. The engineers had known how to calculate the load that the ice could support. In Russia, the army routinely moved artillery across frozen lakes. Closer to home, scaffolding had been placed on the frozen river during construction of the final spans of the Victoria Bridge. The line was abandoned in 1882 when an agreement was finally reached with the Grand Trunk Railway.

In 1880, the poet Louis Fréchette presented two of his works, *Fleurs*

The inauguration of the railway across the frozen St. Lawrence from Hochelaga to Longueuil.

boréales and *Oiseaux de neige*, to the Académie Française to instant acclaim. However, the constitution of the Académie made it impossible to award literary prizes to foreigners. Fréchette was, after all, a British subject. The members decided to make an exception to the offending clause on the grounds that Fréchette was a French-speaking Canadian. Fréchette thus became the first Quebecer to be honoured by the Académie. He was fêted by Montréal's intellectual elite at a magnificent banquet, where he was hailed as the Victor Hugo of North America. Later, he received the more modest title of poet laureate of Québec.

That same year, in December, Sarah Bernhardt visited Montréal where she was greeted as a cultural emissary of France by the same people who had so warmly honoured Fréchette. Her hosts had a change of heart when they learned that she would perform on Christmas Day. Their opposition stiffened when they learned that she would perform in Scribe's *Adrienne Lecouvreur*, which Bishop Fabre described as an "immoral drama" and a "pathetic lesson for Christian families." The bishop added that the actors' talent would only serve to heighten the danger and increase the audience's fascination with the evil passions lurking in the depths of the human heart.

Bernhardt was nevertheless given a warm welcome and when she climbed in the carriage escorting her back to the Windsor Hotel after her

MONTREAL. — Laval University and St Denis street
MONTRÉAL: — L'Université Laval et la Rue St-Denis

Laval University's Montréal building, located on the east side of Saint-Denis Street south of Sainte-Catherine, in the early twentieth century. The Université de Montréal was founded in 1920.

performance on Christmas Eve, students took the place of her horses and pulled the carriage themselves. It was said that Louis Fréchette led the procession. Perhaps he hoped that Bernhardt would one day play the leading role in one of his plays. Alas, it was not to be.

McGill University had served the English-speaking population of Montréal for many years. In 1852, Université Laval had been founded in Québec City. The bishop of Montréal decided to found a university in his diocese and enlisted the help of the Sulpicians. His first attempts were unsuccessful. Université Laval objected, stating that Québec's population was not large enough to support two universities. Politics also played a role. It was not until 1876, when the Holy See was made aware of the problem, that Laval agreed to create an affiliated college in Montréal. The Québec legislature authorized the founding of faculties of theology, medicine and law in 1881.

In 1894, the Sulpicians donated land on Saint-Denis Street for the building, and three years later funded a chair in French literature. Over the years, Laval's authority over the branch became a source of tension; it was not until 1920 that the institution became a separate entity, the Université de Montréal. The building on Saint-Denis Street has housed the École des Métiers Commerciaux and, more recently, the Institut de Tourisme et

Drawings for a building of Université Laval, to be built at a cost of $1 million, were never used.

d'Hôtellerie du Québec. When a fire and explosion destroyed the building in 1969, the land was incorporated into the block where the Université du Québec now stands.

Laval's faculty of medicine in Montréal was the work of Dr. Emmanuel Persillier-Lachapelle, treasurer of the College of Physicians and Surgeons and a professor at the École Victoria, a French-language school affiliated with a Methodist institution, Victoria University in Cobourg, Ontario. It will come as no surprise that the religious authorities were anxious to bring the teaching of medicine back into the fold. To provide students with practical clinical training to supplement their theoretical education, Dr. Lachapelle together with two colleagues founded Notre-Dame Hospital in 1880. This was undoubtedly his greatest accomplishment, although it could be argued that he played an equally important role five years later when he campaigned in favour of vaccination against smallpox, a measure that incited people to riot, as we shall see later on.

Historians familiar with the development of sports in Canada agree that Montrealers were responsible for hockey supplanting lacrosse and becoming Canada's national sport. The sport of pushing disks across the ice with curved sticks had long been popular in Ireland and Scotland, but it was in Montréal that rules for the game of hockey were established jointly by a group of McGill students and members of the Victoria Club in 1881. Some historians claim that the sport dates from games played on the Victoria Rink in 1875 and 1876 and that students at Collège Sainte-Marie played the game of shinny, which had been brought from Ireland, but it is only logical to date the beginning of a sport from the moment when its rules are officially codified.

Up until 1882, the only transatlantic steamers that made regular stops at Montréal came from England. That year, the French postal service began offering service between Le Havre and Montréal. The *Ville de Para* was officially welcomed by city officials in mid-September. At a banquet aboard the steamer, the French consul, Comte de Sesmaisons, expressed the view that the new social, financial, industrial and commercial relations between the peoples of Québec and France would provide new opportunities for strengthening the ties that bound them.

In 1882, the railway line between Montréal and Sorel went into service. On April 1, trains left from either end of the line and met in Verchères where, to the sound of deafening musket fire, the last four spikes were driven home. The line would be used not only by business travellers but also by those who wanted to take the waters at Varennes, the most fashionable destination in the Montréal region.

For many years, the locomotives used on Canadian lines were built in the United States or Britain. In 1875, when the time came to purchase locomotives for the Intercolonial Railway between Montréal and Halifax, there was only one motor works in Canada that could build locomotives, and it was located in Kingston. In 1883, the Canadian Pacific Railway decided to produce its own locomotives in its shops on De Lorimier Street. The first locomotive, the 285, completed in the fall of 1883, was designed by a Scottish mechanic, Francis R.F. Brown, and remained in service for thirty-seven years. These works were eventually moved to the Angus shops where they remained in production until 1944. A total of 1,200 units were produced there between 1883 and 1944.

Winter sports, particularly snowshoeing, were very popular at this time. However, it was not until January 1883 that Montréal hosted its first winter carnival with an ice palace of breathtaking proportions. The authorities were somewhat reticent about the ice palace, fearing that immigrants would be put off by such an imposing symbol of the Canadian winter. "Each year we spend considerable amounts of money to attract immigrants to our country," wrote one newspaper columnist. "By showing them our country with its snow, with a festival more appropriate for polar regions, are we not working at cross-purposes?" The editor of the paper added that, out of a sense of patriotism, Québec City had decided to postpone its annual carnival to the month of July.

However, shortly after the winter carnival, the paper did a complete

The Ice Palace, centrepiece of the first winter carnival, held in 1883.

about-face: tourism had won out over immigration. "A total success," the editor wrote. "The winter carnival of 1883 will never be forgotten. Foreign visitors to our city, American visitors being the most numerous, will remember their stay with us for many years to come. The ice palace was the centrepiece of the carnival. Lit with electric lights at night, it looks like a fairy-tale palace!"

In 1884, a newspaper was founded that is now into its second century of publication. Shortly after its centenary, it became a truly daily newspaper, printing a Sunday edition. The first issue of *La Presse* appeared on October 20, 1884. Trefflé Berthiaume is often cited as the founder, but in fact it was William Edmond Blumhart who founded *La Presse* with the help of his father-in-law, Louis-Adélard Sénécal, the keen entrepreneur who had built the first railway on ice.

La Presse grew out of a split in the Conservative Party between Sénécal and Joseph-Adolphe Chapleau on the one hand and Hector Langevin on the other. At the federal level, Langevin represented Conservatives who were faithful disciples of John A. Macdonald. A printer at *La Minerve*, Trefflé Berthiaume took the risk of accepting the paper as a gift – and assuming its debts. In 1893, *La Presse* could claim a circulation of 31,477, more than all of the other French-language dailies in Montréal combined. Berthiaume had not only saved the paper from extinction: he had made it a national institution.

At around this time, Montréal began to develop a keen appetite for expansion. In 1883, under Mayor Jean-Louis Beaudry, Montréal annexed the village municipality of Hochelaga. In the space of a decade, Montréal's population doubled as a result of similar annexations, and over forty years it absorbed almost one town per year on average. Its most recent acquisition is the city of Pointe-aux-Trembles. When the first acquisition took place in 1883, French-speaking Montrealers represented just over half of the population. By 1920, Francophones represented three quarters of the city's population.

In 1885, Montréal experienced a smallpox epidemic that claimed 3,164 lives. Smallpox is highly contagious. In fact, at the time of the Conquest, Field Marshal Lord Amherst had wanted to use smallpox as a weapon by distributing pox-infested blankets to natives who had aligned themselves with the French.

In 1885, the mayor of Montréal was Honoré Beaugrand. Beaugrand was not only a liberal thinker but proved to be a progressive mayor on almost every issue. He bravely introduced highly unpopular measures, including a health commission whose job it was to halt the epidemic. Homes affected by the pox were placed under quarantine, and a sign was posted outside. Angry citizens expressed their outrage by destroying the signs. The city took responsibility for feeding affected families, spending a total of $185,000. On the evening of September 28, some 2,000 people gathered in front of the health commission offices. Although police were present, the angry crowd began breaking windows, entering the building and destroying the offices.

Louis Riel was hanged on November 16, 1885, and it was a day of mourning for all French Canadians. Five days later in *Le Monde illustré*, Léon Ledieu wrote a passionate editorial framed in a heavy black border. Queen Victoria had turned a deaf ear to appeals for clemency. Addressing his editorial to "the ruler of three hundred million subjects," Ledieu wrote, "May you be spared in your dreams the sight of the body of the martyr of freedom swinging above the gallows that your representatives have erected in your name."

Elegant sleighs on Place d'Armes. Passengers kept warm under luxurious buffalo robes. (Engraving, 1886.)

Emotions ran high in Montréal. On November 22, a crowd of 30,000 people gathered on the Champ-de-Mars to hear some of the greatest orators of the period. Wilfrid Laurier accused the Macdonald government of cowardice. Journalist and senator F.-X.-A. Trudel reminded the crowd that a young girl had been burned at the stake for defending her country and that "those who sent Joan of Arc to her death were English, just like those who hanged Riel." Member of Parliament Charles-Joseph Coursol likened Riel to Danton who, as he was about to be beheaded, declared that he was taking Robespierre with him. Coursol concluded by saying that "in surrendering to the sheriff of Regina, Riel could also say that he was taking the ministry with him, because the voice of the people would execute those who sent the brave Métis leader to his death!"

La Presse also voiced its outrage. "Montréal is in mourning," it wrote. "Montréal, Canada's metropolis, the birthplace of every major patriotic movement and national enterprise, is grieving because the nation has just committed a grave error, a criminal error, one for which the price remains unknown."

The year 1886 was marked by many events. In the spring, the city experienced unprecedented flooding. On April 17, those who wished to travel from the foot of Beaver Hall Hill to Saint-Jacques Street had to hire either a

The militia holds drills on the Champ-de-Mars under electric light produced by a technician who had visited the 1878 Paris World's Fair.

carriage or a rowboat. The impromptu ferrymen charged five cents for the trip. In early June, Montrealers were overjoyed to learn that the man who had been their bishop since 1876, Édouard-Charles Fabre, had been made an archbishop and would now wear the pallium.

The previous year, the last spike of the transcontinental railway had been driven in the Rockies. On June 28, 1886, the first train for the Pacific coast prepared to leave Dalhousie Station. Mayor Beaugrand and officials from Canadian Pacific were on hand. Cannons were fired as the train, composed of three baggage cars (including a mail car), a first-class carriage, a sleeping car and several cars filled with immigrants left the station. In 1893, 132 trains arrived in Montréal each day, a clear indication of the city's importance before the turn of the century.

In 1886, a bazaar lasting many weeks was held to raise money for the new cathedral. One of the most popular events was a visit from the chief of the Blackfoot Indians of Alberta, Crowfoot, and his brother, Three Bison. The famous Oblate missionary Albert Lacombe arranged the visit at the request of charity organizers. The "royal visitors," as they were referred to by some Montrealers, arrived on September 27.

Crowfoot wore the traditional Blackfoot costume: doeskin garments ornamented with pearls and feathers, and ermine on the shoulders and

The sled run on Place Jacques-Cartier during the 1887 winter carnival.

sleeves to symbolize his rank. He wore three silver medals on his chest, one awarded to him by Queen Victoria in 1877 on the signing of a peace treaty, the second by the Marquis of Lorne for his refusal to align himself with the Sioux during their revolt against the American government, and the third by the Marquis of Lansdowne the previous year for his loyalty to the crown. Mayor Beaugrand gave Crowfoot an address illuminated by the Soeurs du Bon-Pasteur, which he accepted "in a booming voice." The presentation ceremony had to be cut short, because the crowd had become so large that there were fears that panic would break out.

When Crowfoot and Three Bison returned home, they were able to tell their families and friends about the benefits of electric street lights. Montréal's first electric street lamps had been installed in July. Eight years earlier, J.A.I. Craig of Montréal had returned from the Paris world's fair with the principle of the arc lamp or electric candle. The following year, in 1879, he succeeded in lighting the Champ-de-Mars so that the militia could hold training exercises at night. There was fierce competition to provide electric lighting, but on July 17, 1886, the streets of the city were lit with arc lamps. The company that supplied the city with gas lamps opposed electric

The *City of Montreal* catches fire in the Atlantic, 650 kilometres off Newfoundland, in August 1887.

lighting, its arguments extending to the claim that the new lighting system was detrimental to the complexion of women.

The year 1887 opened, as usual, with the winter carnival and an ice palace near the new cathedral. For fresh-air enthusiasts, a sled run was built. The run started at the Nelson Column on Place Jacques-Cartier, overshot Saint-Paul and Commissioners streets and ended on the icy wastes of the St. Lawrence – a total distance of more than 350 metres.

For a number of years, the country's civil engineers had wanted to form a professional organization and, in June 1887, their association was incorporated in Montréal, which became its headquarters. The association's first president, Thomas Coltrin Keefer, was a very prominent engineer at the time. He had helped build the canals of the upper St. Lawrence, the Montréal-Toronto railway line and the Victoria Bridge line.

In August, Montrealers were saddened to hear of the sinking of a transatlantic steamer named after their city. The *City of Montreal* had departed on August 6 for Liverpool. Six hundred and fifty kilometres off the coast of Newfoundland, a fire broke out in the hold, which was filled with bales of cotton. Lifeboats were lowered into the water, but another steamship, the

Vessels at the western end of the port of Montréal are decorated to celebrate Queen Victoria's golden jubilee (1887).

York City, arrived in time to take all those on board the vessel, with the exception of eleven people who had taken to a lifeboat and could not be found.

In mid-January 1888, plans were announced for a building for Université Laval to be built on Saint-Denis Street, between Sherbrooke and Ontario. It was to have been a majestic building. No doubt it was the cost of the project, estimated at $1 million, that prevented it from ever being built.

The Lenten sermon at Notre-Dame was introduced in 1888. The sermon attracted large crowds because of the quality of the religious figures who were invited to speak. Oldtimers will remember Lenten sermons preached by Abbé Thellier de Poncheville in 1917 and 1921.

For more than a century, Montrealers have been celebrating Labour Day with a day of rest. The first Labour Day parade in Montréal was staged on September 3, 1888. Five thousand workers marched through the streets before a crowd of 25,000 onlookers.

November 11, 1888, marked the inauguration of the Canadian College in Rome. The work of the Sulpician superior, Frédéric Louis Colin, the college was founded to provide a home for priests who wanted to study in the Eternal City. The Sulpicians assumed the cost of building and

In the mind of architect Bruce Price, Windsor Station's epic proportions reflected the future of the railway.

maintaining the college. Before construction was begun, Father Colin had gone to London seeking assurances that the seminary could invest funds outside of Canada.

The year 1889 began with the passing of a singular and sympathetic figure. Charles McKiernan, known as "Joe Beef," was a veteran of the Crimean War. His charity was legendary, and when he died a large crowd of mourners – beggars and gainfully employed citizens alike – followed the hearse, drawn by four horses draped in black. Joe Beef was a publican and it was as the owner of the Crown and the Sceptre that he became the father of the disinherited. He collected every penny that changed hands in his establishment in a jar and donated the proceeds to charity. Not counting the silver and bank notes, his estate was estimated at $80,000. Charity does not always make a person poorer.

The decade ended amid a great deal of pomp and ceremony with the inauguration of Windsor Station, offered to the city of Montréal by Canadian Pacific on completion of the transcontinental railway. In the mind of the architect, Bruce Price, the epic proportions of the station reflected the prosperity that rail travel would bring to the whole country. The station opened to passengers in 1889. Price went on to design a series of distinctive château-hotels that boosted Canada's popularity as a tourist destination. The Château Frontenac in Québec City and the Banff Springs Hotel in Banff, Alberta, are two examples of his work.

Montréal Comes of Age

————————— ⇥⇤ —————————

As Montréal entered the last decade of the nineteenth century, preparations began for its 250th anniversary. Montréal was beyond question Canada's largest city. According to the 1891 census it had a population of 216,650, compared to Québec City's 63,090 and Toronto's 181,220. That same year, 725 ocean liners and 5,268 Great Lakes vessels, weighing a total of two million tons, visited the port of Montréal. The city covered a total area of 2,170 hectares, excluding parks, and had 214 kilometres of roads and streets.

At the beginning of the decade a Jewish Montrealer, Louis Rubenstein, was the city's ambassador to the world. Rubenstein won an international skating competition in St. Petersburg against competitors from Austria, Finland, Norway and Sweden and from the cities of Moscow, Stockholm and St. Petersburg itself. Rubenstein was also adept at political figure eights: he later became an alderman. A fountain has been dedicated in his honour at the corner of Park and Mount Royal avenues.

In 1891, for the first time in Québec, a woman was granted a degree in medicine. At the time, McGill University and the School of Medicine, a faculty of Bishop's University, at the corner of Ontario and Jeanne-Mance, were great rivals. On March 31, Bishop's medical student Grace Ritchie received her degree in the Anglican Synodal Hall behind Christ Church Cathedral.

No doubt alluding to McGill, which had refused to admit Ritchie, Dr. Bradford McConnell, a professor of pathology, declared that the problems that skeptics had predicted would occur with coeducational classes were "imagined." Problems did, however, arise over admitting women to internships in hospitals with more than one hundred beds. The problem was only resolved in 1905, when the two faculties of medicine were merged.

The year 1891 ended with the founding in Montréal of the Canadian Bankers' Association. In the nineteenth century, people were reluctant to entrust their savings to banks, as many had become insolvent. In an effort to make these institutions more stable and safeguard their own interests, bankers decided to form a professional association. The site for the annual meetings of the association rotated among Montréal, Toronto, Halifax, Québec City and Ottawa.

The year 1892 was an important milestone in the city's development. It was the 250th anniversary of its founding. As early as 1879, it had been suggested that a monument be erected to the memory of Chomedey de Maisonneuve, but nothing had come of the suggestion. In the February 1890 issue of *Le Monde illustré*, É.-Z. Massicotte, who would later become the director of Montréal's legal archives, deplored the fact that there was still no monument to Chomedey de Maisonneuve. "Is there no one," he wrote, "to form a committee? Is there not a historical society, a literary circle, a patriotic journalist or a common citizen that recognizes his contribution?"

The January 23, 1892, issue of *Le Monde illustré* contained a sketch of the statue commissioned from the sculptor Philippe Hébert. It was to be his greatest accomplishment. As often happens, when a provisional committee was set up in the spring of 1891 to organize a program of activities to mark the anniversary, it was already too late. The enthusiasm of the organizers was also dampened by the 1892 Chicago World's Fair marking the 400th anniversary of the discovery of America by Christopher Columbus. In 1888, a pamphlet promoting Montréal as a venue for the world's fair had been produced.

Justice Louis François Georges Baby, president of the Société d'Archéologie et de Numismatique de Montréal and one of the founders of the Société Historique de Montréal, was made chair of the committee organizing the festivities. It quickly became clear that not enough time had been allowed to organize an appropriate celebration of the founding of Ville-Marie; however, the monument committee would not be dissuaded. On September 4, 1892, the first stone of the statue's pedestal was put in place. The statue itself was not completed until three years later. We will return to this story later on.

Montréal's public transportation system had gone into service in 1861. For the next thirty years, horse-drawn streetcars were used. On September 21, 1892, an electric streetcar called the *Rocket* was tested; however, the curve at Bleury and Craig streets proved too much for the *Rocket* and it left the tracks. It redeemed itself by coming to a stop at the foot of Amherst Street and travelling back up the street in reverse. According to one

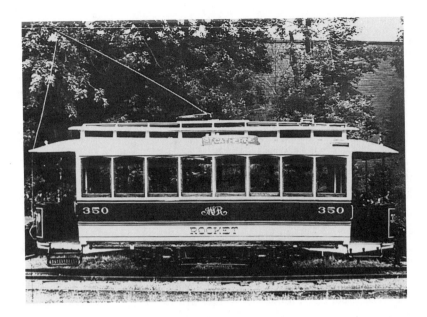

Montréal's first electric streetcar, the *Rocket,* delighted onlookers when it travelled up the Amherst Street hill in reverse.

onlooker, an electrician was perched on the roof to ensure that the streetcar remained connected to the overhead electrical wires.

These early technological feats may seem amusing, but it would be interesting to assess the role that public transportation has played in Montréal's development. For many years, Montréal's streetcars served other functions as well: cleaning the city's streets, collecting milk cans and transporting prisoners from Bordeaux Jail to the Court House on Notre-Dame. The streetcars could even be equipped with a hearse carriage to transport Montrealers to their final resting place.

The month of June 1893 began sadly with a fire at Villa Maria Convent. Luckily, the students were not present at the time; however, many firefighters were gravely injured and one died in the fire.

On June 14, a monument to Jacques Cartier was unveiled in Saint-Henri Square. It is, to our knowledge, the first statue of the discoverer of Canada. The statue on the ramparts of Saint-Malo, his birthplace in France, dates from 1905.

June 24, 1893 marked the inauguration of the Monument National by the Saint-Jean-Baptiste Society of Montréal. It has been hailed as a bastion

Cutting blocks of ice on the St. Lawrence at Montréal (1889).

of the French fact in North America, and judging from the long list of international stars who have performed on its stage it has played a key role in the history of Québec nationalism and Montréal's cultural development. The Monument National was, in fact, Montréal's first "place des arts." In addition, many brilliant orators, including Wilfrid Laurier, Henri Bourassa, Olivar Asselin, Lionel Groulx and André Laurendeau, have spoken there. The year after it opened, *La Presse* proposed a "Boulevard de l'Opéra" linking Saint-Denis Street with St. Lawrence Boulevard and ending in front of the Monument National, but the proposal was rejected.

In early December 1893, the Royal Victoria Hospital was opened by the governor general, Lord Aberdeen. According to *La Presse*, it was dedicated by Lord Mount Stephen and Sir Donald A. Smith to the suffering.

To mark Montréal's 250th anniversary, the Société Historique de Montréal decided to present a monument to the first settlers as a gift to the city. The seventeen-ton obelisk was placed on its pedestal on May 17, 1894, even though one of the four bronze plaques on the statue mentions the date May 18, 1893. Work on the monument must have been delayed as a result of unforeseen circumstances. Over the years, the ground under the monument shifted to the point where the obelisk began leaning dangerously. In 1939, the Société Historique recommended that it be moved to Place Royale, where it still stands. Its new home is actually closer to the site where Ville-Marie was built in 1642.

The events marking the 250th anniversary of the founding of Ville-Marie sparked new interest in and recognition of important figures in the

Royal Victoria Hospital, for which plans were drawn up in 1889.

city's history. And so it was that in 1894, opposite Sainte-Cunégonde church, a statue was erected to the memory of Pierre Le Moyne d'Iberville, whom some historians consider the first great Canadian. Like the statue of Jacques Cartier, this statue also was the work of J.-Arthur Vincent.

In late October 1894, Montrealers mourned the passing of a great Québec statesman, former premier Honoré Mercier. Setting aside their partisan differences, politicians recognized that Mercier had had a profound impact on the history of Québec and had played an important role in bringing the Québec government closer to its cultural roots. Mercier's trip to France in 1890 to arrange a $10-million loan had strengthened ties between France and Québec immeasurably. Funeral services were held on November 2, 1894, and the funeral procession was the largest Montréal had seen since the death of Georges-Étienne Cartier in 1873.

Mid-February 1895 marked the inauguration of the Chemin de Fer des Comtés-Unis, roughly ninety kilometres in length, which ran from Montréal to Sorel on the south shore. It passed through Iberville, Rougemont, Saint-Hyacinthe and another dozen or so parishes along the line. In their haste to open the line on time, the railway's promoters had not taken into account the rigours of the Canadian winter. On its maiden voyage, the train became stuck in a snowdrift near Saint-Robert. Neither the

St. Helen's Island was proposed as the site for the 1896 world's fair.

presence of Lieutenant-Governor Chapleau nor the locomotive rushed in from Sorel could free it. Finally, horses were brought in and pulled the train and its passengers free.

Judging from all of the grandiose plans that were proposed for Montréal, civic pride was firmly in place in the 1890s. In the spring of 1895, St. Helen's Island was proposed as the site for a world's fair the following year. The artist A.-S. Brodeur drew up plans that included a tall tower in the centre of the island, a huge waterfall and a bridge connecting St. Helen's Island and Île Ronde. At night, wrote *Le Monde illustré*, the festivities would be truly wonderful. St. Helen's Island would be like the Venice of the St. Lawrence. The illuminated fair grounds, with the cascade and brilliantly lit pavilions, would present a truly enchanting spectacle. It was anticipated that after the fair, most of the pavilions would be preserved and St. Helen's Island would become a public park, the only one of its kind in the world. Less than three quarters of a century later, what began as a modest plan would become a world's fair of epic proportions, thanks to the creative genius of Mayor Jean Drapeau.

In 1895, three statues were unveiled in Montréal. On April 24, the statue of the Patriote Jean-Olivier Chénier was unveiled on Saint-Denis Street.

Viger Station-Hotel, inaugurated in 1898, brought many illustrious visitors to Montréal's east end.

Plans for a statue put forward in 1887 on the fiftieth anniversary of the rebellion had met with opposition, and the archbishop of Montréal had refused to exhume Chénier's ashes. In 1893, Honoré Mercier raised the idea again. This time, however, protests from the descendants of those who had taken up arms against the Patriotes were not enough to stop the plan from going through. Could it be a coincidence that six weeks later, on June 6, a statue of John A. Macdonald, who had let Louis Riel hang ten years earlier, was unveiled in Dominion Square?

On July 1, 1895, Lieutenant-Governor Joseph-Adolphe Chapleau unveiled a monument to Maisonneuve on Place d'Armes. The statue of Montréal's founder, the four figures on the pedestal and the bas-reliefs decorating the pedestal represent the most important work of sculptor Philippe Hébert. In late August 1990, Maisonneuve, Charles Le Moyne, Jeanne Mance, Lambert Closse and the Unknown Indian who looked down on them were removed from their perches to be restored in time for the festivities marking the 350th anniversary of Montréal.

During the fall of 1895, the Montréal building of Université Laval on Saint-Denis Street, just south of Sainte-Catherine, was inaugurated. The official opening ceremony, which took place on October 8, 1895, coincided with the first council of the ecclesiastical province of Montréal.

In early December, the city authorities approved the final plans for a Canadian Pacific Railway station in Montréal East. On the upper storeys of Viger Station-Hotel, which had a façade more than ninety metres long, was

The steamer *Valleyfield* docked at St. Helen's Island. In the nineteenth century, the island was a favourite site for picnics and public gatherings.

a hotel, for Mayor Raymond Préfontaine wanted to attract visitors to Montréal's east end. The hotel was inaugurated in 1898 and served its original purpose until 1932. It now houses municipal offices.

In 1896 Emma Lajeunesse, known to opera lovers in Europe by her stage name Albani, returned to her native Québec. The prima donna was given a very warm welcome by Montrealers at the Monument National.

The 1967 World's Fair was not the first time that the construction of a tower on Mount Royal was proposed. On March 21, 1896, *La Presse* published an article on a Montréal architect, then living in Chicago, who wanted to build a small-scale replica of the Eiffel Tower. With its base at the centre of the park, the top of the 150-metre tower would have risen 380 metres above the river.

At a time when "moving pictures" were still a fantasy in the minds of most people, Montrealers were treated to "one of the wonders of the century." On June 27, 1896, the French cinematographer Louis Lumière projected moving images of a cavalry charge on St. Lawrence Boulevard. "The instrument moves so quickly," reported one spectator, "that in the space of a fifteenth of a second, it can reproduce 960 difficult movements."

Although the art of cinematography was still in its infancy, the Lumière brothers would probably have appreciated the sleight of hand of those who practised a far more ancient art: law. As the light brigade charged across Lumière's screen, Montréal's lawyers decided to close ranks and form a

In the parade celebrating Queen Victoria's diamond jubilee (1897), the Société Saint-Jean-Baptiste float is decorated with a bust of Ludger Duvernay, for whom an arrest warrant had been issued in Victoria's name in 1837.

professional association. On September 15, 1896, the Canadian Bar Association held its first meeting. The first president of the association was Joseph-Émery Robidoux, who went on to a career in politics before coming attorney general of Québec and later provincial secretary.

In the early summer of 1897, Montréal celebrated Queen Victoria's diamond jubilee, the sixtieth anniversary of her accession to the throne. There was a procession with an altar of repose and the papal delegate, Mgr. Merry Del Val, carried the holy sacrament himself. There were floats, some driven by electricity. During a fireworks display, a colossal monogram "VR" appeared in the sky over Mount Royal. One journalist reporting on the celebrations remarked that the empress had always had a soft spot for the French Canadians. "She has always protected the rights of minorities in her colonies," he wrote, "and if events such as those that occurred in 1837 were necessary, it was not because of the queen but because of those who had abused her authority in order to oppress minorities. French Canadians spilled their blood for their queen, but they were also prepared to spill their blood for their rights and their faith, as they had done in Rome between 1868 and 1870."

Over the years, an increasing number of conventions were held in

Notables fill the square in front of the university as Joseph-Adolphe Chapleau's remains are carried to the Gesù church.

Montréal. In 1897, the Canadian Medical Association and the British Medical Association held a joint convention in the city. It was the first time that the British organization had held its convention outside the United Kingdom. At this time, Canada had close to 5,000 doctors, one hundred of whom were women. The convention drew to a close on August 30 with Montréal's hottest tourist attraction, a trip down the Lachine Rapids by steamer.

That same day, Sir Wilfrid Laurier returned from Europe aboard the *Druid*. In England, Laurier had attended celebrations marking the diamond jubilee and had given many eloquent speeches. In France, he had been made an officer of the Legion of Honour, the first French Canadian to receive such an honour. Laurier received a warm welcome on his return. From the *Druid*, an elegant carriage drawn by four white horses carried Laurier through the crowded streets of Montréal to the Champ-de-Mars, where he made a speech.

In June 1898, Montréal mourned the loss of another great leader, Sir Joseph-Adolphe Chapleau, former premier and lieutenant-governor. Chapleau died suddenly at the Windsor Hotel after a political career spanning thirty years. He lay in state at the new university building on Saint-Denis Street, and the catafalque was erected at the Gesù church. Chapleau's strong attachment to the French language and culture and his great eloquence were recalled. He had been given the name "Bouche d'or" and, as one editorial writer put it, if anyone in Canada deserved such a name, it was Joseph-Adolphe Chapleau.

During 1898, Canada found itself in the grips of a debate over the prohibition of alcohol. A Canada-wide referendum was held. Québec was the only province that wanted to maintain the sale of liquor. In Montréal, every ward except Saint-Antoine came out against prohibition, contributing close to 22,000 votes to the province's anti-prohibition stand.

In late December 1898, the École Littéraire de Montréal opened its meetings to the public. The movement had been founded three years earlier by leading literary figures. In 1897, the school offered courses in natural history, architecture, literature, poetry and Canadian history. The Société d'Archéologie et de Numismatique de Montréal later allowed the school to use one of the halls at Château de Ramezay where, on December 29, 1898, the school held its first public meeting. "It was a school in name only," wrote Victor Barbeau, "but it deserved more than a simple epitaph in the cemetery of good intentions." Mgr. Olivier Maurault was less harsh in his criticism of the school, pointing out that it had "produced remarkable authors and counted among its members Nelligan, Gill, Lozeau and Désaulniers." Louis Fréchette was the school's honorary president.

In 1899, Notre-Dame hospital became the proud owner of a Roentgen machine. The physician after whom the machine was named had discovered the invisible rays, which he called "X-rays," only four years earlier. It was reported that the machine could "locate a foreign body through flesh and blood" and that it could "locate a fracture or an inflammation" and "monitor the healing process day by day." The machine was on the cutting edge of medical technology at the time.

On October 29, Montrealers gathered to watch a regiment of volunteers parade on the Champ-de-Mars before leaving for the Transvaal, where the Boers were challenging British sovereignty. Other contingents would later follow. The Boer War ended in 1902. Five years later, a monument to the memory of the Canadians who had lost their lives in the war was unveiled in Dominion Square. On a pedestal is a soldier of the Strathcona Horse Regiment reining in his mount.

It will be recalled that the Victoria Bridge, inaugurated in 1860, had only one track. The bridge was entirely covered, with openings in the roof to allow fumes to escape. At the end of the century, it was decided that the bridge should be rebuilt so as to accommodate two tracks, two carriageways and two footpaths. Building on either side of the existing bridge made it possible to carry out the expansion without interrupting train service, an ambitious undertaking at the time. One of the tracks was used by electric streetcars serving the counties on the south shore; however, the streetcars were pulled across the bridge by locomotives.

The bridge was originally opened in 1860 by Queen Victoria's son, the Prince of Wales, later King Edward VII. It would be officially reopened in 1901 by his second son, who also bore the title of Prince of Wales and would later be King George V. In the meantime, however, the bridge had been unofficially opened and used by trains since the fall of 1899.

The carriageways were originally designed for horse-drawn traffic; gradually, however, four-footed traffic yielded to four-wheeled traffic. As the century drew to a close, Montréal entered the era of the motorcar. On November 21, 1899, real estate agent Ucal-Henri Dandurand had the honour of taking Mayor Raymond Préfontaine for a spin in his Crestmobile, which had just arrived from the New England Motor Carriage Company in Boston. It was the first horseless carriage to grace the streets of Montréal, but it would not be the last.

The Curtain Rises on the Twentieth Century

———————— ⟩⟨ ————————

Wilfrid Laurier had said that the twentieth century would belong to Canada. In Montréal, however, the century opened with a racially motivated riot. It will be recalled that Canadians had volunteered to defend Britain in the Boer War. The British suffered heavy losses early on, but rallied valiantly in 1900. Students at McGill took to the streets of Montréal, blaming French Canadians for Britain's plight – even though French Canadians, no doubt aware of the declaration of loyalty to the British crown made by Archbishop Bégin (later Cardinal Bégin) of Québec, were already fighting in the Transvaal.

The McGill students tore up news bulletins posted outside the offices of French-language newspapers, stormed into the city hall and forced the authorities to hoist the flag, then headed for the university building on Saint-Denis Street, where violence broke out. Someone called the fire department, and fire hoses were used to disperse the crowd. Several students and members of the police force were injured. The story in *La Presse* covering the events ran under the headline "War in Montréal."

Strikes in those days did not always end peacefully. In some cases, strong-arm tactics and even bayonets were used. During the fall of 1900, soldiers from the Montréal garrison were called in to end a strike at a factory in Valleyfield where more than 200 workers working on the expansion of the Montreal Cotton Company plant had struck, demanding that their wages be increased by twenty-five cents a day. When the company did not respond, the workers decided to prevent the company's 3,000 regular employees from entering the plant. No doubt to avoid any loss of earnings by the regular employees and to forestall the possibility of violence, the mayor called in the army.

The first contingent boarded a special train at Bonaventure Station on the afternoon of October 25, 1900. Tension mounted and when a confrontation between the strikers and the army resulted in fifteen people being injured, a second contingent was dispatched on a night train. The army now had 400 men, including forty-five cavalry and a small cannon, to restore order and ensure that the plant reopened.

In January 1901, a fire broke out at the intersection of Saint-Pierre and Le Moyne streets in the heart of the city's business district, destroying close to fifty businesses. It took the firefighters five hours to get the blaze under control and damages were estimated at $2.5 million. Among the buildings destroyed was the Board of Trade, erected only seven years earlier.

The dredging of the St. Lawrence channel and the construction of new port facilities made it possible for ocean liners to reach Montréal. Having a seaport so far inland had brought prosperity to Montréal, but some deplored the loss of revenue during the winter months when the river was closed to traffic. Some felt that the St. Lawrence could remain open year-round; ice-breaking vessels had been in existence for a number of years.

If it could not actually spearhead the campaign to keep the St. Lawrence open year-round, *La Presse* decided that it would at least be its most enthusiastic supporter. Some said that the campaign was the work of a very determined *La Presse* reporter named Lorenzo Prince. Prince organized an expedition from the Gulf of St. Lawrence to Québec City aboard a steamer commissioned by *La Presse* to prove the feasibility of such an undertaking. The final leg of the trip from Rivière-du-Loup nearly ended in disaster. Just as the steamer passed the westernmost tip of Île d'Orleans, it collided with a treacherous piece of ice, damaging its propeller shaft and engine. Flags had already been hoisted and a little cannon made ready in anticipation of the

Market day, Place Jacques-Cartier, at the turn of the century. (Photograph: Notman.)

steamer's arrival. Luckily, the steamer was equipped with auxiliary sails. The mizzen and mainsail were bent and on April 11, 1901, the vessel reached its destination under sail.

Perhaps vexed by his misadventure, Lorenzo Prince immediately embarked on a race around the world organized by the Paris newspaper *Le Matin*, in which participants could use only means of locomotion available to the public. In addition to Prince, journalists from Paris, Cherbourg, New York, Chicago and San Francisco participated. On July 30, Prince arrived in triumph at Windsor Station. It had taken him sixty-four days and eleven minutes to circle the globe. Clearly, resorting to outlandish stunts to boost newspaper circulation is not a new invention.

Montrealers were soon caught up in another race, the first of its kind in Québec. This time, the race was between the most recent makes of automobiles, or "bone shakers" as they were called because of their internal combustion engines. Ucal-Henri Dandurand, who had driven a Crestmobile in 1899, now had a De Dion-Bouton that he had imported from France. There were at least three rival models: the Rambler, the Stanley and the Winton.

In 1898, a theatre troupe called Les Soirées de Famille had been founded at the Monument National by Elzéar Roy. Hoping to establish Québec's first national theatre, Roy had travelled to Paris to study theatre companies. The company got off to a shaky start, but under the patronage of the Société Saint-Jean-Baptiste Les Soirées de Famille soon became very popular with Montréal's cultural elite. In 1901, the company toured the United States where many French-speaking émigrés looked to Québec in the hope of preserving their cultural identity.

It will be recalled that on October 16, 1901, the Prince of Wales, the future King George V, inaugurated the new Victoria Bridge. In actual fact, he was still the Duke of York at the time of the inauguration, and only became the Prince of Wales the following month. Downtown streets were decorated with garlands and triumphal arches and there was a spectacular fireworks display on Mount Royal. His Royal Highness was given a tour of Montréal's most recent architectural achievement, the Université de Montréal.

In November, two events caused quite a stir in Montréal. Early in the month, a whale was found in the port. Soon the quays were lined with curious spectators. Some brought their hunting rifles to use the poor beast for target practice. "If people continue to shoot at it today," reported one newspaper, "and if every shot finds its mark, the bewildered whale will inevitably sink under the weight of all of the bullets."

A few days later, the whale was brought ashore. It weighed nine tons. Canadian Pacific offered $1,500 for the carcass, which it intended to exhibit across Canada. Taxidermists spent a month stuffing the carcass.

In mid-November, it was reported that plays threatening public morality were attracting large crowds to the Théâtre Royal, which was labelled a place of corruption. The plays must have been running for some time, because some young women claimed that they had been so influenced by

Inauguration of the new Victoria Bridge in 1901. In the front row, from left to right, the Duchess and Duke of Cornwall and York. The Duke of York would soon become Prince of Wales and later reigned as King George V.

them that they had turned to prostitution. The church, the police, the city council and even the courts intervened. The *Herald* pointed out that while large sums were being spent to wipe out smallpox and tuberculosis (a massive vaccination campaign was being conducted at city hall at the time), little was being done to suppress a calamity that was threatening the morality of the city's young people. The public outcry finally paid off, and the producers rewrote the scripts.

It might be thought that Montrealers did not have access to tropical fruits at the turn of the century, given the city's distance from the countries in which these fruits were grown. However, in the spring of 1902, two ocean freighters, the *Fremona* and the *Jacona*, arrived in the port of Montréal carrying 120,000 crates of oranges, lemons and other fruits from the Mediterranean. The food terminal on Rue de la Montagne had cellars in which the fruit could ripen. Wholesalers came to the terminal from as far away as New York, Chicago and Boston to purchase the fruit at auction.

It will be recalled that as early as 1876, there were plans to link Montréal to the south shore by means of a second bridge, to get around the Grand Trunk's refusal to allow other railways to use the Victoria Bridge. The plans called for a bridge across the river using St. Helen's Island as a stepping stone and promoting the development of Montréal's east end. Unfortunately, the plan was not approved by the Board of Trade and had to be shelved. Four years later, Anthony Ralph proposed that a tunnel be dug between Hochelaga and Longueuil. Ralph estimated the cost of the undertaking at $1 million, but his comments clearly indicate that his grasp of the technical details was scanty at best. "If investors had my faith," he said, "the tunnel would be finished in two years."

Montréal's capitalists were not lacking in faith, however, and some time later, Louis-Adélard Sénécal founded a company with fifteen other businessmen for this purpose. Given his past record, no one could accuse Sénécal of dreaming. The company obtained a charter from the provincial government for the construction of a tunnel with two railway lines. Unfortunately, Sénécal's energy and enthusiasm were not boundless. He died before the project could be carried out. "Had Sénécal not died in 1887, at the age of fifty-eight," wrote the *Album universel* in 1902, "we would now have the tunnel for which he had obtained a charter."

In 1902, plans for a tunnel were dusted off. This time, however, the tunnel would be dug only between Montréal and St. Helen's Island, and a tenspan bridge would then link the island to the south shore. In this way, the promoters claimed, ocean steamships would still be able to enter the port.

Plans for this tunnel were mothballed as well. Bridges were still the public favourite. As if to prove the point, a 1,700-ton caisson had just been put in place for a bridge at Québec City. After the inauguration of the Victoria Bridge, Canadian Pacific built its own bridge between Lachine and Kahnawake.

While government officials were poring over the plans for the tunnel-bridge, the Montreal and St. Lawrence Bridge Company came up with a plan for a bridge for railways that could use neither the Grand Trunk nor the Canadian Pacific line. The plan offered two scenarios. In the first scenario, the bridge would stretch from Sainte-Marie ward to Longueuil, supported in the middle by Île Ronde. The main arch would provide clearance of 45.72 metres, allowing ocean steamers to pass beneath. The other scenario also provided for a bridge between Île Ronde and Longueuil, but replaced the bridge over the seaway by another bridge from St. Helen's Island over the Lachine Canal at a height that provided clearance for Great Lake steamers, coming to rest at the west end of Montréal harbour near the foot of McGill Street.

Although none of these projects ever materialized, they are nevertheless worth mentioning because they illustrate the extent to which the problem of transportation across the St. Lawrence hampered Montréal's expansion. The Montreal and St. Lawrence Bridge Company plan called for two tracks for trains, two tracks for electric streetcars, two carriageways, and footpaths. A quarter of a century went by before the Harbour Bridge, now called the Jacques Cartier Bridge, was built. The problem of accommodating railway traffic no longer existed, but some old-timers will recall that space was provided for streetcars. This space was never used, and eventually it was taken up by wider lanes for vehicular traffic.

The beginning of the twentieth century spawned many projects, some fantastic or incredible, others less visionary. Some actually came true. Expo 67 was one such dream. The creative spirit is always there, waiting to be tapped.

In 1902, a young lawyer by the name of J.-R. Mainville suggested that towers be built on St. Helen's Island and Mount Royal from which electrical cables could be strung. Mainville claimed that an aerial railway, worthy of a Jules Verne fantasy, would make the perfect centrepiece for an international exhibition.

A manufacturer of ploughing implements who shall remain nameless suggested that Montréal be girded by a band of iron to protect it from the threat of an attack. A set of tracks on a raised structure would support

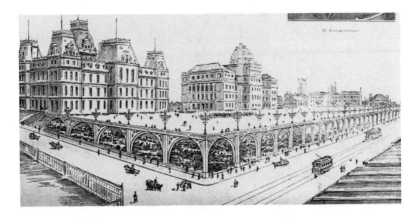

As a means of clearing the quays, it was suggested in 1902 that a public market be built under the Champ-de-Mars.

cannons on carriages linked to a circular chain mechanism, similar to the mechanism used in threshing machines – no doubt the source of his inspiration. In times of peace, he explained, the cannons could be replaced with sightseeing cars.

A European schemer whose name has also escaped mention felt that open quarries were unacceptable. Open stone quarries were commonplace in Montréal, particularly at Carrières Street, the "Kingdom of the Black Foot." The man claimed that in Paris, enormous quantities of stone had been quarried underground, creating huge catacombs in which row upon row of neatly arranged tibias and femurs from millions of skeletons removed from old cemeteries can be seen today. Sheltered from the blazing sun and the biting cold, he continued, the workers could quarry enough stone under Mount Royal to rebuild the entire city. The result, he added, would be beautiful underground water basins in which stalactites would be reflected.

Such schemes were not in short supply. In 1902, it was proposed that Saint-Louis Square be converted into a watering place for the neighbourhood children. The project's promoter had seen a public bath used by children in Buffalo. The health benefits of bathing, he noted, were widely recognized.

Regret was often expressed that the area under the Champ-de-Mars was not put to some practical use. It was suggested that the earth beneath it be removed and a large public market built, freeing the embankments of merchandise and vehicles and providing the militia with a training ground as

At the turn of the century, Montréal's terminal building on Rue de la Montagne had cold cellars in which fruit from the Mediterranean was ripened for sale.

smooth and clean as a church courtyard. Another Montrealer recommended that the space be used for a zoo, a swimming pool and even a skating rink. On a visit to Paris, he had seen an ammonia solution turn a pool of water into a solid sheet of ice in a matter of moments. In the time it took to whistle a tune, he noted, bathing beauties would be replaced by skaters.

There were far too many farfetched proposals for us to mention them all here, but not all proposals were farfetched. Some were even realizable within the foreseeable future. For example, in August 1902, it was suggested that a station for motor cars be built where cars could be maintained and where one might perhaps find an experienced chauffeur. The man who came up with the idea, A.J. de B. Corriveau, had had the honour of driving a French touring car in New York. He knew what lay ahead for the horseless carriage. Another visionary was Councillor L.A. Lavallée who, that same year, proposed the acquisition of the land needed to build a divided multi-lane boulevard from one end of the island to the other – what is now the Metropolitan Autoroute.

When the shipping season opened in 1903, there was chaos in the port. The longshoremen had gone on strike. On the evening of April 28, the

U.-H. Dandurand driving his second motor car, a De Dion – Bouton.

army occupied the port and forbade access to everyone except authorized personnel. It was decided that nothing should interrupt the unloading of the vessels and since there were no regulations preventing the owners from hiring scabs, fifty longshoremen were brought from Halifax aboard the *Lake Champlain*. The men went to work under the watchful eye of the soldiers; hours earlier, the strikers had attacked teams of workers sent by the Bureau Indépendant du Travail. "Martial law in the Port of Montréal," reported *La Presse*.

The port had also been the subject of front-page news only a few weeks before. It was clear that any vessel named after the city would meet an untimely end. It will be recalled that when the *City of Montreal* caught fire off the coast of Newfoundland, lives and property had been lost. On March 7, 1903, the *Montréal*, a luxury liner belonging to the Compagnie de Navigation Richelieu et Ontario, caught fire near the customs dock where workers were making preparations for her launching. The fire broke out in the evening and the news spread almost as quickly as the flames. Downtown theatres and stores emptied and, before long, thousands of people were gathered on the shore, watching the demise of a liner that was to have been the flagship of the company's fleet. Soon all that remained of her upper deck was the two chimney stacks and the frame of the paddle wheel.

In the early twentieth century, strikes became a common means of trying to bring about change in the workplace. When the Montreal Street Railway Company refused to allow its workers to form a union in February 1903, the conductors went on strike. Despite the general manager's efforts to explain that the company was trying to keep its employees happy by providing them with uniforms, caps and cardigans, the workers who gathered in the great hall of Bonsecours Market stood their ground. After forty-eight hours the company yielded, recognizing the workers' right to form a union and giving them a 10 per cent raise. Soon electric street cars were once again travelling back and forth along the streets of Montréal.

January 1904 was an important month in the history of Montréal's east end. That month, Canadian Pacific opened the new Angus shops where its locomotives and passenger and freight cars would henceforth be built. There were approximately twenty shops in all, providing work for some 5,000 workers. This huge industrial complex was named after the financier Richard Bladworth Angus, who in 1880 joined the syndicate that was established to build the transcontinental railway. During the Second World War, close to 1,500 tanks were built at the Angus shops.

With a total area of barely fifty hectares, the town of Sainte-Cunégonde, later annexed to Montréal, was considered the smallest municipality in Canada. From a religious standpoint, Sainte-Cunégonde was considered a part of the parish of Saint-Henri until 1875, when it became a separate parish. Work began on a church that was to take ten years to build. On January 19, 1904, the church, whose spire rose seventy metres from the ground, burned to the ground as the firefighters watched helplessly. It was so cold that most of the fire hydrants had frozen.

We have already mentioned how Montréal's expansion was greatly accelerated by its policy of absorbing adjoining municipalities. The Lachine Canal had led to the establishment of many industries, including a number of tanneries at Saint-Henri-des-Tanneries, which obtained the status of a municipality. In October 1905, the municipality's property owners unanimously approved its annexation to Montréal, which gained 172 hectares of land and 25,000 new citizens.

When the St. Lawrence froze, it was an easy matter for anyone who had a horse and carriage to cross the river on a cleared path of ice; however, there was no public transportation system to replace the ferries that operated during the summer months. In December 1905, two men decided to test an omnibus that could carry fifty passengers in two separate compartments, the front compartment being reserved exclusively for smokers. The omnibus was, in effect, a streetcar on runners. It was equipped with a motor that drove a wheel connected to a metal cable more than two kilometres long, firmly anchored on either shore. The cable car or "funicular" would have run every half hour between 6 a.m. and midnight and the entire trip would have taken only three or four minutes.

There were other, more enduring, wonders. January 1, 1906 marked the first public viewing of the Ouimetoscope at the Salle Poiré at the corner of Sainte-Catherine and Montcalm streets. Montrealers had already been exposed to the strange phenomenon of moving images. Now J.-Ernest Ouimet offered them the first cinema in North America. For more than an hour, reels of film lasting three to four minutes were projected, each containing four or five subjects. Between reels, the audience was entertained by a popular singer. Twenty months later, a new Ouimetoscope accommodating 1,200 spectators opened. It was the first theatre designed specifically for the projection of films in North America.

In Québec, the public had fallen in love with another invention: the automobile. It will be recalled that the first automobile was brought to Montréal in 1899. Seven years later, a car rally organized by the American Automobile Association included Québec in its itinerary. Close to one hundred cars from Chicago and Buffalo drove through Québec in July 1906, en route to Bretton Woods, New Hampshire, near Mount Washington. The rally was greeted enthusiastically and the horseless carriage increased in popularity.

Progress carries a price. On August 11, 1906, *La Presse* reported that the automobile had claimed its first victim on the streets of Montréal. Two mechanics were driving east along Sainte-Catherine Street when a streetcar appeared. The driver veered to the right just as Antoine Toutant, his wife, and their son Oswald prepared to cross the street. Antoine Toutant suffered

In the nineteenth century, the army maintained a garrison on St. Helen's Island. In this engraving, the new Gilbert cannon is being tested.

a fractured skull and died, becoming Montréal's first automobile accident victim. That very day, Montrealers learned that Pope Pius X had made St. Christopher the patron saint of automobile drivers.

In 1873, the city had been given authorization to establish a park on St. Helen's Island; however, the decision could be revoked at any time. In 1907, Montréal finally purchased the island at a cost of $200,000, but the federal authorities retained the right to take it back in the event that it was needed for military purposes, a right that it exercised during the Second World War when the island was used as a prisoner-of-war camp. Over the years, Montréal developed a beautiful sanctuary on the island, accessible by a ferry belonging to the Compagnie de Navigation Richelieu et Ontario. To city-dwellers seeking fresh air and diversion, the park offered live music from bandstands, merry-go-rounds, shooting galleries and refreshment stands in a pleasant natural setting.

In the spring of 1907, the salons of Montréal buzzed with talk of an interdict issued by Archbishop Paul Bruchési. The Théâtre des Nouveautés was putting on a play entitled *La Rafale* that had met with diocesan disapproval. The archbishop quickly denounced the play and banned Roman Catholics from attending. The director of the theatre responded immediately, apologizing and asking that the interdict be lifted. He agreed to the creation of a committee to censor plays before they were presented.

Liberal ideas were beginning to peep through the conservative vestment of the defenders of social order. Celebrations on May 1, 1907, International Labour Day – "the only day that workers take without the authorization of Capital" – nearly degenerated into a riot. A large socialist demonstration was to take place on the Champ-de-Mars, but the police had forbidden the demonstrators to organize a march to the square for fear that violence would break out. The celebrations began with speeches at Salle Saint-Joseph, at the corner of Sainte-Catherine and Sainte-Élisabeth streets. A large crowd gathered, and carriages were waiting outside to take the speakers directly to the Champ-de-Mars. The police ordered the carriages to disperse.

After a few heated exchanges the organizers, carrying red flags and roman candles, arrived at the Champ-de-Mars where, according to newspaper reports, 10,000 people had gathered. The demonstration took place without any major incidents, although at one point the police did move in to protect the people on the platform.

On May 31, 1908, Quebecers mourned the death of their poet laureate, Louis-Honoré Fréchette, whose poetry had reached deep into the Québec psyche. Fréchette was made a member of the Académie Française in 1880. He had been living at the Institut des Sourds-Muets on Saint-Denis Street for a year, and it was there that he died of apoplexy. A lawyer and a journalist, Fréchette had been clerk of the Legislative Council since 1889. He received honorary degrees from McGill University and Queen's University in 1881 and from Université Laval in 1888. His body lay in state at the home of his son-in-law, Honoré Mercier (son of the Québec premier of the same name), on Saint-Denis Street. Fréchette's funeral service was attended by every major figure in the Québec literary world.

Shortly thereafter, Québec experienced a wave of euphoria as Québec City, the "City of Champlain," celebrated its three hundredth anniversary.

The program of events was inspected by the Prince of Wales, the future King George V himself, but in any event influential "cousins" came from France, and Montréal had an opportunity to welcome them. On Bastille Day, July 14, the Union Nationale Française organized a party in Bout-de-l'Île Park. Particularly touching was the gesture of an English-speaking newspaper columnist, John Boyd, who wrote for papers in Montréal and Toronto. Boyd wrote a poem to the memory of Fréchette that he dedicated to the brave captain Jean Vauquelin and his ship the *Atalante*. The festivities drew to a close with a magnificent fireworks display. In June, Mayor Payette of Montréal had made official visits to Paris and Honfleur.

In September 1908, 5,000 fans of the new sport of automobile racing flocked to De Lorimier Park. In order to avoid any risk of accident, the participants "refrained from demonstrating the full potential of their machines." The papers did report, however, that a young millionaire named Walter Christie drew thunderous applause from the crowds by establishing a new world record, travelling one mile in two minutes and ten seconds.

Montrealers were passionate about politics as well. On October 26, 1908, despite bad weather, a huge crowd gathered at the offices of *La Presse* as the results of the election came in. Wilfrid Laurier was returned to office for another term. His reputation was, of course, a key factor in the crowd's enthusiasm, but the paper also used a completely new technique. As the results came in, J.-Ernest Ouimet, owner of the Ouimetoscope, projected them on a screen on the other side of the street.

In late November 1908, Montrealers were treated to what could only be described as a festival of lights. On November 9, the day of its inauguration, the Forum was lit by 13,000 sixteen-candle electric bulbs. Three thousand citizens wearing roller skates celebrated in the "palace of electricity" with which the Association du Montagnard had provided the west end of the city. According to one journalist, the Forum "eclipses all other establishments of its kind in North America and Europe in beauty, comfort and sheer size." Its design was considered simple and tasteful; the reporter added that its many windows made it look like a crystal palace.

However, the first decade of the twentieth century closed on a sombre note. On March 17, 1909, the locomotive of a train arriving from Boston experienced an explosion just as it was approaching the city centre. To escape the scalding steam, the engineer and the mechanic jumped to safety. The mechanic suffered fatal head injuries. The conductor, realizing that the train was gradually gathering speed after it passed the Montréal West

Station, applied the emergency brake, but it was too late. The locomotive finally came to a stop in the waiting room at Windsor Station. Four people died and eleven more were injured.

On the last day of the year, there was another accident at Viger Station. A gas pipe exploded under a platform where a hundred people were waiting for a train; approximately twenty were taken to hospital with injuries.

Also unsettling was the report of a royal commission, submitted to Premier Lomer Gouin fifteen days earlier by Justice L.A. Cannon, accusing eight city councillors and a number of city officials of negligence in awarding contracts that had led to an unnecessary increase of about 25 per cent in the city's expenditures. Two King's Counsels, N.-M. Laflamme and J.-L. Perron, had pressed the case on behalf of a citizens' committee.

The Year of the Eucharistic Congress

———————— ✕ ————————

The grandiose ceremonies marking the Eucharistic Congress of 1910 were so deeply etched in the collective consciousness that, for close to half a century, many old-timers referred to 1910 simply as "the year of the congress."

The papal legate, Cardinal Vannutelli, opened the twenty-first International Eucharistic Congress in Montréal's cathedral on the evening of September 6, 1910. Some forty cardinals and 100 archbishops and bishops attended the week-long conference. On at least five occasions, Notre-Dame Basilica was packed with enthusiastic crowds. At one midnight mass, 5,000 faithful took communion. There was a choir of 300 voices, accompanied by forty instruments. The basilica had been specially decorated for the occasion with flowers, lights, silk and lace.

During the week, a grand procession made its way through the streets of Montréal to the chiming of Notre-Dame's great bell. After two and a half hours the procession, led by the papal legate, stopped at the foot of Mount Royal. More than 400,000 people gathered to reaffirm their faith, and it was reported that 115 trains carrying pilgrims had arrived in Montréal that morning.

Two evenings were devoted to assemblies at which, as Mgr. Olivier Maurault wrote, "prelates, priests and laypeople competed with one another in their eloquence and expression of faith." Those who attended will long remember the orator Henri Bourassa's speech in response to Archbishop Bourne of Westminster. Under the vaulted roof of Notre-Dame, Archbishop Bourne declared that in Canada, where English had become the language of the majority, the only way of bringing the Catholic faith to the nation was to explore the mysteries of the faith in that language. He expressed the hope that this would result in the unity of the faith.

When Bourassa rose, there was an audible murmur in the crowd. He put his prepared speech back in his breast pocket and delivered, instead, a rebuke that was spoken from the heart. Christ, Bourassa declared, had died for all men. He did not require men to deny their race as a condition of faith. "We are but a handful," Bourassa conceded, "but the school of Christ did not teach me to measure moral strength in numbers or in riches." He ended his speech with an impassioned plea: "Do not take away from men that which is dearest to them after their faith in God!" Bourassa's determination in delivering a rebuke to an archbishop in a church in 1910 can only be admired.

While some Montrealers were concerned with lofty questions, others were trying to raise themselves up by purely mechanical means. Even as the technology of the automobile was in its infancy, the technology of aviation was taking flight. On July 25, 1909, Louis Blériot became the first person to fly across the English Channel. Less than a year later, Montrealers waited eagerly in anticipation of a visit from one of his imitators, Count Jacques de Lesseps, son of Ferdinand Vicomte de Lesseps, the man who had built the Suez Canal. The *Scarabée*, the plane flown by the younger de Lesseps, was equipped with a Gnome seven-cylinder rotary engine and was similar to Blériot's.

On July 2, 1910, the *Scarabée* was readied for takeoff on the tiny airstrip by the shore of Lac Saint-Louis. After circling the landing strip twice, de Lesseps announced that he would now fly over Montréal, an announcement that was met with much head-shaking and skepticism. The *Scarabée* left the strip, rose to a height of 150 metres, selected a course for St. Helen's Island, circled over city hall, and then, after flying over Saint-Henri, returned to the airstrip. De Lesseps' flight was a complete success. The first airplane voyage in Canada had lasted forty-nine minutes and three seconds.

On February 23, 1909, Douglas McCurdy had lifted his *Silver Dart* off the frozen surface of a lake at Baddeck, Nova Scotia, in what was Canada's first heavier-than-air machine, but his accomplishment could not exactly be called a voyage. The reporter for *La Patrie* explained the difference: the young count had flown a total distance of approximately thirty-five miles, including detours, without making any stops. De Lesseps' flight was an important event. Archbishop Bruchési, no doubt somewhat overwhelmed by the weighty issues of the Eucharistic Congress, tore himself away to greet the pilot and offer his congratulations.

An event in August sparked further interest in flying machines. Native son Jean-Baptiste Moisan had just flown across the English Channel – with a passenger. The following month, journalists in Montréal were given an opportunity to inspect a monoplane, called the *Montréalaise*, built entirely of Canadian materials. Real estate agent Max Daoust declared that he was prepared to invest a quarter of a million dollars in a facility to produce copies of the prototype. However, the *Montréalaise* never got off the ground and the dreams of its promoters were never realized. In 1911, two mechanics named Anctil and Reed built a monoplane which they flew, albeit very briefly. The following year, Anctil built a biplane that made several flights over Cartierville, some with passengers.

In 1910, another major project took flight. *Le Devoir* was founded by Henri Bourassa, who had raised $100,000 through donations from 500 citizens, to ensure "the triumph of ideas over appetites, of the public good over partisanship." Bourassa and his brilliant team produced a paper that was devoted to defending the interests of the French Canadian people by providing a platform of reasoned, well-thought-out patriotism "to help it learn, love and practise national duty, namely the preservation of its faith and traditions, true understanding and advocacy for its constitutional rights."

Since its founding, *Le Devoir* has consistently promoted the rights of French-speaking Canadians. When Bourassa stepped down after more than twenty years of active journalism, one of his closest collaborators, Georges Pelletier, took over as editor. Bourassa could not have chosen a better replacement. Pelletier remained editor for a period of fifteen years, until his death in 1947.

Bourassa had already taken steps to safeguard the paper's original mandate. "Should the paper fail in or betray the mission that I have chosen for it," Bourassa said, "should I see the end of all my ambitions and of all my hopes, I will kill it with my own hands." When he took over as editor, Pelletier adopted the same tone: "If by some misfortune *Le Devoir* should fall into the hands of an individual who wanted to make a departure from its founding principles, this individual would find an empty hull." In other words, not only Pelletier but also his two closest collaborators, Omer Héroux and Louis Dupire, would abandon ship. The successors to Bourassa

Steam-pressured pumps were still in use in 1910 when the offices of the *Herald* caught fire.

and Pelletier – journalists such as Gérard Filion, André Laurendeau, Claude Ryan and many others – have always steered *Le Devoir* on a true course.

Tragedy struck on June 13, 1910, at the *Herald*, which would celebrate its centenary the following year. That day, as the staff went about their duties, the roof of the building collapsed under the weight of an enormous water reservoir, which then fell through each of the floors below. A fire broke out almost immediately. The floors had held around the huge holes left by the tank as it fell, and more than one hundred employees were able to escape through windows and fire escapes; however, thirty-two did not leave the building. Their bodies were found in the basement when the debris from the fire was finally cleared away. When the accident occurred, the *Herald*'s offices were located on Saint-Jacques Street opposite Victoria Square. The paper ceased publication in October 1957.

Horse-drawn carriages were the only passenger vehicles for hire until June 1910, when the first motorized cabs went into service. When they arrived at Montréal by steamer, large crowds gathered on the quays to watch.

During the previous thirty-year period, ties between Québec and France had grown stronger. Curé Labelle and two Québec premiers, Honoré Mercier and Joseph-Adolphe Chapleau, had made official visits to Québec's cultural mother country. Hector Fabre, who became Québec's commissioner general in Paris in 1882 and was subsequently made Canada's commissioner general as well, paved the way for the mutual rediscovery, of which these visits were an expression.

Fabre died on September 2, 1910, but the contacts that he had made with the French continued to be fruitful ones. In 1911, for example, the Société du Parler Français au Canada organized the first conference on the French language under the aegis of Université Laval. It was a resounding success. The conference took place in Québec City, from June 24 to 30, 1912, but France's delegates were first welcomed in Montréal. The delegation was made up of many dignitaries, including three members of the Académie Française, Gabriel Hanotaux, Étienne Lamy and René Bazin; Comte de Chambrun, representing Premier Raymond Poincaré; and Louis Barthou, a former justice minister and future premier. One of the fifteen delegates was Louis Blériot, who had crossed the English Channel in his tiny airplane only the year before.

The Comité France-Amérique hosted a huge banquet at the Windsor Hotel and the guests were treated to a "flight of fancy" by Blériot: "If France had wings," he declared, "she would no doubt fly to you." At the Monument National, a crowd of 2,000 people turned out to welcome the French delegation, and the chamber of commerce and the Board of Trade also arranged talks to discuss trade between the two countries. The conference itself went a long way towards making the civilized world aware of the existence of a vibrant French nation in North America. A young history professor, Lionel Groulx, made a name for himself by reminding the delegates that "we are the French sentinels on duty whom France forgot to relieve. We are still standing on guard on the old rock of Québec."

On November 10, 1912, Montréal mourned the death of a man who had done as much as anyone, perhaps even more, to make Québec known abroad. Louis Cyr, an unchallenged champion, was known to his admirers as the "strongest man of all time." The list of his exploits is very long indeed. Without using his knees for support, Cyr lifted 251 kilograms with one finger, 449 kilograms with one hand, and 862 kilograms with both hands. He could withstand the strength of four horses weighing 550 kilograms each tied in teams to his arms while their owners whipped them so that they would pull with their full strength. A statue was erected in his honour in Saint-Henri, where he had worked as a police constable, making life miserable for troublemakers.

In April, several Montréal families had been personally struck by the tragedy of the *Titanic*. Charles Melville Hayes, president of the Grand Trunk Railway, and Harry Markland Molson, a prominent businessman, were among the victims. When the death of Charles Hayes was confirmed, every Grand Trunk train from the Atlantic to the Pacific stopped for five minutes.

In the wake of the success of the first conference on the French language, ties between France and Québec were once again strengthened in 1913, when the cruiser *Descartes* spent several days in Montréal. Its crew was given a warm reception and many parties, and on July 13 its officers attended the unveiling of a monument representing France opposite Viger Square. The monument was the work of the sculptor Paul Chevré, whose statues of Samuel de Champlain and Premier Honoré Mercier already stood in Québec City. The monument was later joined by a statue of Joan of Arc, unveiled in early October 1912.

In 1907, a group of dynamic Montréal women opened a hospital for children at the urging of Dr. Irma Levasseur, the first French-speaking woman in Québec to be admitted to the medical profession. Dr. Levasseur had received her degree seven years earlier in St. Paul, Minnesota; at that time, Québec's schools of medicine did not admit women. In its first year of operation, Sainte-Justine Hospital counted 4,400 patient-days, thanks to the "suffragettes of charity," as the hospital's founders were called. The hospital underwent a transformation in 1913, when work on a new 540-bed facility on Saint-Denis Street was completed. At the inauguration, Édouard Montpetit coined a new expression: "Let us start building for tomorrow today by saving lives."

In December 1913, teams drilling from opposite sides of Mount Royal finally completed a tunnel that many had doubted would ever be dug. Although it is Montréal's crowning glory, Mount Royal had always presented a problem for rail links between the city centre and neighbourhoods to the north. Two entrepreneurs, William Mackenzie and Donald Mann, who had founded the Canadian Northern Railway, wanted to build a railway from the city centre to the north. Mackenzie and Mann realized that building the railway around the hill was unthinkable and came up with the idea of acquiring the land they would need for the rights to build the line and establish a model city, now known as the Town of Mount Royal.

On July 8, 1912, the first team began work on the north side of the hill. On August 3, a second team commenced work near Dorchester (now René-Lévesque Boulevard). On December 10 of the following year, the two teams met 189 metres under the summit. Even though the tools they used were not nearly as sophisticated as those available today, the two sections were within a few centimetres of being perfectly aligned. More than

300,000 cubic metres of rock had been extracted to create the tunnel, which was 5.63 kilometres long. That very afternoon, the first train with twenty cars, each occupied by four guests, entered the north portal of the tunnel, stopped at the place where the two teams had met, then emerged from the tunnel on Dorchester two and a half hours later. Regular train service through the tunnel, which brought Mount Royal within seven minutes of the city centre, did not start until 1918. The tunnel was considered a remarkable feat of engineering.

While we are on the subject of Mount Royal, I should point out that in early 1914, the former postmaster general, Rodolphe Lemieux, tabled a proposal in the House of Commons for a world's fair atop Mount Royal. According to the proposal, the fair was to mark the fiftieth anniversary of Confederation in 1917. Lemieux was not lacking in imagination. His plans for the fair included a tall tower with a huge clock on top. When the fair opened, the king of England and the president of France would push a lever atop the Eiffel Tower that through wireless telegraphy would create a giant spark that would light up the monument to Confederation and all of the pavilions at once. It will come as no surprise that Rodolphe Lemieux is referred to as a "luminary" in the annals of French Canada. At any rate, he must have been an avid reader of Jules Verne.

On May 25, 1914, the port of Montréal had a brush with disaster. The steamer *Berthier* had just docked at Victoria Pier with 135 passengers when a fire broke out on the aft bridge. Luckily, all of the passengers were able to disembark before the fire spread, but three of the crew were trapped on the vessel. Firefighters managed to rescue them. As the lines holding the vessel to the pier burned, it floated away from the quay, saving other vessels from destruction.

The First World War

———————— >< ————————

On August 5, 1914, Montrealers learned that at 7 p.m. the previous day Britain had declared war on Germany. For the next four years, the terrible tragedy of war would be part of daily life. In Montréal, as in other parts of Canada, the news would be dominated by themes of patriotism, recruitment campaigns, clothing drives, Red Cross fundraising efforts, appeals

Two First World War posters. One invites French Canadians to "help the Gallic cock beat the Prussian eagle," while the other warns, "Are we going to wait until our own [churches] burn? Let us enlist right away in the 178th French Canadian Battalion." (Social Science Library, Université de Montréal.)

ATTENDRONS-NOUS QUE LES NÔTRES BRÛLENT?

ENRÔLONS-NOUS et tout de suite

Dans Le

178ième

Bataillon
CANADIEN
FRANÇAIS

Commandé par le
Lt.Col.Girouard
et six autres officiers du
22ième tous de retour du
Front.

INFORMATIONS:
AUX QUARTIERS GÉNÉRAUX, SHERBROOKE, P.Q.
OU COIN   St ANDRÉ ET Ste CATHERINE
MONTRÉAL.—

from the government for support of the war effort through Victory Bonds, political conflicts and – especially in Québec – the impact of conscription.

Canada's involvement in the conflict was almost instantaneous; a saying had it that "Canada is at war when the Empire is at war," although not everyone agreed. Even though Ottawa acknowledged that the country did not have the materiel or the officers to field more than 20,000 men, the governor general assured the king that Canadians "were united from sea to sea in their determination to maintain the honour and traditions of our Empire."

On August 7, Canada declared that it was ready to send 22,500 men to Europe. Three weeks later, training began at Valcartier, near Québec City. On September 22, 32,000 men left for Britain. Canada contributed to the war effort in other ways too. On August 6, London learned that Canada was donating a million bags of flour. Two hundred trains, each pulling thirty cars, were needed to transport the flour to the east coast.

Rumours circulated that parish priests in rural Québec were against recruitment. Early in September, *L'Action Catholique*, a Québec City daily considered the official organ of the cardinal-archbishop, stated that the clergy owed their allegiance not to the principles of any political authority but to the pope and bishops. It did add, however, that in such difficult times the clergy, rural or otherwise, would be remiss if they provided any excuse for those who questioned their loyalty and adherence to the cause of the motherland.

While these statements no doubt helped cool the fervour of Catholics who might have opposed the country's involvement in the conflict, Ottawa still did not feel secure about everyone's loyalty. It censored all incoming and outgoing messages sent by wireless or cable and the German and Austrian consuls were asked to leave the country forthwith.

European animosities were echoed among Montrealers who traced their origins to countries at war. On October 20, 1914, a bomb exploded on Frontenac Street where Russian and Polish immigrants lived opposite immigrants from Austria. According to *La Presse*, two people were killed and several others injured. Nine homes and three stores were also destroyed. The newspaper reported that there had been frequent outbursts between "these foreigners since the war broke out in Europe." It talked of espionage and called for the severest punishment for the perpetrators, adding that the impact on nearby houses was so severe that for a few moments, occupants believed that the Germans had invaded Montréal.

Then, as now, the papers had an insatiable appetite for the offbeat. *La*

Presse reported, for example, that the Canadian troops overseas were as resourceful as they were brave, "putting their aptitudes to work for the noble cause they are defending." Some, for example, were using lacrosse sticks to hurl grenades into the enemy trenches. The paper reprinted a story from a Toronto newspaper according to which the military, having weighed the merits of this initiative, purchased several hundred lacrosse sticks.

Recruiting campaigns were stepped up across the country. In Québec, a French Canadian recruiting service was established and candidates were directed to seven centres, the largest of which was in Montréal. The posters used in the campaigns relied far more heavily on the French Canadians' sense of attachment to their history and cultural homeland than on their attachment to the British Empire. One poster carried a drawing of Dollard des Ormeaux fighting the Iroquois at Long-Sault. The inscription urged French Canadians to follow his example. "Don't wait for the enemy to attack! Strike first! Join a French Canadian regiment!"

The French Canadian regiments had their own posters. One poster showed the French cock attacking an eagle holding France in its talons against a red, white and blue background. An officer beckoned to passersby to follow him to Europe. "French Canadians," the inscription read, "join the 150th Battalion C.M.R. and help the French cock triumph over the Prussian eagle." The message was signed by Lieutenant-Colonel Barré, Chevalier of the Legion of Honour – Arsenal of the 65th Battalion, Pine Avenue; Drill Room, Craig Street. Another poster showed Rheims cathedral in flames and Marianne, symbol of the French republic, imploring, "Are we going to wait until our churches burn? Sign up now. Join the 178th French Canadian Battalion under the command of Lieutenant-Colonel Girouard and six other officers of the 22nd, who have all returned from the front."

In 1915 and 1916 the church did little to stimulate recruitment, although it upheld the justice of Britain's cause. On December 8, 1915, Archbishop Bruchési of Montréal praised Laval University's Military Hospital in Montréal. "The university," said the prelate, "has understood Canada's role in the conflict and has made a patriotic gesture, helping to dispel the notion that French Canadian Catholics are not helping to defend the law, civilization and humanity. Thank God, our people have understood their duty and have offered up their gold and their sons. They have not avoided sacrifice."

Between January 1 and November 1, 1916, 39,907 volunteers signed up in the military districts of Montréal and Québec City. The following year conscription was imposed, even though Prime Minister Robert Borden had said repeatedly that it would not be necessary. On July 13, 1917, he wrote the mayor of Montréal: "These statements were absolutely and literally true when I made them. No one could have guessed or imagined the scale of the effort that victory and the preservation of our nationhood would require."

Québec City was not the only scene of violent confrontations and protests over this coercive measure. During the night of August 8, 1917, an attempt was made to blow up Elmwood, the sumptuous home of Lord Atholstan, the owner of the Montreal *Star*. Elmwood stood in the middle of a huge estate in Cartierville on the banks of the Rivière des Prairies. The *Star* supported conscription, and Lord Atholstan, the former Hugh Graham, had been given his title in recognition of his fierce loyalty to the British Empire.

The Red Cross appealed to Canadians to give generously. By late October 1917 it had raised more than half a million dollars in Québec, most of it in Montréal. The government issued Victory Bonds to help fill its coffers, severely strained by the war effort. On November 19, 1917, there was a military parade with floats, a tank named the *Britannia* that had been used by the Canadian troops in Flanders, and a Canadian Pacific locomotive. Soldiers wounded at the front waved to the crowd from armoured cars as did detachments of American sailors and French soldiers, drawing cheers and applause from the crowd. In the port, a German submarine brought from Halifax by railway was put on display.

Then in November 1918, the war ended. On November 7, Montrealers were caught up in a wave of euphoria when it was announced that a peace treaty had been signed. Even though the announcement was premature, fire trucks drove through the streets sounding their sirens. The port was lit up by Bengal lights from ships at anchor. Many houses were decorated with flags. Four days later, it was finally true. The Germans accepted Marshal Ferdinand Foch's terms and, after 1,560 long days, the nightmare was over.

On May 19, 1919, 758 officers and soldiers of the 22nd Regiment were given a very emotional welcome. Press accounts of the homecoming bordered on the poetic. One reporter wrote that "a ray of sunshine from Austerlitz flickered on the bayonets of the men who had taken Courcelettes, descendants of the men who had fought under Napoleon." It was estimated that 200,000 people lined the sidewalks all the way from Viger Station to Fletcher's Field, where the troops were decorated, and from there to the barracks. Triumphant, proud, delirious with joy, our boys were finally home.

Life Goes On

—————————— ✄ ——————————

Europe had been ravaged by a bloody war and there were urgent issues to be addressed at home, but on the local level life went on pretty much as usual.

At the turn of the century, the Sulpicians had decided to give Montréal a library. In 1860, they had established the Cabinet de Lecture Paroissial or parish reading room, where Montrealers could read and attend lectures. The reading room was a great success and played a key role in the cultural life of French-speaking Montrealers. Over the years the city had expanded northward and the reading room, located near Notre-Dame Basilica, was no longer readily accessible. There was another factor too: Université Laval had established a campus on Saint-Denis Street. The Sulpicians felt that the time had come to build a library that would provide the general public with an opportunity to read and students at Laval with the reference works they needed.

The city's cultural elite was putting pressure on the city to establish a municipal library; although parish libraries served a purpose, they could not meet the needs of the city as a whole. Among those who supported the idea was Ægidius Fauteux who, in 1912, became the first curator of the Bibliothèque Saint-Sulpice. The previous year, the Sulpicians had chosen the plans of architect Eugène Payette for the new library. Work on the new building began in the early summer of 1911 and was not completed until May 1914. During this time, Fauteux travelled throughout Europe building the library's collection. On September 12, 1915, the Bibliothèque Saint-Sulpice, one of the Sulpician fathers' many gifts to the city of Montréal, was inaugurated. It later became Québec's national library, the Bibliothèque Nationale du Québec.

When Montréal's first telephone line was installed in 1879, a central office was established on Saint-François-Xavier Street to handle calls within the city. The telephone became increasingly popular. On January 14, 1916, during a banquet at the Ritz-Carlton Hotel, the first long-distance telephone call was patched through to Vancouver via Buffalo, Chicago, Omaha, Salt Lake City and Portland, Oregon, a distance of 6,800 kilometres. Another five years would elapse before such long-distance calls could be made entirely through Canada.

It is said that bad luck comes in threes; perhaps this is true of good luck as well. As mentioned previously, Montréal's cultural elite had tried to get the city council to build a municipal library. Perhaps the Sulpician fathers had an influence on the city fathers. In 1915, the year the Bibliothèque Saint-Sulpice was inaugurated, work began on the Municipal Library, also designed by Eugène Payette. In May 1917, there was a ceremony to celebrate the founding of the new library's collection. Initially, it contained 23,000 volumes, although it was designed to hold 250,000 volumes. The ceremony was timed to coincide with a visit from Marshal Joffre, famous for his stand at the Marne. Montrealers prepared a hero's welcome for "Papa" Joffre, called "the saviour of civilization." At first, Joffre had allowed the French troops to fall back towards Paris. When the Germans crossed the Marne, he led a general offensive against the enemy flanks, forcing them into retreat.

At the base of the Georges-Étienne Cartier monument in Parc Jeanne-Mance, Marshal Joffre inspected troops that had returned from the front and received honours from the French Canadian people. "What the soldiers of Montréal and Canada did will always be remembered by the French. Canada's soldiers were brave; they were not afraid of death and their courage equalled that of the French soldiers." Joffre was given a gold key with which he opened the heavy bronze doors of the new library. He then signed the registry, and Mayor Médéric Martin, Premier Lomer Gouin, the city councillors and the library's first curator, Hector Garneau, followed suit.

On December 16, 1917, Catholics attended the consecration of the crypt of the future basilica of St. Joseph's Oratory by Archbishop Bruchési. Thirteen years earlier, Brother André's little mountainside sanctuary had been consecrated. With money that he had earned cutting the hair of children at Côte-des-Neiges school, Brother André had built the sanctuary at the foot of Mount Royal with the help of a friend, Calixte Bouchard, who wanted to thank God for being cured of a longstanding illness. Over the years, Catholics attributed thousands of miraculous cures by St. Joseph to Brother André. Their offerings made it possible to enlarge the sanctuary, and as the number of pilgrims increased it became necessary to add a crypt. Before long, there were 500,000 visitors each year. Saint Joseph's Oratory is now the most popular pilgrimage site in Québec.

In mid-February 1918, one of Montréal's worst fires destroyed the west wing of the Grey Nuns' convent at Dorchester and Guy. On February 14, the sisters were tucking 170 young children, ranging in age from a few days to three years, into their beds on the fourth floor of the building. On the floor below, soldiers wounded in Europe were convalescing. On a lower floor, elderly residents were resting until it was time for bed.

At about 7 p.m., one of the nuns came on duty and turned out all the lights in the children's dormitory except the night lights. About ten minutes later, flames spread across the floor. As the firefighters hooked up their hoses, the nuns and the soldiers formed a human chain to carry the children to safety, while others ran for stretchers to save soldiers and nuns immobilized by injuries and infirmities. The firefighters tried in vain to put out the flames, but insufficient water pressure made their task an impossible one. The next morning, the bodies of fifty-three children were found beneath twisted metal bed railings. The bodies of eleven other children, presumed to have died in the fire, were never found. The cause of the fire was never determined, but it was blamed on an improperly wired X-ray machine that had been brought in to treat the soldiers.

In 1909, the Sun Life Insurance Company decided that it had outgrown its offices at Notre-Dame and Saint-Jean streets. For the site of its new headquarters, the company purchased a parcel of land on Dominion Square occupied by a beautiful red brick and stone building belonging to the YMCA, which it tore down. Work on the new building began in 1913 and it was officially opened in March 1918. Initially, it had only six floors. It was completed in 1933; with twenty-six floors, it was the tallest building in the British Commonwealth.

After Count de Lesseps' flight over Montréal in 1910, small planes became increasingly popular. A polo field at Bois-Francs, Cartierville, became a centre for amateur flyers. Later, Curtiss Reid Airport was built there, and today it is the headquarters of Canadair. It was there that air mail delivery began. On the morning of June 24, 1918, Brian A. Peck took off in a JN 4 Curtiss with a bag containing 120 letters. Because the plane could not fly at altitudes of more than 300 metres, Peck had to fly under the electric wires at the end of the strip before veering towards the St. Lawrence and setting a course for Toronto. After stopping twice to refuel, he landed at Leaside, outside of Toronto. Peck then drove the mail to the main post office himself.

In the fall of 1918, an influenza epidemic broke out in Europe; it spread to North America with surprising speed. Influenza is sometimes considered a disease of the modern era, yet newspaper reports dating back to 1826 describe epidemics affecting half the population of Québec City. The epidemic of 1918 was particularly virulent and because it was first publicly identified in Spain, it was called the Spanish flu.

On July 19, 1918, a vessel from India moored in the port of Montréal. When it was noted that some of the crew of the *Somali* had flu-like symptoms, the vessel was quickly directed to the quarantine station on Grosse-Île. All vessels from overseas were henceforth required to stop at Grosse-Île, where they were scrubbed from stem to stern and all passengers and crew members were subjected to a medical examination. Two members of the *Somali*'s crew died. By mid-September, the flu had spread to the general population. It ultimately claimed more than 30,000 victims.

On September 27, Montreal General Hospital received the first cases. Fifteen days later, sixty people had died and another 400 had been infected. Theatres were closed and camphor disappeared from the drugstores. In mid-October, police constables were ordered to enforce a city bylaw forbidding spitting in the streets. Stores were ordered to close at 4:30 p.m. On October 23, doctors were instructed to post signs outside the homes of flu victims.

The epidemic provided an excellent opportunity for quacks to market "home remedies," of which there were many. To contain the epidemic, the city's churches were closed. The army was particularly hard hit – 622 victims at Saint-Jean and 213 at Montréal as of October 7. Nonetheless, conscription was still enforced and efforts were made to track down conscripts who had left home to avoid the military police. It was pointed out, not without reason, that it was senseless to take drastic measures to stop the spread of the disease when soldiers were allowed to continue spreading it.

Upon the urging of the Conseil d'Hygiène du Québec, Catholics were given dispensation from attending Sunday mass. On Sunday, November 10, the city's churches opened for worship for the first time in weeks. Of the 30,000 people who became infected with the flu in Montréal, 3,000 died. In Québec as a whole, 460,000 people had been infected and 13,000 had died. It was said that the epidemic had claimed more lives than the war.

In 1892, public transportation had been transformed by the introduction of the first electric streetcars. When buses were introduced in 1919, it became possible to have more flexible routes and serve neighbourhoods that were not equipped with streetcar tracks. The prototype was a thirty-passenger vehicle designed and built at the Youville works of the tramways company. The bus was built on a truck chassis and equipped with noninflatable tires. There was no mechanical starter and no heater. Utility had clearly taken precedence over comfort.

On March 24, 1919, Montréal lost its largest recreation centre, Sohmer Park, created thirty years earlier on a huge lot situated east of Panet Street, bordering on Notre-Dame and extending down to the river. More than an amusement park with animal exhibits, Sohmer Park was an important

The first bus was built on a truck chassis. Inflatable tires were not yet in use.

venue for urban popular culture. The park's developers were Ernest Lavigne and Louis-Joseph Lajoie. Music lovers knew Lavigne as the conductor of the city's concert band, which had given many open-air concerts in the gardens of Viger Square. In 1892, the city's largest concert hall was built in Sohmer Park. The hall had 4,400 seats on the ground floor and 1,400 seats on the balcony.

The park did offer a variety of popular attractions, including circuses, vaudeville acts and strongmen, but Lavigne, an accomplished cornet player, also brought a symphony orchestra to the park, culling many of its forty musicians from orchestras in Belgium. Well-known artists and ensembles performed, to the delight of music lovers. Under the baton of founder Theodore Thomas, the Chicago Symphony Orchestra performed for three evenings in a row. Accompanied by both orchestras, Charles Labelle conducted the Association Chorale de Saint-Louis-de-France in the "Choeur des Romains" from *Herodiade*. When the great amphitheatre was destroyed in a fire, it was not rebuilt. Two other amusement parks, Royal and Dominion, had already begun drawing crowds away from Sohmer Park.

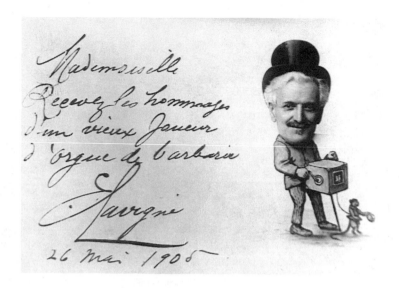

Although he was a serious musician, Ernest Lavigne did not lack a sense of humour. The inscription reads: "Mademoiselle, Sincere Regards from an Old Organ-Grinder. E. Lavigne. May 26, 1905."

Less than five months later, however, the facilities at Dominion Park were also destroyed in a fire. Just as the John Philip Sousa Concert Band was wrapping up its concert on the afternoon of August 10, 1919, a fire broke out in the stalls under the roller coaster and quickly spread to the roller coaster itself. As the firefighters prepared to rescue those trapped on the "scenic railway," it collapsed in flames. Seven people were killed.

Montrealers were gradually becoming accustomed to the phenomenon of small planes, although they still looked up when they heard the drone of an airplane's engine. In late September 1919, another page was added to the history of air travel. Taking off in Burlington, Vermont, the Curtiss *Seagull* became the first hydroplane to fly over the city before touching down in the harbour. The *Seagull* was flown by two English pilots, Captain Wilcox and Major Parker.

The year 1919 was an important one for the Université de Montréal. A branch of Université Laval until May 1919, it finally ended what had been a very strained relationship. The university had barely had time to test its new-found freedom when, on November 22, a night watchman making his rounds at the building on Saint-Denis Street spotted a fire in the elevator well. Climbing the stairs to the top floor, he watched in horror as the

LIFE GOES ON

elevator, cut free of its cables, hurtled downwards. Responding to the alarm, the firefighters soon found their task complicated by strong winds and by an explosion that completely destroyed a chemistry laboratory. Many of the firefighters were posted to protect Saint-Jacques and Notre-Dame-de- Lourdes churches.

Superstitious souls saw the fire, which completely destroyed the upper floor of the beautiful building on Saint-Denis, as an act of punishment. To obtain a separate charter for the university, Archbishop Bruchési had gone to the pope himself; it had fallen to Bruchési's successor, Georges Gauthier, to announce that his efforts had been successful.

In August 1920, a seemingly trivial news item made the front page of Montréal's dailies. Antiquated covered bridges linking Montréal to the south shore caught fire fairly frequently, but on August 22 it was the carriageway of the Victoria Bridge that caught fire, making it impossible for automobiles or horse-drawn carriages to use the bridge. The only means of transportation was the *Longueuil*, a Canada Steamship Lines steamer.

For many years, Montrealers had been calling for a second bridge. In 1876, the Royal Albert plan had been rejected. There had been other proposals, equally unsuccessful. This time, however, the pressure was stepped up. Even though the steamer sailed twenty-four hours a day, there were long waiting lines. One argument for a second bridge was tourism. Tourists unable to find accommodation in Montréal had to cross the Victoria Bridge and continue their search on the south shore. A few years later the Harbour Bridge, now known as the Jacques-Cartier Bridge, would provide the answer.

Two French marshals paid visits to Montréal in 1921. Following in the footsteps of "Papa" Joffre, who had visited the city in 1917, Marshal Émile Fayolle arrived in Montréal in June 1921 aboard the *Paris*, a new steamship of the Compagnie Générale Transatlantique, to thank Canadians for their support during the First World War. For his role in the second stand on the Marne and as president of the allied control commission, he had been promoted to the rank of marshal shortly before leading the official visit to Canada. Fayolle brought with him a bronze bust by Rodin symbolizing France, a gift from Académie Française member Gabriel Hanotaux to the Canadian government. Many events were organized to celebrate his visit.

July 14, 1921 marked the first of many visits to Montréal by the French escort vessel *Ville d'Ys* under the command of Captain Ruffi de Pontevés de Gévaudan. The *Ville d'Ys* docked at Victoria Pier in time to help Montrealers celebrate Bastille Day.

l'Hôtel de Ville.

The new city hall ablaze with lights in December 1878 to celebrate the visit of the governor general, the Marquis of Lorne, and Princess Louise, daughter of Queen Victoria.

In early December, Marshal Ferdinand Foch received an almost delirious welcome. After securing the victory of the Allies on the Marne, Foch launched the counteroffensive that brought about the negotiation of an armistice ending the war on November 11, 1918. He was enthusiastically welcomed into the Académie Française. On December 12, the papers reported that more than 100,000 people gathered to see the "great liberator of the world," the largest crowd since Marshal Joffre's visit. Like Joffre and Fayolle, Foch signed the registry at the Municipal Library, of which Mayor Médéric Martin was justifiably proud. In March, the "âme de la France glorieuse" was made an honorary colonel of the 22nd French Canadian Regiment, as he called it. Earlier that year, he had sent a souvenir flag with Marshal Fayolle destined for the commander of the regiment, Colonel Henri Chassé.

Visits from French dignitaries did much to strengthen the ties between Québec and France, and the tradition was continued after the war. In December 1921, the great composer Vincent d'Indy and the famous conductor Pierre Monteux were warmly received by Montréal audiences.

The cable car to the top of Mount Royal started at Fletcher's Field, now Jeanne-Mance Park. The first cars were open on all sides.

Montréal's city hall dates from 1878. Its architect, Henri-Maurice Perrault, had taken his inspiration from the city hall in Paris and the Palais du Commerce in Rennes. The result was a very imposing structure that came to be known as the *palais municipal*, the municipal palace. Forty-four years later, the building was gutted by fire. Only the exterior façade remained. On the evening of March 2, 1922, a guard on night duty noticed smoke escaping from a top-storey window. He roused the concierge, who immediately called the fire department. Steam-driven water pumps were quickly put in place around the building, but it was too late. The building was engulfed in flames and the floors toppled one after the other. The water from the pumps flooded nearby streets. Several firefighters had to be taken to hospital. The light from the fire was such that the snow on the Champ-de-Mars was a brilliant white.

Mayor Médéric Martin arrived on the scene with Sergeant Ferdinand Lafleur of the police department and the two men ran into the building. Overcome by the smoke, the mayor was forced outside, but Sergeant Lafleur made his way to the offices of the chief magistrate and returned with an armful of files and the famous chain of office worn by Montréal's "first citizen" at official functions. Mayor Martin watched the building's final moments from the driver's seat of a van on Notre-Dame Street. Although it had cost approximately $500,000 to build the city hall, damages were estimated at twenty times that amount. It was immediately decided that the city hall would be rebuilt with funds collected through a special tax, as the building had not been insured.

As early as 1884, Montrealers had taken full advantage of the beautiful park atop Mount Royal, thanks to a cable car that travelled from Fletcher's Field to the summit, where passengers alighted at a chalet. Two rail cars secured by cables met midway up the incline. The cable car was abandoned in 1919 when it was decided that it no longer met minimum safety standards. It was estimated that seven million citizens and tourists had taken the car. Three years later, it was suggested that twin elevators, accessible through a sixty-metre tunnel, be built. At this time, the only way to reach the park was to climb several long flights of steps, which was impossible for the elderly, or to rent a carriage, which not everyone could afford. In 1922, it was decided that streetcar service would be provided along Shakespeare Road. As the line would cross the northwest slope of the mountain, it was felt that this service would be adequate. In 1952, a city councillor came up with a plan to link Fletcher's Field to the summit by means of an aerial cable car, similar to those he had seen in Europe; however, this plan was never adopted.

The year 1922 was a very important one for radio enthusiasts, as it marked the beginning of French-language radio service in Canada. In its May 3 issue, *La Presse* reported that it was planning to erect an antenna on the roof of its building for a broadcasting station. A contract had been signed the previous day with the Marconi Company. The manager also had a famous name: he was A.H. Morse. The call signal was CKAC and antennas mounted on pylons were soon to be seen atop the building. At the time, the station's signal was stronger than that of any other station in North America. CKAC began broadcasting on September 27, sharing the antenna with

CFCF, which had been founded three years earlier. People in Montréal and the surrounding region who were fortunate enough to have a receiver could now hear French-language radio. For the first ten years, however, CKAC provided programming in both English and French.

It is interesting to note that the pioneers of French-language broadcasting were newspaper publishers. After CKAC, there was CHLP, which was established by the daily *La Patrie* and began broadcasting in 1932; CHLT, established by the Sherbrooke daily *La Tribune* in 1937; CHLN, established by *Le Nouvelliste* in Trois-Rivières in 1937; CJBR, established by *Le Progrès du Golfe* in Rimouski in 1937; and CKCH, established by *Le Droit* in Hull in 1939. In 1929, CKAC decided to set up its transmitter in Saint-Hyacinthe.

On October 2, 1922, two stars of the silver screen, Mary Pickford and Douglas Fairbanks, visited Montréal after a stay at Lake Louise. As both spoke fluent French, they took part in a program on CKAC and their message was relayed by many stations across the continent. When complimented on his knowledge of French, Fairbanks expressed surprise: "It is a skill that one must have to be a good actor," he replied modestly.

Three days before Christmas, there was a wonderful party with more than a thousand guests to celebrate the inauguration of the grandest hotel in the British Empire, the Mount Royal Hotel. Although it had 1,046 rooms, the hotel was built in 469 days, at a cost of $10 million. The Mount Royal was a wonderful asset to a great city that received visits from an increasing number of convention-goers and tourists.

Near the end of the nineteenth century two women with charitable inclinations, the Genéreux sisters, had opened a home on Saint-Hubert Street for people suffering from tuberculosis, for which there was no known medical treatment. The modest home quickly established a reputation as a hospital for incurable diseases. Shortly thereafter, the Sisters of Providence took over the home and, in 1901, acquired a building on Décarie Boulevard built five years earlier as a convent for the Sisters of the Precious Blood. Over the years, the hospital was gradually expanded to accommodate 400 beds, but in March 1923, it was totally destroyed in a fire. The hospital's residents were wrapped in blankets and placed on the snow until they could be taken to other institutions. Thanks to the firefighters and the nuns, no lives were lost. Following the disaster, a hospital for people with incurable diseases was built in Cartierville.

The court house on the north side of Notre-Dame Street, built in 1856 according to the plans of architect John Ostell, no longer met the needs of the judicial system. On March 22, 1923, the Québec government signed a

High technology in 1923: train travel and radio broadcasts.

contract for the construction of a new court house, to be built on the south
side of Notre-Dame, at a cost of close to $2 million. A remarkable building,
it did much to enhance the reputation of architect Ernest Cormier. Cormier also designed the bronze doors. Restoration work on the building
began in 1986, after the department of justice moved to its new quarters in a
lofty steel and glass tower at Notre-Dame and St. Lawrence.

Radio programs had gained widespread popularity. In 1922, the year
that CKAC began broadcasting, Sir Henry Thornton was appointed president of Canadian National Railways. Thornton thought that radio would
provide a welcome distraction for railway passengers and challenged his
technicians to come up with a plan. In July 1923, American tourists passing

through Montréal on their way to Alaska became the first to hear a radio program in their estate car. Each seat was equipped with headphones, tuned to Northern Electric's station, CHYC. In 1925 thirty-seven cars were equipped with headphones and by 1930, the number had risen to eighty. Uniformed technicians helped passengers get the best possible reception.

Exchanges between Canada and France were not always cultural in nature. On July 2, 1923, an "exhibition train" from Montréal was loaded onto the *France*, a steamship of the Compagnie Générale Transatlantique bound for Le Havre. The exhibition was a convoy of trucks and trailers that would tour France. The trailers had been transformed into exhibitions displaying a wide variety of products. France had agreed to put five million francs towards the cost of the tour. It was estimated that fifteen million people visited the exhibition, which ended its tour with a two-month stay in Paris at the Orangerie des Tuileries. In all, the exhibition toured forty-six cities.

In October, the master organist of Notre-Dame Cathedral in Paris, Marcel Dupré, gave a series of recitals in Montréal in which he performed the entire works of J.S. Bach for organ, a total of 151 compositions. Dupré was the first artist to agree to a public broadcast of his concerts, engineered by CKAC. Dupré later became the organist at Saint-Sulpice.

In late September, Montréal received a visit from Édouard Herriot, who had been the mayor of Lyon since 1905. Herriot was a member of the French National Assembly and a former minister of public works. The purpose of his North American tour was to refute accusations that France had imperialist designs on the Ruhr and the Rhine and to promote a huge exhibition that would be held in Lyon. In 1924, he was called upon to form a government and assumed the foreign affairs portfolio himself. Under Herriot France did, in fact, withdraw from the Ruhr.

In 1924, the Saint-Jean-Baptiste Society donated the huge illuminated cross atop Mount Royal to the city of Montréal. For many years, the association had wanted to create a permanent monument to Maisonneuve, who had fulfilled a promise on January 6, 1643, by carrying a cross to the top of the mountain, thanking God for sparing Ville-Marie from floods that had threatened to destroy it.

According to the plans drawn up in June 1924 by Father Dupaigne, a Sulpician attached to the seminary, the cross would have an eleven-metre-high base of cut stone, decorated with elaborate balusters, supporting a cross nineteen metres high. The base of the cross would have a welcoming area. The association, which had raised the funds for the project by subscription, preferred a base that was not enclosed. Once completed, the cross stood thirty-one metres high and nine metres across. It was lit for the first time at 5 p.m. on Christmas Eve. Since then, it has provided a beacon for Montrealers and tourists alike.

In 1925, another invention swept Montréal: the rotary telephone dial. The construction of the Lancaster telephone exchange at the corner of Ontario and Saint-Urbain streets made it possible for all subscribers whose telephone number started with 52 (LA) to place calls without going through an operator.

That same year, Montréal paid homage to the great diva Albani, born Emma Lajeunesse in Chambly, who had brought Canada's name to every great stage in the world and enchanted devotees of London's Covent Garden. On a visit to London, Prime Minister Mackenzie King learned that Albani now lived in poverty and, at the age of seventy-three, was forced to give music lessons to support herself. King returned to Canada with a plan to launch a nationwide fundraising campaign. The daily *La Presse* quickly responded and organized a concert in her honour at the Théâtre Saint-Denis. Under the direction of Louis-H. Bourdon, artists performed for an audience of 2,400 music lovers. Thanks to CKAC, Albani was able to hear a broadcast of the concert and the thunderous applause at the mention of her name. The program included a song that had been her signature tune, "Les souvenirs du jeune âge sont gravés dans mon coeur." No doubt it reminded her of her early days in Montréal. Even though Parliament was in session, the prime minister insisted on attending the concert.

In mid-February 1926, Montréal officially opened its new *"palais munici-pal,"* built after the fire of 1922. Containing a grandiose marble hall of honour and much intricately carved wood, it was indeed a palace. Unfortunately Médéric Martin, who had watched "his" city hall burn to the ground, was no longer at the helm and did not attend the inaugural ceremony.

In October, there was further cause for celebration. Pope Pius XI had bestowed on André Grasset de Saint-Sauveur the title of "Blessed." Born in Montréal in 1758, Grasset travelled to France with his father after the signing of the Treaty of Paris. There he entered a religious order, becoming a canon of Sens Cathedral. When the Constituent Assembly abolished religious orders during the French Revolution, Grasset withdrew to the Carmelites in Paris. During the night of September 2, 1792, Grasset and more than one hundred other priests were murdered. All were beatified on

The stained glass window in Collège André-Grasset to the memory of André Grasset de Saint-Sauveur, beatified in 1926.

October 17, 1926. A college was named after the Montréal priest and, in the faculty dining hall, there is a stained glass window to his memory.

It will be recalled that in 1903, work was completed on a luxury liner, the *Montreal*, that was subsequently destroyed by fire. Perhaps to tempt the fate that had befallen other vessels of the same name, another luxury liner was baptized the *Montreal*. On November 18, 1926, it too caught fire off Sainte-Anne-de-Sorel. Luckily, its cargo on this voyage consisted entirely of livestock. The *Montreal* was taken out of service for the remainder of the shipping season.

When Sacha Guitry visited Montréal in January 1927, Médéric Martin was once again mayor of Montréal. "Martin speaks with a Lisieux accent," the playwright later wrote. "He is more Norman than Alphonse Allais himself." After performing in New York, Guitry and his theatre company performed for eight days in Montréal. During a speech before the Club Saint-Denis, Guitry responded to the charge that Quebecers had an accent that was not French. An accent is not a defect or even an oddity, Guitry declared. It is a trait, just like eye colour and cheekbones. At this point in his speech,

Guitry may have turned to his lifelong companion, Yvonne Printemps. "One wears one's language like a costume. Yours is a lawn headdress, a fine satin skirt, woollen petticoats and a lace shawl. If you add a hat with a long feather, the effect is ruined. In my opinion, this would be a mistake." Guitry concluded his speech by saying that he hoped that one day Canada would have its own literary and theatrical tradition. "I hope that, one day, one of your novelists will receive the Prix Goncourt." If Guitry were here today, he would be overjoyed to find a vibrant community of authors and play-wrights, and he would be happy to shake Roger Lemelin's hand.*

The year 1927 began with one of the greatest tragedies Montréal has ever known: the fire at Laurier Palace. On January 9, the movie theatre located almost directly opposite a fire station on Sainte-Catherine Street was filled with children when a fire broke out. When the children smelled the smoke, they began running for the exits. The doors opened inwards and the children, in their panic, were crushed to death. Seventy-seven children died in the fire. A family living on Joliette Street lost three children in the fire. One of the policemen helping to remove the bodies from the theatre found the body of his own son, age six, under several other bodies. For days, the papers ran gruesome accounts of the tragedy. The authorities banned children under the age of sixteen years from attending movies and decreed that henceforth the doors of all public buildings should open outwards.

That fall, flooding made it painfully clear just how vulnerable Montréal's public transportation system was. On November 17, torrential rains caused the Saint-Pierre rivulet to overflow its banks in the area known as Village Turcot, near the shunting station of the same name. It was not long before there was two metres of water in the streets. Streetcar service in Lachine ground to a halt, but a bus service from Ville-Saint-Pierre was provided.

Not long before, Montrealers had learned of the death of Count de Lesseps who, it will be recalled, had flown over Montréal's city hall in 1910, becoming the first person to fly a plane in Canada. In 1927, the department of lands and forests completed a topographical survey of the Gaspé Peninsula using two small planes out of Gaspé and Val-Brillant. When de Lesseps' death was announced Québec's minister of lands and forests, Honoré Mercier (son of the former premier of the same name), was in Val-Brillant, monitoring the progress of the survey. De Lesseps, with whom Mercier had originally planned to make the return trip, was in Gaspé. He had decided to return to Val-Brillant with his mechanic. Their plane entered a mass of

* *Unfortunately, Roger Lemelin died after the original French version of this book was published.*

dense fog and crashed off Matane. De Lesseps was buried in Gaspé, where a stele was erected in his memory. It bears a high relief by sculptor Henri Hébert in which humanity is depicted as defying gravity in a flying machine.

In 1928, a colourful and engaging character entered municipal politics. Camillien Houde, "le p'tit gars de Saint-Henri," won the mayoral election over Médéric Martin by more than 20,000 votes. The son of a carpenter and the only surviving child of a family of ten, Houde was only seven when his father died. As a child, he had worked every day, after school, as a butcher's helper to support his mother. At the Collège de Longueuil, Houde met Brother Marie-Victorin, who found him a position as a bank clerk. In 1923, Houde got his first taste of politics. When he promised to put his fist through the top hat of Premier Taschereau, he won the hearts of the working-class voters of Sainte-Marie riding, and went on to represent them in Québec City. Houde decided to enter municipal politics and became known as "Mr. Montréal."

On May 5, barely a month after being elected mayor, Houde presided over the official opening of Montréal's largest stadium at the corner of Ontario and De Lorimier streets. It was here that 22,500 spectators watched the Montreal Royals of the International League beat Reading, after patiently sitting through a concert by the Grenadier Guards. Politics and sports were closely interconnected at this time: the president of the Montreal Royals was none other than the provincial secretary, Athanase David.

On October 1, a crowd gathered at the airport in Saint-Hubert for the official start of airmail service between Canada and the United States. The premier of Québec, Montréal's new mayor and Canada's postmaster general were all on hand as the Canadian Colonial Air Lines monoplane *Fairchild* landed and then took off for Albany with a sack of mail. Houde gave the pilot a teddy bear for New York Mayor Jimmy Walker. Canadian Colonial provided daily mail service in both directions; later, it would carry passengers to and from New York.

It was not until 1930 that the Harbour Bridge linked Montréal with Longueuil on the south shore. When the bridge was officially opened on May 24, all of the vessels moored in the harbour sounded their horns. Four years later, on the 400th anniversary of Cartier's claiming of Canada for France, it was renamed the Jacques-Cartier Bridge.

The Harbour Commission had received permission to build, finance and operate a bridge in 1924. Two Montréal engineers, C.-N. Monsarrat and P.L. Pratley, and an engineer from Chicago, J.B. Strauss, were instructed

It was estimated that 40,000 people gathered to see the R-100 tethered to a tower at the Saint-Hubert airport.

to select the best possible location for the bridge and to draw up plans, specifications and estimates. Work on the bridge began in May 1925. It was agreed that the Harbour Commission, the government of Québec and the city of Montréal would share the cost of the loan for the project. Work progressed quickly, despite challenges presented by the span over the shipping channel, and the bridge was completed fourteen months ahead of schedule. The total cost was $18,571,308; modifications to the design following the opening of the St. Lawrence Seaway required an additional $3 million. During construction of the span providing access to St. Helen's Island, there was no interruption in shipping. Similarly, when the span across the Seaway was built, there was barely any interruption in ship movement.

Also in 1930, Montrealers were dazzled by another feat of engineering: the R-100. Germany had already built several zeppelins, but after the Treaty of Versailles, was not allowed to produce zeppelins capable of holding more than 28,000 cubic metres of gas. Inspired by the design of a German L-33 shot down over its territory, Britain designed and launched the R-33 and R-34. When the R-34 successfully completed an Atlantic crossing in 1919, work began on larger zeppelins, the R-100 and R-101.

On July 29, 1930, the R-100 left Cardington, Scotland, with forty-four passengers, 23.75 tons of fuel and 5.4 tons of ballast. On August 1, as 40,000 spectators watched, it was tethered to a tower built especially for this purpose. Old-timers will no doubt remember seeing the huge blimp fly over Montréal. The zeppelin's designer was invited to talk about the craft, and he predicted that eventually weekly service between Britain and Montréal would be provided. His dream was shattered the same year when the R-101 crashed at Beauvais, France, en route to India. Its sister ship was dismantled six years later in Cardington, where it had been built.

Since the beginning of the century, a city bylaw had blocked the construction of buildings taller than 130 feet. As downtown Montréal developed, city authorities decided that the bylaw was an unnecessary restriction on attractive and desirable construction projects. In 1927, it was amended to allow for the construction of taller buildings, provided that the mass of the building was reduced by means of setbacks. Two years later, work began on the Aldred Building on Place d'Armes, named after the president of the Shawinigan Water and Power Company, J.E. Aldred. Twenty-three storeys high, the new skyscraper had a huge mass. Because the clay on which it was built was unstable, beams were erected on a reinforced concrete base, poured in one piece. With the construction of the Aldred Building, the towers of Notre-Dame Basilica no longer dominated the skyline. And when the glass cube of the Banque Nationale Building appeared, Notre-Dame seemed to shrink even more.

It will be recalled that Brother Marie-Victorin had found employment for a student of the Collège de Longueuil. Several years later, Camillien Houde returned the favour, to the delight of Montrealers.

In 1885, plans to develop a botanical garden on the slopes of Mount Royal were abandoned. In 1929, returning home from a long voyage that had spanned three continents, Brother Marie-Victorin reintroduced the idea. "I am now convinced," he said, "that a city such as ours and a university such as the Université de Montréal needs a botanical garden with scientific stature." Some months later, the outspoken botanist proposed that the garden be constructed in Maisonneuve Park. On March 4, 1932, the municipal council passed a resolution establishing the Botanical Gardens. That year, Montréal elected a new mayor, but Camillien Houde had ensured that the commitment of $100,000 to the project could not be withdrawn by the new council. The project initially consisted of levelling the site and building a small greenhouse; over the years, despite a number of setbacks, it has become one of the best-known botanical gardens in the world.

At noon on July 14, 1933, a Canadian Airways D-H Oragon left Cartierville airport with a team of journalists to escort a squadron of twenty-four Italian hydroplanes. It was the only plane to receive this mission from the Department of National Defence, which feared that a larger contingent might interfere with the squadron's progress towards its final destination, Chicago. The winged armada was under the command of General Italo Balbo, the Italian minister of the air. The crowd watched in amazement from the shore as one by one the planes glided to a stop in the harbour opposite Fairchild Pier.

Complete with a top hat, the federal minister of the navy, Alfred Duran-leau, was on hand to welcome General Balbo. From the Harbour Bridge, twenty-one hydroplanes positioned themselves between Sainte-Marie cur-rent and the jetty; those of the general and his officers moored nearby, offer-ing a wonderful spectacle. Balbo had been one of Mussolini's closest allies during the march on Rome in 1922 and had personally commanded several long-distance flights, such as the flight to North America in 1933. Pro-moted to the rank of marshal, Balbo was so popular with the Italian public that Mussolini, fearing for his own image, appointed him governor of Libya. Balbo died shortly after the Second World War broke out. He was shot down by Italy's own DCA. According to the Italian government, his death was accidental.

In mid-March 1934, Montréal welcomed Julien Duvivier, the great French screenwriter. Duvivier hoped to shoot winter scenes for *Maria Chapdelaine*, a film that would later cement his reputation. Customs officials demanded that Duvivier pay the equivalent of 11,000 francs to bring camera equipment into Canada and refused to reimburse him when he left. The matter was resolved when Duvivier declared that if he was not reimbursed, he would shoot the film in France using French actors.

It is impossible to have too much of a good thing, especially where land transportation is concerned. With the inauguration of the Harbour Bridge in 1930, seventy years after the construction of the Victoria Bridge, Montréal finally got a second bridge across the St. Lawrence. Four years later, a third bridge was built between Ville LaSalle and Kahnawake. The first caisson was put in place in 1932 on the north side and on June 22, 1934, Premier Louis-Alexandre Taschereau officially opened the Honoré-Mer-cier Bridge, declaring that, for the first time, a team of French Canadian engineers, all graduates of Montréal's École Polytechnique, had built a bridge over the St. Lawrence without the help of engineers of any other ethnic origin. Later, when the Seaway was developed, the bulkhead of the southern section was dynamited and replaced by a span that provided thirty-six metres of clearance over the Seaway. In 1964, a second Mercier Bridge was built to double the carrying capacity of the first bridge.

Celebrations in the Gaspé marking the 400th anniversary of Jacques Cartier's first voyage to Canada drew a prestigious delegation from France. In late April, Paris radio stations had begun broadcasting programs featur-ing French Canadian literature and music, with the help of artists from the

Opéra-Comique and the Comédie Française. In June, the Quatuor Alouette and the Troubadours de Bytown left Montréal to join in the celebrations.

The French delegation arrived in Canada aboard the *Champlain*, the most recent addition to the fleet of the Compagnie Générale Transatlantique. Seventy fishing vessels wearing the colours of France's former provinces set out to meet the *Champlain*. Mooring at the first buoy in Northumberland Strait, the *Champlain* transferred its passengers to the *Cartier* for the trip to Charlottetown. There, a cairn commemorating Cartier's description of the "fair isle" in his journal was unveiled. There were speeches, including one by Henry Bordeaux of the Académie Française. "M. Bordeaux addressed his audience in French," reported a Montréal daily, which might seem a statement of the obvious. For several months, however, concerns had been raised about the commemoration of the event.

In *L'Ordre*, Olivar Asselin wrote that every effort should be made to avoid the mistakes committed at the 300th anniversary of the founding of Québec City where the machinations of the governor general, Lord Grey, had turned the program into "a commemoration of the British Conquest and a celebration of Anglo-Saxon imperialism." Perhaps this is why the August 27 issue of *La Presse* carried the headline "Cartier Seals Anglo-Canadian Friendship," and at a banquet offered by the province of Québec, the British representative, Hon. A.L. Fisher, spoke in French, saying, "The British Empire has nothing to fear from you. Treat your French culture and freedoms with care."

In addition to writer Henry Bordeaux, the delegation from France included several well-known individuals. Representing the French government were Public Works Minister Pierre Étienne Flandin and Sébastien Charléty, rector of the Université de Paris. Two well-known historians, Charles de La Roncière, assistant curator of the Bibliothèque Nationale, and Firmin Roz, director of Canada House at the Cité Universitaire de Paris, also attended. They were accompanied by eminent French journalists who were attending a convention of the French-language press being held in Québec City and came to Montréal to meet their colleagues there.

La Presse decided to organize a public festival at Lafontaine Park in honour of Cartier. The following day, it was estimated that 300,000 people had taken part. The festivities ended with fireworks that included a display in the likeness of the French explorer. Henry Bordeaux declared that he had not seen such a joyous celebration since the Armistice ending the First World War.

The president of the Comité France-Amérique de Montréal was Senator Raoul Dandurand. At a dinner offered by the Comité France-Amérique de Paris on August 31, he publicly announced that for many years he had dreamt of establishing a French *lycée* in Montréal. And so it was that Collège Stanislas was born.

That year, the French committee had commissioned a bust of Jacques Cartier, which can been seen today on the Place du Canada in Paris. Montréal also has a tangible souvenir of the celebrations. France presented Montréal with a replica of the bust, which was placed on a pedestal where the great span of the former Harbour Bridge, since renamed in honour of Jacques Cartier, comes to rest on St. Helen's Island.

The following year, Firmin Roz's history of Canada was published in Paris. The preface was written by Sébastien Charléty who, along with Étienne Flandin, had represented France at the 400th anniversary celebrations.

The Société des Concerts Symphoniques, founded in 1934 through the efforts of Mrs. Athanase David, Henri Letondal and Jean Lallemand, provided a venue for French Canadian conductors, composers and soloists who were refused admission to the Montreal Orchestra. Mrs. David's husband, the provincial secretary, succeeded in convincing the conductor of the Metropolitan Opera of New York, Wilfrid Pelletier, to become its musical director.

Like Emma Lajeunesse, Pelletier had helped to make a name for Québec in international music circles. Pelletier learned the rudiments from his father, a musician in the 65th Regiment band. He later learned music theory and harmony from an accomplished musician, Mrs. François Héraly. He played the drums in the Dominion Park Concert Band, then the piano in a small ensemble. Through Mrs. Héraly's efforts, he met many great musicians and was eventually made choirmaster of the Montreal Opera Chorus. A scholarship made it possible for him to study music in Paris, where he met Pierre Monteux, conductor of the Metropolitan Opera, who took Pelletier on as assistant conductor in 1917. Pelletier became the conductor himself when it came under the management of the Canadian musician Edward Johnson.

In recognition of his contribution to the field of music, the Université de Montréal gave Pelletier an honorary doctorate on February 29, 1936. His mother and father attended the ceremony. In 1954, the Société des Concerts Symphoniques became the Orchestre Symphonique de Montréal. Wilfrid Pelletier died in 1982. A concert honouring him was held in the

Salle Wilfrid-Pelletier, the main concert hall of the Place des Arts. The world of music has changed radically since Pelletier first raised his baton in Plateau Hall.

The year 1936 was an important one in the history of rail travel. Work on five locomotives of the 3000 series, offering rapid service to Québec City, had just been completed. Canadian Pacific's most powerful locomotive, the 8000, measuring thirty metres with its tender and weighing 398 tons, rarely exceeded speeds of 128 kilometres an hour. It was estimated that locomotives of the 3000 series, measuring twenty-four metres and weighing a mere 215 tons, would reach speeds of 176 kilometres an hour on a straight track, which meant that the distance between Montréal and Québec City could be covered in three and a half hours.

Canada did not escape the Depression that followed the crash of the New York stock market. Montréal was particularly hard hit, as plant after plant ceased operations. Charitable organizations received innumerable pleas for help, and endless lines of unemployed workers formed outside soup kitchens. Unemployment was endemic and city authorities were forced to set up a system offering financial assistance to those most in need. Various measures to revive the economy were tried. In 1936, the Québec government began a massive public works project, which included the Repentigny Bridge, the construction of a major portion of the Botanical Gardens and the restoration of the historical park on St. Helen's Island.

After the official opening of the Harbour Bridge in 1930, architect Frederick G. Todd, who had designed the model city that became the Town of Mount Royal, was asked to come up with a design for the island. Todd's design included the current configuration of roads, an expansion of the park and a swimming lagoon. Unfortunately, the Depression prevented implementation of the project. It was revived in 1936, when the province decided to restore the military buildings and clear the underbrush. Construction work began on a magnificent tower to adorn the water works and on two large buildings, the Pavillon Hélène-de-Champlain and the Chalet des Baigneurs.

In 1937, the lieutenant-governor opened a folk art fair in the military barracks, organized by Léon Trépanier, who had been appointed director general of the celebrations marking Montréal's 300th anniversary. This event was of particular importance because it marked a resurgence of interest in folk art. Its champion was Jean-Marie Gauvreau, director of the École du Meuble, which later became the Institut des Arts Appliqués. On the afternoon of June 25, 1938, the new park was officially opened. The inauguration was organized by journalist Louis Francoeur, president of the technical committee of the Montreal Metropolitan Commission. It was a very public event: Public Works Minister William Tremblay had invited all those who had worked on the restoration and their families to a picnic. The landscape architect had suggested that the park be expanded to include Île Ronde and Île Verte, as well as a string of little islands off the south shore. Because of the war, the plan was postponed until the 1967 world's fair.

In early 1937, Montréal mourned the loss of a man who although he shunned the public eye was one of the city's greatest citizens: Brother André, the miracle worker of Mount Royal. We have already mentioned the little sanctuary on the mountainside that became St. Joseph's Oratory, one of the most popular destinations for pilgrimages in North America. Brother André's death was a great shock to the Roman Catholic community and unprecedented numbers came out to pay their last respects. Despite snow and cold, it is estimated that a million people visited the church where he lay in state. Special trains were reserved for pilgrims from New England. Brother André was beatified in 1982.

In 1937 Canada's first airline, Trans-Canada Air Lines, was established. The forerunner of Air Canada, TCA was a wholly owned subsidiary of Canadian National. On April 1, 1939, transcontinental flights linking Montréal and Vancouver left simultaneously from both cities. Four months later, Imperial Airways began offering transatlantic airmail service between Canada and Britain, using two four-engined hydroplanes, the *Caribou* and the *Cabot*, equipped with three-blade propellers. The planes took off from the St. Lawrence River off Boucherville and landed at Southampton on England's south coast. The inaugural voyage took place on August 5 and lasted thirty-three hours.

Over the course of its history, Montréal has had a number of princely visitors, but it was not until 1939 that it received a visit from a reigning sovereign. On May 18, 1939, King George VI and Queen Elizabeth "visited their Canadian metropolis," as *La Presse* phrased it. The royal party were taken on a forty-kilometre tour along the city's major arteries with an escort of motorcyclists from the 8th Duke of Connaught's Royal Canadian Hussars and cavalrymen of the 17th Duke of Connaught's Hussars. The King and Queen admired the city from atop Mount Royal, then withdrew to the Windsor Hotel, where they attended a banquet hosted by the city of Montréal.

Journalist Roger Champoux, whose articles recounted all the visits of visiting dignitaries, had eyes only for the queen. "In tulle of a blue so pale that it was almost white, accented with silver clasps, Her Majesty wore a crown of diamonds and the sober insignia of the Order of the Garter with true majesty. Her smile filled the room and beside all the gold, silver and crystal, her eyes were the most beautiful jewels in the world." This was a portrait that the Paris broadcaster Léon Zitrone would have been proud of. Mayor Camillien Houde was the master of ceremonies and toasted the royal couple in both languages. The splendour of the evening must have come back to him in full force a few months later when he was transported to an internment camp. But we are getting ahead of ourselves.

On July 23, 1939, the second convention of the Jeunesse Ouvrière Catholique du Canada opened at De Lorimier Stadium with a ceremony in which 106 couples belonging to the movement were married simultaneously. They came not only from Québec, but also from Ontario and the Maritimes. The archbishop of Montréal, six bishops and dozens of priests presided over the ceremony attended by 20,000 JOC members and various political figures of the day, including federal Public Works Minister P.-J.-A. Cardin, provincial Labour Minister William Tremblay and Montréal Mayor Camillien Houde. It was an event that participants will long remember.

The Second World War

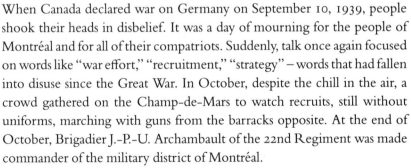

When Canada declared war on Germany on September 10, 1939, people shook their heads in disbelief. It was a day of mourning for the people of Montréal and for all of their compatriots. Suddenly, talk once again focused on words like "war effort," "recruitment," "strategy" – words that had fallen into disuse since the Great War. In October, despite the chill in the air, a crowd gathered on the Champ-de-Mars to watch recruits, still without uniforms, marching with guns from the barracks opposite. At the end of October, Brigadier J.-P.-U. Archambault of the 22nd Regiment was made commander of the military district of Montréal.

Posters calling on Canadians to sign up began appearing everywhere. Like those used during the First World War, Second World War recruitment posters were illustrations of historical figures designed to inspire pride and patriotism in young French Canadians. Many were reproductions of paintings commissioned for the campaign from artist Adam Sherriff Scott. Using the theme "Yesterday - Today," Scott painted a magnificent portrait of Lieutenant-Colonel de Salaberry, victorious at Châteauguay. In a small inset was an illustration of a modern soldier in the same stance. Another poster depicted Madeleine de Verchères with a musket and powder horn. In the background is the Verchères fort, which she had successfully defended against an Iroquois attack. This time, the inset was of a woman in modern uniform, a reminder that women had recently been allowed to join the armed forces.

The first recruits, drawn largely from the unemployed, learned quickly and when they paraded in Lafontaine Park the following spring, they were a tightly disciplined group. Montréal had been transformed; the two French-language regiments, the Régiment de Maisonneuve and the Fusiliers Mont-Royal, both wanted to be the first to have a battalion of 800 men.

France suffered one defeat after another. "We love France as she is, with all her imperfections and weaknesses, the way a son loves his mother," wrote Louis Francoeur in *La Patrie* on March 26, 1940. "We owe it to the blood that flows through our veins to keep our morale high. Our cousins, for whom this war is an immediate reality, are surviving with the quiet strength they have always shown when their nation was in danger. To those of us who stand behind them, oceans away, they offer a lesson in moral strength, which we would do well to heed." Up until June 16, the papers tried to reassure their readers. The following day, France was in total disarray and sued for peace; still, *Le Devoir* reported that France was "a country of resurrections."

Montrealers established a branch of the Assistance aux Oeuvres Françaises de Guerre, a civilian organization to assist the war effort. According to Francoeur, the association offered "one of the most practical and straightforward means of thanking France for everything we owe her – our blood, our spirit, our civilization, two thousand years of collective consciousness."

The papers reported worrisome stories of subversion. During the night of June 17, the RCMP arrested "a considerable number of communists and fascists." In early July, *La Presse* announced that the RCMP and the provincial police had discovered a house of Nazi propaganda on St. Lawrence Boulevard north of Sherbrooke. A short-wave radio capable of transmitting and receiving messages from Berlin was found, along with approximately 15,000 magazines, brochures and pamphlets written in German. The authorities quickly posted messages directed at sailors, dockers and stevedores warning them that the enemy was listening to everything they said: "Watch out! The enemy is listening. Information that is useful to the enemy can be fatal to you. Serve your country by being discreet."

On August 6, there was a bombshell: it was announced that the previous day, Mayor Camillien Houde had been arrested and taken to an internment camp. More than half a century has elapsed since the day Houde was arrested, which makes it important to recall briefly what prompted the authorities to act in this manner. Before the First World War, no doubt to win votes, the ruling Conservatives in Ottawa had made a commitment never to impose compulsory military service. And yet, in 1917, Prime Minister Borden had introduced conscription, stating that when the commitment was made, no one could have imagined the scale of the effort that would be required to achieve victory.

Once bitten, twice shy, as they say. Even the least astute leaders in Québec knew what was coming when Ottawa decreed compulsory national registration at the beginning of the Second World War, despite its commitment to rely on voluntary service in the event of another conflict. Although he was the mayor of Montréal, Camillien Houde had the courage to speak out. His gesture was one less of political opportunism than of deep personal conviction. For Houde, and for many others, the purpose of national registration was crystal clear: to identify future conscripts. But when he called on the population not to submit to national registration, what he was suggesting amounted to civil disobedience.

Perhaps Houde believed that his position offered him some sort of immunity. This was not the case. As he was preparing to leave city hall on Place Vauquelin at 11 p.m. on August 5, he was arrested. A meeting of the city council had been called for August 7. At Houde's request, the first item on the agenda was to have been "national registration and conscription." In the internment camp, Houde did not receive special treatment. He was assigned physical labour commensurate with his state of health. Just like his fellow prisoners, he rose at 5:30 a.m. each morning and his lights were turned off at 10 p.m.

Factories across Canada converted their machinery to begin producing armaments. In Montréal, the Canadian Pacific Railway's huge Angus shops stopped producing locomotives and railway cars and began producing tanks. On May 22, 1941, the first heavy tank rolled off a Canadian assembly line. In size and weight, it was vastly different from the first "landships" used by the Allies at the Somme in 1916 and designed by the British to reduce infantry casualties. The Angus shops turned out a total of 1,420 tanks during

MADELEINE DE VERCHÈRES · 1678-1747

NÉE à Sorel, l'héroïne nationale du Canada français. Le 22 octobre 1692, à l'âge de 14 ans et demi, avec l'aide de ses deux frères âgés de 12 et de 10 ans respectivement, elle défendit avec succès le Fort de Verchères contre 45 Iroquois. Elle symbolise l'héroïsme féminin de la Nouvelle-France. Décédée à Sainte-Anne de la Pérade.

HIER

AUJOURD'HUI

Second World War posters evoked heroes of French Canada's past to stimulate commitment to the war effort.

LE LIEUT.-COL. CHARLES M. DE SALABERRY · 1752-1829

Né à Beauport, près de Québec. Officier, député,
magistrat, conseiller législatif. A l'âge de 61 ans, à la tête de 300
voltigeurs, avec le colonel Macdonell, qui commande la réserve,
il met en déroute 7,000 adversaires aux alentours de Châteauguay.
On a appelé Châteauguay les Thermopyles du Canada. Lord
Sherbrooke l'appela au Conseil législatif; le duc de Kent
accepta d'être parrain d'un de ses enfants. Décédé à Chambly.

HIER

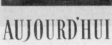

AUJOURD'HUI

the Second World War. In 1990, a Canadian tank that had fallen through the ice during the Russian campaign was pulled from its icy grave and offered to Canadian Pacific by the town council of Telepino, a town about 200 kilometres from Kiev.

Those who took part in the catastrophic raid on Dieppe will long remember August 19, 1942. The Allies wanted to test the defences put in place by the Germans to repel any attempts at landing. Hundreds of Canadian soldiers lost their lives during the raid, and 697 of them are buried in a little military cemetery near Dieppe. The population of Montréal was particularly sensitive to this holocaust; on the beaches at Dieppe, there now stands a stele honouring the members of the Fusiliers Mont-Royal who lost their lives in the aborted landing. On September 4, a crowd of 8,000 Montrealers gathered at the Forum to honour the troops who had landed at Dieppe. Colonel Dollard Ménard's battle cry had been, "My soldiers are the best in the world!"

Three weeks later, there was a ceremony to honour seventeen soldiers wounded during the raid. The site chosen for the ceremony was the monument to Dollard des Ormeaux and the other heroes of Long-Sault in Lafontaine Park; it is difficult to know whether this was coincidental or intentional. Attending the ceremony were Justice Minister Louis Saint-Laurent and Air Minister C.G. Power representing the federal government, Québec Premier Adélard Godbout and Montréal Mayor Adhémar Raynault. Many of those who attended the ceremony were moved to tears as Brigadier General E. de B. Panet read out the names of the veterans and described their injuries and decorations.

It is not the intention of this book to give a detailed description of the war and its many battles. However, we would like to mention one event that took place at 12:45 p.m. on July 12, 1944. A four-engined plane from the United States landed at Dorval Airport and a general emerged who, with his patriotism, sense of honour, fierce loyalty to his country and unflagging ability to rally his people, had managed to triumph over the haughtiness of Churchill and the reticence of Roosevelt, both of whom believed that France would remain forever under the German boot. General Charles de Gaulle had not forgotten that the offspring of the cultural homeland had flourished on American soil.

Torpedo attacks on vessels in the St. Lawrence and the arrest of Nazi spies, particularly in the Gaspé, made the war very real for the people of Québec. Public awareness of the conflict was also heightened by commentators like Louis Francoeur, whose broadcasts on the CBC program *La*

Situation ce soir provided daily updates. Direct radio contact with France had been established in 1941 through an arrangement between the Canadian Broadcasting Corporation and WRUL in Boston. The official host of these programs, broadcast on short-wave frequencies, was Roger Baulu. Among the members of the French-speaking elite who provided moral support by broadcasting messages of hope to their cousins in France were the archbishop of Québec, Rodrigue Cardinal Villeneuve; Premier Adélard Godbout; and two former Canadian ambassadors to France, Georges Vanier and Jean Désy.

Charles de Gaulle was no doubt aware that French Quebecers were generally sympathetic to his cause, although Marshal Pétain did have supporters in Québec. Among de Gaulle's supporters was Élisabeth de Miribel, who was in charge of information services for the Free French in Canada.

That General de Gaulle should visit Montréal and Québec City after visiting Washington, New York and Ottawa should come as no surprise. On August 2, 1940, de Gaulle had spoken directly to French Canada, which he remembered as a branch of Old France that had taken root on American soil: "The soul of France is appealing to you, as French Canadians, for help. France is calling on you for help because she knows you. She knows your stake in the country, in the people, in the State to which you belong." After declaring that the branch had grown into a mature tree, he concluded by saying: "French Canadians, I greet you confidently as a French soldier who, for the time being, has the very great responsibility of speaking alone on behalf of France." By 1944, de Gaulle no longer spoke alone. Churchill, who had grumbled about wearing the Croix de Lorraine, symbol of the Free French forces, was now proud of it. Together with Roosevelt, he now understood that when Europe was liberated, de Gaulle would be equal to the task of rebuilding his country.

General de Gaulle spoke to French Canada again when he sent a message to the mayor of Montréal in 1942 on the 300th anniversary of the city's founding: "France has not forgotten her sons who have carried her cherished name and traditions over the seas. The Comité National Français, which draws its strength from the greatest victories of France's glorious history and from the certainty that, in collaboration with civilized peoples, it will be victorious, sends you this day a message of hope and confidence."

In 1944, de Gaulle had only a few hours to spare. Two days before his arrival, Canadian troops had liberated the city of Caen in France. At Dorval Airport, he was officially welcomed by Mayor Raynault and representatives of the Canadian army, navy and air force. After inspecting a company of

Canadian airmen, he inspected two groups of French pilots who were training in Québec, then departed for city hall where he signed the golden book.
A few hours later, the general boarded his plane once again. "Over the roar
of the engines," *La Presse* reported "could be heard cries of 'Vive de Gaulle!
Vive la France!' Spectators watched as the plane grew smaller, carrying with
it the man whom many countries recognized as the head of the provisional
French government."

Less than a year later, Nazi Germany was defeated. In the streets of
Montréal, the atmosphere was one of euphoria. On May 7, 1945, *Le Petit
Journal* printed a special run of 50,000 copies that were distributed free of
charge on every street corner. "War Ends in Europe" read the headlines.
And yet the war continued in the Pacific; it was not until mid-August that
the Japanese flag was lowered.

Peace is Restored

———————— >‹ ————————

Although the imperatives of war were uppermost in the minds of most public officials, legislation was adopted in Québec City that had a profound
effect on the way the city of Montréal was administered. Passed on June 5,
1940, the bill stipulated that as of the elections to be held in December of
that year, the city council would be made up of a mayor and ninety-nine
councillors. Property owners would elect one third of the councillors, the
general public another third, and the remaining third would be appointed
by various organizations. Some wondered whether this system, which was
destined to last only a relatively short time, was democratic. Montréal was to
have eleven districts, replacing the existing thirty-five wards. Perhaps
because of the logistics of bringing together such a large group, the new
council was to meet only four times a year.

In 1939, Montréal had established a commission to organize the celebrations for its 300th birthday in 1942. Léon Trépanier was put in charge of
organizing the festivities. A historical committee was also created, chaired
by Ægidius Fauteux, curator of the Municipal Library, who selected twelve
historians, notably Abbé Lionel Groulx, archivist É.-Z. Massicotte and
Mgr. Olivier Maurault, rector of the Université de Montréal.

Trépanier announced a competition for the publication of a popular

history of Montréal and commissioned costumes to be worn by participants. The celebrations began with an evening at Bonsecours Market on
March 30, 1940, having as its theme *"Jacques Viger reçoit"* (An evening with
Jacques Viger). Lawyer and humorist Gérard Delage was asked to write the
script for the evening's performance, a reenactment of the very first meeting
of Montréal's city council. Montréal's first mayor, Jacques Viger, was played
by eminent actor J.-P. Filion. Civil servants in period costumes danced the
gavotte and the minuet. It was estimated that some 3,000 people attended
the March 30 event and a repeat performance on April 6.

The festivities were also to include an exhibition of folk art in the fort on
St. Helen's Island, one of the goals of which was to encourage the design of
articles that could be sold to visitors and tourists. However, plans for the
anniversary were cut short by the war – this was hardly a time for rejoicing –
and the celebrations were far more modest than originally planned. It will
also be recalled that Camillien Houde, here in the role of chief commissioner, had been interned.

After the war, the American aeronautics industry was impatient to
reconvert to civilian aircraft production, and one of the first companies to
undertake this transformation was Lockheed Aircraft of Burbank, California. In 1945, Lockheed showed the world the prototype of the Constellation. Thirty metres long and 37.50 metres from wing tip to wing tip, the
Constellation could cross the Atlantic with sixty-four passengers. Some of
the aircraft were actually equipped with berths for sleeping.

On September 17, 1945, the first Constellation touched down at Dorval
Airport outside Montréal. The 1,735-kilometre trip from Winnipeg had
taken three hours and thirty-three minutes, at an average speed of 512
kilometres an hour. The aeronautical industry had become increasingly
sophisticated during the war. There were now regular flights to European
capitals. In 1947, Trans-Canada Air Lines offered flights from Montréal to
London via Prestwick on its North Star, a four-engined plane built on
Montréal's own Canadair assembly lines. The North Star may not have had
the Constellation's sleek lines or its triple steering rudder, but it proved to be
a workhorse, enabling TCA to become a major international carrier and
Canadian Pacific Airlines to become a competitor in world travel. It provided the Canadian armed forces with a heavy transport carrier as well.
British Overseas Airways Corporation also purchased North Stars for its
fleet.

Interest among young people in science and technology had grown to
such an extent that *Sciences et Aventures*, Québec's first popular science

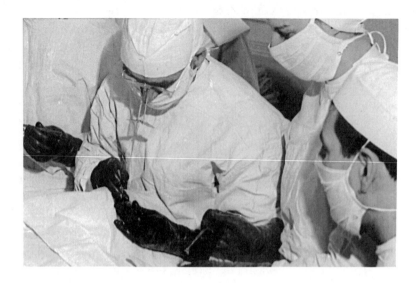

Dr. Jean Audet-Lapointe at Sainte-Justine Hospital, performing Canada's first cornea transplant.

magazine, was founded in 1946. The following year, it reported that McGill University had developed a particle separator called a cyclotron. *Sciences et Aventures* also explained to its readers in January 1948 why balloons were sometimes seen floating over Mount Royal. Pierre Demers, a professor of nuclear physics at the Université de Montréal, was releasing the balloons into the stratosphere to take photographs of cosmic rays. Five months later, the magazine reported that Dr. Jean Audet-Lapointe had performed the first successful cornea transplant in Canada. In a later issue, it would feature the work of Dr. Hans Selye on the bane of modern existence, stress.

In February 1948, Mayor Houde presented the Société Historique with a painting of the church at Neuville-sur-Vanne where Maisonneuve was baptized. Houde's gesture recalled a gift of one hundred tons of flour donated the previous fall by the people of Montréal to the people of Troyes, home of Marguerite Bourgeoys, to help them deal with problems resulting from the Nazi occupation. The woman who organized the relief effort was journalist Odette Oligny, who like Maisonneuve and Bourgeoys came from the Champagne district of France.

Montréal's medical practitioners continued to make headlines. At Sainte-Anne-de-Bellevue, war veteran Gustave Gingras worked with amputees to develop artificial limbs that would help them lead a normal life. In the beginning, Dr. Gingras worked alone with one assistant who was confined to a wheelchair, but in 1949, the Montreal Rehabilitation Institute was founded and quickly gained a wide reputation. Thousands of people from around the world, notably Morocco and Vietnam, owe a debt of gratitude to Dr. Gingras for artificial limbs that have made their lives better and happier.

Mention should also be made of microbiologist Armand Frappier who, despite his modest beginnings, was to develop vaccines that would save thousands of lives. Frappier was one of the founders of the Institut de Microbiologie et d'Hygiène of the Université de Montréal, renamed the Institut Armand-Frappier in 1975. With twenty buildings and 1,700 research publications to its credit since its inception half a century ago, the Institut Armand-Frappier has also helped to make Montréal a household name throughout the world.

The aeronautics industry continued to grow. In addition to the *North Star*, the Canadair plant in Cartierville began producing the F-86 for the Royal Canadian Air Force in August 1950. On August 9, the prototype was taken on its first test flight over Dorval.

Flights between Montréal and Paris went into service in 1950. On October 3, an Air France Constellation touched down at Dorval. The plane had left Orly Airport in Paris the previous day and arrived in Montréal after a fifteen-and-a-half-hour flight that included two one-hour stops at Shannon, Ireland, and Gander, Newfoundland. Among the thirty-four passengers was an official delegation led by the French minister of the merchant marine, Gaston Defferre. On its return flight, the Constellation carried a Canadian delegation headed by federal Transport Minister Lionel Chevrier. Not to be outdone, a TCA *North Star* left Dorval for Orly on March 30, 1951 with a delegation of government officials and journalists, on the first flight of its regular service between Montréal and Paris.

In 1943, architect Ernest Cormier's first independent project, the main building of the newly established Université de Montréal, was officially opened. The university staff had left the building on Saint-Denis Street a few months earlier, taking up residence in the new building on Mount Royal. As impressive as the new building was, it was just the beginning. In late April 1951 the rector, Mgr. Olivier Maurault, announced plans for a new university campus designed by architect Ludger Venne.

Each year brought its share of joy and grief. On June 15, 1951, a fire broke out at the Sainte-Cunégonde Hospice. Six bodies had already been recovered from the ruins when the roof caved in, killing many pensioners. Forty-five people lost their lives in the fire, including the mother superior and six nuns.

In 1948, the Québec government set up a commission to examine Montréal's public transportation system and make recommendations for improving it. Two years later, the commissioners recommended that the system be run by the city and that any subway system built be administered separately from the streetcar network, a rather surprising proviso. On June 14, 1951, the Montreal Transportation Commission took over control.

In 1952, television was introduced in Toronto and Montréal simultaneously. The previous year, Mayor Camillien Houde had turned the first sod on Mount Royal for Montréal's first television antenna. The same year, Marcel Ouimet, Alphonse Ouimet, Aurèle Séguin and Augustin Frigon had offered to provide a parliamentary committee in Ottawa with a demonstration of television. The first television program was broadcast on September 6, 1952. That year, the mayor was a guest on *Le nez de Cléopâtre*, a television series that became a runaway success.

With regular transatlantic flights, the ties between Québec and France grew even stronger. In the spring of 1951, Montréal received a visit from Vincent Auriol, president of the French republic. The following year, forty journalists from weekly regional newspapers were given a reception at the Élysée Palace. Winning 80,000 votes – three times as many as his closest rival – a young lawyer named Jean Drapeau became mayor of Montréal in 1954. Drapeau was only thirty-eight years old and his success was no doubt due to his involvement as a member of the Civic Action League in an investigation into organized crime. The findings were released twenty days before voters went to the polls.

One of the freighters moored in the harbour in April 1955 was the *Ville de Montréal*. It was one of five freighters belonging to the Compagnie Générale Transatlantique that carried merchandise as far as the Great Lakes. One hundred years earlier, in 1855, the *Capricieuse* had become the first vessel wearing French colours to travel up the St. Lawrence since the Conquest in 1760. The *Capricieuse* had come to the New World to establish trade relations with Canada. Mayor Drapeau greeted the president of the French shipping company with the very words with which his predecessor, Wolfred Nelson, had welcomed the captain of the *Capricieuse*.

In May 1957, the city announced preparations for a sports complex to be built in the city block bounded by Sherbrooke, Boyce, Pie-IX and Viau.

The plans called for a 10,000-seat arena, named after hockey star Maurice Richard, a baseball diamond and playing fields. The sports centre was the first sign of the role that this part of Montréal would later have as the site of the Olympic Stadium and other Olympic facilities.

Camillien Houde died on September 11, 1958. He had been mayor through many critical years. On his release from the internment camp, Mr. Montréal had been carried on the shoulders of his supporters. Three hundred thousand Montrealers paid their last respects to Houde as he lay in state at City Hall. Mayor Sarto Fournier and former mayors Jean Drapeau (whom Fournier defeated in 1957) and Adhémar Raynault were part of the funeral cortege carrying his body to Notre-Dame. Not since the death of Brother André had such large crowds lined the streets.

Since its introduction six years earlier, television had become a part of daily life. On December 19, 1958, seventy-five producers at the Société Radio Canada went on strike because the public corporation would not recognize their union. Several public figures supported their move. They returned to work on March 9, after winning the right to organize.

In 1959, Montréal lost an important asset that had contributed to its prosperity over the years. The port of Montréal was no longer the final destination for all river traffic from the east, a strategic advantage that it had held since the digging of the St. Lawrence channel nearly a century earlier. Merchandise bound for the Great Lakes would no longer be unloaded on its docks. On June 26, Queen Elizabeth and American President Dwight Eisenhower officially opened the St. Lawrence Seaway, making it possible for ocean-going ships to travel right to the heart of the continent.

In 1895, Canada and the United States had set up an international commission to determine the feasibility of digging a deep-water channel. Work on the seaway did not begin until 1954. It was to be a huge undertaking, and the total cost of the project was more than $1 billion. Twenty thousand workers were employed and more than 275 million cubic metres of earth and stone were removed. More than 6,500 Canadians had to evacuate their homes and settle elsewhere.

On August 30, 1959, another chapter of Montréal's history drew to a close. Although Montrealers loved to complain about their electric streetcars, several thousand of them turned out to say "adieu" as the last streetcar, the *Papineau 3517*, made its final run. Montréal's buses, with their flexible routes, had finally won their half-century-long competition with the streetcars, confined to narrow rails. Later, however, Montrealers would come to realize that their "new and improved" transportation system consumed large quantities of gasoline. Perhaps the trolley bus offered the ideal balance between flexibility and energy conservation.

Sumptuous Years of Prosperity

——————————— ➤< ———————————

It was during the sixties that Montréal, jealously defending its title as Canada's largest city, began a series of undertakings designed to project it on to the international scene. The complete transformation of the downtown core, the construction of a subway reflecting the latest technology and opportunities to host several coveted international events brought phenomenal changes over the next twenty years.

Most of these developments are of too recent memory to warrant more than a passing mention here.

Montréal's rebirth began with the expansion of Dorchester Street (now René-Lévesque Boulevard), for which rows of beautiful Victorian houses were torn down. It continued in 1958 with expropriations for the construction of Place Ville-Marie. The talks that led to Place Ville-Marie began in 1955 under Mayor Jean Drapeau. Mayor again from 1960 on, Drapeau was to become the architect of the transformation that catapulted Montréal into the twenty-first century. In 1967, he would find himself on the balcony of city hall with French President Charles de Gaulle. While one reflected on the grandeur of France, the other reflected on the stature of his great city. On September 13, 1962, the mayor attended the official opening of Place Ville-Marie's cruciform tower. "Having a centre, a real centre like New York's Rockefeller Centre is more than an event; it marks the founding of a truly world-class city."

Not three months before, Montrealers had been given another source of civic pride: the forty-three-storey Canadian Imperial Bank of Commerce Tower. Standing at 184 metres, it was the tallest building with prefabricated walls in the world; it contained 17,000 tons of steel and 30,560 cubic metres of concrete – "a symbol," the mayor said, "of the progress that Montréal has made and the confidence of the Canadian business community in its future."

It was not only above ground that Montréal was being transformed.

Excavation for the city's new Metro had already begun. The previous year, on a visit to Paris for the official opening of the Québec delegation, Premier Jean Lesage had spent two hours touring the Paris Metro. He was particularly interested in gathering information about rubber tires, an innovation being used in Montréal, needing the information in case the financing being arranged by the city for the Metro required provincial guarantees.

That year, Montréal Island was linked to the south shore by a new bridge, the Champlain Bridge, which opened to the public on June 29, 1962, although some of the access lanes were as yet incomplete. The bridge cost $35 million and has served Montréal well; it is estimated that 12,000 vehicles pass over the bridge every hour. With the exception of the span across the Seaway, which is 758 metres long and weighs approximately 11,000 tons, the 6.5-kilometre bridge is built entirely of prestressed concrete.

On March 28, 1963, Montrealers were overjoyed to learn that Montréal had been chosen as the site of the 1967 world's fair. On his return from Paris on September 3, 1962, Mayor Drapeau had expressed his conviction that the Bureau International des Expositions would choose Montréal if it received an official bid from the Canadian government.

The first question to be resolved was the selection of a site that was large enough for the fair while still being close to the city centre. The city administration headed by Drapeau and Executive Committee Chair Lucien Saulnier responded with a plan to expand St. Helen's Island – which would remain completely accessible to Montrealers – and to create an artificial island by linking Moffat's Island and a little string of islands just north of the Seaway. Landscape architect Frederick G. Todd's plan to transform St. Helen's Island, Île Verte and Île Ronde into a single park suddenly took shape, along with the rather bold plan to create an entirely new island, Île Notre-Dame, for the fair's pavilions. Some critics – who seemed to feel more comfortable with extravagant plans than with actually getting things done – called it "a hare-brained scheme." What they did not know was that the word "impossible" was not part of the vocabulary of the dynamic team that would bring the project to fruition.

It was three long months before Ottawa – concerned that creating new islands with fill might damage the shipping lanes – finally approved the project and its share of the financing. In his determination to see the plan go through, the mayor moved mountains. This was evident time and again during construction of the site. When the engineers announced that the riverbed would not provide the material needed, Drapeau turned to the excavation of the Metro tunnels for the answer. For twenty-two hours each day, a steady stream of trucks could be heard rumbling across the Jacques-Cartier Bridge. Against all odds, the site was ready on time.

When the Monument National outgrew its usefulness, it was decided that a new home for the arts was needed. On September 21, 1963, after much trepidation and dissension, the Place des Arts was officially opened with a concert attended by 3,000 people. While the guests admired the interior of the new arts centre, hundreds of people gathered outside, singing the hymn of the French Revolution, the *"ça ira, ça ira,"* and demanding Québec's independence from the rest of Canada. Police on motorcycles and on horseback managed to disperse the crowd. A few months earlier, there had been other signs of social unrest in the immediate vicinity of the city. Twelve bombs had been placed in letter boxes in the English enclave of Westmount; another bomb had exploded behind an army recruitment centre, killing one person.

In October 1963, an exhibition from France was officially opened at Montréal's trade centre, the Palais du Commerce, by French Culture Minister André Malraux. Noting that the ties that had developed between Québec and France extended beyond the sphere of culture into trade and commerce, Malraux stressed that in the minds of the French people, Canada must show itself in a new light: "We don't want you to think of France as champagne, and we don't want to think of Québec as cradles." He added that France's future depended on the union of science and culture and reminded his audience that French technology had been used in building Québec's dams and the Montréal Metro: "This French exhibition is an important step along the path bringing our destinies together."

Entrepreneurs saw the new Metro as an opportunity to develop the city centre. In late June 1965, plans were unveiled for the redevelopment of McGill College Avenue; the plans called for the avenue to be expanded to a width of thirty-five metres between Place Ville-Marie and the McGill University campus, opening up a view of Mount Royal. Montrealers are now able to enjoy the fruits of this urban redevelopment plan.

In mid-June 1965, the Canadian Broadcasting Corporation was authorized to convert its transmitters, which had provided black and white programming to Montréal homes since 1952, to colour. The coming world exhibition may have helped spur this decision. The CBC planned to broadcast in colour programs produced in its new studios on Mackay Pier, where radio and television crews from around the world would gather in 1967.

A work of art in stained glass at the Berri-UQAM subway station commemorates three of the founders of Ville-Marie: Jérôme Le Royer de la Dauversière; Paul de Chomedey, Sieur de Maisonneuve; and Jeanne Mance. The cartoon by the artist Pierre Gaboriau was executed by the master glazier Pierre Osterrath.

The building and facilities would require an investment of $14 million. The CBC also planned to convert its main broadcast facilities in Montréal and Toronto to colour transmission starting in 1968.

For more than four years, Montréal was an immense construction site. Above ground, there was the development of St. Helen's Island and the creation of Île Notre-Dame; below, a network of Metro tunnels and stations was being built. But good things come to those who wait, and on October 14, 1966, all twenty-six stations of the first Metro network went into service. For the first time, Montrealers got a taste of a world-class, ultramodern public transportation system. The first line had to be in place for the millions of people who would visit Expo 67. The Metro was initially undertaken by the city of Montréal, but it was the Montreal Urban Community that later added another thirty-nine stations. Each station has a distinctive design and is decorated with works of art.

Montrealers remember 1967 either as "the year of Expo" or as "the year of General de Gaulle."

"I declare the Montréal Universal and International Exposition officially open." As Governor General Roland Michener pronounced these words on April 27, the Expo Carillon rang out and all the church bells in Montréal joined in. Vessels anchored in the harbour sounded their sirens and water gushed forth from fountains around the site and even from fireboats. Against a brilliant blue sky, the Snow Birds of the Royal Canadian Air Force described perfect arabesques. At Place des Nations on the Expo site, 6,000 Montrealers greeted representatives from sixty nations gathered to give flesh to the theme of Man and His World, which characterized the fair that had gradually taken shape after years of hard work and painstaking planning. Mayor Jean Drapeau, without whom Expo would never have taken place, was in attendance, as was Commissioner General Pierre Dupuy, whose job it had been to secure the participation of the greatest possible number of countries. "Expo 67," he declared, "is an act of faith in the creative genius of man."

A detailed description of the fair, which lasted six months, is beyond the scope of this book; however, certain events stand out. One such event is the visit of General de Gaulle.

The arrival of the ocean liner *France* in Québec City on May 9 could not have gone unnoticed; 315 metres in length, the *France* was the longest vessel in the world. However, another French ship, the *Colbert*, attracted even more attention. Bonfires burned brightly on either side of the St. Lawrence to greet the *Colbert*: Quebecers were looking forward to the visit from the president of the French republic. As President de Gaulle alighted, Québec Premier Daniel Johnson greeted him with these words: "There isn't a son of the French people in America who does not join with me in saying, 'Welcome to New France.'" Johnson's greeting set the tone for the general's visit. In an outpouring of support, people lined the Chemin du Roy between Québec City and Montréal. It is hardly surprising that, after such an effusive welcome, General de Gaulle responded to the expectant crowd as he did when he stepped out on the balcony of Montréal city hall.

"Vive Montréal! Vive le Québec! Vive le Québec libre!"

"What we are witnessing here," de Gaulle had declared in Québec City, "is the emergence of a people that, in every sense of the word, wants to create its own destiny." From the balcony of city hall, de Gaulle propelled Québec onto the international front pages.

Expo 67 received thousands of visitors each day. On September 13, it received its forty millionth visitor and when it ended, fifty million people had passed through the turnstiles. "Great fairs leave marks," wrote *Life* magazine. "The skyline of Paris was changed forever by the Eiffel Tower, built for the 1889 World's Fair. Expo 67 changed an entire country. For visitors from other countries, particularly Americans who knew nothing about their neighbors to the north apart from Mounties and lumberjacks, it was a revelation. For Canadians, it was much more; it helped shape their self-image." Several pavilions remained standing after the last visitor went home. Two in particular had been built to last. The French pavilion and the Québec pavilion still stand like sentinels on the shore of the St. Lawrence.

In May 1967, Québec mourned the loss of a great thinker, Lionel Groulx. From the sanctuary of his office, Groulx had done much to stir his compatriots' love of their homeland, and he was worthy of a state funeral. As he lay in state in Notre-Dame Basilica, religious and political figures came to pay their last respects. The archbishop of Montréal, Paul-Émile Cardinal Léger, recalled that Groulx's work had roused an entire generation from its slumber, challenging those who hesitated, remained undecided or lacked faith. He added, "If we had become what he wanted us to be, our morality and humanity might have commanded the respect of all ethnic groups that make up the Canadian nation. We might have received, as a matter of course, recognition of the fundamental rights that Abbé Groulx worked so hard to achieve. Whether or not we achieve this becomes a matter of individual responsibility."

In 1931, the Sulpicians had been forced to close the prestigious library that they had donated to the city of Montréal because of financial difficulties. The 170,000 volumes in its collection now became inaccessible. Ten years later, the Québec government purchased the library, reopening it in 1944. In 1961, responsibility for the library was transferred to the province's newly established department of cultural affairs, and plans got under way to make it Québec's national library, with all of the rights and obligations that such libraries carry. In 1967, a bill was tabled in the National Assembly transforming the Bibliothèque Saint-Sulpice into the Bibliothèque Nationale.

Expo 67, which brought Québec to the world and the world to Québec, provided a shot in the arm to the Québec tourist industry. In 1968, for

St. Helen's Island was expanded and Île Notre-Dame, in the foreground, was created for Expo 67.

example, Québec began exploring the potential of the western European market, and especially France, for the first time. If tourism was to grow, Québec would also need workers trained in tourism and hospitality. For a number of years, the École des Métiers Commerciaux, located in the building previously occupied by the Université de Montréal on Saint-Denis Street, taught professional food preparation, baking and pastry-making. In July 1968, the Institut de Tourisme et d'Hôtellerie opened in the same building. The building was destroyed by a fire some months later, and the institute eventually moved into new quarters on Carré Saint-Louis. The building's design was extremely controversial, as it marked a sudden departure from the other buildings on the square. In terms of enrolment, the institute is the largest of its kind in the world.

The building on Saint-Denis was not rebuilt, but another project, much larger in scale, was about to begin. Until 1968, Montréal, Québec City, Sherbrooke and Lennoxville were the only cities in Québec to offer university-level education. Québec needed a system that brought university-level education to other cities while also expanding it in Montréal.

On December 18, 1968, the legislature passed a bill establishing the Université du Québec. One of the campuses of the new university would be in Montréal. The province-wide university opened its doors in the fall of 1969 and grew rapidly. Ten years later, work was begun on the first phase of the campus of the Université du Québec à Montréal in the Latin Quarter, where Montréal's first university had been located.

In late May 1968, Montrealers learned that Dr. Pierre Grondin, chief surgeon at the Institut de Cardiologie, and his assistant, Dr. Gilles Lepage, had performed the first heart transplant in Canada with the help of a team of twenty doctors and nurses. A few days later, Montrealers had another cause for celebration, somewhat more lighthearted this time. In Chicago, the National League announced that it had granted Montréal the first Canadian baseball franchise. The Expos were born.

Alas, the events of those years were not all happy ones, especially starting in 1969. On the morning of September 29, 1969, a bomb exploded at the home of Mayor Drapeau. The explosion was labelled a terrorist attack. Luckily, the mayor was not home at the time and his wife and son escaped unharmed. During the police strike of that year there was rioting and looting along Sainte-Catherine Street, and the firefighters' strike was marked by *le week-end rouge*.

The Montreal Metropolitan Commission, established in the late 1920s, provided Montréal and neighbouring communities with a means of reaching mutually beneficial agreements for managing municipal debt and for major public works projects such as the Metropolitan Autoroute. In 1964, a commission established to examine intermunicipal problems on Montréal Island tabled its report. It recommended that a regional council be created and given a mandate to amalgamate services deemed regional in scope and to divide the cost of these services among the member municipalities.

Following the commission's report, the Montreal Urban Community was established in 1969 along with two other supramunicipal bodies, the

Communauté Urbaine de Québec and the Outaouais Regional Community. The MUC is administered by a council and an executive committee. The executive committee includes six representatives of the city of Montréal and six representatives of the island's other municipalities, in addition to the chair, chosen by the council from among its members. The council's eighty-six members include the chair of the executive committee, the mayor and councillors of the city of Montréal, and the mayors of the other member municipalities. In 1982, five permanent commissions were established for urban development, the environment, assessment and finances, public security and public transportation. Their role is to study the needs of the MUC in these areas and to report to the council.

In May 1970, bombs exploded in the most affluent parts of Westmount, presaging the October Crisis later that same year. In October 1970, British diplomat James Richard Cross and Québec Labour and Immigration Minister Pierre Laporte were kidnapped. Cross was eventually released, but Laporte's kidnapping ended in his tragic death. His body was found in the trunk of the car used in the kidnapping. Hundreds of citizens suspected of being activists were arrested under the War Measures Act and the army was brought in to occupy strategic areas of the city. Twenty years later, the memory of these dramatic events brought back bitter memories.

The tragic events of the October Crisis overshadowed news that should have been cause for rejoicing. Word arrived from Amsterdam in early May 1970 that Montréal had been chosen as the site for the 1976 Olympic Games. The hardhearted were convinced that the honour would go to Moscow for political reasons, or to Los Angeles because of its financial clout. But they underestimated the prestige that Montréal had gained through Expo 67 and the charismatic figure of Mayor Jean Drapeau.

At the Centre Maisonneuve on April 6, 1972, a scale model of an Olympic stadium was unveiled. It was anticipated that the stadium would cost $55 million. The plans called for a capacity of 50,000 seats for baseball and football games, expanded to 70,000 seats for the Olympics. With a plastic roof supported by the highest inclined tower in the world, the stadium would operate year-round. The model was impressive, to say the least. "Anyone who knew Mayor Drapeau," reported *La Presse*, "also knew that the 1976 Olympic Stadium would not be your average stadium. And they were right!" There were many unforeseen obstacles: the stadium's bold design, the use of avant-garde techniques, and labour disputes to mention only a few. In spite of these challenges, the stadium whose panoramic view and inclined tower became symbols of Montréal just as the Eiffel Tower had become a symbol of Paris, opened on schedule. The cost was astronomical. As in the case of the expansion of St. Helen's Island and the creation of Île Notre-Dame, the least costly of all factors – determination – was what made it possible to finish on time.

In late July 1973, the House of Commons passed a bill providing for funding of the Olympics. Although the Velodrome was ready in time for the games in 1976, it was not ready for the world cycling championships, held two years earlier. Instead, the championships were held on a temporary track, erected in record time at the Université de Montréal.

Television crews brought the opening ceremony of the twenty-first Olympiad into Montrealers' living rooms. Some of the world's finest athletes appeared at the games. Athletes from the USSR won the largest number of medals: forty-seven gold, forty-three silver and thirty-five bronze. The atmosphere at the closing ceremony was festive. Five hundred young women formed the five Olympic circles around five wigwams. Lord Killanin, president of the International Olympic Committee, was still delivering his official speech when the crowd began chanting, "Drapeau! Drapeau! Drapeau!" and rose to give the mayor a standing ovation. As the sun set in Montréal, it rose over Moscow, the site of the next Olympic Games. Giant screens in the stadium carried images of dancers and singers in Moscow saluting Montréal as the host city.

Much has been written and said about the Olympic Stadium. Ten years later, when the 1976 gold medallists were invited to attend the tenth anniversary of the Montréal Olympics, the stadium still did not have a retractable roof and its tower was still incomplete. However, the Olympic facilities were eventually completed and are a source of collective pride for Montrealers.

Unfortunately, Montrealers were forced to turn their attention to another event. A fire set by arsonists in a nightclub on Union Street on September 1, 1972, claimed forty victims. Forty others were injured. The fire had taken the staff and the 200-odd people present in the nightclub completely by surprise.

In February 1974, Notre-Dame Hospital achieved international fame as the site of the first liver transplant, performed by Dr. Pierre Deloze. The young patient survived for two years.

Montrealers had learned to take their Metro for granted when, in August 1974, service was interrupted by a forty-day strike by the system's maintenance and garage workers.

For the holiday season, the Québec government flew a thirty-five-metre pine tree to Paris, where it stood opposite the convention centre on the Place de la Porte-Maillot. It was flown to Paris in the hold of Air France's *Super Pelican*, a 747 cargo jet making regular flights between Charles-de-Gaulle Airport and Mirabel.

By now, Montrealers had clearly acquired a taste for events of international importance. In 1977, they were thrilled to learn that St. Helen's Island had been chosen as the venue for the Grand Prix automobile race. The 1980s began with another international event, the Floralies or international flower show. Because Montréal had hosted Expo in 1967 and the twenty-first Olympic Games in 1976, the Bureau International des Expositions had no hesitation in choosing Montréal for the world's most important horticultural event. The Association Internationale des Producteurs de l'Horticulture, with representatives from nineteen countries, also gave its approval. It was the first time that an event of this magnitude had been organized in North America.

The Floralies lasted three and a half months. From May 17 to May 29, the Olympic Velodrome was transformed into a valley of intricate floral arrangements by horticulturists from twenty different countries, including Québec and other parts of Canada. The 6,000-square-metre Velodrome was transformed into an earthly paradise. On May 31, the outdoor exhibits opened on Île Notre-Dame: forty hectares of ornamental trees and shrubs, evergreens, fruit trees and an infinite variety of plants, arranged to please the eye. Seven Expo 67 pavilions were refurbished with information counters, a children's garden and child care centre, and other amenities. The show lasted until September 1.

In 1982, Montrealers were overjoyed to learn that one of the great figures of Ville-Marie's early days was to be canonized. In 1950 the founder of the Congrégation de Notre-Dame, Marguerite Bourgeoys, had been beatified by Pope Pius XII before a crowd of 30,000 people and now, in 1982, she took her place among the saints.

Québec's engineering community had already established an international reputation when the Montréal chamber of commerce founded the Centre International de Gestion des Grands Projets in 1984 in an effort to promote Québec technology abroad. One hundred businesses and associations became members of the centre. They helped identify high-ranking officials in public and private corporations in other countries who could be invited to the province to meet industry leaders and become acquainted with Québec technology, especially in the energy sector.

When the International Civil Aviation Organization and the International Air Transport Association decided to move their headquarters to Montréal, the city's reputation as an international centre for transportation technology grew. In 1987, delegations from fifty-five countries met in Montréal to reach an agreement on the environment. The outcome of the meeting was an agreement that became known as the Montréal Protocol on the ozone layer. Montréal was subsequently selected as the site for the permanent secretariat of the multilateral funds that administers a budget of $200 million under the aegis of the United Nations to help developing nations implement measures to phase out products that destroy the ozone layer.

Progress was also being made in medicine. In February 1988, the first successful lung-only transplant operation was performed at the Royal Victoria Hospital. The following year, medical history was made once again when a Québec woman danced with a man who earlier had received her original heart in a transplant operation. In late June, the woman had been on the waiting list for a double-lung transplant that would save her life. The transplant would be a domino, with the recipient getting both the lungs and the heart of the donor. Because the recipient's heart was healthy, it was decided that it, in turn, could be given to a patient awaiting a heart transplant in a nearby room. He became the first person to thank a donor for having offered her heart. Both operations took place at the Royal Victoria Hospital. A few days later, at the Hôpital Général, a team of thirteen specialists successfully transplanted two lungs without replacing the patient's heart, using a technique developed in France. Such operations, which to the layperson seem like science fiction, demonstrate just how determined Montréal's medical community was to stay in the forefront of scientific progress.

In 1985, the international women's decade proclaimed by the United Nations drew to a close. It was no coincidence that, during this period, women began occupying positions that had previously been off-limits to them. At thirty-seven, Louise Roy became the chief officer of the Montreal Urban Community Transportation Commission. Lorraine Pagé was elected president of the Alliance des Professeurs de Montréal, then president of the Centrale de l'enseignement du Québec, Québec's largest teachers' union. Nycol Pageau-Goyette became chair of the Chambre de Commerce du Montréal Métropolitain. Following the 1990 municipal election, Léa Cousineau was chosen to head the city's executive committee. But while there are many, many examples of social progress, Montréal was also the scene of an unspeakable tragedy. On December 6, 1989, fourteen female engineering students were killed by a lone gunman at the École Polytechnique.

Mention must also be made of Phyllis Bronfman-Lambert's contribution to the arts. Through her personal financial contribution and the support of various levels of government, the Canadian Centre for Architecture building was opened in May 1989. The modern building elegantly incorporates Shaughnessy House, recognized as a heritage site by the province in 1974.

In December 1988, Montréal established a commission called the Corporation des Célébrations du 350ᵉ Anniversaire de Montréal to organize events marking the city's 350th anniversary in 1992. It is made up of twenty-four people from all walks of life and is headed by Patrick Kenniff, rector of Concordia University. The commission's board of directors is complemented by a board of governors chaired by former Bell Canada chief executive officer Jean de Grandpré.

In addition to promotion, program development and fundraising, the corporation received a clear mandate from Mayor Jean Doré to strengthen Montrealers' sense of partnership and pride in their city. In mid-January 1991, the corporation announced that more than $2 million would be made available in the form of subsidies to some sixty different projects and that the program of festivities would be made public in mid-October. The corporation was counting on support not only from the government but from the private sector as well.

Past, Present and Future

———————— >< ————————

The chronicling of events in Montréal's history has brought us up to the present. As we write this, 1991 has just opened and Montréal is 348 years young.

In late May 1990, more than 3,000 architects from around the globe gathered to discuss the future of the profession on the threshold of the twenty-first century. It was only the second time that the international union of architects had met in North America. In early June, Montréal hosted the first international summit on women and the dimensions of power. The delegates, many of international repute, studied issues relating to political, economic, media and religious power. In mid-October, the International Centre for Human Rights and Democratic Development opened in Montréal with a budget of $15 million. Plans were already underway to subsidize a dozen agencies working in various parts of the world to secure the rights of women, aboriginal peoples and the poor.

If Montrealers had any doubts about the merit of clinical research conducted at the Clinical Research Institute, they would have been reassured by a survey of the most frequently cited authors in 3,200 internationally recognized scientific journals. Dr. Jacques Genest and Dr. Marc Cantin were cited 5,931 and 5,429 times respectively. Unfortunately, Dr. Cantin died before these figures were published. For many years, the two conducted research on a synthetic substitute for a hormone produced by the heart to control high blood pressure.

In recent years, Montréal engineering firms have been involved in large-scale projects throughout the world, including the construction of hydroelectric dams and public transportation systems. A Montréal consulting engineering firm and a Montréal firm of chartered accountants are now working in Moscow to put structures in place for the introduction of a market economy.

In early November, the Université du Québec à Montréal founded the Institut des Sciences de l'Environnement to bring together graduate-level environmental science programs, departments, laboratories and research groups and to conduct research into global warming, forest ecology and environmental management.

As we have already mentioned, Montréal's first teacher, Marguerite Bourgeoys, was canonized in 1982. On December 9, 1990, Marie Marguerite Dufrost de Lajemmerais, Mère d'Youville, was given the same honour. The first female saint to be born on Québec soil, the founder of the Sisters of Charity of the Hôpital Général of Montréal, St. Marie-Marguerite toiled ceaselessly for the Hôpital Général, overseeing its reconstruction on two separate occasions.

The year 1990 also brought an event worthy of an entire page in our history books. In 1979, the Fondation Émile-Nelligan had been founded by Gilles Corbeil, a nephew of the Québec poet. When Corbeil died tragically seven years later, he left instructions for the founding of a prize for literature worth $100,000. To be given out every three years, the Prix Gilles-Corbeil was first awarded in 1990 to writer Réjean Ducharme who, with character-istic humility and self-effacement, sent his mother to accept the award in his place. Traditionally, Québec's literary awards have been rather modest in scale, a pattern that the Prix Gilles-Corbeil has changed forever.

After *"Forum SOS l'eau c'est la vie"* was held in Montréal in June 1990, the Secrétariat International de l'Eau decided to make Montréal its perma-nent headquarters. This organization works to bring potable water and rudimentary hygiene measures to countries of the South.

Three and a half centuries is not a long time in the history of a city. Cities the size of Montréal have existed in France for more than a thousand years. Montréal is still young; plans for its 350th anniversary augur well for the future. At this point, it is difficult to say what 1992 will bring.

Early in the summer of 1991, the *Corporation des Célébrations du 350ᵉ Anniversaire de Montréal* announced that the opening ceremonies would take place between May 15 and May 17 in the Old Port and on Mount Royal. There would be an all-night celebration, with a parade and a mass at Notre-Dame Basilica where the Orchestre Symphonique de Montréal and a 250-voice chorus would interpret Berlioz's *Te Deum*.

The city is planning to develop the western portion of St. Helen's Island for the celebrations. Important components of Expo 67 including the American pavilion (now the Biosphere), what remains of the Place des Nations, the Alexander Calder sculpture and the Concordia Bridge will be incorporated into the site, accessible from the city centre by Metro.

The Université du Québec à Montréal has announced the construction of a new concert hall with 800 seats, at the northwest corner of de Maison-neuve Boulevard and Sanguinet Street. The Québec government has announced plans to build a national archive centre in the heart of Montréal, at a cost of $25 million.

Work on the Centre de Commerce Mondial, to be located in the heart of an international district, is nearing completion. It will mean complete redevelopment of the city block bounded by McGill, Saint-Antoine, Bleury and Saint-Jacques streets. It is anticipated that the centre will open in the fall of 1991. In addition to boutiques and offices, the complex will con-tain special facilities for corporations that operate internationally. A twenty-six-storey hotel is planned, and a glass canopy will be built over the historic Ruelle des Fortifications.

Technoparc, a high-technology industrial park located near the

Bonaventure Autoroute, will become a campus of sorts with the redevelopment of Adacport, which will become a kind of prestigious antechamber to the business centre. The development will include public areas and urban appointments designed to give it an upscale corporate profile.

The Biodôme is scheduled to open on June 24, 1992 in the former Velodrome in the Olympic Park. With a botanical garden, aquarium, zoo, nature museum and interpretation centre, the Biodôme will faithfully recreate four ecosystems. Close to 5,000 species of fish and mammals and more than 2,000 species of plants will be introduced into four distinct zones: a tropical forest, a boreal forest, a polar region and the St. Lawrence estuary. The Institut de Recherche en Biologie Végétale, launched jointly in November 1990 by the Université de Montréal and the city of Montréal, will occupy its own building in 1992, an extension of the Institut Botanique founded half a century ago by Brother Marie-Victorin.

In 1992, Montréal will also create Place Charles-de-Gaulle. It was hoped that the size of the square would be commensurate with de Gaulle's stature as a statesman, but its prestige is derived more from its geographical location than its size. Place du Québec in Paris is a tiny crescent-shaped area, barely large enough to hold a fountain, yet twelve million people visit it each year. Paris has donated a sculpture by Olivier Debré to decorate the square. The sculpture is based on the flame Debré is creating for Place de la Porte-Maillot and will be lit by laser beams. Perhaps this is an attempt to symbolize the progress that Montréal has made since the day when pioneers used fireflies to light the holy sacrament on the day of Ville-Marie's founding.

Three religious communities that have been active in Montréal during its 350-year history will receive subsidies from the federal government to restore heritage buildings and collections carefully preserved over the years. The Hospitalières de Saint-Joseph, who founded the Hôtel-Dieu, will open a museum dedicated to the history of the hospital, Montréal's first. The Congrégation de Notre-Dame will restore the stone barn adjacent to Saint-Gabriel house, creating an interpretation centre on the early settlement of Montréal Island. Finally, the chapel of the former Frères Charon hospital will be restored. Mère d'Youville took over the hospital and converted it into the Hôpital Général.

Another major project to coincide with the 350th anniversary is the creation of an archeological and historical interpretation centre on Pointe à Callière, on the very spot where Ville-Marie's fort was erected in 1642. Over the years, the Société du Vieux-Port has conducted a number of archeological digs on the site, notably in 1989. With funding from all three levels of government, the centre will require an investment of approximately $30 million.

In 1992, Montréal's three major museums will double, and perhaps triple, their floor space. The Musée d'Art Contemporain will take up lodgings in a new building in Place des Arts and the McCord Museum and the Montreal Museum of Fine Arts will both be expanded. These changes will cost a total of $150 million. There are also plans to renovate the Palais de la Civilisation, the French pavilion dating from Expo 67, so that artistic events can be held there, even during the winter months.

There has been talk of restoring the Monument National, an exceptional heritage site, for many years. Acquired by the National Theatre School in November 1971, it was declared a historical monument in 1976. The plans for restoration have been dusted off and it is anticipated that the work will be completed in time for the 350th anniversary celebrations.

Montréal has had an international reputation as a venue for major conventions for many years, particularly since the opening of the Palais des Congrès. The Fédération Internationale des Journalistes will meet in Montréal in 1992, the first time that it has held its convention outside Europe. Representatives of unions and professional associations from fifty different countries will take part. In February, Montréal will host the fifth biennial meeting of winter cities, a conference of mayors of northern communities, accompanied by an exhibition on the theme "Winter in the City." Forty mayors from northern communities in eighteen countries will take part.

In September, the twelfth international archives convention will be held at the Palais des Congrès, bringing together 1,300 specialists in the conservation and classification of paper documents, magnetic tapes, optical disks and other archival materials. Then, in October, the world's third largest conference on advertising, the Mondial de la Publicité, will return to Montréal. The newly formed organization first met in Montréal in October 1990.

Shortly after its 350th birthday party, Montréal will be honoured by its sister cities around the world when it hosts Metropolis '93, bringing together 2,500 representatives of the thirty-eight largest cities on five continents. The decision to hold this conference, the fourth of its kind, in Montréal in June 1993 was made in Melbourne in October 1990. Montréal's Metro, Place des Arts and Place Ville-Marie make up an underground city that continues to attract tourists. In five years, it has almost doubled in size from twelve to twenty-two square kilometres. Corridors, tunnels, atriums and boutiques spread out from downtown Metro stations over a total distance of twenty-two kilometres. Taking into account major above-ground building projects underway at the end of 1990, it is estimated that by 1992 the underground city will contain twenty-nine kilometres of passages spreading out from ten Metro stations, offering access to 80 per cent of the offices in the business district, 1,700 stores, 1,615 apartments and 1,700 hotel rooms, as well as a university, two train stations and two bus terminals.

The city of Montréal and real estate developers are planning a cruciform "Cité Internationale" with Victoria Square at its centre. The Cité would build on the Palais des Congrès through the addition of a large convention centre. Close to a hundred well-known architectural firms submitted tenders for the project. The project went to New York architect Steven K. Peterson, who also won first prize in an international competition to redevelop the Les Halles district in Paris.

Another "foolish venture"?

Index

Printed in Canada